Teaching Lawyers' Skills

Teaching Lawyers' Skills

Edited by
Julian Webb and Caroline Maughan

Butterworths
London, Dublin, Edinburgh
1996

United Kingdom	Butterworths, a Division of Reed Elsevier (UK) Ltd, Halsbury House, 35 Chancery Lane, LONDON WC2A 1EL and 4 Hill Street, EDINBURGH EH2 3JZ
Australia	Butterworths, SYDNEY, MELBOURNE, BRISBANE, ADELAIDE, PERTH, CANBERRA and HOBART
Canada	Butterworths Canada Ltd, TORONTO and VANCOUVER
Ireland	Butterworth (Ireland) Ltd, DUBLIN
Malaysia	Malayan Law Journal Sdn Bhd, KUALA LUMPUR
New Zealand	Butterworths of New Zealand Ltd, WELLINGTON and AUCKLAND
Singapore	Reed Elsevier (Singapore) Pte Ltd, SINGAPORE
South Africa	Butterworths Publishers (Pty) Ltd, DURBAN
USA	Michie, CHARLOTTESVILLE, Virginia

A CIP Catalogue record for this book is available from the British Library.

ISBN   0 406 05216 6

Typeset by B & J Whitcombe, Nr Diss, Norfolk, IP22 2LP
Printed by Redwood Books, Trowbridge, Wiltshire

Foreword

Avrom Sherr

Woolf Professor of Legal Education, Institute of Advanced Legal Studies, University of London

This is an appropriate time to consider the progress of the legal skills movement from an English perspective. It is clear why skills teaching within law should have taken a firm root in North America. The lack of both a formal apprenticeship system and vocational training, the postgraduate nature of university legal education and therefore its dedication to a more vocational model, and also a more mechanistic tradition in educational approach, are all strong reasons for the clinical method and skills teaching to have started in North America.[1] If clinical method and legal skills had not already had their seeds in the realist movement,[2] they would probably have had to be invented.

But what of the other common law jurisdictions with their strong tradition of both apprenticeship and formal vocational legal education? Why should skills be of interest and have become so much a part of the professional legal educational system in jurisdictions which possessed articles of clerkship, pupillage and practical, vocational courses? A partial rationalisation is that because skills teaching became the norm in North America it became recognised as 'best practice' to be followed in the rest of the common law world. But this best-practice reasoning is unlikely to be the most important. The fossilising effect of 'last year's notes' on teaching in an increasingly pressurised environment might well have been

1 See A H Sherr (1995) 'Clinical Legal Education at Warwick and the Skills Movement: Was clinic a creature of its time?', chapter in G P Wilson (ed) *Frontiers of Legal Scholarship*, Wiley.
2 See eg W Twining (1993) 'The Idea of Juristic Method: A Tribute to Karl Llewellyn' 48 *University of Miami Law Review* 119.

stronger than any feeling that others might be doing it rather better elsewhere. A number of other factors have come into play.

The explosion of law graduates into what appeared to be an expanding market in the late 1980s fostered a need for a teaching approach and curriculum which was less élitist and, more basically, for a larger and more heterogeneous group of lawyers than had previously been involved in the vocational legal education system. At the same time, the two professional bodies, the Bar Council and the Law Society were making their decisions about the educational needs of the future profession. They found themselves looking to North America and to receivers of that tradition in Australasia and Hong Kong, who had faced the difficulties of setting up vocational programmes where apprenticeship was not always available. To some extent there was also a move afoot to break the seeming hegemony of the College of Law for solicitors' training. When the Law Society finals had been refashioned in 1980 there had been an attempt to make them more practical as they moved from a six months' to a nine months' course. Somehow, this appeared not to have been successful. By opening up the market of course-providing institutions further and moving over towards more of a skills base, the competition and sense of change might produce a more effective vocational course. Until recently this was not the picture for the Bar, whose course was only run (and said to be heavily subsidised) at the Inns of Court School of Law. This monopoly is also now to be removed and other institutions will be able to compete for authorisation.

But by far the most important reason for the general move towards skills in the UK has been the changing nature of work in law and the changing nature of the legal profession itself. The growth in the output of parliamentary and delegated legislation has meant an outpouring in every subject area of law only paralleled by an equivalent growth in case law. The result is that no lawyer can be expert and up-to-date in every area of law or even in more than one or two areas. Therefore, educating new lawyers at an across-the-board level of expertise, even in half a dozen core subjects which they must memorise and learn over one year for an examination, becomes an impossible feat. It is also a pointless exercise, since so much of the law will change even by the time they are two to three years into qualification. Partly as a result of this sheer growth in law, and the growth in size of firms, lawyers have become much more specialised in the areas in which they work. By 1990 the Law Society's own research showed almost 70% of solicitors to be declaring themselves to be specialists in one or more areas.[3] If law is too large to learn everything about and if lawyers in any event are going to become specialised in a few discrete areas, then what is most sensible and most appropriate for them to learn? Clearly, within each subject area it must be the concepts that encapsulate the meaning, the process and the substance of law in that area, and also the legal skills which enable a lawyer to find and to deal with that law and with the legal process and all those who come into contact with it. Add to this the constantly changing nature of not only the practice of law, but also the important subject areas within it and the impossibility of predicting what will be important in ten, twenty or thirty years, and there exists a very clear set of reasons for looking towards a more direct teaching of those concepts and skills rather than an indirect ingestion of the raw material of law itself in the hope that the skills will somehow come with it.

There is more within the practice of law to add to this argument beyond the first stage of specialisation. Larger enterprises begin to form teams working on particular types of transaction or case. In order to progress as large a number as possible of such files in the shortest possible time, the work becomes routinised in such a way that lower level lawyers can handle as much of it as possible. As the work moves into this factory form of industrialisation, the level of discretion or prior knowledge and experience becomes lessened for routinised portions of the work. It therefore becomes deskilled. But at the lower levels, where new lawyers and trainee lawyers operate, what they actually need is the basic skills to get started. If they have these skills when they arrive in a firm, they can show their prowess on lower-level tasks and soon advance to tasks which involve more discretion and understanding. When they arrive in the law firm, in theory, they can already pay their way.

This presents a strong picture of reasons for moving towards a skills-based approach to legal education at the vocational level and for the basic needs of the new trainee and newly qualified lawyer. But the needs do not end, or begin, there. An interest in skills, as shown most particularly by this book, is developing among those

---

3   G Chambers and S Harwood 'Solicitors in England and Wales: First Report' Law Society RPPU.

involved in undergraduate legal education and continuing beyond the early vocational training within practice. The demands of practice within more highly specialised firms begin to need a form of training which can allow qualified lawyers to operate at increasingly high levels and upon increasingly complex tasks. These include areas of skill such as the ability to interview directors of large corporate concerns, to negotiate on takeovers, mergers, and financing or to take cases under higher court advocacy qualifications as full-blown advocates. And it is not just professional skills which now need to be learned or updated at higher levels of experience. Managerial and administrative skills have also become part of the necessary armoury of the senior lawyer. Managing people, managing projects, managing time, marketing and analysing finance are all areas which more senior managers within the larger law practice need to learn about. The most appropriate way to be introduced to the techniques, skills, concepts and even the basic information involved at the adult stage of learning is in the context of 'learning by doing' – in other words, either apprenticeship or skills. Firms are less willing to allow the mistakes of apprenticeship to be made at higher levels of legal work and legal management, and so the direct teaching of skills has become more popular at these upper levels as well. This form of training is so ingrained in many larger firms that it is probably not recognised any more as something separately called 'skills training', but is simply 'how it is done'.

Why then should skills training have become such an important part of the undergraduate curriculum? Well, it is not absolutely clear that it has. The bulk of undergraduate legal education is still very much at the 'black letter law' level which seems to be entirely necessary and entirely appropriate. Where differences do seem to be beginning to emerge are in certain subject areas. In terms of teaching legal research and legal writing and even sometimes problem-solving, the approach seems to have moved more towards a direct skills method than simply pushing people through three years of organised cases and statutes and hope they will be able to come out the other end able to do things one would expect from a well-trained law student. But it is largely these skills that have begun to be taught at undergraduate level.

Increasingly, though, there has also been a feedback into undergraduate legal education of some of the needs of vocational training. Partly in order to introduce students to what it may be like to behave as a lawyer, and to show the context in which real legal problems are dealt with, client interviewing is beginning to be studied either as part of the curriculum or as an extracurricular activity leading to the national and international Client Interviewing Competitions (see the Introduction). Mooting had already been a fairly important part of extracurricular activities at many universities and now seems to be more carefully prepared and channelled, and sometimes even appears as part of the general curriculum. The presence of skills training at the undergraduate level, then, is partly because it has been shown to be 'best practice' for teaching some of the work of undergraduate legal education, partly as a preparation for vocational training and partly as an exercise in providing context to the otherwise possibly sterile world of undergraduate legal problem solving (and thereby producing the holistic approach mentioned by so many of the contributors to this book).

How does it help us to know *why* the skills movement took off in this way in the English and Welsh jurisdiction? If we are correct in our assumptions about the reasons for this movement, then we can begin to evaluate whether the progress of legal skills training has actually satisfied the needs which brought it about. Such needs, of course, change with time and therefore a continuing evaluation is necessary. Furthermore, people and systems find uses for existing phenomena which might not have been thought of prior to their existence. But, in general, if the above comments are correct, we should be able to assess what has happened in the last ten years by reference to them.

As the reader reads this book the following questions should be kept in mind. How far has the progress in legal skills been in accordance with the factors which brought it about? How far have we progressed educationally in providing skills-based education? How far have we discovered in research terms what are the ingredients of the actual skills lawyers use which we are trying to teach? The answers to these questions should provide us with the research agenda for the future.

The contributors

Andy Boon is Head of the Law School at the University of Westminster and an Associate Research Fellow of the Institute of Advanced Legal Studies, University of London.

Hugh Brayne is Professor of Law and Head of the Law School at Kingston University. He was formerly Director of Professional Legal Education at the University of Northumbria at Newcastle.

David Cruickshank is Adjunct Professor, University of British Columbia Faculty of Law, and Director of Professional Development, Gowling, Strathy and Henderson, a national law firm in Canada.

Richard Grimes is a Senior Lecturer in Law at Sheffield Hallam University. He is currently on a two year secondment to the University of the South Pacific as Director of Vocational Legal Education.

Philip Jones is Director of Legal Practice at the University of Sheffield, and a member of the Institute for the Study of the Legal Profession.

Peter Kilpin is an independent training consultant and a Visiting Lecturer on the Legal Practice Course at the University of the West of England, Bristol.

Caroline Maughan is a Senior Lecturer in Law, and a member of the Legal Education and Professional Skills Research Unit at the University of the West of England, Bristol.

Mike Maughan is a Senior Lecturer in Organisational Behaviour at Cheltenham and Gloucester College of Higher Education.

Joanna Shapland is Professor of Criminal Justice and Director of the Institute for the Study of the Legal Profession, University of Sheffield.

Diana Tribe is Professor of Law and Head of the Law Division at the University of Hertfordshire and an Associate Research Fellow of the Institute of Advanced Legal Studies, University of London.

Julian Webb is Director of Graduate Studies in Law and Director of the Legal Education and Professional Skills Research Unit at the University of the West of England, Bristol.

Richard Winter is Professor of Education at Anglia Polytechnic University.

Contents

Introduction

Legal skills in the 1990s
Julian Webb and Caroline Maughan

The origins of the skills movement

Skills education in law has a variety of progenitors.[1] Most commentators agree that the story starts in America. However, it is a matter of some debate whether it starts with the Realist attempts to reform legal education, such as Llewellyn (1945), or the clinical movement of the 1960s. Its more recent expansion across the Common Law world has been fuelled primarily by changes to vocational education and training, with a consequent focus on lawyering skills and the development of professional rather than academic competencies: see Roper (1988). In the UK too, the most visible manifestation of the 'skills revolution' has been the development and launch of the new professional courses for the English Bar (in 1989) and the Law Society (in 1993).

However, the impetus towards skills education in the English law schools has a more complex pedigree than this suggests. To some extent, as the sceptics have always been quick to point out, skills are not new; there has always been an element of skills teaching in the law schools, given the problem focus of much legal education. But beyond this there have been two discrete elements.

First, interest in the *applied* or 'lawyering' skills arose originally as an incidental attribute of the early clinical courses that developed in the UK from the mid-1970s. By the mid-1980s a relatively small number of institutions also began experimenting with interviewing skills courses, many outside the formal curriculum, as an activity

---

1 Aspects of this history have been discussed more fully by inter alia Spiegal (1987) and Twining (1988), (1993).

directed towards student participation in the UK Client Interviewing Competition, which was launched at Warwick University in 1984. This has since expanded into separate competitions for England and Scotland. In 1989 we saw the publication of *Learning Lawyers' Skills* by Gold, Mackie and Twining (1989). This landmark publication showed the educational establishment that legal skills were indeed to be taken seriously, and provided an invaluable set of materials for developing skills courses around the DRAIN typology – ie, Drafting, Research, Advocacy, Interviewing and Negotiation skills. Since then, there has been a dramatic upsurge in the level of skills-based and clinical education in the United Kingdom: see Harris et al (1993). This has been particularly marked by the formation, in 1994, of CLEO – the Clinical Legal Education Organisation – a loose association of individuals from nearly 20 university sector institutions offering (or interested in developing) live client and simulated clinical programmes.

Second, the later 1970s also saw an expansion in courses developing *foundational* legal skills. These started out as courses which attempted to teach the 'applied science' of legal reasoning by focusing, often in a fairly technical 'black-letter' fashion, on the principles of precedent and statutory interpretation. These basic legal method courses have not only become increasingly common, they have often evolved into far more multifunctional courses, fusing a range of basic legal, general study and other transferable skills (eg, library research; understanding legal sources; legal writing; legal argumentation) with the substantive legal method and, perhaps, some introduction to jurisprudence and/or the legal system in context.[2]

So, what are the reasons underlying the movement towards skills-based learning in law and why has the skills movement developed in the way it has? These are quite complex questions, which we do not intend to address fully here. Nevertheless, as the answers go some way to explaining our motivations in putting this collection together, we offer some pointers along the way.

2   To some extent this process is reflected by the development of general student texts in the area. The whole history can almost be traced through the transformation of Farrar's *Introduction to Legal Method* (1977) to its present format: Farrar & Dugdale (1991). The other seminal text is, of course, Twining & Mier's *How To Do Things With Rules* (first published in 1976). The more recent focus on a combination of basic study skills, or a mix of study skills and applied skills, with 'legal method', is reflected not only in the latest editions of those texts, but in more recent additions such as Holland & Webb's *Learning Legal Rules* and Lee & Fox's *Learning Legal Skills*, both first published in 1991.

Why skills?

Undoubtedly, knowledge of the American and Commonwealth experience and of the reforms at the vocational stage have played a major part in encouraging and opening up the skills debate. But there have been other factors as well.

Firstly, the law schools have not been immune from pressures for skills from outside and inside the university. Employer and student demand for 'practical relevance' is the most obvious and most commonly cited example, as in Bright (1991); Halpern (1994), pp 36–7. There are others. In the former polytechnic sector, Her Majesty's Inspectorate and the Council for National Academic Awards both encouraged a greater diversity of teaching and learning methods, and particularly a shift from teacher-centred to student-centred forms of learning in which skills-based methods have played a leading role. Following the abolition of the old binary divide, it is perhaps unsurprising that similar noises are now being heard from the Scottish Committee of University Principals (1992) and, if the evidence of a fairly recent seminar described by Entwistle (1994) is anything to go by, from the Committee of Vice-Chancellors and Principals. Other wider developments, such as the Royal Society of Arts' 'Higher Education for Capability', the (former) Training Agency 'Enterprise in Higher Education' and the PICKUP[3] initiatives, have also played their part (i) in creating a connection between the academy and the world of work[4] and (ii) in moving the university's perspective away from the learning needs of its traditional post-A level 'clientele': for example, see Duke (1992), Chapter 2. Pressure from teaching assessments and quality audits may also have a similar effect.[5]

Second, skills-based approaches have fitted in with certain kinds of institutional ethos. It is recognised that the move towards more

---

3   'Professional, Industrial and Commercial Updating'.
4   As Boon (1990) points out (at p 25), these wider initiatives are therefore at odds in many respects with the attitudes of those in the legal profession who see a continuing demarcation between academic and vocational skills.
5   However, not all such pressures are supportive of skills developments. Demands to increase research output in order to capitalise on the financial benefits of the Research Assessment Exercises certainly create a significant counter pressure. Inevitably, most law schools face a trade-off. Staff cannot easily increase research output *and* develop labour-intensive skills programmes or other student-centred approaches. One or other objective is likely to suffer, perhaps both: see eg Brownsword (1994); Jenkins & Gibbs (1995).

skills-based teaching and learning has been most widespread in the new university sector: see Jones (1992); Tribe & Tribe (1992); Harris et al (1993). This has much to do with the institutional framework and structures involved – the oft-cited 'practical' bent of the former polytechnics being the most amorphous example of this. More pragmatically, the incorporation of law teaching within wider interdisciplinary structures at institutions like Leeds Metropolitan, Anglia Polytechnic and Central England Universities has meant that law has, for good or ill, been unable to lock itself into a disciplinary cocoon. Cross-fertilisation of methods between, say, the law schools and the business schools has taken place. In some instances, the law programmes have been tied into inter-departmental modular schemes, with the result that law teachers have had to take on board the wider skills objectives of the modular programme.

Conversely, in the old university sector there has been some greater reluctance to accept that skills teaching (other than research skills or 'legal method') is not so tainted with vocationalism as to fall beyond the academic pale: see Bradney (1992), and also Jones (1992) for some empirical evidence.[6] This reluctance now appears to be less marked than it was. Certainly there is evidence of a settlement on pluralist terms which accepts that a balanced undergraduate legal education requires an appropriate mixture (however that may be defined) of skills, substantive law and legal theory: for example, Birks (1993); Twining (1994); ACLEC (1994).

Thirdly, at a more theoretical level, the process of widening participation to higher education for non-traditional students has created new challenges for university teachers. We have been made increasingly aware that non-traditional adults may possess different needs from our traditional 18–21 year old post-A level students. As Alan Tuckett (1990) has noted: 'Adults need a system that can measure what students know, are capable of doing, can show they have learned...' (p 131). Higher education accordingly has shown a growing awareness of andragogy – the processes of adult education – and discovered that these may have something to offer all students, not just the non-traditional: see Macfarlane (1992). A particular facet of this has been a growing concern for the development

---

6   It is easy to overstate the case here. In reality, studies such as Macfarlane et al (1987) suggest that most law teachers accept that the degree should have some vocational relevance, but argue that it is not a major function of the degree to prepare students for the world of work.

in students of a capacity for 'lifelong learning'[7] rather than simply preparing them for the particular hurdles required by (say) the initial or vocational stage: see ACLEC (1995), paras 2.11, 3.4. Lastly, this process of 'skilling' the initial stage has arguably received a further push with the deconstruction of the law degree through the widespread modularisation of courses, and (more debatably) following the relaxation of prescription in the Law Society/Bar *Joint Statement* of 1995. Some institutions[8] have clearly used modularisation as an opportunity to create or extend the range of skills-based modules within the degree programme.

Whither skills?

Learning Lawyers' Skills has become part of the iconography of the skills movement. It was – and is – not just a useful toolkit for skills teachers. It has helped create a powerful image of what elements constitute lawyers' skills, and of how they should be taught and assessed. At the same time, like all texts, it describes ideas that are of a given moment. For many of us now engaged in skills, it provided a springboard which gave us a firmer base for our own teaching and learning. However, the skills debate has moved apace since 1989, and we hope the authors will forgive us therefore for treating their book as a representation of a number of key ideas that have dominated the skills debate into the 1990s. There are three particular ideas we wish to address.

7 The notion of lifelong learning is generally taken to imply a process with most if not all of the following characteristics:
  1. learning that is intentional rather than spontaneous or unplanned learning;
  2. learning that has a definite goal rather than a simple concern with 'broadening the mind';
  3. learning that equips individuals with the knowledge, skills and attitudes to cope with change, either in their occupational or social sphere; and
  4. learning that is acquired with the intention that the knowledge/skill is to be used *immediately* (this is a key distinction, following Piaget, between pedagogy and andragogy).
  See generally Knapper & Cropley (1985); Ball (1989).
8 For example, the LLB at Anglia Polytechnic University offers five skills modules: Research, Writing & Communication at level 1 and Fact Investigation & Analysis (level 2) are compulsory; Interviewing & Counselling, Negotiation & Advocacy, and a further Research module are all optional at levels 2 or 3. Staffordshire University's LLB similarly contains three skills modules: Interviewing (level 1, compulsory), Negotiation (level 2, compulsory) and Advocacy (level 3, optional). The influence of the DRAIN skills approach on these structures is plain to see.

The division between foundational and applied skills

For whatever reason, the professions have, in the past, sought to distinguish the generic and specific intellectual skills of the law degree from the applied skills of vocational and continuing education. This approach was central to the Marre Committee (1988) recommendations on legal education, and it certainly informs the present division of skills between the initial and vocational stages of legal education. Certainly part of the value of *Learning Lawyers' Skills* is that it contains materials from undergraduate and vocational programmes, and it does not attempt a strong differentiation of the two. But neither does it ultimately deny the distinction. To be fair, that is not really its function.

Skills teachers at the academic stage, however, have long had their doubts about the logic of a divide which overlooks the extent to which all legal education has as a central concern the development of the knowledge, skills and attitudes necessary to engage in effective legal problem solving: see Wangerin (1986); Nathanson (1989). The approval of a four-year exempting law degree at Northumbria University, and the less prescriptive approach to skills favoured by the Lord Chancellor's Advisory Committee, ACLEC (1994), suggest that the lines of demarcation are breaking down.[9] It is perhaps no coincidence that a recurrent theme in a number of the contributions which follow is the continuity, if not the inseparability, of the academic and the professional.

The emphasis on competence

Learning Lawyers' Skills also reflected the centrality of competence and outcome-led approaches to the first wave of skills-based learning. That is, there was an emphasis on teaching and assessment methods that focus on developing and assessing appropriate performance in particular skilled activities, such as client interviewing, etc. This has not been the only approach to skills-based learning, however, and our own experiences suggest that an increasing number of skills teachers are starting to look for models of teaching and

---

9   However, the fact that ACLEC's aims for the initial stage (1994) give way, at the vocational stage (1995), to the general aim of 'developing the capacity to apply lawyerlike thought to lawyerlike action' (para 3.2) could be read as suggesting the primary emphasis on problem solving skills remains at the vocational stage.

learning that take us beyond competence. The exploration of alternative models is a key feature of the present collection.

The dominance of DRAIN

Attempts to develop lawyering skills courses have largely reflected the practice of both the Commonwealth vocational courses, and the American competencies movement to identify lawyers' skills according to the DRAIN (Drafting, Research, Advocacy, Interviewing and Negotiation) categories. This distinction is well established and has the advantage of task-based coherence. Perhaps it is also limiting for the same reason. It can disguise the extent to which many of the basic skills lawyers use are common to a range of these tasks. How far the ideological dominance of the DRAIN model has restricted both research and teaching initiatives which attempt to construct/use alternative models, which might better reflect the cognitive as opposed to behavioural basis of lawyers skills, is a moot point. A number of papers in this collection begin to point us in this direction, though we take the view that there is much work that remains to be done on the nature of legal problem solving before we can realistically progress towards alternative conceptualisations of legal skills that will work in the classroom.

A prospectus

Looking back, some six years on from *Learning Lawyers' Skills*, we therefore felt it was time to publish another book on legal skills education, with four aims in mind:
- To illustrate how the skills debate has developed since the late 1980s, particularly at the initial stage, with an emphasis away from the relatively behavioural, outcome-led models of the legal practice courses, to increasingly holistic and reflective approaches.
- To provide practical guidance on the development of skills in a variety of legal educational contexts.
- Given the broader base of experience in skills teaching in the UK, to reflect on issues of delivering applied skills courses at both the initial and vocational stages of legal education.
- To reflect on a variety of course design, assessment and evaluation issues.

In attempting to meet these aims we have divided the collection into three parts. In Part I we have included two introductory essays on the learning process; these papers consider the research on student learning and look at the role of educational theory in informing curriculum design. The contributions in Part II, when taken together, identify a variety of models for skills education, and reflect on their authors' concrete experiences of designing and delivering skills-based courses for both academic and professional programmes. Part III then focuses on issues of assessment and evaluation. In our view this aspect of programme design and implementation has long been treated as the poor relation in the legal education literature.

We have tried to put together a collection that blends theory and practice and that contains something of value to both the novice skills teacher and the more experienced. We hope you find the result not just interesting but an encouragement to experiment with your own teaching. If there is one single message that comes out of this collection, it is that the skills movement is still evolving, and (appropriately enough) learning from its own experience.

References

ACLEC – Lord Chancellor's Advisory Committee on Legal Education and Conduct (1994) *Review of Legal Education. Consultation Paper: The Initial Stage*, ACLEC, London.

ACLEC (1995) *Review of Legal Education. Consultation Paper: The Vocational Stage and Continuing Professional Development*, ACLEC, London.

C Ball (1989) 'Should education continue?', in 1(1) *Adults Learning* 7.

P Birks (1993) 'A Decade of Turmoil in Legal Education' in P Birks (ed) *Examining the Law Syllabus: Beyond the Core*, Oxford University Press, Oxford.

A Boon (1990) 'Enterprise in Higher Education: A New Agenda for Educational Change?', 24 *Law Teacher* 14.

A Bradney (1992) 'Ivory Towers and Satanic Mills: Choices for University Law Schools', 17 *Studies in Higher Education* 5.

S Bright (1991), 'What, and How, Should We Be Teaching?' 25 *Law Teacher* 11.

R Brownsword (1994) 'Teaching Quality Assessment in Law Schools: A Cause for Concern?', 21 *Journal of Law & Society* 259.

CSUP – Committee of Scottish University Principals Working Party, (1992) *Teaching and Learning in an Expanding Higher Education System*, CSUP, Edinburgh.

C Duke (1992) *The Learning University: Towards a New Paradigm?* SRHE/Open University Press, Buckingham.

N Entwistle (1994) *Teaching and the Quality of Learning* CVCP/SRHE, London.

N Gold, K Mackie & W Twining (eds) (1989) *Learning Lawyers' Skills*, Butterworths, London.

D Halpern (1994) *Entry into the Legal Professions*, Research Study No 15, the Law Society, London.

P Harris & S Bellerby with P Leighton & J Hodgson (1993) *A Survey of Law Teaching 1993*, Sweet & Maxwell/Association of Law Teachers, London.

A Jenkins & G Gibbs (1995) 'Scandal of postgrad army' *Times Higher Education Supplement*, 15 September, p 13.

P A Jones (1992) 'Skills and Assessment in Undergraduate Law Courses – A Survey', *CASEL Working Paper No 1*, CNAA, London.

C Knapper & A Cropley (1985) *Lifelong Learning and Higher Education*, Croom Helm, London.

K N Llewellyn (1945) 'The Place of Skills in Legal Education', 45 *Columbia Law Review* 345.

J Macfarlane (1992) 'Look Before You Leap: Knowledge and Learning in Legal Skills Education', 19 *Journal of Law & Society* 293.

J Macfarlane, M Jeeves & A Boon (1987), 'Education for Life or for Work?', 137 *New Law Journal* 835.

S Nathanson (1989) 'The Role of Problem Solving in Legal Education', 39 *Journal of Legal Education* 167.

C Roper (1988) 'The Legal Practice Courses – Theoretical Frameworks and Models', 6 *Journal of Professional Legal Education* 77.

M Spiegal (1987) 'Theory and Practice in Legal Education: An Essay on Clinical Education', 34 *UCLA Law Review* 577.

D M R Tribe & A J Tribe (1992) 'The Law Teacher's Dilemma' in R Barnett (ed) *Learning to Effect*, SRHE/Open University Press, Guildford.

A Tuckett (1990) 'A higher education system fit for adult learners' in G Parry & C Wake (eds) *Access and Alternative Futures for Higher Education*, Hodder & Stoughton, London.

W Twining (1988) 'Legal Skills and Legal Education', 22 *Law Teacher* 4.

W Twining (1993) 'The Idea of Juristic Method: A Tribute to Karl Llewellyn', 48 *University of Miami Law Review* 119.

W Twining (1994) *Blackstone's Tower: The English Law School*, Sweet & Maxwell, London.

P T Wangerin (1986) 'Skills Training in "Legal Analysis": A Systematic Approach', 40 *University of Miami Law Review* 409.

Part I

The learning process

In this section we present two papers which address the role of learning theory in legal education in rather different ways.

In the first of these papers, Diana Tribe stresses the importance of learning theory as a means to greater understanding of how students learn and as a basis for optimising our teaching. Tribe begins her analysis by drawing the classic distinction between learning *models* and learning *styles*. By focusing on two models which have been particularly influential in higher education, the work of D P Ausubel and Benjamin Bloom, she emphasises the importance of (i) student participation and (ii) the need for tutors to structure learning so as to encourage understanding and to foster a 'deep' style of learning. Tribe then goes on to consider evidence from studies of student learning to support the development of more 'experiential' and student-centred approaches to learning the law, and their implications for law teaching and assessment.

Julian Webb's paper builds on a number of Tribe's themes to offer an analysis and critique of legal education that focuses more on the epistemological failings of the traditional approach to law teaching, than on the psychology of student learning. He particularly explores the significance of a number of approaches to legal skills education. The approaches he explores, which he terms competence, capability and holistic approaches, share a common grounding in experiential learning theory, but stress markedly different outcomes of the learning process. Webb concludes his paper by exploring one particular holistic approach and offering a brief SWOT analysis for theorising legal skills education.

Chapter 1

How students learn
Diana Tribe

Introduction

Law lecturers will often attribute student failure to laziness or lack of intellectual ability; however, there are many students who, having failed in one subject at one University, go on to perform perfectly satisfactorily at another. What is it about this second experience which produces success in such a student? The cynical might attribute the change in level of performance to a variance in standards of assessment at differing institutions; however, it may equally be the case that the subject content, curriculum design or method of teaching at the second University is more suitable to the individual student's intellectual needs:

> Law Teaching is conducted in a variety of ways; some subjects are taught in large lectures with small tutorials; others in large tutorial groups; others in seminars; others on the basis of self study and self directed learning. Some courses offer a clinical programme; others a skills programme. There is already considerable variety.
>
> Partington (1994)

Indeed, there is a wealth of impressionistic evidence describing teaching methods that are said to lead to effective and high quality learning, as opposed to those which do not. All law lecturers have their own ideas about what constitutes a proper learning environment in which their students can prosper. Some are committed to student-directed learning and the integration of skills, others believe that the more hours spent in the classroom the better will be the

5

student results, whilst yet others believe that a well produced set of learning materials with minimum staff–student contact should be sufficient to ensure student success. Attempts to obtain rigorous, objective evidence of the effectiveness of the various innovations in higher education have, however, run into intractable problems due to the difficulty of defining what actually characterises 'effective' learning. Despite the now widespread use of student feedback questionnaires, students remain notoriously poor judges of how much they learn from one method compared with another, whilst law lecturers are similarly poor at judging the most effective methods of motivating students and conveying information to them. The student feedback questionnaire is in serious danger of becoming a form of 'beauty parade' in which the most favoured (for whatever reason) lecturers get the highest grades!

Most of the research examining the relationship between teaching methods and their products, in terms of what and how students learn, has been based on the undifferentiated criterion of 'achievement' or 'academic performance':

> The precise definition of achievement varies from institution to institution, from discipline to discipline and even from department to department . . . thus there is often rather little objective evidence available to indicate the strength and consistency of the influence of particular teaching methods on specific learning outcomes.
>
> Entwistle (1992)

The truth of Entwistle's statement is borne out by analysis of the present position in the University sector in the second half of the 1990s. In some law schools students are recruited from the very highest band of school achievers whilst other institutions have as an integral part of their university mission the aim of recruiting students from groups who have had limited formal education, and some law schools recruit students from both groups. It is important to note that Partington (1994), commenting on the Lord Chancellor's Consultation Paper on the Initial Stage of Legal Education, specifically stated that 'there is the reassertion – which does now need making – of the importance of ensuring that access to the initial stage of legal education is afforded to students from as wide a range of backgrounds as possible'.

It is not possible, however, to compare the effectiveness of similar teaching methods on such dissimilar groups of students, for what is appropriate and effective with one group may be inappropriate and ineffective with another. Nonetheless, Universities find themselves under increasing pressure to ensure that the drop-out and failure rate of students on their courses is kept to a minimum (note that impressionistic evidence obtained by the writer would seem to imply that the drop-out/failure rate amongst law undergraduates is a high one by comparison with other disciplines). For this reason, if for no other, a basic knowledge and understanding of learning theory is helpful for law lecturers, since it provides information about how students learn, which in turn provides the foundation for decisions about optimum methods of teaching which should produce better results for students and for their Universities. The section below outlines some aspects of psychological learning theory which are believed to be of importance in the education of law students.

Learning theory

Meaningful reception learning

One of the most common models for learning utilised in higher education is based upon the work of D P Ausubel (1961), (1978). The main propositions upon which the model is based seem particularly relevant to higher education. For Ausubel, meaningful learning is a distinctive process with distinctive outcomes which require active student participation for its success; it is qualitatively different and distinct from the rote learning of material that is short on meaning. Law lecturers are only too familiar with the conscientious student who 'learns his notes' and yet can neither analyse them constructively nor elicit from them basic legal principles for application to real or hypothetical situations. Ausubel rejects this kind of learning in favour of more active student participation with the aim of developing meaning. He suggests that lecturers should explicitly relate each learning task to previously acquired knowledge, for the importance of pre-existing cognitive structures, to which new learning is potentially related, is a central theme of his work. These structures comprise existing organisations of knowledge which are stable and clear. It has been empirically demonstrated that new material will be more readily understood and remembered when it is linked in this way to earlier learning:

> If we had to reduce all educational psychology to just one principle, we would say this: the most important single factor influencing learning, is what the learner already knows.

On the other hand, if earlier material has been learned in a disorganised and unstable way, then it has also been empirically demonstrated that new material will tend to be learned in a rote manner because the learner cannot imbue it with meaning. Discussions with law students on their preferred style of learning indicates that in many cases students do learn in a disorganised and unstable way. They learn by rote without relating the current topic to earlier ones, failing to make those connections between different parts of the syllabus which are so necessary for meaningful learning. Thus, in Tort, students frequently fail to comprehend that breach of duty alone does not establish liability, whilst Criminal Law examination scripts regularly demonstrate the misunderstanding of students who believe that 'recklessness' is a crime. These mistakes appear to arise from a partial rote learning of the syllabus by students anxious to pass examinations through the last-minute revision of lecture notes which were barely comprehended at the time of taking, and the meaning of which has long since been forgotten.

Ausubel's model can be applied to the planning of lectures so that at the start of each session students' existing knowledge of relevant legal concepts can be elicited through questioning or other teaching devices. For instance, in the first Criminal Law lecture of the year students might be encouraged to reflect on relevant knowledge acquired through the media and through earlier study of the criminal justice system, so that this can form the basis for discussion of the criminal law principles of actus reus and mens rea.

A second aspect of 'meaningful reception learning' in Ausubel's model involves the induction in the student of what is described as a 'learning set' to operate in a meaningful (ie: non-rote) manner. Ausubel argues that however inherently meaningful material may be, unless the learner approaches it with the active intention of acquiring meaning (as opposed to an arbitrarily related set of facts and notions), the learning outcomes are unlikely to be meaningful (Gagné describes this as 'attention set'). Thus, for instance, a meaningful learning set may be developed in students through the deliberate selection of materials for student study which pose cognitive conflict. Following Dewey, it is generally agreed that learning requires recognition by the learner of a problem and of his initial inability to solve it. The result of this first step is the development in the learner of a feeling of dissatisfaction known variously as disequilibrium (Piaget), cognitive dissonance (Festinger), or conceptual conflict (Berlyne). All these models are based on the assumption that human beings experience a strong motivational drive to seek more knowledge in order to relieve conflict. In fact both Berlyne and Ausubel have advocated the deliberate induction of cognitive conflict on the part of the lecturer, to arouse motivation and attention in the student. This can be achieved by presenting students with materials in which apparently conflicting decisions have been reached by the courts. Questions should then be posed which motivate the students into meaningful intellectual activity which in turn assists in the resolution of the conceptual conflict and the development of sound legal concepts. Thus, for instance, a comparison of the decisions in *R v Deller* and *R v Dadson* at the commencement of a criminal law course will lead students to perceive the ratio of the two cases as being apparently inconsistent, until they can develop a legal concept that can account satisfactorily for both decisions.

A third important aspect of Ausubel's model is the use of appropriately clear and inclusive introductory materials which operate as 'advance organisers' for the learning that is to follow. These organisers are introduced in advance of the material to be learned to facilitate the establishment of a general and inclusive explanatory basis for the subsequent content. It must be emphasised here that 'advance organisers' do not consist of an overview of the material to be covered, but rather that they serve to set the material in an explanatory context which can provide the basis for the retention and incorporation of the more detailed and differentiated subject matter that is to follow. The effect of 'advance organisers' on learning has been empirically demonstrated by Postman and by Ausubel. New material is rendered more familiar to the student through their use, while much of the undesirable rote memorisation to which students resort when they are made to learn the details of a discipline before acquiring a sufficient number of subsuming key concepts is made unnecessary.

Thus questions about hypothetical problems may be used to lead students towards a general concept underpinning the subsequent detailed understanding to be acquired. For example, in considering, in the law of Tort, whether damage is too remote to give rise to liability students may be asked to compare the decisions in cases such as *Hughes v Lord Advocate* [1963] and *Doughty v Turner Manufacturing* [1964].

An analysis of these decisions, which appear at first sight to be inconsistent with each other, enables students to develop the general tort principle that the fact that damage occurred in an unforeseeable way does not necessarily mean that the damage itself was unforeseeable (and thus non-compensatable).

Taxonomy of educational objectives in the cognitive domain

The work of Benjamin Bloom on learning objectives has also been of considerable influence in higher education. Bloom (1956) identified six hierarchical levels of learning objectives in the cognitive domain.

The six fundamental levels are labelled:

> knowledge;
> comprehension;
> application;
> analysis;
> synthesis; and
> evaluation.

According to Bloom these levels represent a hierarchy based upon the increasing complexity of intellectual behaviour required to achieve each succeeding objective. Moreover, the hierarchy is cumulative, since the attainment of an objective at a given level will be dependent upon the attainment of objectives at lower levels. Underlying much of the current criticism of law teaching is the view that traditional law teaching does not promote thought at the higher levels. This is borne out by observation which indicates that in many lectures there is a heavy emphasis on knowledge acquisition at Bloom Level 1 (and sometimes on associated note-taking skills). This emphasis is underlined by the current practice of providing law students with detailed lecture handouts which obviate the need for note-taking: many students fail to attend lectures on the grounds that they already 'have the notes', and those that do attend have no need to concentrate on the lecturer's meaning since the printed notes are to hand for later perusal.

However, Petter believes that law schools should provide for all six levels of cognitive learning within their curricula:

... it is necessary that they should teach students (1) to know the law; (2) to comprehend it; (3) to apply it to particular fact situations; (4) to break it down into its component parts; (5) to reorganise it and apply it creatively to serve clients' interests; (6) to evaluate the strength of its authority and its probable impact upon clients.

This does not mean that giving students factual information is not helpful in developing high level intellectual skills, but it does mean that information conveyed through the lecturing mode can only be assimilated by the learner and converted into higher order cognitive functioning by the exercise of higher order cognitive skills. Hence the need for practice, information and feedback. It is axiomatic, as Petter has pointed out, that one cannot teach a student to learn at a higher cognitive level by addressing him at a lower cognitive level. Thus law students cannot be expected to answer hypothetical problems at anything other than the knowledge level, if that is the level at which they are addressed.

Curriculum implications of different student learning styles

Entwistle and Ramsden (1983), Marton (1976), Pask (1976) and many others have, in their research, identified student approaches to learning which may broadly be categorised as either 'surface' or 'deep' processing of information. Some students (who, it would appear, tend to be less successful in examinations) take a passive approach and are mainly concerned with the surface-level processing of academic knowledge. Typically such students are primarily concerned with 'getting the notes' (see above) and 'covering the content'; how many cases or pages they have learned; finding the 'right' answers; and assimilating unaltered pieces of knowledge (ie those upon which they have performed no intellectual operation themselves) by a process of rote learning. It is possible that such students may have found this approach suitable for school learning in some subjects, and attempt to apply it to the university situation without being made aware of its very great disadvantages at the level of higher education.

By contrast, other students, who employ deep-level processing of material (and who it would appear from the research cited above, tend to be much more successful in examinations) are typically concerned with identifying the central point of an argument; what lies behind the argument; the overall picture; the logic of an argument; points that remain unclear; and with questioning conclusions reached by others. In other words, deep processors tend to process the information actively: they are more concerned with *understanding* and *thinking things through* than with the pure assimilation of facts. These deep-processing students are also shown to be more versatile, and find it easier to tackle hypothetical questions than do surface processors whose style is simply to reproduce on the paper in the examination situation the facts that they have already learned, regardless of their application and relevance to the question under consideration.

For the sake of those students whose cognitive style leads them to operate a deep-processing approach to learning, it is important to provide an academic opportunity for them to do so. This is best achieved, as Entwistle suggests, through facilitating student learning by means of large and small group methods. Group work as a part of the undergraduate law curriculum has become increasingly common over the past 15 years despite the firmly entrenched view of many law lecturers that such work is inappropriate to study at degree level.

Examples of group learning for law students in HE include group reports and videos made on the working of the courts, group working on fact management files, and contract and environmental law workshops in which students work co-operatively together on problems. The recently introduced Legal Practice Course utilises this method in many law schools through the operation of small groups of four or six students within a workshop of about 60 students. Whilst this approach to learning is vital for the deep processors among the student body, it is also important to demonstrate this style for the sake of surface processors, to give them the opportunity to model their behaviour on that of their peers. It is likely, moreover, that there are some versatile students who actually employ both deep and surface techniques interchangeably and these students will also benefit from a learning environment which provides the opportunity for both deep and surface processing of information.

Experiential learning

In his seminal text *Remembering*, Sir Frederick Bartlett (1932) demonstrated a variety of ways in which the mental processes of students who listened to (or read for) information made an active contribution to how much information they actually learned.

From Bartlett's findings it is clear that the processes that make meaningful learning possible are by no means restricted to what is generally perceived by lecturers to be the passive storage of information for subsequent recall. By contrast, the individual student actively sets out to develop a range of coding processes (whether she knows it or not), through which the received information is acted upon in ways that select, scan, modify and integrate that knowledge. This may of course have the result that a student may make mistakes and may internalise a severely distorted version of what was presented to her, depending upon the way in which the knowledge is processed. The form taken by such coding operations depends largely upon the *existing knowledge and the mental processes already possessed* by the particular student who is attempting to assimilate the material. Thus, as many law lecturers will testify, there is an important distinction to be drawn between the form in which knowledge is presented to students by their lecturers, the way in which students process that knowledge, and the form in which it is eventually recalled at the point of assessment. Indeed it is a painful, but nonetheless salutary process, for a lecturer to read a set of student notes of a lecture that she has recently delivered: the discrepancy between the meaning that was intended to be conveyed and the meaning that was actually conveyed can be considerable.

Howe (1970), replicating an experiment carried out by one of Bartlett's pupils, Kay (1955), set out to test the validity of this proposition; he presented postgraduate students with a learning task in which they were required to listen to information made available in meaningful prose form, and were then asked to reproduce it. The material was repeated on a number of occasions at weekly intervals, and the learners were allowed to make a number of separate recall attempts, usually also at weekly intervals. The results, which showed overall increasing accuracy of recall in successive sessions, are unsurprising; what was surprising, however, was the very small scale of the week-by-week improvement. One might have anticipated that providing repeated opportunities for students to remember the content of the passages would lead to dramatically improved rates of retention and recall. In the event, the improvements, when they did occur, were very modest indeed. Examination of the results showed that, on average, an item recalled correctly on the first recall trial had a 0.7 probability of being recalled again on the succeeding trial, whilst if this item was recalled over three successive attempts, the probability of further correct recall was as high as 0.98. However, the probability of an item which was not recalled on the first occasion being correct on the subsequent attempt was only 0.2, and even on the third and fourth repetitions the probability remained at a very low level. In short, the probability of an item being recalled was only weakly related to the number of times that the subject had heard it, and probability of recall was strongly influenced by the contents of the students' own previous experience.

What emerges strongly from these findings is that, however frequently a lecturer repeats information or gives correct answers to a piece of coursework carried out by a student, the repetition, of itself, will not improve the level of her understanding. The evidence suggests that the knowledge that an individual will retain is very strongly determined by the work that *she herself has previously carried out*. It is the materials which the student has produced or reproduced that will be remembered in the future: presumably this is because some of the coding and processing that the individual must undertake with meaningful verbal materials, in order to be able to reproduce information on subsequent occasions, has the effect of ensuring that those materials have a highly stable place in the cognitive structure of the individual's memory system. Whatever the detailed processes involved, the findings have practical implications for those who teach law students.

Indeed, it will not have escaped the reader's attention that the research design of this project was in many ways similar to the still widely prevalent practice of lecturing to law students on a weekly basis, with assessment points occurring at regular points throughout the learning period. Lecturers commonly adopt a pattern of instruction followed by in-course assessment, subsequently going over the problem in class to provide the correct answers and often providing students with a model answer, on the assumption that informing a student what the answer should have been, will help learning. Indeed, the publication of law texts giving questions together with model answers has been highly popular with students, although there is no evidence that their performance has benefited in any way from the possession of these texts. The experimental findings indicate that such practices are likely to be unsuccessful: where a student's version is incorrect, simply being told the right answer would appear to be insufficient to ensure its adequate understanding, retention and subsequent recall. In fact, the evidence would suggest that lecturing to large groups of students, where the only voice that is heard is that of the lecturer, tends to be an inefficient use of time and energy. Students are more likely to learn in a situation where they are required to process information actively, seeking solutions and discussing problems with their teachers and their peers.

A broader implication of the work of such authors as Bartlett and Kolb is that, as law lecturers, we should pay far more attention to learners' previous experiential learning (ie earlier activities and knowledge) and attend less exclusively to our own instructional variables and manner of presentation, for the variables associated with learner activity, rather than teacher activity, are the most crucial ones.

The term 'experiential learning' is currently used to describe two rather different broad concepts. '*Prior* experiential learning' describes the relevant learning which has already been acquired in some experience prior to the particular teaching and learning situation under consideration. Thus, many law students have experience of note-taking, revision prior to examinations and the taking of examinations which will affect the learning strategies which they utilise at university; similarly, students studying employment law who have already studied the law of contract will have acquired relevant information upon which the new learning can be based and from which it can be developed.

> *Further* experiential learning describes the active and interactive situations within which higher level cognitive and affective goals are attained, and in which the lecturer is involved as a facilitator.
>
> Cowan (1988)

Here the student, through strategies devised by the facilitating lecturer, operates on and internalises new information, integrating it with that previously learned. This would seem to be the foundation stone for effective teaching and learning in higher education.

Once the undoubted existence of these types of prior experiential learning is accepted by law lecturers, there are clear implications for the methods of instruction that those lecturers will use. The time-honoured and simple expedient of treating all students in a class in the same way is clearly inappropriate; this is particularly true in the light of the increase in the proportion of 'non-standard' student entrants who are studying law.

It is becoming increasingly common for international students with varying qualifications and home students without prior 'A' Level experience, but with acceptable alternative learning experiences (APEL; APL), to form a significant percentage of the normal law class. Under such circumstances it becomes necessary, therefore, for lecturers to devise and offer appropriate learning instruction to all such students. It can be argued that the need for students to learn in an experiential and self-directed way requires traditional law lecturers to pass over the:

> absolute control which has previously rested with them as didactic instructors, with authority over the passive recipients of learning who make up their classes. Instead the (lecturer) must now become a resource, a facilitator of learning, supporting and not directing the autonomous learners.
>
> Cowan (1988)

Cowan suggests that firstly, individual students' needs should be identified by reviewing their own prior experiential learning. Secondly, after the learner has been offered the opportunity to explore new concepts or experiences in further experiential learning, she should be encouraged to reflect on that experience, analyse it and generalise from it to formulate a sharper definition of what has been learnt and what remains to be learned. This is a constructive preparation for the third level of experiential learning in which concepts are consolidated and refined, in preparation for the fourth level, which is their subsequent application elsewhere. Those readers who are familiar with Bloom's taxonomy of educational objectives (1956) (see p 10 above) will observe some similarities here with the levels in his taxonomy described as 'knowledge', 'understanding', and 'application'.

Similarly Kolb's Learning Cycle (1979), (1984) is based on the principle that, when adults undertake to learn something for themselves, there is a natural learning cycle which follows four stages.

Firstly, there is the starting point which is the individual student's concrete experience; secondly, students will then make observations and reflections on this experience; the third step involves the student in making abstract concepts and generalisations about the new information to make sense of their reflections, which then leads on to the final step, the testing of the implications of those concepts in new situations.

The implication of all these different models of the learning process for law lecturers is that they must be made aware that *prior experiential learning* affects the ability of students to respond to the learning environment offered; that higher level cognitive abilities and interpersonal and communication skills are only capable of being developed in *active learning situations* (ie not lectures); that students must be encouraged to *appraise their own level of learning* rather than simply relying on the lecturer's appraisal, because the lecturer's role as facilitator is of vital importance and quite different from the traditional role of didactic lecturer. These implications fit in well with the current preoccupation within higher education with student self-directed learning, non-taught modules, distance learning and credit accumulation and transfer, all of which are based, at least theoretically, upon the desirability of students managing their own learning.

Interestingly, these conclusions are supported by the Lord Chancellor's Advisory Committee on Legal Education and Conduct, ACLEC (1994), which emphasised the importance of developing 'student centred learning' in law, in which students take active responsibility for their own learning rather than being the passive audience in a didactic teaching situation.

A number of practical classroom problems are suggested by Cowan's analysis: the variable prior learning experiences within a normal class group can lead to difficulties for those who feel themselves to be at a disadvantage in terms of prior learning experience (eg, first year law students who have not recently completed a course of 'A' Level study, or acquired an 'A' Level in Law, or for whom English is not their first language). If a substantial minority of students feel themselves to be at a disadvantage in the learning situation, in these kinds of ways, this can have, as many lecturers will agree, negative and disruptive effects on the class dynamic.

Conversion of students to the methodology of self-directed learning can be a slow process: most students, when they arrive at university, have been trained to be passive learners who depend almost entirely for their learning on input from a teacher. They are doubtful of their ability to be successful with student-directed learning packages and self-study modules, and often doubtful of their academic validity. They frequently express these doubts as criticisms of the course, its style and its objectives. This in turn has the effect of making academic staff doubtful of the validity of self-directed learning, group study and distance learning activities.

Implications of learning models for the assessment and evaluation of student work

> One of the marked changes that has taken place over the last twenty years has been the acceptance that the three hour unseen examination may not be the best, certainly not the exclusive, way of assessing the outcome of student learning.
>
> Partington (1994)

Whilst the easiest and probably the cheapest method of assessing students is by means of the three-hour written examination, other processes like coursework, projects, and dissertations have all become accepted ways of assessing student learning. In addition, some institutions assess students' oral performance in tutorials or other forms of oral contribution, and some assess the outcomes of jointly prepared work. Although the ACLEC Consultation Paper certainly encouraged law lecturers to utilise more progressive and innovative methods of assessment, there are fears that the introduction of semesterisation throughout the sector will lead staff, who are often labouring under an assessment 'overload', back into the traditional 'formulaic' methods of assessment rather than experimenting with new methods.

If the implications of the learning theory referred to above are taken seriously, however, this will lead to the further development of student-directed and self-managed learning, which in its turn must lead to the development of new assessment strategies.

The criteria by which such work is to be assessed require careful consideration, however, particularly where the work to be assessed is non-traditional. The South Bank case study in the CASEL project indicated that however carefully criteria for the assessment of skills were constructed, law lecturers tended to base their assessment on intuition which was then justified against the criteria. This finding was also duplicated by the University of Hertfordshire team's investigations for the CASEL project: Jones (1994). However, criteria do need to be clearly understood by markers and transmitted to students, especially where they are engaged in group work and self-directed study: see Tribe (1996).

New assessment practices based on learning theory should, it is argued, be built around the eight key principles outlined by Barnes (1991):

(i) Assessment is a teaching strategy. Staff should base their assessment on the understanding that it forms an important part not simply in assessing students but also in teaching them how to improve their work.

(ii) Assessment schemes should be consistent with teaching philosophy and objectives. They should be designed at the same time as, and give effect to, the stated learning objectives of any programme of study. Thus, for example, where an objective is to encourage students to think analytically about the law, they should not be asked to answer questions which simply require a repetition of learned facts.

(iii) The setting of assessments should be co-ordinated. That is, between subjects, so that too great a burden is not placed on the staff who mark and the students who write the assessments. The co-ordination should also occur between schemes in these days of modularisation to ensure that students on different schemes of study taking the same or overlapping courses are not overburdened with assessment tasks at any one time.

(iv) Fair procedures should precede the implementation of assessment schemes. That is, students should be at least informed in full about the details of an assessment regime at the beginning of the module and, where possible, should be involved in discussing and setting criteria for assessment.

(v) Assessment should be broadly based. That is, students should be required to carry out at least three different types of task in any assessment regime; these tasks might include as well as essay and problem questions, moots, drafting exercises, classroom performance, group activities or oral examinations.

(vi) Assessment schemes must be based upon, and correspond to, the syllabus. That is, the assessment must correspond as far as possible with material taught in lectures and seminars, documentation handed out to students as a part of the syllabus and any other activities in which students have been required to be involved (for instance, court or tribunal visits).

(vii)   Assessment schemes should seek to minimise expenditure of resources. That is, marking should not be resource intensive but wherever possible involve such assessment strategies as group work, in-course assessment, shorter examinations and self and peer assessment.

(viii) Assessment schemes should seek to give a proper account of a student's achievement. That is, any mode of assessment dominated by a single strategy is unlikely to give a full account of the range of an individual's skills and knowledge.

References

ACLEC (1994) *Review of Legal Education. Consultation Paper: The Initial Stage*, ACLEC, London.

J Barker and R Tucker (1990) *Interactive Learning Revolution*, Kogan Page, London.

J W Barnes (1991) 'The Functions of Assessment', 2 *Legal Education Review* 177–217.

F C Bartlett (1932) *Remembering*, Cambridge University Press, London.

N L Baumgart (1976) 'Verbal Interaction in University Tutorials', 5 *Higher Education* 301–17.

J B Biggs (1987) 'Individual and Group Differences in Study Processes', 48 *British Journal of Educational Psychology* 266–79.

B S Bloom (1956) *Taxonomy of Educational Objectives: Cognitive Domain*, Longmans, New York.

J Cowan (1988) 'A Model of Experiential Learning and its Facilitation' *Learning for Action*, Standing Conference on Educational Development, Occasional Paper no 51.

N Entwistle (1992) *The Impact of Teaching on Learning Outcomes in Higher Education*, Committee of Vice Chancellors and Principals, USDU, Sheffield.

N Entwistle & P Ramsden (1983) *Understanding Student Learning,* Croom Helm, London.

M J Howe (1970) 'Note Taking, Strategy Review and Long Term Retention of Verbal Information', 64 *Journal of Educational Research* 61.

P Jones (1994) *Competences, Learning Outcomes and Education,* Chapters 3 (Neil Kibble) and 6 (Diana Tribe & Phil Parry), Institute of Advanced Legal Studies, London.

H Kay (1955) 'Learning and Retaining Verbal Material' 44 *British Journal of Educational Psychology* 81.

D A Kolb (1981) 'Learning Styles and Disciplinary Differences' in A W Chickering et al (eds) *The Modern American College,* Jossey-Bass, San Francisco.

D A Kolb (1984) *Experiential Learning: Experience as the Source of Learning and Development,* Prentice Hall, Englewood Cliffs, NJ.

F Marton (1976) 'On Qualitative Differences in Learning', 46 *British Journal of Educational Psychology* 1–21.

M Partington (1994) 'Maintaining Quality in Legal Education' in ACLEC *Review of Legal Education: Second Consultative Conference,* 18 July 1994, ACLEC, London.

N Pask (1976), 'Styles and Strategies of Learning', 46 *British Journal of Educational Psychology* 2.

D M R Tribe (1994) 'Group-Based Learning: An Overview in Higher Education', in Thorley and Gregory (eds) *Using Group-Based Learning in Higher Education,* HEC, London.

D M R Tribe (1996) 'DIY learning: self and peer assessment', this collection.

D M R Tribe & A J Tribe (1986) 'Assessing Law Students', 20 *Law Teacher* 160.

Chapter 2

Why theory matters
Julian Webb

Anyone who says that they approach teaching without any learning theory is being disingenuous at best. Most of us probably spend very little time actually thinking about why we teach the way we do, but that is not to say that there is no tacit theory bobbing around somewhere below the surface. To adapt Hanson's (1958) observation: teaching, like seeing, is a theory-laden activity (p 19).

Theory matters because, without it, education is hit-and-miss: the quality of education suffers; student choice suffers; and ultimately we risk misunderstanding not only the nature of our pedagogy, but the epistemic foundations of our discipline. It is only by articulating and engaging with our tacit theories that we can begin to rethink the process of legal education.

In this paper I will examine each of those contentions and suggest an alternative, holistic, framework within which to review the teaching and learning process. In this way I hope this paper provides a pointer to a range of issues and possibilities that will be explored more fully in the various contributions which follow.

The hit and miss approach to legal education[1]

My starting point is that at present the quality of legal education is largely a 'hit and miss' affair. I suggest that this is for two main

---

1   It was only after devising the title of this section that I found it echoed Alan Blake's '"Hit-and-Miss" Legal Education' (1987), p 4. While the context has changed somewhat, clearly some of the concerns have not.

reasons: our uncertainty about our functions, and our uncertainty about our methods. These uncertainties have a number of negative consequences for the law school experience.

What do we teach?

The modern history of legal education is a story of boundary disputes and skirmishes. Black-letter, contextual, critical and skills-based approaches vie for space. However, these skirmishes have taken place within a broader framework – the notion of the qualifying law degree, to be followed by a shorter period of vocational education – that has remained largely unchallenged for nearly 30 years. This framework, and much of the content, has been determined by what Twining (1994) has aptly called 'a neutral expository, descriptive science of law' (p 155). This is hardly earth shattering news, and the expository tradition has been attacked so often that it hardly needs me to stick yet another knife in the corpse. Nevertheless, there are a number of implications which flow from this expository base which are relevant to our discussion, and which will, I hope, bear one further, brief repetition.

First, one result is that academic law has tended to be defined primarily as (i) those areas of technical knowledge[2] which the professions deem it appropriate for academic lawyers to teach and (ii) a rule-focused 'task' scholarship, monitoring what Schlegel (1984) calls 'the small changes in the law: a new development in an eminent domain, a new wrinkle in consideration' (p 107), rather than a concern with the wider picture.

Secondly, as is well known, the formalist tradition has tended to expose teachers and students to no greater raison d'être than to know 'the law'. The result has been to overload the curriculum with substance at the expense sometimes of conceptual understanding – the phenomena of the 'creeping core' and the 'dragon of coverage' are testament to that. This creates a source of dissatisfaction for both teachers and students. Teachers recognise that coverage does not necessarily equate to learning. We become frustrated by our students' lack of 'understanding' and their adoption of an instrumental focus to their studies. They, on the other hand, are likely to become disenchanted with aspects of the curriculum which divert

2   And skills: see Marre (1988).

them from their true purpose of learning the law: see Halpern (1994), pp 38–40.
Thirdly, it supports the 'Life Begins at Law School' syndrome. This is the tendency, already alluded to by Diana Tribe, to exclude the relevance of all other forms of experience from the process of learning the law. Students are exhorted to forget what they learned 'outside' – a lesson in hyperbole, perhaps, but one which some clearly take to heart.

This has at least two consequences:

(a) It creates an image of legal education as a totally self-contained and transformative experience. We tell students that what they have learned before is nowhere near as important as what they are about to learn. We emphasise that they 'will never think the same way again': see Foster (1981), p 181. What I find particularly frustrating is the way that this seems to encourage students to switch off their 'common sense'. Their perspective on the world changes: problems are to be resolved with legal solutions; non-legal solutions, if considered at all, are second-best. However, I suggest the effect goes deeper than that. The notion of a *discipline* of law begins to take on almost Foucaultian overtones of social control. It is interesting in this context that, in our own research, see Webb (1995a), students have used manufacturing and industrial analogies to describe the 'process' of legal education. They recognise from their own experience that they are the raw material which is being moulded and re-shaped before being sent out as a partly finished product.

(b) It encourages us to advance an image of the law (and the lawyer) as amoral: never mind whether the outcome is 'just', is it the law? This, I believe, is a primary consequence of the expository tradition. Legal academics have spent years hiving theory and ethics off into discrete little boxes labelled 'jurisprudence' or (sometimes) 'sociology of law' and marginalising them in the curriculum: see Hunt (1989). Much substantive law teaching is thus taught divorced from any form of explicit social or legal theory, a position that is often defended by a kind of naive vocationalism: for example, in Barrett (1986). This separation of fact from value and of knowledge from the means for its evaluation is a feature which still distinguishes much modern legal scholarship from work in other fields in the humanities and social sciences.

How do we teach?

The stereotypical image of law school teaching was well represented by Alan Blake when he wrote (p 3) that:

> Traditionally law is taught through a series of lectures, with little or no student involvement, and a tutorial programme. Sometimes tutorials are referred to as seminars but the terminology used is often insignificant: both terms refer to probably the only form of student participation that takes place throughout the student's academic legal education. The tutorial consists of analysing the answers, prepared in advance, to artificial Janet and John Doe problems or esoteric essay questions.
>
> Blake (1987)

One hopes that, even in 1987, that picture was something of a parody. Nevertheless, concern continues to be expressed:

- about the quality of law teaching, both per se and relative to that in other disciplines;[3]
- about the narrow range of outcomes being prescribed and met by much law teaching and assessment: see Tribe & Tribe (1986); Maughan et al (1995);
- about the extent to which student learning becomes focused on narrow knowledge-based objectives.[4]

A recurring theme has been one of concern at the passivity of law students, and their emphasis on knowledge acquisition over other outcomes of learning. Passivity is a recognised problem in higher education more generally (Williams & Loder (1993)), where it is

---

3 A widely cited study in Australia reported that law students rated the quality of their teaching, the appropriateness of assessment and the emphasis on independence below the average score recorded for a total of nine fields of study: Ramsden (1991). See also the HEFCE final report on the law teaching assessments which identified a certain amount of teaching that lacked 'intellectual challenge': HEFCE (1994), para 19.

4 As Halpern shows, acquiring legal knowledge was rated 'very important' by 78% of new university students, 68% of old university students and 63% of 'Oxbridge' students: Halpern (1994), p 40. This finding could be ambiguous. All learning, at some level, involves the acquisition of knowledge; but it does not necessarily involve the absorption of propositional knowledge or 'content', ie substantive or adjectival law, or (possibly) context. This interpretation therefore makes the assumption that most of Halpern's respondents interpreted 'legal knowledge' as propositional knowledge. Given the epistemological sophistication of this criticism, this seems highly plausible.

widely seen as indicative of a surface approach to learning: Entwistle & Ramsden (1983). Often this approach is something the student arrives with.[5] It is part of their prior learning experience. But passivity may be developed or reinforced by the experience of higher education, particularly where teaching methods emphasise the passive acquisition and reproduction of propositional (content-based) knowledge. A strong focus on the acquisition and reproduction of content-based knowledge is a feature of such surface approaches.

My role here is not to deny the value of traditional methods, though their role in skills-based teaching is bound to be limited. Rather I wish to emphasise a number of particular concerns about teaching methods.

Fundamental to our concerns is the fact that the issue of teaching has been so little debated outside the privacy of law school common rooms or (more recently) law school teaching and learning committees. In debates about legal education, the impression is that the question of *how* we teach has always taken a poor second place to the question of *what* we teach.[6] In part, of course, this represents an artificial separation of two fundamentally linked questions. Whether one explicitly adopts an outcomes-driven approach to teaching or not, it is axiomatic to suggest that decisions about what we want students to learn should in large part determine how we teach.

The lack of debate is symptomatic of both a content-led approach to course design and, perhaps more generally a deep-rooted conservatism towards the question of how we teach. Such conservatism is a feature that is not unique to legal education, as Apps points out:

There is great irony involved in examining the faculty at most colleges and universities. On the one hand, most faculty members pride themselves on being liberal and open-minded and constantly searching for new ideas and new approaches, particularly when they are related to their disciplinary interests. But on the other hand, when it comes to their own teaching, their own departmental structure, and their view of educational

5 Cf the student quoted by Boon (1996) in Chapter 4.
6 Even within the recent HEFCE review, although concern with innovation was apparent, excellent teaching was characterised by '*content* of a high quality, *offering* up-to-date and reflective *commentaries* on the law': HEFCE (1994), para 16 (my emphasis).

aims, they are extremely conservative. They generally see no
need to change and resist change at every turn . . .

Apps (1988)

Classic symptoms of this malaise include:

The 'let's concentrate on improving the basics' philosophy: Defenders of
the traditional pedagogy rightly argue that much can be achieved
through the traditional lecture/tutorial (or seminar) format, and that
we should focus on getting the most out of these approaches. But
even if the traditional pedagogy is well used, we ought at least to
question whether three years' exposure to broadly the same teaching methods with broadly the same aims really meets the
educational needs of our students. Lectures and seminars, even at
their best, require students only to undertake a limited range of
activities, and as Diana Tribe (1996) has noted, need meticulous
construction if learning at the higher cognitive levels is to take
place.

One virtue of this approach is that it can serve as a salutary
reminder that, in the current climate of audit and review, there is a
great temptation simply to be seen to be instituting change. We
need to be sure it is for the right reasons and properly planned. This
is particularly relevant to developments in skills-based learning.
Relatively few law teachers are trained in the teaching methods
appropriate to skills-based learning and much of the legal skills
material on the market also takes a restricted, functional and didactic approach to skills. It is accordingly very easy to develop skills
courses which confirm the critics' worst fears by functioning at the
lowest cognitive levels and offering students little of real intellectual
worth.

The NIMBY[7] approach to innovation: This is the view that change is
fine, so long as it does not affect me. Today, clinical education,
performance-based work and assessment, peer-group teaching, supplementary instruction and innovations in small and large group
teaching exist in many institutions across the old binary divide.[8] But
impressionistic evidence suggests that many of these developments

---

7   NIMBY – Not In My Back Yard.
8   See eg, in the law school context, Jones (1994); Murdoch (1994); Oliver (1994);
    Grimes (1995). Unfortunately, much of this innovative work remains unpublished.

are patchy and isolated to particular courses, and then chiefly in the later stages of the degree. Is this symptomatic of some tendency to play safe by allowing innovation on the fringes of the curriculum, but leaving the core untouched? I do not know. But, if that is the case, it could prove a highly divisive policy. As the American experience with clinical education shows, this can have the effect of marginalising both the method, the content, and the teachers of such options within the law school: see eg Tarr (1993).

The 'students aren't what they used to be' defence: True. They are under greater social and financial pressure than for many years. They are (for the time being at least) the product of far wider social and educational backgrounds than ever before. But to say that the problem lies with our students' abilities, not in our teaching, smacks of a prejudice that sits uncomfortably with the liberal tradition we supposedly espouse:

... when we try to make teaching more effective by clarifying its goals and the conditions needed to improve its efficiency, we clash with the pedagogical philosophy of academics, whose disdain for the 'elementary' nature of a reflexive pedagogy reflects the superior level of the education system which they occupy. Their rejection of an explicit teaching practice follows from a perception of the student favoured by the professorial craft, one which is armed with all the certitudes and all the blindness of cultural ethnocentrism. Defined by their lesser knowledge, students can do nothing which does not confirm the most pessimistic image that the professor, in his most professional capacity, is willing to confess to: they understand nothing; and they reduce the most brilliant theories to logical monstrosities or picturesque oddities, as if their only role in life was to illustrate the vanity of the efforts which the professor squanders on them and which he will continue to squander, despite everything, out of professional conscience, with a disabused lucidity which only redoubles his merit. By definition, the professor teaches as he ought to teach, and the meagre results with which he is rewarded can only reinforce his certainty that the great majority of his students are unworthy of the efforts he bestows upon them. Indeed, the professor is as resigned to his students and their 'natural' incapacities as the good colonist is to the 'natives', for whom he has no higher expectations than that they be just the way they are. Attempts to combat linguistic misunderstanding are widely absent among academics because, for one thing, teaching naturally implies poor reception of the best messages by the worst receivers.

                                           Bourdieu et al (1994), pp 6–7

If we are to live with a system of mass higher education (and that is a political fact), we need to adjust our pedagogy, not expect our students to adjust to a model that was designed for the elite institutions of a system that in turn catered primarily for an educational elite, who were, perhaps, at least better able to cope with the inadequacies of some of the teaching they received.

Legal education and legal skills – more hit and less miss?

What has not accompanied the 'skilling' of the law school curriculum is a widespread and explicit debate about the role of educational theory in the revision that is going on. As Julie Macfarlane (1992) has cogently argued, without theoretical debate there is a danger that courses will be poorly constructed; confusion will abound as to the appropriateness of aims and outcomes of skills-based learning, and courses will be designed imitatively of each other, with a consequent loss of diversity and student choice (pp 294–5). I would add that law teachers will also waste resources in trying to tackle problems that are widely understood, and often resolved, elsewhere in higher education. The adoption of skills-based methods does not automatically mean that legal education becomes 'more hit and less miss'. Indeed, the reverse may be true if all we end up doing is bolting-on a fairly low-level, mechanistic, amount of skills-based learning to the established, knowledge-based curricula.

Legal education and educational theory – making connections

The essence of my argument is quite simple. If we are to become more effective teachers, we need to become more reflective teachers. To be reflective we need to articulate our theories of learning, critically examine them and replace those parts which, we suspect or, better still, can show do not work.

Paul Ramsden (1992) has usefully identified three 'models'[9] for lecturers' theories of teaching in higher education. These he labels 'teaching as telling'; 'teaching as organising student activity'; and 'teaching as making learning possible' (pp 111–16). I propose using this framework for the remainder of this section, and will try and spell out the implications for each in the context of legal skills education.

Teaching as telling

This model, of course, essentially describes the content-led approach already discussed. It focuses, as Ramsden puts it, 'on what the teacher does to the student' (p 112) by way of transmission of information. Problems of learning in this model may be resolved by technical fixes – better and more sophisticated mechanisms for the transfer of knowledge (computer-assisted learning; better structured lectures with good audio-visual aids, etc).

It is a model which, theoretically, rests on an implicitly behaviourist model of learning. It assumes that if we get the input right, the output will be right, and the obverse.[10] It thus tends to overlook the individual process of learning and the significance of learner differences. It also overlooks the extent to which, in higher education, the quality of learning depends on the quality of the whole learning environment: library and research resources; space and opportunity for students to undertake independent study, learning support and study skills provision, as well as face-to-face teaching: see Entwistle (1994).

In the skills context, 'teaching as telling' theoretically plays little or no part. However, it can break through as an inappropriate reliance on directed learning and over-emphasis on the use of specific techniques. The obvious example, which I have met too frequently in vocational education, is a narrow checklist approach to skills, particularly where the criteria are introduced by the tutor, rather than developed experientially from the student's learning. Teacher domination of feedback can also emphasise the technical and informational aspects over the process dimension of learning.

9 As Ramsden also points out, these are 'ideal types' in the Weberian sense. They are logical but nonetheless artificial constructs rather than complete and accurate descriptions of practice.
10 Computer programming serves as a good analogy. Programmers thus talk of GIGO (garbage in – garbage out) as a consequence of poor programming.

Teaching as organising student activity

This model recognises that the teaching role is far more interactive and supervisory rather than directive. It is essentially student-centred:

> teaching is no longer . . . mainly about telling or transmission: it is also about dealing with students, and above all about making them busy, using a set of efficient procedures to cover the ground.
>
> Ramsden (1992), p 113

It thus offers a more sophisticated base than the first theory. It recognises the importance of active methods of learning, though teachers using this model treat these primarily as new techniques which are added to their repertoire of methods. The individual teacher's understanding of the learning process may not be much changed thereby, and it is debatable whether this rather instrumental approach to teaching equips us to apply and develop our knowledge in new teaching situations.

This is probably the model that underpins much skills teaching as presently practised in the universities. It represents a pick-and-mix approach to teaching which remains under-rationalised. It can overlook the fact that students do not necessarily learn better by doing than by any other means. Doing things does not, of itself, lead to understanding of 'practice' or of underlying theoretical concepts. We need to understand what students are doing and why in terms of the cognitive or affective processes involved. For this reason it is sometimes important to recognise that there are widely different psychological bases to the different approaches to learning that have evolved.[11] Moreover, we may not be very good at relating the techniques to our students' learning needs. We may fail to integrate what is taught through 'trendy' skills-based exercises to students' learning of the more traditional substantive content.

Teaching as making learning possible

Ramsden's third model is, he argues, a more complete and systematic approach. It treats teaching and learning as a complex and

---

11   For example, experiential learning may be based on 'scientific' cognitive developmental models, as described by Macfarlane (1992) or on humanistic psychology – particularly the Rogerian learner-centred approach – see eg Withall (1991).

dynamic process. Teaching using this model has a number of characteristics: see Ramsden (1992), pp 114–15:

- It defines learning as an active and co-operative process in which both teachers and students engage.
- It recognises that learning begins by identifying the learning needs of the students.
- It then seeks to develop a learning process, focusing particularly on the critical barriers to understanding and using whatever tools are capable of meeting those particular students' needs.
- It is 'imaginative' in that it transforms 'knowledge' from something that is received from outside, to something that we each construct within ourselves.

This, Ramsden argues, requires us as teachers to rethink the epistemological basis of our teaching, and to view it as a reflexive and context-related activity. We need to respond experientially to our teaching in the same way as we expect our students to respond experientially to their learning. So what can we say about the epistemological assumptions of skills-based learning?

Epistemology and legal skills

Ramsden is by no means the only educationalist to stress the importance of epistemology to teaching. Ronald Barnett, in one of the most perceptive contributions to the modern debate on teaching and learning in higher education, also places that debate within an epistemic context:

> the modern society is reaching for other definitions of knowledge. Notions of skill, vocationalism, transferability, competence, outcomes, experiential learning, capability, enterprise, when taken together, are indications that traditional definitions of knowledge are felt to be inadequate for meeting the systems-wide problems faced by contemporary society. Whereas those traditional definitions of knowledge have emphasised language, especially through writing, an open process of communication, and formal and discipline-bound conventions, the new terminology urges higher education to allow the term 'knowledge' to embrace knowledge-through-action, particular outcomes of a learning transaction, and transdisciplinary forms of skill.
>
> Barnett (1994), p 71

Evidence for such an epistemic shift in legal education is partial only, and far more apparent at the vocational and continuing stages than at the initial stage. However, I would suggest that the following developments in undergraduate legal education are consistent with it:

• an increasing emphasis on inter-disciplinary and critical approaches to legal scholarship, rather than reliance on the closed world of legal formalism;

• the growing acceptance that some element of both general and specific intellectual and problem-solving skills need to be taught at the initial stage;

• a recognition that traditional treatments of the law as text disregard the extent to which law constitutes a basis for action;

• doubts that the distinction between academic law and law as practised can be sustained at a deep level.

What is commonly lacking, however, is a unifying epistemology that is capable of incorporating these new definitions of knowledge while preserving those elements of the liberal tradition which we wish to preserve, and without becoming, as Barnett puts it, 'a form of epistemological closure' (p 71). The question for us thus becomes, not *why* theory but *which* theory is most likely to deliver the goods?

Theory, which theory?

All forms of skills-based learning rely on active, student-centred, approaches to learning. However, beyond that there are critical differences, particularly regarding the definition of aims and objectives and assessment criteria, which have major ramifications for the learning process.

In skills-based legal education as presently defined, there appears to be a choice emerging between three dominant paradigms: outcome/competence; capability; and holistic models. I will take them in this order, not least because the first two are closely interrelated.

Outcomes/competences approaches

Outcomes-led approaches to learning have a substantial history, which can be traced back to attempts at inventorying lawyers' skills in the American law schools of the 1950s: Strong (1951), Maughan et al (1995). An outcomes approach enables us to focus on the product of learning – what students should know and be able to do by a given point in their studies. The logic behind this is that if we can clearly define the outcomes of learning, this should enable us more accurately to determine the learning necessary to produce those outcomes and the assessment methods appropriate to measure them.

Competence-based education is essentially a development of the outcomes approach.[12] It has been widely influential in the development of the Commonwealth professional training courses: see Roper (1988). In England, it also has roots in vocational, and particularly work-place, training, now typified by the work of the National Council for Vocational Qualifications: see Jones (1994), pp 11–22. The basis of competency tends to be a functional analysis of vocational tasks – ie, an assessment of what it is a professional needs to be able to do to perform her job 'competently'. While there have been a number of attempts to define broad or generic competences for legal education (see Jones, ibid) the NCVQ competence approach has so far been eschewed, even in the context of vocational legal education.[13]

I would submit that outcomes and competence approaches are inadequate for the epistemological task Barnett identifies, particularly because they tend to throw out much that is of value in the traditional liberal educational model:

• They can lead us to focus on low-level procedures and attributes that are easy to define, at the expense of developing and assessing the higher skills of critical thinking, judgment and evaluation: see Atkins et al (1993).

• They encourage us to focus too much on the behavioural outcomes of learning, rather than the underlying process of *how* students become effective and reflective learners: see Maughan et al (1995).

• Both approaches tend towards assessing *understanding* by looking at observable competences and outcomes. This is ontologically flawed because the student actors' understanding is constitutive

---

12 Though there are differences, notably in that outcomes can be the product of negotiation between teacher and students. Competences, by definition, are an externally imposed standard and are therefore a far greater constraint on the learning autonomy of students.

13 Though paralegal training is now being developed within the NCVQ framework.

of their action. We cannot rationalise their action without en-
quiring of their understanding: see Barnett (1994).

● The methodology reflects the course designer's assumptions
about what constitutes competent and *appropriate* forms of practice. These issues are not to be the subject of analysis and
critique by the class.[14]

● Competence approaches in particular can dehumanise learning:
'a sense of persons as thinking, thoughtful, discriminating individuals is absent' (Barnett, ibid, p 76). The learning experience
may therefore be even more alienating than that I have already
criticised.

In the context of the initial stage of education, we could also add
that:

● Competence approaches specifically may lead to too great an
emphasis on vocational outcomes, at the expense of more appropriate aims for undergraduate education: see Jones (1994).

Capability approaches

Building on an alternative approach to competence, a recent corpus
of work in the UK has sought to distinguish more closely between
the demands of 'professional' and 'vocational' education in terms of
'capability': Stephenson & Weil (1992); Eraut & Cole (1993). This
offers a way forward specifically for higher education to:

–   [give students] confidence in their ability to (1) take effective and appropriate action; (2) explain what they are
about; (3) live and work effectively with others and (4)
continue to learn from their experiences;

–   [enable them to take] effective and appropriate action
within unfamiliar and changing circumstances;

–   [give] students confidence and ability to take responsibility for their own continuing personal and professional
development;

14   Cf Neil Gold's observation that:

'On a basic level learning legal skills is about competence and client service . . . its aspirations are not only to aid lawyers to be more skilful and
therefore more helpful, but also to seek to implement a variety of values
inherent in the instructional choices [the course designers] have made . . .'

Gold (1989), p 322

- [prepare] students to be personally effective within the circumstances of their lives and work.

Stephenson & Weil, ibid, pp 1–2

A capability approach is thus one which seeks to supplement evidence of task-oriented competence with other data which is capable of eliciting more direct evidence of:

- the substantive knowledge underpinning competence;
- the cognitive processes constituting professional thinking;
- commitment to appropriate standards of professional service which may exceed the merely competent.

Although the labels are different, one might argue that elements of a capability approach appear to underpin recent attempts to define the nature of legal problem-solving. These have commonly stressed the need to develop capacities (or competences) across three dimensions: see eg Ayling & Costanzo (1984); Cruickshank (1991); Slorach & Nathanson (1995):

KNOWLEDGE	– substantive law/procedures;
	– theories of action (eg, negotiation theory);
	– appropriate strategies/tactics;
	– rules of professional conduct;
SKILLS	– research and analysis;[15]
	– numeracy;
	– communication (written and oral);[16]
	– organisation and planning;
	– process skills relevant to specific legal transactions;
ATTITUDES	– interpersonal;
	– ethical.

Such approaches tend to adopt a transactional base for learning which seeks to integrate these various dimensions into an overall problem-solving methodology: see Nathanson (1994); Slorach & Nathanson (1995). However, experience suggests it is difficult to meld these elements into something akin to a genuine capability

---

15 This category could easily be extended to incorporate the range of intellectual skills currently seen to fall within the initial stage: cf Marre (1988); Twining (1993b).

16 I have used this umbrella category to subsume the various communicative competences implicit in the DRAIN skills.

approach. At present skills-based programmes having these objectives may still:

● adopt a fragmentary approach to the teaching and, particularly, the assessment of knowledge and skills by an inadequate development of the transactional basis of learning;

● be heavily directed towards 'symbolic learning' in the form of competent performance of a set of skills, rather than focusing on effective change or personal growth;

● face considerable difficulties in determining the best sequence in which knowledge and skills are to be learned so as to maximise learning for capability: cf Nathanson (1994), p 231.

The capability approach also shares many common features with (indeed, some might argue that it is an example of) what I shall here call a 'holistic approach' to learning.

Holistic approaches

In educational theory generally, the term 'holistic approach to learning' is used to describe a way of structuring learning. Students who adopt a holistic approach experience problems and organise them by focusing on the whole in relation to the integral parts, not just on each part atomistically. The approach is one which seeks to identify and preserve the overall framework and structure of knowledge: see Marton (1988).

In English legal education, holistic approaches to learning exist, but they have been even less widely written about than the models we have already discussed. Indeed, it remains difficult to define the ambit of such approaches, so what follows is inevitably a fairly personal description of the theory underpinning one such approach. Accordingly, I suggest holism is a term that describes those approaches to education which stress the relevance of the range of knowledge forms – the propositional, the practical and the personal. To put this in simple terms, learning becomes holistic when it encompasses the development of theoretical knowledge, values and skills, in the context of individual experience and the heuristics this creates.[17]

Epistemologically, my starting point is that a holistic theory builds on the assumption that legal education constitutes a socio-practical

---

17   See eg, in the context of English legal education, Webb (1995a); Boon (1996).

field: see Webb (1995b); de Castell & Freeman (1978). This allies law more with areas of study such as medicine, engineering or social work than, say, the pure sciences, or philosophy. So what does this mean?

The characteristics of the holistic, 'socio-practical' model

Put briefly, this model has the following characteristics.

OUR PERSPECTIVE IS 'PHENOMENOLOGICAL'

Our perceptions of law are not inevitable or natural constructs, but a product of a particular way of seeing the world and interacting with it. This reality is reflected across the law curriculum, though formalist approaches may obscure that fact. We contrast different theories of law which illuminate (or not) different 'truths' about the law. We get students to compare and analyse different interpretations of legal rules. We spend large parts of our working lives telling them there is no right answer to 'hard cases'. We stress the social or historical contingency of particular rules. The logic of this approach ought to make apparent the limitations on our own capacities to offer authoritative ways of seeing the legal world. Our approach to teaching therefore needs to create the space for students to develop this phenomenological understanding for themselves.

IT STRESSES THAT THE RELATIONSHIP BETWEEN THEORY AND PRACTICE IS REFLEXIVE

This recognises the point made by Rubinstein that:

> Knowledge is originally directly interwoven with practical activity; only then it detaches itself and forms itself into a special cognitive 'activity'. It is not correct to oppose action and knowledge and treat them as external to each other.
>
> Cited in Marková (1982), p 175

It implies that what Schön (1983) terms technical-rational knowledge – ie 'specialised, firmly bounded, scientific and standardised' knowledge (pp 21–30) – is actually transformed by its application to a particular situation. Let's think about this in the legal context.

In practical terms, the law of contract has a number of dimensions. The technical rational knowledge is made up of a variety of legal rules.[18] There is the *directional law* – the substantive principles of contract; the *answering* and *accomplishing law* which respectively lay down the remedial basis of the law (eg action for damages for breach of contract) and the procedural rules and conventions which govern the process of initiating an action (eg the need for a summons or writ and statement of claim to commence the action); there is also the facilitative law which defines the ways in which the accomplishing law is administered (eg knowledge of the drafting conventions and filing requirements for a statement of claim). This technical knowledge is then bounded in particular cases by a range of strictly non-legal, strategic, considerations: the relations between the parties; the possibilities for informal dispute resolution, and so on.

How is this model traditionally divided up in teaching? Academic law courses provide one site at which part of the technical rational knowledge is taught – normally the directional law and possibly some element of the answering law. The non-legal dimensions may not be taught at all, unless they are introduced through a 'socio-legal' discussion of research into the realities of contractual disputing.[19] The accomplishing and facilitating law is left to the vocational stage. This is partly because it is debatable whether it has acquired the status of technical-rational knowledge at all, or whether it is simply 'practice' – an area of non-rigorous inquiry that is of little intellectual significance. The strategic dimensions will also be addressed at the vocational stage, though because they are so difficult to generalise, in a fairly anodyne fashion. Yet, once the student enters practice, it is often those same strategic considerations that will assume centre stage and thereby transform not just the student's perspective on a particular dispute, but on the nature and role of the law of contract.

The point is an obvious one. Our division of 'knowledge' from 'practice' is highly artificial and limiting in the understanding it gives us of the phenomenon of law in action.

IT STRESSES THE PRACTICAL USE OF LEGAL KNOWLEDGE

The orientation of a socio-practical legal education is on the use of knowledge to solve real human problems. Traditional approaches to the law curriculum constitute both an epistemological and a

18 The following analysis follows Ayling & Costanzo (1984).
19 In which case they may remain a side issue for the students, particularly as (in this context especially) their main effect is to emphasise just how little impact the formal law –which students have just invested a substantial amount of effort into understanding – has on commercial practices!

moral failure by disregarding the human dimensions of legal problems: see Radin & Michelman (1991); Williams (1993). It is a moral failure because it prevents our students from working through the interpersonal dimensions of lawyering and experiencing the ethical demands these create. As Williams (p 1573) argues, this is at the same time an epistemological failure because epistemology and ethics are closely interlinked. Our claims to knowledge involve the making of value judgments, and those normative judgments are themselves based on certain foundational knowledge claims about human experience and human life.

Our traditional emphasis on technical rational, 'Janet and John Doe' problem-solving overlooks the extent to which the real problems of law lie outside the realm of traditional enquiry. The beauty of technical rational problems is that they are capable of 'scientific' resolution, at least within reasonably definable parameters. This is comforting for both teachers and learners. Within the socio-practical terrain of unstable knowledge, problem solutions may be deeply uncertain. To confront such problems is unsettling because it confirms the limits of our traditional knowledge. It is an uncomfortable reminder of the limits of scientific scholarship and of our own lack of omniscience. To confront students with such problems challenges their passivity, their certainties about the discipline, perhaps even their own 'professional' identities. Robert Pirsig offers a nice analogy. In his philosophy class he once set an assignment on 'What is quality in thought and statement'. The students' reaction was hostile:

> 'How are *we* supposed to know what quality is?' they said. 'You're supposed to tell *us!*'
> Then he told them he couldn't figure it out either and really wanted to know. He has assigned it in the hope that somebody would come up with a good answer. That ignited it. A roar of indignation shook the room. Before the commotion had settled down another teacher had stuck his head in the door to see what the trouble was.
> 'It's all right,' Phaedrus said. 'We just accidentally stumbled over a genuine question, and the shock is hard to recover from.'
>
> Pirsig (1974), p 199

IT IS 'LIBERATING'

It follows from the above practical emphasis that this approach to education is 'liberating' in the sense that it creates a capacity for action. David Bridges (1993) has cogently argued that an underlying rationale of liberal education is its capacity to enable us to understand the choices we have, to make decisions based on those choices, and to pursue those choices in the social world. But this is, he argues, an insufficient guarantee for the individual's positive freedom within most social contexts, unless she is also skilled in acting upon the world (p 44).

In essence, it is not enough to be able to think: one must also be able to do, and teaching someone to think does not of itself enable them to act.

IT IS EXPERIENTIAL AND REFLECTIVE

Holistic learning is commonly associated with experiential learning; that is, knowledge acquired by personal encounter, reflection and experimentation: see Kolb (1984); Boud et al (1985). Experiential learning is holistic in the sense that it addresses all the dimensions of the classical, Platonic construction of the 'person' – the cognitive (thinking), the conative (willing) and the affective (feeling) – at least in theory. It is arguable, however, that basic experiential learning theories have themselves become locked into an overly positivist framework that underplays the role of the affective and emotive – of feelings, intuition, empathy: see Heron (1992), (1993); Mulligan (1993). For me, certainly, it is these more 'human' dimensions that much skills-based learning in law has yet to address. Skills-based learning only becomes genuinely holistic when we begin to explore its capacity for developing self-awareness and awareness of others. This is essential if we are to enable our students to question critically – with an *internal* rather than just external perspective – their perceptions of themselves as 'lawyers' and the roles that they must play in that guise.

As part of this process holistic learning starts by making students self-aware of their own learning.[20] This is an essential first step, as one influential Working Party has suggested:

> Students find it difficult to apply general skills to their specific subject area. It is essential for students to see the purpose of the work they have to do, to devise an appropriate strategy, and to

---

20   For examples, see Webb (1995a); Maughan & Webb (1996); Boon (1996).

monitor the outcome of their learning for themselves – in other words to become more consciously aware of the process of studying. The most recent approaches are directed essentially towards 'learning to learn' or *self-regulated learning*. These skills are of such importance to the continued professional development of students once they complete their courses, that they should not be left to chance.

CSUP (1992), para 2.9.2

Holism has its critics: see Mackie (1989). Holistic approaches can, relative to competency models, be unstructured and suffer from a lack of precision in their objectives. I suspect also that holistic approaches, almost by definition, are more likely to be constructed around a wider range of learning objectives than competence-based programmes, with consequently a greater risk of overstretching the students and thereby encouraging a surface approach to at least some aspects of the learning process. By stressing personalised learning holistic courses also create difficult questions for assessment – do you assess performance by an external competency standard (and if so, what?) or by some measure of individual growth, ie focusing on how much that individual has learned or 'improved' over the period of study? Either way this has implications for the individual's self-development and confidence, especially if they progress to later skills courses which adopt a different criterion. From my own experience of teaching skills both on the Legal Practice Course and a holistic LLB skills module, the holistic approach creates a learning experience that is far more open-ended, and makes the learning process much more difficult to manage. This may prove quite threatening for some teachers.

The potential for holistic approaches, in my view, far outweighs these disadvantages. They have a real capacity to link the academic and practical and to overcome the knowledge/skills divide. Even though, in theory, this has long been a dead letter, yet it continues to surface in staff development programmes and particularly in discussions of the LPC and its assessment: see Brayne (1994). Holistic approaches do not treat knowledge and skills as separable: they are intermingled as the basis for professional 'artistry': see Schön (1983); Webb (1995a). The potential for using a holistic perspective to construct curricula around problem-based learning methods is particularly exciting.

Conclusions: theorising skills – a SWOT analysis

In this paper I have attempted to highlight the importance of theorising skills-based learning. In this final section I will briefly outline some of the key issues that this raises in the form of a SWOT analysis; ie strengths/weaknesses; opportunities/threats.

Strengths

Appropriate use of theory should enhance our capacity to:

- know what is possible by way of skills-based learning and to make informed decisions in the light of our own epistemological assumptions about the discipline;
- select a theoretical framework (or range of frameworks) that is (are) consistent with the learning needs of our particular students;
- construct courses which have a clear range of achievable objectives and/or outcomes;
- develop techniques to encourage students to take greater responsibility for their own learning;
- enable students to develop their reflective capacities and take on the habits of lifelong learning;
- enable students to make choices in the real world and to cope with change.

Weaknesses

I suggest there are few weaknesses in theorising per se. The dangers lie primarily in ignorance, or an inappropriate use of particular theory. We need to be cautious in how we use theory. It would be ironic if experiential learning theory was to become another kind of technical rational knowledge which actually retarded rather than enhanced the intuitive dimensions of the learning process. We also need to know our limitations and to be willing to learn from the experience of others. Anecdotally, I have the impression that much UK staff development in the legal skills domain has drawn chiefly on the experience of other law teachers.[1] Perhaps there is an insularity

---

1   Cf Birks (ed) (1994); it is symptomatic of this tendency perhaps that only two of the substantive contributions to that volume contained any reference to educational material outside the legal domain.

or arrogance within us which makes us, as an 'academic tribe' (Becher (1989)) relatively unreceptive to experience or expertise that is not domain-specific. If so, this is a pity, as there is a great deal we could learn from outside.

Opportunities

The opportunities for skills-based learning are almost endless. Yet to exploit these opportunities to the full also requires some grounding in learning theory. Rather than explore themes in detail which, in some cases, are to be raised by other contributors to this collection, I will do no more than briefly set out the key opportunities, especially for holistic methods, as I see them:

● to close the knowledge/skills divide;
● to increase the capacity for legal education to function within the affective and ethical domains;
● to increase the use of clinical and other skills-based methodologies as a means of enabling students to become self-critical and reflective learners;
● to create an intellectual environment in which legal education is more generally viewed as a continuum, rather than in terms of the present milestones of the LLB, vocational education and continuing development.

Threats

The greatest threats on the horizon are the continuing structural changes faced by higher education.

At the initial stage, the impact of modularisation may equally either enhance or detract from skills developments. It is difficult to say which. The break-up of the traditional curriculum that can flow from modularisation of courses certainly creates new opportunities for including free-standing skills modules, or devising problem or transaction based modules out of old, content-led, courses. Equally, modularisation by its very fragmentation of the teaching year may make it more difficult to develop holistic approaches to skills, or modules that build on more complex transactional bases. There is limited evidence emerging from some law schools of student concerns that the shift to modularisation is leading to an overloading of teaching and assessment which increases rather than reduces the tendency towards surface learning.[2]

Resourcing also remains an issue for skills-based education, both at vocational and initial stages. Skills courses tend to require substantial physical resources and relatively low staff-student ratios (SSRs) for workshop activities. Experience suggests that clinical approaches tend to function on a lower SSR than the competence-based professional training courses.[3] Research has consistently shown that deep learning is greatly facilitated by small group sizes, which has been taken to mean, for all purposes other than lecturing, no more than 32 students to a class, and for contexts where extensive student-tutor or student-student interaction and feedback is required, no more than 14: see Andresen (1993). Clearly, this is not just an issue for skills-based learning, but the impact of pressure to increase class sizes would be particularly devastating for skills-based learning. If the unit of resource for law continues to fall, this may create pressures to counter the expansion of such courses. The ability to justify those courses on the basis of a sound pedagogy, student demand and evidence of quality outcomes (see Andresen, p 3) may help.

References

L Andresen (1993) *What's the use of small group teaching?* Centre for Legal Education, Sydney.

M J Atkins, J Beattie & W B Dockrell (1993) *Assessment Issues in Higher Education,* Employment Department Group, Sheffield.

J W Apps (1988) *Higher Education in a Learning Society,* Jossey-Bass, San Francisco & London.

2   This evidence emerges from interview data with non-traditional students at eight university law schools in England and Wales. The data has been collected as part of an on-going research project for ACLEC into Access and Participation in Undergraduate Legal Education, presently being conducted by the Legal Education & Professional Skills Research Unit at UWE, Bristol and the School of Law, Middlesex University.

3   For example, LPC courses commonly operate with an SSR of between 1:15 and 1:20; the UWE and Warwick simulation clinics both operate on a ratio of about 1:12; the Northumbria clinic functions, I believe, on a current SSR of about 1:14 for live client work. These figures, of course, disguise the fact that the effective ratio for different activities may vary widely above and below those indicative levels.

R Ayling & M Costanzo (1984) 'Towards a Model of Education for Competent Practice', 2 *Journal of Professional Legal Education* 94.

R Barnett (1994) *The Limits of Competence: Knowledge, Higher Education and Society*, SRHE/Open University Press, Buckingham.

B Barrett (1986) 'What Should be Conserved?', 20 *Law Teacher* 187.

T Becher (1989) *Academic Tribes and Territories: intellectual enquiry and the cultures of disciplines*, SRHE/Open University Press, Milton Keynes.

P Birks (ed) (1994) *Reviewing Legal Education*, Oxford University Press, Oxford.

A Blake (1987) 'Legal Education in Crisis: A Strategy for Legal Education into the 1990s', 21 *Law Teacher* 3.

A Boon (1996) 'Skills in the initial stage of legal education: theory and practice for transformation', this collection.

D Boud, R Keogh & D Walker (eds) (1985) *Reflection: Turning Experience into Learning*, Kogan Page, London.

P Bourdieu, J-C Passeron & M de Saint Martin (1994) *Academic Discourse: Linguistic Misunderstanding and Professorial Power* (trans R Teese), Polity Press, Cambridge (first published 1965).

H Brayne (1994) 'LPC Skills Assessments– A Year's Experience', 28 *Law Teacher* 227.

D Bridges (1993) 'Transferable Skills: A Philosophical Perspective', 18 *Studies in Higher Education* 43.

D A Cruickshank (1991) 'Training mediators: moving towards competency-based training' in K J Mackie (ed) *A Handbook of Dispute Resolution: ADR in Action*, Routledge/Sweet & Maxwell, London.

CSUP – Committee of Scottish University Principals Working Party (1992) *Teaching and Learning in an Expanding Higher Education System*, CSUP, Edinburgh.

S de Castell & H Freeman (1978) 'Education as a socio-practical field: the theory-practice question reformulated', 12 *Journal of Philosophy of Education* 12.

N Entwistle (1994) *Teaching and the Quality of Learning*, CVCP/SRHE, London.

N Entwistle & P Ramsden (1983) *Understanding Student Learning*, Croom Helm, London.

M Eraut & G Cole (1993) *Assessing Competence in the Professions*, Employment Department, Sheffield.

J C Foster (1981) 'The "Cooling Out" of Law Students: Facilitating Market Cooptation of Future Lawyers' in R A L Gambitta, M L May & J C Foster (eds) *Governing Through Courts*, Sage, Beverly Hills & London.

N Gold (1989) 'Learning Lawyers' Skills: Research, Development and Evaluation – the Future Prospectus' in N Gold, K Mackie & W Twining (eds) *Learning Legal Skills*, Butterworths, London.

R Grimes (1995) 'Reflections on Clinical Legal Education', 29 *Law Teacher* 169.

D Halpern (1994) *Entry into the Legal Professions*, Research Study No 15, The Law Society, London.

N Hanson (1958) *Patterns of Discovery: an inquiry into the conceptual foundations of science*, Cambridge University Press, Cambridge.

HEFCE – Higher Education Funding Council for England (1994) *Subject Overview Report: Quality Assessment of Law 1993–94*, HEFCE, Bristol.

J Heron (1992) *Feeling and Personhood*, Sage, London.

J Heron (1993) *Group Facilitation: Theories and Models for Practice*, Kogan Page, London.

A Hunt (1989) 'The role and place of theory in legal education: reflections on foundationalism', 9 *Legal Studies* 146.

P A Jones (1992) 'Skills and Assessment in Undergraduate Law Courses – A Survey', *CASEL Working Paper No 1*, CNAA, London.

P A Jones (1994) *Competences, Learning Outcomes and Legal Education*, Institute of Advanced Legal Studies, London.

D A Kolb (1984) *Experiential Learning: Experience as a Source of Learning and Development*, Prentice Hall, Englewood Cliffs, NJ.

J Macfarlane (1992) 'Look Before You Leap: Knowledge and Learning in Legal Skills Education', 19 *Journal of Law & Society* 293.

K Mackie (1989) 'Lawyers' Skills: Educational Skills' in N Gold, K Mackie & W Twining (eds) *Learning Legal Skills*, Butterworths, London.

I Marková (1982) *Paradigms, Thought and Language*, John Wiley, Chichester.

F Marton (1988) 'Describing and Improving Learning' in R R Schmeck (ed) *Learning Strategies and Learning Styles*, Plenum Press, New York.

Marre Committee (1988) *A Time for Change: Report of the Committee on the Future of the Legal Profession*, General Council of the Bar/The Law Society, London.

C Maughan, M Maughan & J Webb (1995) 'Sharpening the Mind or Narrowing It? The Limitations of Outcome and Performance Measures in Legal Education', 29 *Law Teacher* 255.

C Maughan & J Webb (1996) 'Taking reflection seriously: How was it for us?', this collection.

J Mulligan (1993) 'Activating Internal Processes in Experiential Learning' in D Boud, R Cohen & D Walker (eds) *Using Experience for Learning*, SRHE/Open University Press, Buckingham.

J Murdoch (1994) 'Using Group Skills in Honours Teaching: The European Human Rights Project', 28 *Law Teacher* 258.

S Nathanson (1994) 'Developing Legal Problem-Solving Skills', 44 *Journal of Legal Education* 215.

D Oliver (1994) 'Teaching and Learning Law: The Pressures on the Liberal Law Degree' in P Birks (ed) (1994) *Reviewing Legal Education*, Oxford University Press, Oxford.

R M Pirsig (1974) *Zen and the Art of Motorcycle Maintenance*, The Bodley Head, London.

M Radin & F Michelman (1991) 'Pragmatist and Poststructuralist Critical Legal Practice', 139 *University of Pennsylvania Law Review* 1019.

P Ramsden (1991) 'A Performance Indicator of Teaching Quality in Higher Education: The Course Experience Questionnaire', 16 *Studies in Higher Education* 129.

P Ramsden (1992) *Learning to Teach in Higher Education*, Routledge, London & New York.

C Roper (1988) 'The Legal Practice Courses – Theoretical Frameworks and Models', 6 *Journal of Professional Legal Education* 77.

J H Schlegel (1984) 'Searching for Archimedes', 34 *Journal of Legal Education* 103.

D A Schön (1983) *The Reflective Practitioner: How Professionals Think in Action*, Basic Books, New York.

S Slorach & S Nathanson (1995) 'Design and Build: The Legal Practice Course at Nottingham Law School', 4 *Nottingham Law Journal* 75.

J Stephenson & S Weil (1992) *Quality in Learning: A Capability Approach to Higher Education*, Kogan Page, London.

F Strong (1951) 'The Pedagogical Implications of Inventorying Legal Capacities', 3 *Journal of Legal Education* 555.

N Tarr (1993) 'Current Issues in Clinical Legal Education', 37 *Howard Law Journal* 31.

D Tribe (1996) 'How students learn', this collection.

D Tribe & A J Tribe (1986) 'Assessing Law Students', 20 *Law Teacher* 160.

W Twining (1993a) 'The Idea of Juristic Method: A Tribute to Karl Llewellyn', 48 *University of Miami Law Review* 119.

W Twining (1993b) 'Intellectual Skills at the Academic Stage: Twelve Theses' in P Birks (ed) *Examining the Law Syllabus: Beyond the Core*, Oxford University Press, Oxford.

W Twining (1994) *Blackstone's Tower: The English Law School*, Sweet & Maxwell, London.

J Webb (1995a) 'Where the Action Is: Developing Artistry in Legal Education', 2 *International Journal of the Legal Profession* 187.

J Webb (1995b) 'Extending the Theory-Practice Spiral: Action Research as a Mechanism for Crossing the Academic/Professional Divide', 2 *Web Journal of Current Legal Issues* 1.

J Withall (1991) 'Teacher-centred and Learner-centred Instruction' in K Marjoribanks (ed) *The Foundations of Students' Learning*, Pergamon Press, Oxford.

G Williams & C Loder (1993) 'Identifying Priorities' in Newsletter 3 of the project *Identifying and Developing a Quality Ethos for Teaching in Higher Education*, Centre for Higher Education Studies, University of London.

S Williams (1993) 'Legal Education, Feminist Epistemology and the Socratic Method', 45 *Stanford Law Review* 1571.

Part II

Approaches to skills teaching

The contributors to this section introduce us to a wide range of learning approaches. What these chapters have in common, however, is a belief in and quest for an alternative to a curriculum dominated by propositional knowledge for its own sake. Most take the integration of theory with practice as read and deal with learning models and methods that bridge the academic/vocational divide.

Three interlinked themes are disclosed by the contributions: the importance of experiential learning methods and, among these, the role of holistic approaches to learning, and of reflection.

The term *experiential learning* embraces a diversity of teaching techniques and learning environments which promote active learning, or 'learning by doing'. This requires a move from teacher-directed to self-directed learning methods as a means of enhancing personal, intellectual and professional development. David Cruickshank's problem-based learning method (PBL), for example, puts learning squarely into the hands of the learner, as do the clinical and 'discovery' methods discussed by Richard Grimes and Andy Boon. In PBL the learner engages with the problem from scratch, before receiving any instruction in the relevant subject-matter. Cruickshank reviews PBL models currently in operation and discusses ways in which they can be implemented in academic and vocational law programmes. Boon takes as his theme the incorporation of skills into undergraduate programmes and argues that skills education should be spread throughout the curriculum. The live client casework model of clinical legal education, described by Richard Grimes and Hugh Brayne, differs in its focus. It is not primarily a vehicle for skills development, though arguably it provides the most realistic forum for this. Its objective is to foster a deep learning approach to legal study by enabling the learner to get first hand experience of the lawyering process. Both writers discuss the problem of balancing the educational objective against the need to provide a service. Much of experiential learning is based on the learning cycle developed by David Kolb and others. Caroline Maughan introduces Kolb's theory to those readers who may be unfamiliar with it. She goes on to argue that we are in danger of impeding the move towards self-directed learning if we fail to develop the theoretical framework underpinning our skills teaching methodology. Hence she lays particular stress on the techniques and purpose of feedback, which can be a hit and miss process if under-theorised.

It is perhaps such a lack of direction in skills teaching which underpins one of Peter Kilpin's findings in his survey of four institutions running the LPC: that skills are perceived by tutors and students to be less important than propositional knowledge. Kilpin's review of attitudes towards skills shows up the problems of isolating skills from 'knowledge' in foundation courses and assessments, and the limitations of such an approach for professional development.

A *holistic* approach sees learning as a lifelong process which involves the whole person. It therefore integrates propositional, practical, and personal knowledge and encourages the learner to confront and, if necessary, modify her personal and professional values. Whilst LPC and Bar vocational courses, it could be argued, do not have time to devote to searching intellectual enquiry into ethical questions and what motivates people to act as they do, the academic stage is an appropriate forum to do just this. The Boon and Maughan & Webb contributions each describe and evaluate integrated holistic models run on LLB programmes.

Holistic approaches and experiential learning both lay stress on the role of *reflection* in the learning process. At regular intervals throughout this collection we are conscious of a figure: Donald Schön's 'reflective practitioner' who uses her artistry to engage in legal problem-solving creatively and reflexively. Caroline Maughan and Julian Webb discuss their experiences of using Schön's model as a basis for teaching and assessment. They highlight problems of constructing 'reflective' exercises and explain why they found it necessary to 'teach' experiential learning theory to their students.

Peter Kilpin, by contrast, notes the relative absence of student reflection on some LPC programmes, and offers a number of possible solutions. The issue of reflection in professional education is also taken up by Philip Jones, who critically reviews the notions of 'reflective practice' as espoused by Schön, Michael Eraut and Ronald Barnett. He puts forward a careful consideration of how this notion has developed through the work of these theorists to its current state. While recognising the value of reflection in professional development, Jones is critical of aspects of these theories, particularly Schön's, on both epistemological and practical grounds. He ends on a note of disappointment at ACLEC's apparent failure to give greater conceptual clarity to the notion of 'reflective practice' through the development of a post-technocratic alternative model of professional legal education.

Chapter 3

Learning how to learn: the skills developer's guide to experiential learning
Caroline Maughan

Rethinking the familiar

Call yourself a skills teacher?

Articulate your own theory, critically examine it, check for consistency, coherence and adequacy, compare it with alternative theories and reconceptualise it in order to increase the effectiveness of your own professional thinking.

Griffiths and Tann (1992), p 82

Reader: What's this writer on about? What's this got to do with skills? Am I reading the wrong book?
Author: Not at all. These are vital ingredients of experiential learning. In my opinion, the most vital. Please persevere.

If you are involved with course design and teaching on vocational or undergraduate skills courses, then you will be using experiential techniques. However, you may not be aware of the explicit learning theory which underpins them. My purpose in this chapter is to encourage you to reflect on your skills teaching experience to date. Then I shall explain the theory of experiential learning and suggest ways of using the theory to enable your students to learn effectively.

If you are thinking of turning your hand to skills development but as yet have no experience, familiarity with the theory should enable you to plan and teach skills in a systematic way rather than by trial and error. It might be helpful if you begin by reflecting on your current law teaching habits.

TASK 1: METHODS AND ATTITUDES

In what ways does skills teaching differ from your other law teaching? Briefly note down any differences you can think of, and then read on.

You will probably have noted differences in learning methods, the kinds of learning activities and the differing roles and relationships of teacher and learner. You may have noted your feelings about these things.

Now you can compare your notes with the list of comments about skills teaching and learning below. It is based on my own experience and that of colleagues:

- Skills are practised in workshops rather than 'taught' in lectures/ seminars.
- Skills workshops are participative and interactive. In order to learn, students must join in.
- The teacher's function is to facilitate learning. The students therefore take over some control of the learning process.
- Skills learning is about learning *how*, not learning *what.*
- Skills learning can be discomfiting, both for teacher and students.
- Skills teaching is fun.
- Workshop preparation and organisation is complicated and time-consuming.
- I find skills workshops exhausting, even though I am 'teaching' less.
- The learning situation is informal. There is less distance between me and the students.
- I can be myself rather than play the 'teacher as expert' role.
- Skills learning is too 'touchy-feely' for my liking.
- Skills workshops are unstructured.
- Role playing, etc, can lead to displays of emotion in the class-room. This can be hard to handle.

'Learning is a process, not a product' [1]

At times you probably experience exhaustion, enjoyment, anxiety and excitement, whatever kind of teaching you are involved in. If you are new to lecturing, you may suffer extreme discomfort until

1   J S Bruner (1966), p 72.

you are confident you have mastered your content and that you can appear in the lecture theatre without worrying that your mind will go blank or that someone will ask a question you have not anticipated.

All of us, at this stage in our teaching careers, were more preoccupied with the structure and content of what we were delivering to be much concerned about the learning processes of our students. Unfortunately for them, many of us still are. This powerful desire to be in control of what takes place in the lecture theatre has become a habit, so that we still don't pay enough attention to our students' needs. For their part, our students have also become habituated to this approach. They have an expectation of dependency which all too often we do little to dispel.

Moreover, as law teachers we are used to transmitting to students a well-defined and circumscribed body of content.[2] The outcome, or *product*, of this learning experience is clear and certain: assessment of knowledge and understanding of this content by assignment and examination. We tend to be less concerned with the *process* of learning – in other words, what happens during the course of the learning experience which enables the learners to achieve the learning outcomes.

TASK 2: HOW DO STUDENTS LEARN?

Imagine that you are preparing to deliver a course of lectures to a group of first year law students who have never experienced the lecture method before. Some of them have never even heard of a lecture. Assuming your purpose is to enable them to learn, how would you brief them?

You could leave the students to work it out for themselves, and most of them would probably do so eventually, through a process of trial and error. However, they would grasp the process more quickly if you discussed with them:
1.   What they could do during your lectures; how and why they could do these things.
2.   What they could do after your lectures; how and why they could do these things.

---

2   According to Paulo Freire, this is the 'banking' concept of education 'in which the scope of action allowed to the students extends only as far as receiving, filing and storing of the deposits.' (1974), p 58.

You might prefer only to point out what they need to do, and to encourage them to work out how and why for themselves.

The following are some of the issues you might want to discuss under 1:

- Should they listen? Why/why not?
- Should they take notes? Why/why not?
- Should they take detailed notes? Why/why not?
- What should they do with the handout? Why/why not?
- Can they write on the handout? If so, why and what?
- Should they listen/take notes/read handout all at the same time?
- How do you manage to do the above and learn anything?
- Can they speak to you/ask questions/raise issues?
- When can they do these things?
- What should they do if they don't understand something?
- What do they need to remember? Facts? Cases? Theories? Principles? Statutes? Why? Do you make this known to them?

And under 2:

- What should they do if they haven't understood the material?
- Should they reread/rewrite/do anything else with their notes? Why/why not?
- Should they discuss the material with friends/lecturer/seminar tutor? When?
- Do they need to obtain further information on the topic? Why and how?

This activity has focused our attention on the process of learning. Clearly, even for teachers of substantive subject matter, there are issues of how students can get the best out of their learning. For skills teachers this is the main concern. Their role is to provide 'process' knowledge rather than 'content' knowledge: see Webb (1995); Macfarlane (1992).

Process knowledge is by nature open-ended and unpredictable. This can be disconcerting for several reasons.

Firstly, because you are not master of the material, you cannot control the direction a skills workshop will take, and there are limits to how far you can predict its outcome. You define the content, in the sense that you determine the tasks and practice exercises for the workshop session. However, these simply provide the context in which learning takes place. The emphasis and responsibility for the process are placed firmly on the learners. They relieve you of complete control of the situation and its outcomes.

Secondly, you are no longer the expert on whom the ignoramus depends for enlightenment. You have lost your power base. The relationship has to be renegotiated. Your role is now to enable your students to develop expertise, some of which they already possess. Most of the skills that we are trying to develop are adaptations of skills already possessed to some degree. This poses two problems for the teacher:

1. Some will be more skilled than others, so that they will not all be starting from the same point.
2. People learn from experience in different ways. As skills teachers we have to be sensitive to this and understand that there is no one 'best way' to help people learn. For example, in traditional academic programmes theory based on research is presented to students, who are then asked to apply this theoretical knowledge to a problem. This approach will be familiar to many of your students, but will not necessarily be the one they learn best from. In skills development programmes we have to consider that other approaches may suit our students better.

It is tempting to try to reduce the open-ended character of process learning by imposing a 'content' framework on it. For example, a learner searching for a security blanket may interpret a skills checklist as a set of hard and fast rules, rather than flexible guidelines. Because lawyers are so at home with rules, some law teachers may inadvertently encourage this interpretation. I shall give instances of how checklists can seriously damage your learning later, in section 3.

'Teaching, in my estimation, is a vastly over-rated function'[3]

This brings us to the next major difference between content and process-based learning: your role as facilitator rather than instructor. This has a profound effect on your teaching methodology. Your task is to invent and set up situations resembling those of legal practice in which your students can build their skills and experiment with their behaviour. Next, through constructive feedback and discussion, you can guide them towards analysing their behaviour, thoughts and feelings and developing conceptual frameworks in which they organise what they have learnt and how they are going

---

3   Carl Rogers in M Thorpe et al (1993), p 228.

to use this knowledge in the future.

Your aim will be to become redundant as soon as possible, enabling students to discover for themselves what works, why it works and how to capitalise on it.

Many law students will not be familiar with the participative methods of active learning. The more introverted among them may feel inhibited and reluctant to take part at first. Having other people watching you and commenting on your performance can be threatening. How can you develop your skill in creating and maintaining a supportive environment in which making mistakes is not seen as failure? How good are you at persuading your students of this?

This may involve you questioning your own attitudes and behaviour towards students and learning.

One way of building a supportive environment is to agree rules with the group early on.[4] The rules you negotiate will differ from group to group but they will nearly always deal with issues in the following areas:

- Responsibilities of participants and observers during activities.
- The nature and purpose of feedback.
- Management of group work.
- Dealing with disagreements.
- Individual commitment and responsibility.
- Assessment processes. (Tutor, peer, self?)

Informed consent

It is sometimes easy to underestimate the strength of student feelings of discomfort and insecurity towards teaching methodology that is new to them. To illustrate this, let me tell you about one of my early experiences as an inexpert and presumptuous skills teacher.

I was fortunate to train to teach modern languages in the early 70s, when a revolution was taking place in language teaching methodology. Traditional 'book' learning, where you learned lists of noun and verb endings by rote and did written translations in and out of the target language, was becoming as dead as Latin. The new

---

4   Some teachers negotiate a learning contract with the students; Richard Grimes does this at Sheffield Hallam Law Clinic. See also M Maughan (1996), D W Johnson and F P Johnson (1991), G Boak (1991).

emphasis was on the spoken language and language in use. Structure 'drills' replaced noun and verb paradigms of the

I have gone
you have gone
he/she/it has gone

variety. The teacher would isolate a particular grammatical structure and orally present it in a context which would make the meaning clear immediately. Through 'drilling', the learners would hear, repeat and manipulate the structure before seeing it in writing. The 'drilling' would be carried out at a fast tempo, to prevent interference from the learner's mother tongue, ie so that the learner would not have time mentally to translate the structure into their mother tongue and then translate back again – a frequent cause of errors when learning a new language. So, for example, to teach the simple past and present perfect tenses in English – *I did* and *I have done* – you would teach the difference in usage between them. You could present this as follows:

Have you had breakfast this morning?
Yes, I have.
What did you have?
I had a cup of coffee and some Cornflakes.

You would go round the class asking everybody what they had for breakfast, and then drill the structure in a variety of sentences, such as:

Have you seen Klaus today?
No, I haven't.
When did you last see him?
I saw him last night in the pub.

When you were satisfied that all the class could produce the structures correctly and automatically, you relaxed the tempo, wrote the structures on the board and gave any necessary grammatical explanations. This stage also gave you a chance to rest and recover your strength before the next round of drilling!

This was the theory. I went to my first job in a German further education college, all fired up with this new, exciting 'direct method'. I put the theory into practice.

What was the effect on my class of beginners?

My performance gave new meaning to that misguided philosophy which states that students must suffer in order to learn. Before their very eyes I changed from teacher to monster. All were confused; many were hostile. Some had been learning English for some years by the traditional methods. As a more experienced teacher would have expected, they were particularly resistant. At the start they were keen to demonstrate their 'knowledge' of the language to a native speaker and the rest of the class, but that knowledge was in reading and writing. I was more interested in their speech, which was poor. Quite unintentionally I showed them up and destroyed their confidence. Some of them began to disrupt my drilling by asking an unrelated question, or refusing to respond.

Either I had simply not anticipated this hostile reception, or I had refused to face up to its possibility. Now it had happened, what was I to do? I was not prepared to move towards more traditional methods, because I did not believe in them. Moreover, I felt I could rescue the situation because my relationships with the students outside formal classes were good – as long as we talked only German!

I discussed the problem with my college principal and he came up with the solution which, if I had been more experienced, I would have thought of immediately. He recommended that I explain the methodology to the class and why it was more effective than the 'book' learning they were familiar with. In other words, I should teach them some elementary linguistics.

This seemed to work. Quite soon, my students came to understand and even enjoy my approach.

What lessons did I learn? The important one was that students need to be aware of how they are learning and must believe in your methodology. Otherwise they will not be motivated to learn. Students are less likely to take skills learning seriously if they do not know how the process works, because, as I have said, the outcomes are not easily recognisable and measurable in 'content' terms. Still less will they be convinced if their teacher is unsure or unconvinced of the methodology.

And what did I learn about myself? I had assumed that because I was enthused by the method, that I would automatically enthuse my students, too. I didn't take the trouble to prepare them, because I hadn't realised that their previous experience of language learning had habituated them to dependency on other types of activity. Moreover, I hadn't realised how intimidating I had seemed. Drilling is a fast, energetic process which puts individuals on the line to respond quickly and appropriately. I had never intended to intimidate students, and could not believe I would ever do so, or be so insensitive to their feelings. However, it was clear my drilling posture was unacceptably domineering. Why had I adopted this unnatural pose?

I believe the answer lay in an attitude formed during my own foreign language learning at school and university. It went like this: native speakers were not proper teachers because they supplemented the more academic aspects of language study (reading, writing and translation) with 'conversation classes'. Assuming German students would think of me in the same way, I needed to have control in order to gain confidence. I therefore adopted an unnaturally powerful stance, through a medium which lent itself admirably to such a stance – the parade ground!

Learning from doing

Traditional and skills teaching philosophies are not as opposed as some would have us believe. It is often said, for example, that didactic methods make our students passive learners. What does this mean? How can learning ever be passive? The students may not ask questions or move about or even smile in your lecture, but if they are awake and reasonably alert, they will be processing the information through active listening, taking notes, reading the lecture handout, etc. Those students attempting to gain a deeper understanding of the material will be trying to make sense of the subject matter. If they can't grasp it immediately, they may be thinking up strategies which will help them grasp it: should I ask a question, say I don't understand? What book will explain this? Perhaps I'll discuss it with Sarah after the lecture. Or shall I wait for the seminar on the topic? Or do all of these things?

Even those who have adopted a 'surface learning' strategy will be trying to note down all the points you make, so that they can 'learn' them for later regurgitation. Apart from students who have come into your lecture for a rest from the rigours of the day, they will all be working actively to make what they can of your material.

Furthermore, although the techniques of simulation, role play and games are not part of traditional teaching methodology on most academic courses, other experiential methods, such as apprenticeships, articles, pupillage, field and laboratory studies, have long played a part in education. Mooting and library research exercises are common in law schools. Tutors may lay on an experience – a prison visit, for example – and ask students to submit their written reflections on the experience.

If you ask teachers how they would define *experiential learning*, some will reply 'Learning by doing'. Certainly the experience-based activities described above all share this characteristic. Nevertheless, the definition is inadequate, and may help to explain why critics of the methodology regard it as anti-intellectual, concerned with techniques rather than substance.

What this definition ignores are the cognitive processes of *reflection* and *conceptualisation* which enable learning to take place. As I intend to show, reflection is the process which makes most demands on the learner. Conceptualisation – formulating and refining your personal theories of action – is the most important stage of the learning process. It is dependent on searching and considered reflection. Having an experience and thinking about it are easy. But what comes next? Do you always have an answer? It is ironic that both law students and their teachers may pay insufficient attention to this rule-making aspect of the learning process. How do we ensure that it is built into our skills programmes?

Restatement and rebuttal

In this section my aim has been to encourage you to identify and think about the characteristics of 'process' learning and the problems these can raise for students and teachers. This is particularly important for those whose educational experience rests on the didactic methods of information transfer. I have also stressed the importance of explaining learning theory and its purpose to students. This is necessary to win them over to an unfamiliar and unsettling learning process which they perceive to have no clearly defined end. Finally, I have indicated the need to incorporate techniques into skills programmes to encourage conceptualisation.

I have made these points in an attempt to discourage the view that skills learning is 'unstructured'. As we shall see in the next section, nothing could be further from the truth. Skills learning is a highly structured cyclical activity. When it is effective, students are able to articulate very clearly not only what they have learned from a skills workshop but also how they are going to use what they have learned in the future. It should 'create a climate where willing learners realise more and memorise less'.[5]

Experiential learning theory

Learning how to learn: Kolb's learning model

> Experiential learning . . . offers the foundation for an approach to education and learning as a lifelong process that is soundly based in intellectual traditions of social psychology, philosophy, and cognitive psychology. The . . . model pursues a framework for examining and strengthening the critical linkages among education, work and personal development.
>
> Kolb (1984), pp 3–4

Experiential learning theory is therefore not simply concerned with the acquisition of skills. It is about the learner taking control of her learning in a way which enables her to understand herself better as a learner. It is a lifelong, holistic process which integrates knowledge, skills, attitudes and values. It aims to affect the learner in three interconnected ways; see Johnson and Johnson (1991):

1. developing the learner's personal conceptual framework;
2. allowing the learner to articulate and modify her attitudes and values;
3. expanding the learner's repertoire of behavioural skills.

Clearly, the emphasis is not on any one aspect of human functioning, such as cognition or perception. This learning process involves the whole being by integrating thinking, feeling, perceiving and behaving: see Kolb (1984), p 31.

In Kolb's view (p 2), the learning process was distorted, first by the cognitive theories of rationalism, and then by behaviourism: see also Osterman (1990), p 143. The rationalist model of learning is the one we tend to associate with academic education. It is founded on detached, abstract reasoning and the pursuit of apparently objective truth through a research methodology which denies the validity of subjective experience.

---

5   Robert Albertson, cited in A Bailey (1986), p 24.

Behaviourism claims that human learning takes place through responses of the learner to external stimuli and that those responses are encouraged or deterred by negative or positive reinforcements. For example, receiving high marks in a test reinforces the student in the notion that what she is doing is what is required of her as a competent learner. She will therefore be inclined to repeat the process for subsequent tests.[6] Yet behaviourism, too, denies the importance of the personal and subjective by failing to take account of intention, feelings and choice.

Behaviourism has been enormously influential in the domain of vocational training. Thus the cognitive-rationalist type of learning is associated with a higher order of intellectual capacities, while behaviourism is associated with learning the 'lower order' skills needed to perform a narrow range of work-related activities. This may be a contributory factor to the dislike of the whole notion of 'skill' among many traditionalist professionals.

Rationalist and behaviourist concepts of education caused us to 'lose touch with our own experience as the source of personal learning and development': Kolb (1984), p 2. Kolb's model of learning builds on the theoretical frameworks developed by Dewey (1938), Lewin (1951) and Piaget (1952), (1971). These models restore experience to a central role in the learning process, but nevertheless remain cognitive frameworks which resolve and integrate potentially opposed modes of adapting to the world. In Kolb's terms, these conflicting modes are concrete experience/abstract conceptualisation and action/reflection.

Learning is therefore a process of tensions and conflicts which must be confronted. Resolving them will lead to personal growth and creativity.

Going round and round in cycles

The learning process is conceived as a sequential, recurring four-stage cycle: see Kolb et al (1974); Kolb (1984).

Learners have to be able to:

- involve themselves fully, openly and without bias in new experiences (CE);

---

6   The structure drilling referred to on p 65 is an example of a teaching method inspired by behaviourism.

- reflect on and observe their experiences from many perspectives (RO);
- create concepts that integrate their observations into logically sound theories (AC);
- use these theories to make decisions and solve problems (AE) (ibid, p 30).

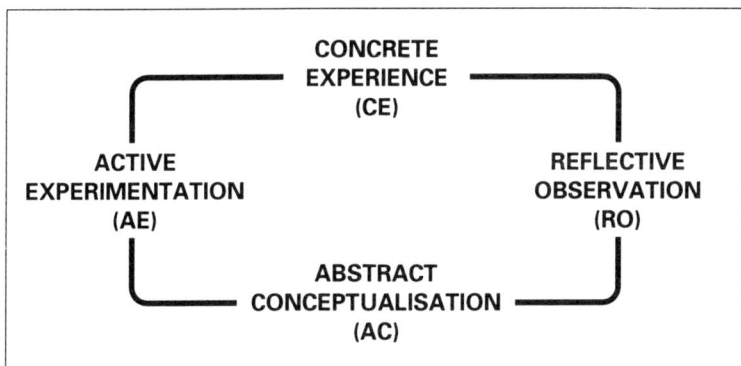

```
                        CONCRETE
                        EXPERIENCE
         ┌──────────────   (CE)   ──────────────┐
         │                                      │
    ACTIVE                                      REFLECTIVE
  EXPERIMENTATION                              OBSERVATION
      (AE)                                        (RO)
         │                                      │
         └──────────────  ABSTRACT  ────────────┘
                    CONCEPTUALISATION
                         (AC)
```

And so the cycle begins again. We experiment with new behaviour, reflect on the consequences, modify and refine our action theories, and try them out in new, uncertain or more complex situations. As the cycle continues we expand the repertoire of the appropriate knowledge and behaviour to use in a variety of situations at home, work, college, etc.

Consequently, as skills teachers, we have to remember that our students' minds are not blank sheets of paper onto which we are imprinting brand new knowledge and ideas. They have already had a wealth of experience from which they will have derived important learning. Some of the values and beliefs they bring with them may conflict with the new ideas which we are introducing to them. They will have to rearrange this new learning so that it is congruent with their previous learning. In this sense, all learning is relearning: see Kolb (1984), p 28.

Identifying learning styles and preferences

In section 1 I recommended discussing the purpose of experiential learning methodology with your students early on in the course. In this context students find it helpful to identify and assess their own learning styles and preferences. Their self-analysis should help them to discover why they are more comfortable with some learning activities than others and so improve their understanding of how they learn.

People have a variety of learning styles and use different ones at different times in the learning process. Generally we are at home with one or two styles, but find it difficult to adapt to styles we are uncomfortable with.

Kolb has identified four learning styles which correspond to quadrants on the learning cycle. The quadrants are created by intersecting the vertical CE/AC axis with the horizontal AE/RO axis. This gives us two opposing pairs of styles (see the diagram opposite). Briefly, these can be characterised as:

Divergers, who prefer to work through concrete experiences followed by reflection and observation – CE/RO. Kolb calls them divergers because they are imaginative and view issues from a number of perspectives. They are good at generating ideas and brainstorming. They value people and are sensitive to their needs.

Convergers have opposite strengths. They prefer to learn by working on abstract conceptualisations and theoretical models and testing these out by experimentation – AC/AE. They are good at problem-solving and decision making, moving quickly to find the one correct answer. They are task rather than people oriented.

Assimilators. This type of learner is able to create convincing generalisable theories from disparate observations – RO/AC. They like to use inductive reasoning and to create abstract models. They are more concerned that these are theoretically sound than that they should work in practice.

The *Accommodator* is the opposite style to this. They learn best by having a go, trying out new things and carrying out plans – AE/CE. They are risk-takers who do well in situations where they have to adapt to meet new circumstances. They will happily challenge and reject accepted theories and ways of doing things if they are not of immediate value.[7]

Peter Honey and Alan Mumford (1992), (1986) identify four styles with similar characteristics, though their styles correspond to the points on the learning cycle. The following diagram illustrates both models.

---

7   Individuals assess their learning styles using the Learning Styles Inventory: see D A Kolb (1985).

```
                    ACTIVIST
                     (CE)
                       |
  ACCOMMODATOR         |         DIVERGER
                       |
PRAGMATIST _____|_____ REFLECTOR
   (AE)                |               (RO)
                       |
   CONVERGER           |         ASSIMILATOR
                       |
                    THEORIST
                      (AC)
```

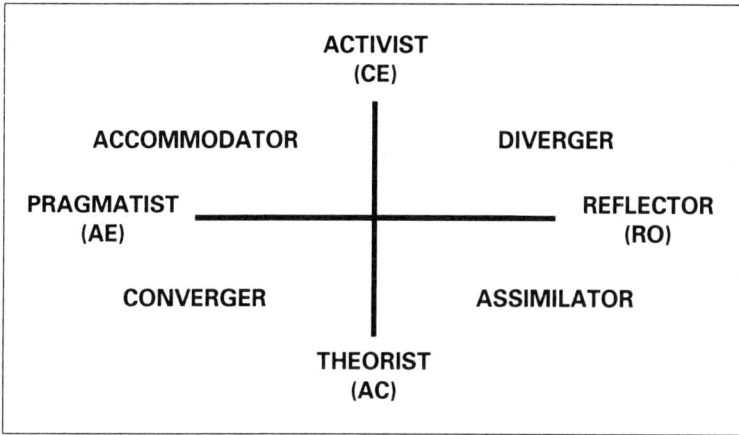

We can summarise the strengths and weaknesses displayed by Honey and Mumford's styles as follows:

STRENGTHS	WEAKNESSES

ACTIVISTS – Try anything once

Flexible	Leap before look
Open-minded	Take unnecessary risks
Like new experiences	Enthusiasm quickly
Optimistic	wears off
Work well in groups	Attention-seeking
and as group leaders	
Lateral thinkers	

REFLECTORS – Like to stand back and ponder

Careful	Reticent
Thorough	Slow to decide
Methodical	Over-cautious
Good listeners	Risk avoiders
Thoughtful	

THEORISTS – Need systems

Logical thinkers	Poor lateral thinkers
Objective	Dislike uncertainty,
Disciplined approach	ambiguity

Probing questioners	Distrust intuition
	Tend to use 'must',
	'ought', 'should'

PRAGMATISTS – Like practical tips, techniques, short cuts

Keen to test out ideas	Reject things having no
Realistic	obvious application
Good at solving practical	Not interested in theory
problems	Take first expedient route
Technique oriented	Task oriented, at expense
Adaptable	of needs of people

Students identify their learning preferences after filling in a questionnaire and plotting their results on a graph: see Honey and Mumford (1992). You may find that some individuals score heavily in more than one style. The resulting profile enables students to assess what kinds of activities they learn best from and which they learn least from.

Activists, for example, like carrying out tasks and tend to learn more from working in groups than working alone. They are happier leading discussions than listening to lectures.

Reflectors like to carry out methodical research and so will enjoy preparing seminar questions in advance. They may dislike role playing in front of an audience or having to make short cuts because of lack of time. However, they will gain a great deal from observing others.

Theorists are happy with interesting ideas, even if not immediately relevant, and like to be offered systems and structured situations with a clear purpose. They may resent being 'pitchforked' into an activity without an apparent purpose. They can feel uncomfortable with open-ended exercises such as client interviewing or negotiation, and tend to avoid activities which emphasise emotions.

Pragmatists want clear links between content and practice and so are happy with 'real life' activities in which they can immediately try out what they have learned. They distrust theory alone and activities which do not appear to be immediately relevant.

Students and teachers, particularly theorists, may be sceptical about the value of attaching rather simplistic labels to the rich diversity of approaches and responses to learning and the apparent ease with which some of us may link these to our 'personality type'. In contrast to personality, however, our learning preferences are not fixed. Questionnaire scores may well vary over time and often depend on the learning approach to which students have been exposed.

You can make it clear to your students that the learning styles questionnaire will not provide them with a solution to all their learning problems. However, it is a useful vehicle for reflection, not only on their own individual learning habits and preferences, but also on the learning process in general. In my experience, students draw a number of general conclusions:

- that the four styles correspond to points on the learning cycle;
- that we tend to prefer styles we are familiar with;
- that no one style is better than any other;
- that some types of learning involve activities appropriate to more than one style;
- that other types of learning are heavily dominated by one type of activity, so that only those learners with the corresponding style will get maximum benefit from it;
- that in their formal education to date theorist/reflector styles predominate;
- that what they now know about their preferences can be put to use in their lectures and seminars;
- that every individual's learning is personal to them;
- that theorist/reflectors should try to develop activist/pragmatist styles to help them feel comfortable with experiential learning.

Maughan and Webb (1995)

This last point makes it clear that learning how to learn means developing abilities in all four styles so that we become all-round, integrated learners. It may be helpful to complete the questionnaire again after a few months to see to what extent the graph has altered.

Encouraging reflection from many perspectives

WHAT HAPPENS WHEN A DOG MEETS A CAT

Dog thinks . . .
1. 'What is this thing I see before me?
2. I saw one of these yesterday and it was as ugly then as it is now.
3. What shall I do? What did I do yesterday?

4. I shall bark at it, because I did that yesterday and it went off and left me to eat and sleep in peace.'

Snow (1993), p 13

Reflection begins the process of translating experience into meaning. The quality of reflection determines the quality of the theories that people (and dogs?) develop for themselves. If students are unable to generate new ideas from the experience, or challenge and revise old ones, then it may be that they are not engaging in reflection from many perspectives.

The purpose of reflection is therefore to bring our reasoning processes and behaviour patterns to the surface and make them explicit. However, uncovering these can be difficult because so much of this knowledge is tacit and spontaneous. When we develop a pattern of behaviour which works in certain situations, we will tend to repeat it until it becomes automatic. We can't describe the processes involved because we are not aware of what is going on. If you are an experienced advocate, for example, you may not be able to explain why you put a particular question to a witness. It is only when something goes wrong or something unexpected happens that we may stop and think about what we did and what we could or should have done in the situation.

Although we use these 'stop and think' processes intuitively and automatically in everyday life, our formal academic education does not generally encourage us to solve problems in this way. Law students tend to be given problems to solve which have been framed in advance, and are asked for a solution from only one perspective – legal knowledge. It is therefore important that we encourage our students to develop techniques of reflective analysis which integrate their technical knowledge with the practical and experiential.

In section 3 I shall discuss methods of feedback which can develop reflection from these three perspectives.

Linking theory and practice

In this section I have introduced you to aspects of experiential learning theory which I hope you can usefully link to the observations about practice discussed in section 1. Now let's go on to consider how we can use these theories effectively in our own teaching and learning.

Testing the theory

From teacher to promoter of learning

As I have suggested in section 1, changing the focus from directive teaching to self-directed learning means we must think about how, why and when learning takes place rather than what is learned. It means trusting the learner to take responsibility for her personal learning and development. Your task is to provide the opportunities for this to happen.

It should happen if you take care to create a positive, open and empathic environment in which all the participants are encouraged to express their thoughts, feelings and attitudes. They should be able to try out new behaviour and attitudes without fearing the loss of their self-esteem.

Encouraging your students (and yourselves?) to 'let it all hang out' can be awkward and embarrassing if you or they do not feel equipped to deal with it. After all, we are accustomed to the dispassionate environment of the traditional lecture and seminar room where powerful norms operate to suppress the expression of emotion: see Bowen (1987), p 196. Linked with this are possibly deeply rooted 'rationalist' attitudes to learning in which we perceive feelings to play no part in cognitive development.

Displays of emotion inside the classroom may manifest themselves during an experiential exercise. More probably, emotions will surface during feedback, when you will help the group to review the experience from as many perspectives as possible. This will inevitably mean that group members have to confront and possibly reassess their values and attitudes. This process can be painful. Displays of emotion should not be upsetting or embarrassing if you have established an atmosphere of support and trust. They will simply be perceived as a necessary aspect of the learning process, to be discussed and reviewed in the same way as all the others.

It is important to remember that you are not the only expert in the group. You will have your own ideas, but so will the other group members who bring their personal experience and perspectives to bear in order to understand and learn from the activities: see Kolb et al (1986), p 22. Furthermore, it appears that adults learn best in situations where they are acknowledged as experts and equals and have the opportunity to teach as well as to learn: see ibid; Freire (1974).

Finally, it is not always easy to find the right balance between over-direction and free choice. Students who find it hard to cope with uncertainty and ambiguity can become immobilised if the process is too open-ended: see Megginson & Pedler (1992), p 50. Having your 'teacher' asking questions yet giving no answers can be puzzling and frustrating for some of these students. Megginson and Pedler suggest that:

> one of the skills in being a developer in this setting is promoting just enough puzzlement to help the learner enquire further but not so much that it leads to complete frustration.
>
> Megginson & Pedler (1992), p 8

Using your other group members as an extra learning resource, you can encourage your puzzled student to discover and evaluate a range of possible 'answers'. You need time and good quality reflection for this. More on this below.

Concrete experience: planning and preparation

TASK 3: DEAR CAROLINE . . .

Imagine you are designing a workshop to introduce your students to the skills of legal negotiation. You have been working with this group of 20 students for three months and they are used to experiential techniques. You plan to 'teach' the workshop yourself.

What factors will determine:
(a)   your choice of learning environment?
(b)   your choice and order of learning activities?

Much will depend on the context in which legal negotiation is covered on your course, so we will ignore issues of broader learning objectives and concentrate on the creation of a forum for skills development.

Below are just some of the issues which might have occurred to you.

Legal negotiation is an extremely open-ended activity, so after determining the content of the exercises I shall have no control over outcomes once the exercises are running. Does this matter?

CAROLINE REPLIES . . .

It will only matter if you feel the need to control. One of the positive aspects of experiential learning is that each individual will take something different from the exercises, depending on their personality, ability, personal history and interests: see Bowen (1987).

Everybody develops the skills of negotiation from an early age. Should I build on that experience? If so, how?

You will probably want your exercises to reflect the reality of legal practice as far as possible, so that students gain experience of the kinds of problems legal professionals encounter. However, you might prefer to begin with a non-legal situation so as to encourage the group to draw on their past negotiating experience. This can serve as a starting point for entering the world of legal negotiation. Your choice here will depend on how much opportunity the group will have to practise and experiment in subsequent workshops.

How do I ensure that all students get a go? What activities should I select? Demonstration? Game? Role play? Short lecture? Research exercise?
    There is a large amount of material on negotiation styles and strategies, legal and non-legal. Should I incorporate any of this into an introductory workshop? If so, why and how much?

Certainly it is important to make sure all the students have an opportunity to practise a negotiation and review their performance. Role play is therefore a suitable activity, but you might prefer to introduce the topic with a live or video demonstration of a legal negotiation, followed by a discussion. By this means you can convey information about negotiating skills and styles without having to go into 'lecturer' mode.

At what point should the students enter the learning cycle? Does it have to be at the concrete experience stage?

When selecting your experiential exercises you will need to know what you want the exercise to do. Should it illustrate a specific learning point which the students work out for themselves? Games are useful for this purpose. Alternatively, you might want the students to carry out a self assessment exercise, such as the Learning Styles questionnaire. In both these cases the learner begins with concrete experience.

Demonstrations followed by discussions are good for strong reflector learners, while introductory explanations begin the cycle at the abstract conceptualisation stage. Both these approaches could lead the group to develop a conceptual framework for the skills of negotiation before they practise them. If this is followed by a negotiation role play exercise, then the students will be actively experimenting with the concepts.

The important thing is not where you get on the cycle, but that you go right round it.

If the purpose of an activity is not immediately clear, should I tell the students the purpose in advance, or hope they will discover this for themselves?

This is an important question to consider when you use an activity to illustrate a learning point. It may well defeat the purpose of the activity to tell the students why they are doing it, if it is to enable them to discover the point through reflection and integrate it into their personal theories of action.

Let me give you an example. At the start of a course on writing skills at UWE we do 'The Brick Exercise'. The purpose of the exercise is as follows:

> To illustrate by means of an intermediate stage the transitions necessary to move from conversing to writing. Students should then be able to identify and describe the differences between the written and spoken language and so have a clearer idea of what is involved in writing – thinking and planning, and keeping in mind the needs and abilities of your audience.

The students are not told the purpose; we only tell them they are going to do an exercise on writing. Two volunteers sit back to back, each with an identical set of bricks. Volunteer A builds a model – anything she likes, so long as it isn't symmetrical. She then tells volunteer B how to build the same model. B is not allowed to ask questions or say anything at all, or indicate that in any way that he doesn't understand. The rest of the group must be able to see, and have to keep quiet.

The two models are extremely unlikely to be the same. We then ask the observers at which points the instructions misled B and why. We list these on the board and then repeat the exercise with one or

two more pairs, to see if they are picking up any of the points raised.
By this stage the students should have noted the similarity with writing and have spotted the features absent from conversation – body language, prosody (intonation, stress, wordless sounds) and immediate feedback. We can then dispel the popular misconception that writing differs from speech because we use more 'formal' language (eg less common vocabulary, passive verb forms instead of active, etc).

We follow this up with a 'thinking and planning' exercise in which small groups construct models and write instructions for other groups to build them. We encourage the students to link the idea of building concrete models with constructing arguments, ideas, facts, etc; building arguments and ideas which need to be put together to achieve the 'construction' they want to communicate.

Clearly, if we made the students aware of the purpose of the exercise in advance, there would be no point in doing it. If we did no exercise at all but simply explained the learning points, the message would have little impact.

In general, however, you should brief your students fully on what it is they are supposed to be doing and why. Until you know the exercise well, it is a good idea to prepare your briefing carefully in advance so that you don't forget anything. Putting it in writing for your students will help to ensure they don't forget anything. Furthermore, a carefully planned briefing will help you remember to bring all the necessary materials – role plays, observation sheets, flip chart, projector transparencies, video camera, playback facilities, etc.

Should I select activities to suit only some learning preferences or all of them?

You will be using all of them anyway if you encourage your students to go round the learning cycle. If your aim is to encourage the students to become all-round learners, then try to design exercises that suit all four styles.

Should I plan follow-up exercises to be completed after the workshop? If so, what, and why?

Follow-up exercises are necessary to allow the learner to reflect further on her experiences and so to develop her conceptual framework. Such exercises could include a written account of the experience, or an entry in the student's learning diary (see below). Or you can provide the students with additional role plays to be performed in small groups and recorded on video. If you have recorded the practice sessions in the workshop, students could take these away for further review.

What will I be doing while the students are carrying out the workshop activities?

Many skills teachers will probably agree that most of the hard work goes into preparing the workshop. If you have done this thoroughly, then you should be able to relax and enjoy yourself during the session. If you have created a climate where it is acceptable for you to go and observe performances and listen in to discussions, you can do this, noting down any points you may want to raise later when the small groups feed back to the whole group.

But beware! If you are like me, you may find yourself falling prey to dictator tendencies. Whenever small groups are reviewing an exercise, for example, I feel an irresistible impulse to interfere and take over the discussion. If this happens to you, you should try to curb this impulse. Just go round noting interesting remarks that you overhear. These are very valuable and amusing to use in feedback sessions.

Sometimes I stop myself succumbing to the urge by moving to the board and noting there the issues I want to raise later. 'No, no, don't look at the board, these are for later,' I tell students whose discussions I have interrupted with this rather more subtle form of interference. 'Oh look! We haven't considered that point,' says a group, pointing to the board. What have I done? I have directed them to discuss *what I want them to discuss.* Let the performance or discussion take its course, even if you think the participants are on the wrong track or ignoring what you think are essential issues. Learn not to interfere.

I don't know anyone who says facilitating is a piece of cake.

Reflective observation: the art of feedback

Our aim here is to ensure that during feedback the learner uncovers her reasoning processes to explain how she framed problems and what motivated her to act as she did. This may involve recognising and analysing processes of discrepant reasoning. This occurs when what we say we should do in a situation is different from what we actually do in the situation.[8] It may not be easy to spot this happening because, as I suggested in section 2, so many of the rules which govern our actions are tacit.

For example, a group of skills teachers attend a workshop on experiential learning. Two of them role play a negotiation, observed by the rest of the group. Before they begin to analyse the performance, the observers agree that feedback to students after role play exercises must be positive and constructive. The observers then proceed to give feedback to the performers. One mentions that the attitude of one 'lawyer' was unnecessarily adversarial. Others agree, and go on to say that his body language could have been interpreted by the opponent as downright hostile. At the time, no one picks up this discrepancy. In time, some participants may make the connection, others may never do so.

Deep reflection needs time. It also needs clear thinking about what students should reflect on, and how they should go about it.

What should we reflect about?

TASK 4: THE ANGRY CLIENT

One of your students interviews a client who came to her for advice after being injured in a road traffic accident. Earlier class discussions had dwelt at some length on the client-centred approach to interviewing. The 'lawyer' decides on an informal environment for the interview – coffee and armchairs with no desk or other barrier between them. The client, in a business suit and carrying a briefcase, is greeted informally by the lawyer, who addresses him by his first name. As the interview proceeds, the client becomes more and more irritated by what he perceives as the lawyer's 'laid back attitude'. His frustration gradually turns to anger as the lawyer persistently refuses to deal with the questions he wants answered (Has he a claim? Quantum of damages). Finally he gets up, saying 'It's quite clear you can't help me. I'll go elsewhere, thank you', and leaves.

What questions would you ask the lawyer, or expect her to ask herself during feedback?

You will want her to look not only at what she did or didn't do, but also why she took certain decisions, acted as she did, responded in a

8   This is discussed in more detail in C Maughan and J Webb (1996), in this collection.

certain way to the client's behaviour; how she felt about the experience; and whether the action theory she used was effective, or needs changing.

It might be useful to start with the well-used technique of questioning for information:

What happened?	*I hit him*
What led up to this happening?	*He called me a liar*
What was the result?	*He hit me back*

We can call this the ABC of reflection: **A**ntecedents, **B**ehaviour, Consequences. However, reflection on behaviour alone will not enable the learner to articulate the feelings, attitudes and values which underpin her action theories. We therefore need a broader category for B. I suggest:

B = R – Responses, reactions
A – Attitudes
V – Values
E – Emotions

Based on this model, here is a list of questions which could encourage the lawyer in Task 4 to reflect on her experience from a number of perspectives:

What happened?

What did I do? What was I thinking/feeling? What did the client do?

I greeted the client in a friendly and informal manner, but he didn't smile or anything. He didn't respond positively to my questions about his case, in fact they just seemed to put his back up. Whatever I tried, I didn't seem to be able to get through. At this point I felt I'd lost control, and I just wanted to leave. I couldn't retrieve the situation. In the end he left. I wasn't at all surprised. Just extremely miserable.

What led up to it happening?

What were the
– circumstances
– assumptions
– feelings

- actions
- reasoning processes

which led me to do what I did?

When I was preparing for the interview I deliberately decided to use an informal, counselling-type approach. I am sympathetic to this approach and it seems natural to me to use it. Also, I used it before in the matrimonial role play and it seemed to work well. So I thought the thing to do was to empathise with the client by meeting him on an equal footing rather than appear to take control of the interaction by 'interrogating' the client.

What was the outcome?

What did I want/intend to happen? Did that happen? If so, was it the result of what I intended or what I did? Or did something else make it happen?

If it was the result of what I intended/did, what theory(ies) of action was I using? Is this theory worth preserving? Can I foresee similar situations and consequences where it might work, or is it a one-off?

If the consequences were not what I intended, was this because I used an inappropriate theory of action? (Because other things intervened, eg I made false assumptions, wasn't prepared for the situation, was insufficiently assertive, felt personally attacked, etc). At the time, what would I like to have done? Thinking about it now, what could I have done to get the response I wanted? Do I need to change my behaviour, action tendencies, attitudes, values, etc, to handle this sort of situation better?

I blew it completely. I thought the informal arrangement of the room and using first name terms would make him feel comfortable and at home so that he could open up and tell me his story without too much prompting. We could then solve the problem together. I kept saying this to him: that I needed all the information for us to be able to resolve it together. That seemed to annoy him, so that when I tried to check if he was to blame at all for the accident he got defensive. When I asked him if he'd been prosecuted he got really angry. Why did I ask him that? Everything I did made things worse. I completely lost my confidence and didn't know what to do. I never even got on to advising him about his claim – he left.

He took a dislike to me from the outset. That must be down to me. He was obviously hostile to my approach. Perhaps his expectations were different from mine. There was a clue – the way he was dressed – a professional-looking client. But I noticed that, and thought he would appreciate being treated as an equal. Obviously not. Perhaps he was uncomfortable because I didn't fit with his image of a lawyer. Why didn't I pick up on that at the time? At the time all I can remember thinking is, *I'm coming to dislike this man more and more.*

Thinking about it now, I shouldn't have stuck so rigidly to my prepared strategy. It clearly doesn't suit all clients. Instead of doggedly proceeding with my 'empathy' line perhaps I should have appeared to take control: asked more closed questions, ASKED HIM STRAIGHT OUT WHAT HE WANTED ME TO DO.

Discrepant reasoning! In reality I wasn't at all client-centred.

My purpose in describing this rather mechanistic A B(RAVE) C approach is to provide a foundation for putting the reflection stage of the learning cycle into practice. It is not intended to be a set of prescriptive rules. For example, students should be encouraged to make their observations freely, so you won't want to prescribe an order in which issues should be discussed. The important thing is to be clear about the purpose of reflection. Otherwise it is possible that students will fail to generate new theories or modify old ones, and so will not make it round the cycle.

Furthermore, reflection is not restricted to introspective analysis by the performer. Feedback from all participants and observers enables the performer to identify differing perceptions, attitudes, and values relating to the experience and what can be learned from it. This feedback from others is important in helping the individual examine the situation in all its complexity. For example, the client in Task 4 above might say that the lawyer's perception of him was mistaken – as was his perception of her:

It's interesting that she found me hostile from the beginning. I wasn't. That came later. It's true I wasn't so sure about the chairs and her general informality. The real trouble was, she was so casual about everything. I was in pain – she didn't even ask me about my injury. So much for a sympathetic approach. I thought she just wasn't interested and didn't care.

TASK 5: ATTEND TO YOUR OWN LEARNING

One way of trying out and developing your approach to reflection is to test it on yourself. For example, think of a recent problem or dilemma which you resolved or failed to resolve satisfactorily. Work through it and identify your reasoning processes and behaviour patterns. Have you identified any discrepant reasoning? What have you learned?

How should we facilitate reflection?

Reflection can take place in small or large group discussions, as soon as possible after the event so that their responses and reasoning processes are fresh in the participants' minds. It is a good idea to allow the performers to feed back first, followed by the observers, and finally, the facilitator. In a client interview, for example, it is common practice to ask the lawyer to feed back before the client. As we have just seen in the Task 4 example, this enables the lawyer to analyse her behaviour and attitudes before the client throws up any possible conflicts in the lawyer's self-perception.

Effective feedback depends on a number of conditions. Here are some of the important ones:

- *Comment on observed behaviour and its effect.* This means focusing attention on what is seen and done, rather than making assumptions about why a person acted or failed to act in a certain way, or being judgmental about behaviour or the attitudes and values of others. Moreover, avoid making vague statements; comment on specific behaviour. For example:

  Did you notice that you interrupted your opponent a few times? Why was that?

  is better than:

  You seemed rather impatient.

- *Be positive.* Many of you probably find that performers tend to select what they consider to be their bad points and ignore the good ones. It will help their confidence if others highlight the good points. In my experience, students are very good at doing this, particularly if you have agreed this rule with them from the start. Teachers, of course, specialise in the art of constructive criticism!
- *Be open and honest.* This rule potentially conflicts with the previous

one; what do you do if a performance was absolutely dire? An abundance of negative criticism from others can make the performer defensive and closed to new ideas. On the other hand, if nobody is honest about it, least of all the performer, she will not learn how to improve her performance. Moreover, asking the performer to acknowledge and explain unsatisfactory behaviour may well reveal a reasoning process which justifies it. From an apparent weakness the performer has identified a possible strength. For example:

> I can't quite remember now, did you ask your client if he had any previous convictions? *(Answer: No.)* Do you think you should have done? *(Answer: I knew I needed the information, but couldn't think how to phrase the question so it wouldn't offend him – he didn't seem to like me much anyway.)* Can you think of a way to phrase the question now? *(Answer: No.)* Can anyone else think of one? . . . and so on.

You can then go back to the perceived 'weakness' identified by the performer and hope to dig out further strengths:

> *(He didn't seem to like me much anyway.)* Why did you say just now you didn't think the client liked you? . . . And so on.

- *Set your priorities in advance.* It won't be possible to cover everything that was done or not done in a particular performance, so concentrate on the important things and those that are capable of change. In any case, there is a limit to the amount of feedback the receiver can take in at one time.
- *Give the performance criteria in advance.* This is especially important when the performance is being assessed. Also, it helps participants to know when they are free to experiment and make mistakes.

Feedback is likely to be much more effective if it can be given and received in a secure and trusting environment. As I suggested in section 1, it is worthwhile agreeing a feedback procedure with your students at the start of the course.

In complex problem-solving situations, reflection will probably continue long after your workshop. It may go on for weeks or months. Where it leads to quite substantial change in behaviour and ideas it will involve a number of experiments and trips round the learning cycle before the change occurs. You can stimulate further reflection by encouraging students to review their performances on video or to write some form of written account or commentary.

This leads us to the most important stage in the cycle.

Keep moving: abstract conceptualisation

Student to Facilitator:

> OK, I can recognise my strengths and weaknesses. What I don't know is what to do about my weaknesses. Tell me how I can improve.

Is this a familiar scenario? If so, it will engender such deep depression that, suddenly, anything must be more rewarding than teaching. Why? Because it means:

(a)   The speaker has not engaged in reflection from many perspectives and so has not uncovered her personal theories.

(b)   Lacking the motivation to learn, she therefore seeks refuge in 'teacher'.

In short, the speaker is stuck at the bottom of the cycle. How do we avoid this happening?

If reflection involves uncovering a personal theory and recognising the need to change it, conceptualisation concerns the question: *What do I change it to?*

Let's continue with the lawyer's reflection in Task 4 above:

> I was really unhappy with the way I handled the situation. It didn't work out as I had planned. I wasn't responsive enough to his needs or to his signals because I was so intent on imposing my agenda. How could I not have picked up the vibes?
>
> How do I stop myself getting into this situation again? For a start, I think I need to accept that not every client will respond favourably to this counselling-style approach. Some may think it unprofessional – after all, they are paying me to solve the problem, not for us to 'solve it together'. If I try to identify the client's concerns at the start, then surely I can take the lead from them. Why didn't I do this? It seems so obvious now. Deep down, I think I was afraid to, because I needed to impose my structure on the interaction so as to feel in control.
>
> Taking the lead from the client – isn't this what client-centred approaches are about? I did exactly the opposite, yet he ended

up controlling the situation in a way I certainly hadn't intended! Next time I shall find out at the start exactly what he wants. And I shall find a way of conveying genuine concern, while maintaining an appropriate 'professional' distance – imagine not asking him about his injury!

The detailed analysis of her behaviour, fears and attitudes has enabled the lawyer to discover her discrepant reasoning and to identify a change she could make which is potentially in line with her espoused theory about client-centred approaches.

Enlightenment may not always come so easily, however. It is possible to generate a rule, or 'learning point' which is unhelpful because it is too general, or because it is inappropriate in the situation.

For example, a lawyer and client meet for the first time. The lawyer instantly takes a liking to the client and senses that the client feels the same. So the lawyer cracks a joke. For some inexplicable reason, it falls flat; the client stares at him, confused, and doesn't even smile. A barrier is set up which remains throughout the interview.

As a consequence of this encounter, the lawyer extrapolates the following 'rule':

I must aim to create a better rapport with the client.

Is this helpful? Surely it begs the questions 'how' and what is meant by 'better rapport'? What situations should the rule apply to? Client interviews? All meetings with the client? Meetings with other professionals? The rule is too vague to be of much use to the lawyer when he is considering what changes he should make to his behaviour.

During reflection, the lawyer should be guided to focus on the specific problem and why it was a problem. We could elicit this by asking:

What was the client's response when you made that joke near the beginning?
Why do you think he responded as he did?
How did you feel about his response?

Once the lawyer has realised that the joke was a mistake and that he misread the situation, we can ask him:

What kind of situation is it?

Would you do the same thing again in this situation?
If not, why not?

With luck, this should elicit a more workable rule:

> *In a professional situation like this it is a good idea to act quite formally until you think the relationship is sufficiently informal to be able to relax a bit.*

Of course, the lawyer might not accept that he misread the situation. He might put the blame on the client:

> *The man obviously had no sense of humour.*

Whilst we may agree that this shows some learning, it is of such a limited kind that it is unlikely to lead the lawyer to modify his behaviour and attitudes.

So there must be a point to 'learning points' and we may need to check that learning has taken place. How can we do this?

Some skills developers ask their students at the end of a skills session to note down their learning points and display them somewhere in the room so that everyone can read them. Unfortunately this may lead some students to think that they can skip the deep reflection stage. They may get into the habit of rationalising intuitive action after the event without having uncovered their reasoning processes. For example:

> *When I see that client again, remember not to make jokes!*

A better way is to ask each student to keep a learning diary in which they record their personal learning in their own time as they become aware of it. Students can record under headings which reflect the learning cycle:

experience;
reflection;
conceptualisation;
experimentation.

This will help them impose a degree of structure on their learning and has the added advantage of reinforcing the learning cycle concepts. However, too much structure may be counter-productive. Some individuals can spend a lot of time deciding whether what they have written falls under the right heading. Not only does this interrupt the flow of their ideas; it may lead them to draw artificial distinctions – between reflection and conceptualisation, for example. It is better to concentrate on making sure that their cycles are completed.

Will you read your students' diaries? This is an ethical dilemma you have to resolve. You might prefer to treat the diaries as confidential and not look at them. On the other hand, you need evidence that the students are refining and reformulating theories, and it won't be practical to set and mark written exercises after every skills practice session. You may prefer therefore to look at the diaries every so often. If you have established a supportive and trusting atmosphere your students should be confident that what they reveal won't be judged.

Active experimentation: planning and testing

The whole learning cycle involves us in experimentation, so I prefer to think of this stage as 'Planning and Testing', or 'Future Action'. We can encourage our students to draw up action plans in which they set objectives for themselves:

> What am I going to try out?
> What event/experience will afford me an opportunity to try it out?
> How am I going to do it?
> How and when am I going to reflect on how it went?
> How and when am I going to record it?
> (And so on.)

How might the 'client-centred' lawyer of Task 4 go about this?

> The next client interview I do, I think I will keep the armchairs and coffee, but after the introductions I shall go straight in and ask the client what I can do for him. At no point will I go on about 'resolving the problem together' unless I am sure that's what the client wants to hear. I shall make sure I remind myself every so often what it is the client wants, so I don't lose track of her concerns.

It will probably take plenty of further experiments and reflection before she is satisfied with her approach. Next time, for example, she may question the wisdom of banning the desk completely and instead allow the client to choose where to sit – by a desk or in a more comfortable armchair.

Interference with tacit knowledge

As part of planning for an interview or negotiation, some skills manuals and skills developers (including me) like to recommend that the students draw up checklists. These enable the performer to check quickly that they have covered everything they planned to cover. However, this practice is dangerous and can result in overdosing if not used in moderation. Here are some examples.

(a)   The client has instructed his lawyer to deal with his house purchase. The two are discussing the property – a small terraced two-bedroomed house in a rather run-down area of urban sprawl:

Lawyer: Are there any fishing rights attached to the property?

Client: *(gapes in astonishment)* I beg your pardon?

(b)   The client has instructed her lawyer to draw up a will:

Client: I've got a list of my assets here if you'd like it.

Lawyer: Yes, but first let me go through my list. Do you and your sister own the property as joint tenants or tenants in common?

Client: *(uncomprehendingly)* I wouldn't know, dear. What on earth do you mean?

(c)   Lawyer and client are discussing the client's house sale:

Client: *(near start of interview)* I'm really worried that Mr Crabbe (the buyer) might convert the house into a bail hostel. I don't think my neighbours would want that. Can I stop him?

Lawyer: We'll come back to that. Did you say you had put the property with an estate agent?

Client: I really need to know this before I decide if I want to accept his offer.

Lawyer: Just let me get some other details first. Who's your estate agent?

(d)   Client: *(clearly distressed)* My mother died two weeks ago.

Lawyer: Right. Have you brought the death certificate?

These examples might seem far fetched, but they are all real. They demonstrate what can go wrong when interviewers turn their checklists into recipes. A student may be tempted to do this when her performance is to be assessed. The more detailed the checklist, the more she thinks she can control the situation by reducing its open-endedness. The unforeseen by-products of this are the use of jargon, apparently irrelevant questions, lack of sympathy and poor eye contact! Most serious, and embracing all of them, is the failure to listen and respond to the client's concerns. The lawyer in (c) surely must be judged not competent on those vitally important criteria.

By allowing students to take detailed checklists into an assessed performance, aren't we encouraging them to use a theory of action which is quite inappropriate in the situation? Moreover, it is a theory which is likely to conflict with the performer's tacit knowledge. What is the source of this theory?

In my view, the over-reliance on checklists stems from students' fears about 'The Law'. They are afraid they don't know it. They are often right about that. Their legal knowledge does not form part of their tacit knowledge because they have not yet learned how to use it in practice. Whereas the interpersonal skills they need may come easily to them, they only feel reasonably confident about law if they have got the details written out in front of them. We encourage them to do this because we know they don't know it either.

Checklists should be used for one purpose: to check you have not forgotten anything. They should be brief and free of legalese. Students should not write their interview notes on them, as doing so focuses their attention on the checklist contents rather than on the client.

In the end was the beginning: preparing for future action

In section 3 above I have discussed techniques we can use to incorporate Kolb's model of the learning cycle into our teaching practice. The value of experiential learning theory is that it integrates knowledge with experience. Kolb's theory gives equal status to the four stages of the cycle. For teaching purposes, however, I have argued that the reflection and conceptualisation stages are the more problematic because it is at these points that learners must use highly developed cognitive and affective processes to learn from the experience. For the teacher it is sometimes difficult to remember that this is a process of self-perception and analysis. Our students will not learn if we tell them what they should have done and why. Such an approach does not attempt to bring to the surface the way the learner deals with the moments of 'not knowing'.

I would like to conclude with a definition of learning which encompasses all that I have been talking about:

> Learning means an approach both to knowledge and to life, that emphasises human initiative. It encompasses the acquisition and practice of new methodologies, new skills, new attitudes, and new values necessary to live in a world of change. Learning is the process of preparing to deal with new situations. It may occur consciously or unconsciously . . .
>
> Botkin et al (1979)[9]

As a skills developer your function is to enable your students to become aware of the processes involved in learning, to internalise those processes, and make them part of their practice so that they never forget them: see Megginson and Pedler (1992).

How are you going to do this?

References

A Bailey (1986) 'Faculty Leaders in Profile', 18 *Change* 24.

G Boak (1991) *Developing Managerial Competences: The Management Learning Contract Approach*, Pitman, London.

J W Botkin, M Elmandra & M Melitza (1979) *No Limits to Learning*, Pergamon, Oxford.

D D Bowen (1987) 'Developing a Personal Theory of Experiential Learning: A Dispatch From the Trenches', 18 *Simulation & Games* 192.

J S Bruner (1966) *Toward a Theory of Instruction*, W W Norton, New York.

J Dewey (1938) *Experience and Education*, Macmillan, New York.

P Freire (1974) *Pedagogy of the Oppressed*, Seabury Press, New York.

M Griffiths and S Tann (1992) 'Using Reflective Practice to Link Personal and Public Theories', 18 *Journal of Education for Teaching* 69.

---

9   Cited in D Thatcher (1990), p 264.

P Honey and A Mumford (1992) *The Manual of Learning Styles*, Honey, Maidenhead.

P Honey and A Mumford (1986) *Using Your Learning Styles*, Honey, Maidenhead.

D W and F P Johnson (1991) *Joining Together: Group Theory and Group Skills*, Prentice Hall International, Englewood Cliffs, NJ.

D A Kolb (1984) *Experiential Learning: Experience as the Source of Learning and Development*, Prentice Hall, Englewood Cliffs, NJ.

D A Kolb (1985) *The Learning Style Inventory* (2nd edn), McBer, Boston.

D A Kolb, I M Rubin, J M McIntyre (1974) *Organisational Psychology*, Prentice Hall, Englewood Cliffs, NJ.

K Lewin (1951) *Field Theory in Social Sciences*, Harper & Row, New York.

J Macfarlane (1992) 'Look Before You Leap: Knowledge and Learning in Legal Skills Education', 19 *Journal of Law and Society* 293.

C Maughan and J Webb (1995) *Lawyering Skills and the Legal Process*, Butterworths, London.

C Maughan and J Webb (1966) 'Taking reflection seriously: How was it for us?', this collection.

M Maughan (1996) 'A capability approach to assessing legal skills: a strategy for developing effective future performance', this collection.

D Megginson & M Pedler (1992) *Self-Development: A Facilitator's Guide*, McGraw-Hill, Maidenhead.

K Osterman (1990) 'Reflective Practice: A New Agenda for Education', 22 *Education and Urban Society* 133.

J Piaget (1952) *The Origins of Intelligence in Children*, International University Press, New York.

J Piaget (1971) *Psychology and Epistemology*, Penguin Books, Middlesex.

C Rogers (1993) 'The Interpersonal Relationship in the Facilitation of Learning', in M Thorpe, R Edwards, A Hanson (eds) *Culture and Processes of Adult Learning*, Routledge, London.

A Snow (1993) *How Dogs Really Work*, Harper Collins, London.

D Thatcher (1990) 'Promoting Learning Through Games and Simulations' *Simulation and Games* 262.

J Webb (1995) 'Where The Action Is: Developing Artistry in Legal Education', 2 *International Journal of the Legal Profession* 187.

Chapter 4

Skills in the initial stage of legal education: theory and practice for transformation
Andy Boon

The focus of this paper is the teaching of skills at the initial stage of legal education. Its principal theme, however, is the transformative functions of skills teaching. The first of these transformations, contentious enough in its own right, is from a curriculum based on the transmission of knowledge to one based on activity and performance. The second transformation, which is less well documented or theorised in the literature on lawyers' skills, lies in the affective domain, that area of learning concerned with perception, attitudes and values: see Krathwohl et al (1964). Early work on this issue, for example Condlin (1983a), (1983b), Stark et al (1987) and Greenebaum (1987), underlines its contentious nature, but it is, nevertheless, one which deserves far greater attention than it has yet received from both academics and policy makers: see Menkel-Meadow (1994). The theme of transformation is explored in the context of the theory underpinning skills teaching and in the light of changes in the professional and academic context in which legal education operates in the United Kingdom. It defines and considers the relevance of 'holistic' and 'competence' based models of skills teaching to higher education and examines the political, practical and pedagogic implications of the choice of approach.

The first section of this paper reviews the various influences on legal education generally, including the Lord Chancellor's Advisory Committee on Legal Education and Conduct (ACLEC) paper on the 'Initial Stage' of legal education: see also Fitzgerald (1993). The second section examines some of the theoretical underpinnings of skills teaching developed more extensively elsewhere: see Macfarlane (1992), p 312; and it offers an expanded conception of the nature and role of skills education in the initial stage. Finally, a programme for undergraduate students is analysed using techniques of action research: see Kemmis (1985).[1] Aspects of this are also reported more fully elsewhere: see Boon and Humphreys (1994), p 71; and, in this paper, the empirical focus is located in student written evaluations of their experience of skills education in the initial stage.[2]

The context of the skills debate in higher education

The Robbins Report (1963) identified the provision of instruction in skills and the promotion of the powers of the mind as the main teaching purposes of higher education. In 1984 the old binary institutions made a more explicit commitment to specified skills because, it was explained, disciplinary knowledge changed so rapidly that teaching disciplinary 'content' was outmoded: see NAB (1984). The identification of specific skills, articulation of course aims and objectives and the collection of assessment evidence were all features of evolving practice in the years following these reports.

The government's agenda for the sector, Higher Education – Meeting the Challenge (1987), was that it should serve the needs of the economy by ensuring that graduates were not only well prepared for employment but also '. . . have the capacity to learn and develop, to move and change with the needs of the organisation; [and] are prepared to break the mould of the past': Bailey (1990). Government sponsored initiatives such as the Royal Society of Arts Capability Programme and the Training Agency's Enterprise in Higher Education Programme promoted the goal of 'developing more autonomous learners with self responsibility for continuing education throughout life': see Williams (1992) and Employment Department Group (1989); and the competence of undergraduates

---

1   While the methodology of action research is particularly appropriate to the problems of evaluation in educational research (Trow (1970), p 302; Parlett & Hamilton (1972), p 6) the absence of anonymity raises questions concerning the reliability of data. To the extent that such concerns can be addressed they are addressed here by triangulation (ie the use of two or more methods of data collection in the study of some aspect of human behaviour) using independent quantitative sources (Cohen & Mannion (1980), p 254).
2   This is drawn from over 60 written 'log books', kept by students for a full academic year and submitted as part of their coursework for the module described in the text.

in the skills associated with superior performance in employment: see Barnett (1994), p 19; Hannon (1991); Jones (1994), p 15. This process may yet culminate in pressure for higher education to embrace the competence based system for national vocational qualifications: see Employment Department (1994) and Jones (1994); and to provide students with:

> first hand work experience and an understanding of the constraints in which employing organisations operate, . . . [together with] the ability to reflect on and learn from practical experiences, . . . to assimilate large quantities of information quickly, and to analyse issues from several perspectives, . . . communication skills including oral presentation and report writing, . . . a foreign language for business, . . . personal qualities including drive, self motivation, self assessment, time management, ability to work without close supervision, leadership potential, enterprise, initiative, . . . working effectively in groups or teams, problem solving and decision making [and] evaluation of risks and consequences . . .
>
> Atkins et al (1993), p 30

These educational aims are, arguably, beyond the compass of higher education's 'traditional' pedagogy (Gow & Kember (1990)) and, further, they threaten traditional academic assumptions. Some academics have therefore equated 'skills' with training, vocationalism or managerialism (Toddington (1994)), and have struck 'an antithesis between 'skills' and 'knowledge and understanding' (Bridges (1993); Barnett (1994)) and seen 'transferable skills' as means of stripping discipline-based academics of their expertise (Barnett, p 93). It is therefore worth briefly examining the nature of the threats posed by skills, particularly to the exclusivity of disciplinary content and to traditional methods of delivery.

Disciplinary content

Legal method is based on the exposition of rules extracted from statute or appellate decisions. Like most disciplines its 'problems' are conceived within the subject rather than being those of the wider society (Barnett (1994), p 20). Not only does the content and method of skills work draw on non-legal social science disciplines, particularly psychology and sociology (Macfarlane (1992)) but its orientation is to the problems of the real world. Therefore, introducing skills to the curriculum is similar to including 'non-legal' subjects in law degrees (Wolstencroft and Van Zwanenburg (1989)). The advantages lie in the potential:

- to enhance understanding of the non-legal complexities of real life problems;
- to limit overspecialisation;
- to introduce content derived from disciplines with different methods of enquiry; and
- in the process to '. . . foster an academic setting which is hospitable to a wide variety of intellectual currents designed to produce lawyers who are creative, sensitive and open to new ideas.'

However, the introduction of skills to the curriculum presents the problems of introducing non-disciplinary material including the risk of rejection by staff and students and of marginalisation of the 'distinctive' material in the curriculum.

Methods of delivery

The introduction of skills also poses problems for methods of delivery. Law teaching, like many other traditional disciplines, has been attacked in terms of both its subject matter and pedagogy. It is not necessary to catalogue the complete list of criticisms which have been addressed elsewhere, both in this collection and outside: see eg Amsterdam (1984); Pirie (1987), p 578. However, points which are relevant to the discussion which follows are that legal education has tended to assess 'symbolic learning'; prized the retention and reproduction of information at the expense of learning outcomes in the affective, perceptual and behavioural domains (Kolb (1984)), encouraged 'surface' approaches to learning at the expense of deep learning which builds on existing patterns of understanding (Marton and Saljo (1976)), and individualised and sharpened competition between students, making them subservient both to authority and to legal authorities (Miller (1994), p 22).

In contrast, skills work requires activity by the learner, usually involving 'performance' in a real life or simulated setting, and is often based on group work. Understanding rooted in direct experience and student-led discussion increases potential for deep understanding and absorption of substantive content, broadens educational experience and expands the range of potential learning outcomes, particularly in relation to personal growth and independence (Clement (1971); Swain (1991)). However, individuals and departments committed to skills face problems which are compounded by sharper competition for government research resources. A skills-based curriculum is relatively demanding in terms of staff time and effort and, therefore, requires a high level of commitment from staff, has radical curriculum and resource implications (Cole (1993)) and may be marginal in terms of providing a field for legal research. Even if teaching quality assessments gave credit for offering skills programmes there would still be less financial incentive to teach skills than to research and publish (Brownsword (1994)). Nevertheless, many teachers and institutions in the higher education sector have embraced the idea of a 'skills curriculum' by, for example, identifying 'core' skills suitable for undergraduate study[3] (Allen (1991)) and by assessing the effectiveness of different teaching methods in enhancing the capability of undergraduates (Falchikov (1988)) including by the use of group work (Murdoch (1994)).

While higher education generally faces a growing demand for flexible provision and a focus on skills (Atkins et al (1993), p 8) the ACLEC consultation exercise on 'the Initial Stage' of legal education (1994) dismisses '. . . artificial divisions . . . between the academic and vocational study of law . . .' (para 1.6). Paragraph 2.1 suggests that 'The Functions of Initial Stage Training' are:

(i)   to develop the intellectual and other skills associated with degree-level education;

(ii) to develop the analytical and conceptual skills needed by lawyers and a proper knowledge and understanding of the general principles, nature and development of law;

(iii) to encourage the development of the independence and robust ethical standards expected of lawyers;

(iv) to provide students wishing to enter the practising profession with skills that will enable them to identify and respond effectively to changes in the law, and in clients' needs; and

---

3   The University of Sheffield's Personal Skills Unit, for example, identified four major skills areas appropriate to all disciplines: communication, teamwork, problem solving and managing and organising. These skills, it was suggested, were best developed through active learning which also stimulated deep learning out of which intellectual flexibility could develop.

(v)　to contain enough conceptual and substantive material for vocational training to be comparatively short.

These aims, it was asserted, are appropriate for 'all skilled in the discipline of law'.

Reflecting pedagogic trends in higher education generally, the consultation paper also asserts that the:

> . . . functions cannot be carried out through learning dominated by passively absorbing or receiving knowledge. It requires an active process which promotes general powers of the mind, and enables students . . . 'not merely to *know* or *know how to* but *understand* why things are as they are and how they could be different' and 'to relate ideas in one subject to those in others, to understand what they read, questioning material, making links, and pursuing lines of enquiry out of interest'.

The professional bodies have been ambivalent in their commitment to undergraduate skills: cf Marre (1988). The Seven Foundations of Legal Knowledge, announced by the Law Society and the Council of Legal Education (1995) expands the subject heads of the 'core' area of undergraduate study. The only references to skills in the Seven Foundations are '. . . the intellectual and practical skills needed to research the law on specific matters and to analyse both statute and case law, to apply it to the solution of legal problems and to communicate – both in writing and orally – the results of such work' and 'the ability to reflect on fundamental social concepts . . .' (page 5, paras (iv) and (v)).

This limited incorporation of skills in the core area of legal study reflects the professional bodies' desire not to 'frustrate or impede' the adoption of 'different scholarly approaches' in the study of law. However, this aspiration apparently conflicts with the assumption made in the Written Standards for the Law Society's Legal Practice Course (LPC) that graduates entering the LPC should have developed '. . . interpersonal skills and . . . , in particular, [they should be able to] listen effectively; engage in oral discussion in a clear and concise fashion; record or summarise a discussion in clear and concise notes; write clearly and precisely with attention to grammar, style, organisation, bibliographies and citations and extract, analyse and apply up to date law from primary sources, including case reports, primary and delegated legislation'. The LPC standards also assume that graduates are able to work 'co-operatively with others in small groups' although this is not a part of the Seven Foundations. This ambivalence reflects a growing tension in professional education. The flirtation with skills reflects the need for a skills-based curriculum, following the 'crisis of confidence' in exclusive disciplinary knowledge as the guarantee of professional status and privilege (Barnett (1994), p 16; Houle (1980); Schön (1983)), in order to respond to concerns about deregulation, competitiveness and the risks of deprofessionalisation and declining ethical standards (Abel (1986), (1989); Glasser (1990); Stanley (1991)). However, the oversupply of graduates with qualifying law degrees fuels concerns about the loss of exclusivity and status and the risk that the profession will fragment into sub-groupings as law graduates find work in the employed sector (Glasser). The risk that law degrees might lose their traditional 'rigour', thus exacerbating the supply problem, apparently underpins the reluctance to reduce 'disciplinary content' at the expense of non-disciplinary content.

This analysis explains the profession's desire to localise skills in vocational courses and to avoid a more extensive commitment to skills at the initial stage. Intending solicitors demonstrate 'competence' in the DRAIN skills[4] in the LPC and then receive a top-up in selected areas in the Professional Skills Course during their training contracts. In terms of scope, and the proportion of education and training time devoted to skills, this represents a limited conception of those skills, abilities, attributes and attitudes required of young professionals. This is illustrated by a small scale survey I conducted among trainees, solicitors and partners in 12 medium to large law firms in 1989[5] in which respondents from 12 solicitors' firms in the UK were asked to identify the 'skills' required of newly qualified solicitors (see table on page 107).

This data suggests two principal 'skills gaps'; first the importance attached to being able to relate to others, including staff, and secondly the importance attached to the qualities of independence, confidence and judgment. These I have labelled, perhaps contentiously, 'intrapersonal' skills. Economides and Smallcombe's (1991) research into

4 Drafting, research, advocacy, interviewing and negotiation.
5 From the 'Skills of Newly-Qualified Solicitors: Is Competence Enough?', a paper presented at the Institute of Advanced Legal Studies' Legal Skills Research Group Colloquium 'Skills and Competence: Questions for the Lord Chancellor's Advisory Committee on Legal Education and Conduct' (1990) (previously unpublished).

the skills required of trainees also recognised personal attributes as important to 'legal competence' (p 26). They identified a further 'skills gap' as the ability to 'break into' new areas of law. This may be seen as a combination of intellectual skills such as analysis and applied skills such as research. However, 'break in' also requires independence, confidence and judgment if the trainee is to make the transition from theoretically 'being able to do' to actually doing.

There is therefore an issue as to whether legal education has achieved the right balance and emphasis in the skills which it deems important. However, a more significant issue is emerging out of the crisis in the profession. This concerns the incapacity of traditional pedagogy to provide students with common professional values. Glasser (1990) suggests that, in the face of market forces, legal education is the 'cement' which can bind the profession together. It is perhaps this notion which underlies the proposal in the ACLEC Consultation Paper to establish ethics in the curriculum. While legal education has, formerly, transmitted values to students in an unconscious way (Stanley (1988)) the explicit adoption of a 'transformative' role in relation to 'common values' would be a radical departure raising serious questions for policy makers and academics alike.

However, it is a direction which has also been taken in the USA, where the MacCrate Report concluded that there was no 'gap' between education and practice as such:

> . . . only an arduous road of professional development along which all prospective lawyers should travel. It is the responsibility of law schools and the practising bar to assist students and lawyers to develop the skills and values required to complete the journey.
>
> MacCrate (1992)

Despite guarded support for the report in general there has also been criticism of MacCrate's weak commitment to 'values' and 'artistry' in its detail: see Costonis (1993); Menkel-Meadow (1994). These themes will be developed in the next section as it is argued that the initial stage of legal education has a critical role in that process because it offers the earliest opportunity to instil in prospective lawyers the attitudes that:

> . . . a proficient practitioner is one who realises the need for continual self education and self evaluation . . . before they

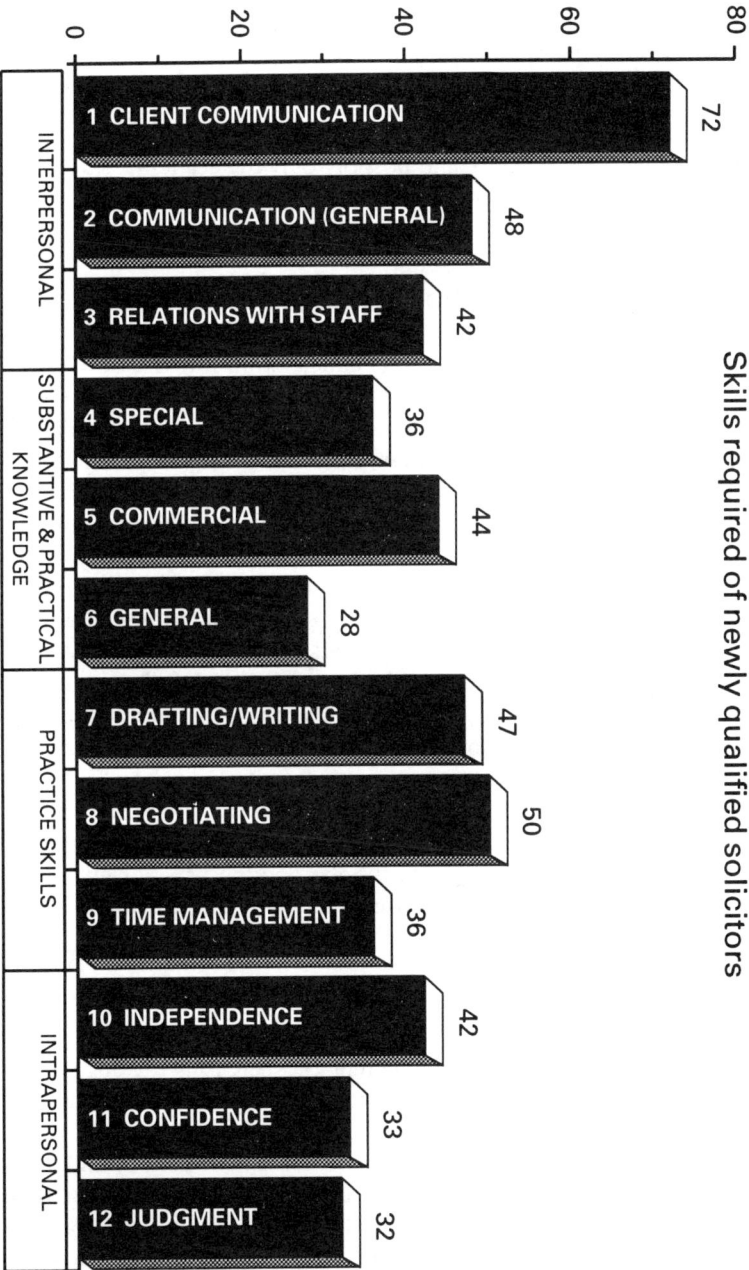

Skills required of newly qualified solicitors

INTERPERSONAL	1 CLIENT COMMUNICATION	72
	2 COMMUNICATION (GENERAL)	48
	3 RELATIONS WITH STAFF	42
SUBSTANTIVE & PRACTICAL KNOWLEDGE	4 SPECIAL	36
	5 COMMERCIAL	44
	6 GENERAL	28
PRACTICE SKILLS	7 DRAFTING/WRITING	47
	8 NEGOTIATING	50
	9 TIME MANAGEMENT	36
INTRAPERSONAL	10 INDEPENDENCE	42
	11 CONFIDENCE	33
	12 JUDGMENT	32

[students] become bored, cynical and anxious about finding
jobs . . .

Maurer and Mischler (1994), p 97

Provided the hegemony of content-based learning can be coun-
tered, the academic stage (and possibly only the academic stage) has
the time or compass to embrace these professional goals.

Skills in legal education in England and Wales

The recent history of skills in legal education in England and Wales
begins in the 1970s and 1980s where, borrowing from experiments
in the USA, programmes of clinical legal education were established
at Kent, Warwick, South Bank and Birmingham (now the University
of Central England). Their methodology was primarily based on the
idea of 'discovery' learning and their rationale was that the study of
law was enriched by direct involvement in legal processes. The
development of 'practice skills' was an ancillary but subsidiary
agenda of such courses and, generally, remains so (Grimes (1995)).

During the same period, law teachers in other common law jurisdictions were experimenting with classroom-based skills instruction,
particularly in relation to professional courses. Their aim was to systematically improve performance of certain lawyerly skills by the use
of criteria checklists, demonstration, performance, analysis and feedback and repeat performance on areas of weakness (Cruickshank
(1994)). These courses were profoundly influential in the design of
new vocational courses for both the Bar and the Law Society which
now, like their Commonwealth counterparts, adopted the DRAIN
skills as their principal vehicle.

Skills and competence

A dichotomy is immediately apparent between skills training, which
was the concern of the Commonwealth skills courses, and skills education, which was the primary concern of the UK clinical experiments.
The goal of skills training is to ensure competent performance of a
work-related task, to raise observable standards of performance
amongst students in the designated tasks, and, in time, amongst the
professional group as a whole. In drafting the standards for the LPC,

the Law Society essentially adopted the language of the occupational competence movement which has struggled to improve the validity and reliability of assessment based on criterion-referenced systems, particularly in relation to the allegations that they are mechanistic and lack breadth (Wolf (1994), p 3). Occupational competence judgments tend to be based on a wide range of evidence, including performance in the workplace over a period of time. Most LPCs, however, assess competence by reference to short role plays and this leads to pressure from staff, students and external examiners to produce competence criteria in the form of checklists of specific and observable performance behaviours. Thus, words and phrases such as 'basic ability' 'appropriate', 'best' and 'professional' in the LPC standards are criticised on the ground that they do not describe what is required of students in behavioural terms (Brayne (1994)). There is also pressure from students for more modelling of the specific behaviours required. Methodology and pedagogy is, therefore, rooted in the Skinnerian behaviourist tradition as exemplified by 'systematic instructional design' of the skills curriculum which demands the analysis of competent performance in relation to specific tasks, the skills required for the performance of the tasks and the production of performance objectives for both tasks and skills (Pirie (1987)).

This is arguably a necessary transitional stage for vocational courses which are developing from a content-based curriculum and which are also concerned to 'prove' the reliability of the form of assessment (Docking (1986)). However, in an academic context the familiar criticisms ring true:

- Some goals are too complex to be reduced to specific behaviours, leading to learning which is narrow and instrumental.
- Flexibility and creativity in course development is restricted.
- It runs counter to the aims of stimulating independent learning and an understanding and critique of the values which underlie practice, performance and assessment.
- The narrowness of the methodology is at odds with the underlying goals of a liberal higher education.

The pedagogy and methodology of the new 'skills courses' has dominated the literature of skills education in law. Learning Lawyers' Skills reflected this. While Mackie (1989), noted (at p 8) that:

. . . the fact of complexity or interdependence in human skills leaves room for varied design approaches from the intuitive or holistic to that of systematic instructional design . . .

all the contributors favoured systematic instructional design in their contributions. Mackie argued that the 'holistic' approach to learning skills was ill-defined and that 'discovery methods', where models of performance emerge from practice, 'possibly concealed an inadequate sense of objectives'. He asked whether such methods were efficient when 'an appropriately structured demonstration' would 'speed learning through imitation'. The question for the behavioural tradition of skills pedagogy is, however: does replication of someone else's performance expand education or does it reduce it by a form of 'closure' (Barnett (1994), p 81)?

Holistic and discovery based methods

Holistic approaches are frequently referred to in the literature on legal skills but are not clearly defined (Macfarlane (1992), p 296). Whereas in the field of occupational competence holism is contrasted with an atomistic approach to defining occupational tasks (Hager et al (1994)), in legal education 'holism' has been contrasted with the methodology of systematic instructional design (Mackie (1989)). We can infer from these polarities that holism is concerned with broad rather than narrow framing of goals, subject matter and delivery, the integration of tasks, the breadth of assessment evidence and 'meta capacities' such as making links between the world of pure understanding and the world of action (Barnett (1994), p 84). In higher education it may be concerned to integrate the world of action with the traditional academic values of understanding, critique, interdisciplinarity and wisdom (Barnett, pp 99–193; cf Webb (1996)).

As with all models, their existence in pure form is unlikely; elements of 'holism' may invade competence-based courses and vice versa. Therefore, for example, the assessment of skills by checklist exemplifies an atomistic approach while the integration of DRAIN skills within transactions is arguably an attempt to make the experience more holistic (Gold (1989)). However, it may only be possible to say that particular aims or content are more or less holistic than other examples and, in time-constrained professional courses, the pressure to adopt an atomistic and behaviourist approach to assessing, and therefore to teaching lawyers' skills, is almost irresistible. Behaviourism is perhaps the least attractive of several theoretical perspectives which can underpin legal education at the initial stage (Bennet (1990)). Degree courses are more able to resist the pressure towards atomistic and behaviouristic teaching and assessment because intellectual development, not competent performance of the skill, is the ultimate goal of law degrees (Jones (1994), p 4). Learning the skill conveys a 'part of the lawyering process we want students to experience, analyse and build upon . . .' (Maurer and Mischler (1994), p 96).

'Holistic' and 'discovery' methods of teaching lawyers' skills are distinguishable from both competence- and examination-based legal education because their learning goals can accommodate notions of increasing competence without being dominated by them. Undergraduate programmes can follow themes and raise questions which vocational education cannot, or does not, raise. For example:

- consciousness of a wide range of skills and the integration of these skills in varying degrees of application to practice (what skills will I need in the future and why?);
- affective and perceptual change in the learner (why, for example, do lawyers need to be independent learners?);
- self awareness and the adoption of the habits of analysis and reflection on performance (am I an independent learner and what must I do to become more autonomous in my learning?);
- understanding of learning and developmental issues as they affect the learner personally (where do I stand in my development now?);
- understanding of contextual issues relevant to personal and professional development (should I take skills seriously?).

Because holistic approaches are not dominated by formal assessment of a skills performance they can be more 'student centred' and more likely to increase student confidence and independence (Greeson (1988)). In this respect holistic methods can aim to integrate a broad range of content including:

> legal reasoning, case and doctrinal analysis and written and oral advocacy skills . . . professional responsibility and a sense of legal ethics, sensitivity to facts, fact gathering, end–means analysis, cost–benefit analysis, hypothesis testing, understanding of the relationship between fact and law, ability to project ideas, common sense, judgment, the ability to work with others in a collaborative fashion and a host of interpersonal skills: communication, the ability to listen and hear, empathy and . . . the ability to integrate heart and mind.
>
> Schneider (1989)

Holistic skills teaching can therefore support underlying goals and curricula which are both consistent with a liberal undergraduate legal education and which can redress some of the problems inherent in learning skills at the vocational stage. While there may be a performance element in a holistic skills programme this can be balanced by a more explicit attempt to examine underlying values and to make connections between 'performance criteria' and underlying ethical or commercial considerations. The starting point is the existing experience of the learner rather than the criteria of competence which must ultimately be met.

This approach is arguably more consistent than an atomistic approach with Schön's (1983) notion of education for the 'reflective practitioner'. According to Schön the development of 'artistry' (as opposed to competence) is dependent on the ability to reflect critically on performance. From the ability to reflect on action the professional develops 'knowing in action', the ability to respond to the novel in the course of complex operations. This ability is a critical element of dynamic professional learning but is perhaps undermined in a context where competence judgments must be based on limited evidence.

Towards holism – a case study

An example will assist in developing these themes. 'Lawyers' Skills' is a module taught on the LLB programme at the University of Westminster. It is a second year optional undergraduate module lasting one semester and is a successor to 'Law in Action', the course from which the data referred to was collected. The current learning outcomes are that, on completion of the module, students should be able to:

1. identify changes in the legal profession which require a new approach to the problems of practice;
2. employ the 'core skills' of communication, problem-solving, teamwork and independent learning in the completion of tasks and the resolution of simulated problems;
3. synthesise theory and their own experience in order to inform their view of the legal profession.

The format of 'lawyers' skills'

The course integrates an introduction to the development and current position of the legal profession, legal education and professional ethics. Drawing on a variety of sources, links are made between skills, the deregulation of legal services, the growth of 'legal consumerism', legal education and legal ethics (Abel (1986), (1989); Glasser (1990); Sarat and Felstiner (1992); Simon (1988); Stanley (1991)).

Classes on these themes are supplemented by practical sessions focusing on the analysis of performance of the skills of group work, presentation, interviewing, drafting and negotiation. Some of these activities are videoed and analysed.[6] Some of the sessions do not deal with legal contexts. The core skills of interviewing, for example, can be introduced in the context of an employment interview rather than a legal interview. This can provide a practical dimension to careers education and opportunities to practise presentational and interrogative oral skills which might be transferable to other contexts such as client interviewing or negotiation (Walker (1993)). Admittedly, there are problems with the course as currently conceived. It has ambitious aims to cover in one module and some students find it difficult to assimilate the different content and methods of working. In the year-long course which preceded it students had more time to adjust to the unusual pedagogic and assessment demands. Nevertheless, a pilot survey of students was conducted by the National Foundation for Educational Research in 1995 (NFER (1995)) and revealed a high level of satisfaction with the course compared even with our more popular traditional courses.

The principal problem the NFER survey revealed was the lack of appropriate text books. Students receive a book of course materials containing short extracts from books and articles, but additional materials are in heavy demand. Other problems relate to finding a format which encourages students to approach the course in a way which is not instrumental or superficial. The lecture/tutorial/practical format proved relatively unsuccessful because some students attended the parts of the course they perceived were relevant to assessment. This meant that practical sessions were poorly attended. The most successful model was a year-long course consisting of a

6   Video is an invaluable vehicle for analysis and discussion (Moberly (1984)), provided exposure is sustained over a period of time. Initial experience of self observation has a number of negative effects, including a focus on personal body image, before positive analysis of *kinesic behaviour* – ie all movements of the body from gestures to posture (see Hargie, Saunders and Dickson (1994), p 43) can begin – see Saunders and Hargie (1989).

two-hour seminar every week. This was sometimes classroom-based, and sometimes based in our Legal Skills Suite, but usually short exposition, discussion and practice were combined in the single session. This is the model which operated during the period described in the extracts of student work which appear below.

Analysis and reflection

Students are encouraged to take a critical perspective on legal education, their own role within it and to anticipate the challenges which face them as legal professionals. The approach attempts to accommodate the observation that an education based on performance must find space for 'insight, understanding and imagination' (Barnett (1994), p 77). Because the purposes underpinning the module are developmental, students are able to experiment with skills performance in a low risk atmosphere. Stimulating students to analyse experience critically is essential in order both to improve performance and to encourage recognition of potential for transfer from one context to another (Bridges (1993)). However, establishing the habit of self analysis and reflection is not a simple process for most students. The most successful attempt to provide evidence of the development of a capacity for reflection was the requirement that students keep a 'learning log'. Such logs are now a well recognised feature of many courses, particularly as a source of additional evidence of competence or in situations where the aim is that students focus on and critically analyse their own performance (Zubrick (1989); Thornbury (1991); Hager et al (1991)). Logs afford opportunities for self assessment, in the sense that judgments can be made by the student on their own work, and for self determined assessment, in the sense that students have some latitude in relation to content and methodology (Baume and Baume (1986); Boud (1992); Boyd and Cowan (1985)).

Students were encouraged to keep a diary note of course and relevant outside activities week by week and to analyse their performance, to consider the multiple influences on that performance and to record their personal feelings. This self analysis was supplemented by peer and tutor assessment of exercises in practical sessions in written and oral form. Detailed written feedback was given by tutors on assessed exercises in interviewing, drafting and negotiation. However, even with a minimum class size of ten students the amount of detailed tutor feedback which could be given in the ordinary weekly practical session was limited and this necessitated the use of additional mechanisms for giving feedback. Further, it seemed in some cases that the requirement of giving feedback to others stimulated the process of self analysis. The student logs were handed in periodically and feedback was given both in the form of written comments and in short individual supervisory meetings held during timetabled sessions. Each of the three assessments comprised three elements: a planning paper which explained the process of preparation, the performance of the task, which in the case of interviewing and negotiation were video recorded, and analysis of the performance of the task. Students were required to conclude their logs with a critical analysis of their own performance throughout the course. Just as they were asked to analyse their own performance they were also invited to analyse the course critically.

Examples of different kinds of reflection and subjects of reflection emerged from this data. These suggest that the experience of learning skills was, in some way unique to each student, a contribution to a deeper moral development than might otherwise have been achieved (Macfarlane (1992), p 305). A limited number of examples may suffice to illustrate the different ways in which structured reflection on performance may help students to articulate and expand their understanding of their subject, themselves and their future plans.

In the early sessions students were asked to reflect on their conception of learning and orientations to learning. Several perspectives were introduced through materials and in the session. These included the completion of the McBer Learning Style Inventory (Kolb (1976)), Perry's work (1970) on intellectual and ethical development in the college years, deep and surface approaches to learning, Taylor's phases and phase transitions in learning for self direction (1986) and Schön's notion of the reflective practitioner (1983), (1987). Some theories immediately struck chords with most students and some had a profound effect on a few. The students' first log entry was an analysis of their personal learning style. Some of this work was particularly anodyne and described how students reacted to the session, whether they enjoyed the session or whether they thought that the theories of learning were 'correct'.

In contrast, a number of students produced perceptive and interesting analyses of their personal orientation to learning. The writing which follows is based on a student's reflection on Perry's stages and transitions in intellectual and ethical development. This, Perry suggests, charts stage changes in many students' thinking during their years at college from a dualist perspective (all questions have right or wrong answers) to contextual relativistic reasoning (even where facts are agreed individuals have different interpretations and therefore identify different solutions). Making a commitment to personal conclusions based on available evidence is the final stage of Perry's developmental stages. The student wrote:[7]

> I think that I am in two very different places [on the scale in terms of my way of learning and my general outlook on life]. I believe I am on the transitional stage 4(a) when it comes to the way I learn [*Where authorities don't know the right answers, every-one has a right to their own opinion; no one is wrong! Then what right have they to grade us? About what?*] but that my overall development and outlook on life is on position 9. [*This is how life will be. I must be wholehearted while tentative, fight for my values yet respect others, believe my deepest values right yet be ready to learn. I see that I shall be retracing this whole journey over and over – but, I hope, more wisely*]. Perhaps it is this state of conflict that is the cause of the sense of fright and frustration I mentioned earlier on. My learning development needs to advance and catch up with my general development. I see now that the way I learn needs to mature drastically – and quickly, too, if I am to do well on this degree and in life generally. The first seminar in Law in Action has really opened my eyes and shown me a lot about myself and others – it has been a frightening experience. Taking this subject may be the best thing for me; perhaps, unwittingly, the best thing I could have done for myself. I know now that I am going to have to change – I also know that doing so is going to be very hard work as old habits die hard . . . and I know that I am still extremely lazy. The way I learn is extremely passive . . . a surface way. I think the first step is to analyse the reason for this. [At school] I had to do little work to pass exams . . . my methods of learning did not evolve or improve with age. [At] . . . academic schools it was always more important to learn the

---

7 The italicised material in square brackets sets out Perry's description of student thinking at the relevant 'developmental stage'.

facts and the well established theories of the authorities. I learnt that the point of education was to pass examinations and that success is to give the examiner what he or she wants – not to risk giving your own opinions. I feel both my learning methods and intellect have stagnated. I realise now that the point of my education was not, ultimately, the examination but was acquiring and developing the skills of learning.

As the course developed, students were exposed to practical exercises. Through the process of writing about the way in which they planned the conduct of these exercises, many appeared to develop a deeper understanding of the processes involved and were encouraged to relate these to previous experience of using similar skills and to the future use of these skills. This is a student's evaluation of the planning stage for an interview in which the student demonstrates the capacity to develop a way of translating theory into action and relating this to previous experience:

> The major aspect of my plan relates to the questioning stage and I was endeavouring to put into practice the skill of using open questions in order to explore specific issues. When I first sat down to try and tailor my questioning approach using this method I found it extraordinarily difficult – questions needing only a yes/no answer flooded my mind! In the end I attempted to work backwards from the information which I was going to need to uncover and thus to the questions which I considered would best facilitate the flow of this information from the client. When I later translated these into written form on my plan I began to see how the technique of open questioning could be used in fact . . . It seemed eminently sensible and workable. I wondered if that was the way one would have instinctively questioned, trying to remember whether I did so in the past when interviewing patients for their medical histories – but I couldn't be sure!

In the next section the student relates the difficulty of translating experience of interviewing gained as a nurse to the task of role playing a solicitor interviewing a client. Despite extremely detailed research and planning the student felt that the interview had gone badly. While all students had received a common set of facts for the interview, sets of 'additional information' were given to interviewees just before the interview. These contained some information about the emotional state of the interviewee which caused the interviewee to behave in a way which the interviewer had not expected. In the initial opinion of the interviewer, the interviewee had 'hijacked' the interview, leading the interviewer to experience feelings of frustration and anger when she could not pursue her personal agenda. However, on reflection she was able to identify, in a balanced way, decisions which had contributed to her difficulties:

> . . . I felt that I began the interview well in terms of introductions and use of an initial open question to assist the client in giving his account of the allegations. In view of the nature of the allegations I also felt it was important to stress the confidentiality of the discussion. I also felt that the questions I had prepared in advance were well chosen. However, I felt that I had not made very good use of the time available to me in that the 20 minute period had expired and I had only reached the questioning stage of my plan. I had the interview plan in front of me which, whilst it made me feel more confident, in retrospect, impeded the spontaneity of the interview in that I made sure I asked all the questions I prepared and perhaps adhered too rigidly to my plan. I also felt that I asked questions too slowly and deliberately. To what extent this can be attributed to the effect of being aware that I was being videoed, I don't know . . .

The interviewer's subsequent analysis was modelled on Taylor's phases and phase transitions of learning for self direction which had been introduced earlier in the course. According to Taylor, meaningful learning is achieved by 'disconfirmation' which upsets an established equilibrium leading to feelings of disorientation, confusion and a crisis of confidence. The crisis in this case was caused by the fact that the student had expected to excel in the exercise because of her experience and extensive planning. However, the student was encouraged by the requirement of written reflection to enter the next transitional phase, of exploration. As a result she was able to identify the problem, the reasons underlying her personal reaction and to synthesise her experience and ideas into a new perspective. In this way, she explained, she had achieved a new understanding or, in Taylor's terms, equilibrium.

Other students came to their own views about how learning experiences could be valued and found that their expectations and attitudes changed during the course. The extract from a student log which follows suggests that the student may have begun to reconceptualise his attitude to learning and to lay a foundation for personal and professional responsibility:

... The initial client interview was the stage at which I probably learnt most about myself and how I could improve my performance over the course. I initially blamed my mediocre showing on an unrealistic atmosphere in front of a video camera with plenty of distracting noise outside the cubicle. But on reflection I came to recognise that there is never going to be a perfect environment for such an interview in real life and that recording equipment may well be used in many situations anyway. It was up to me to treat the exercise as if it were real and then it would automatically seem more realistic. This kind of logic can be applied to the whole course and by doing this I feel I gradually came to get much more out of it. By the time the negotiation came I was in a positive frame of mind ...

An example from the log of another student reinforces the sense that structured reflection can assist students in diagnosing methodological problems:

... my attempt at co-operative negotiation was perhaps a good deal less than co-operative. However, I have recognised my initial mistakes and confusion in drawing up the plan and feel that this has taught me a valuable lesson for the future. I feel that the confusion I displayed in my plan was caused by too much in-depth reading which concentrated on comparisons of the co-operative and competitive negotiation models. Although I tried to be co-operative, a sense of defending my position mixed with this confusion caused some problems ... I relish the next time I have to mediate between two hostile parties ...

Other students were able to transfer skills covered in the course to other areas of their academic work. One student said of the McBer learning inventory:

Even though I did not feel the inventory was entirely accurate it suggested some general ways in which I could improve my learning skills. I looked at planning and the conceptualisation of ideas: this has actually helped me in my Criminology presentation which required careful organisation of material. Because I am not very good at large scale research I panicked on seeing so much material. By using the diagram of suggested improvements I found my presentation became organised. For a student like myself, this really is quite an achievement.

Students also began progress from using 'taught' skills to developing a language for identifying, discussing and using skills 'out of context'. One student volunteered that:

... The writing of the log also involves a number of skills eg keeping accurate records; writing skills; analysing and selecting information; flexibility; a sense of independent learning (since it is I who chooses what is to be covered); creativity/experimentation and the ability to review learning experience ...

Another area in which students were able to identify development was in the classification of 'personal qualities', such as confidence, motivation and judgment, which I earlier identified as 'intrapersonal skills'. In a number of cases students related ways in which their experience of 'learning skills' had affected their daily lives, not only in terms of their increased awareness of how to behave, but in terms also of the confidence and motivation which that knowledge and experience gave them:

... My son was attending a certain school, and was in the first year of the seniors, when I realised that I had made a mistake in sending him there. I applied for a transfer to another school which I felt he would be better suited to ... I appealed [against the refusal of a transfer] and I was asked to represent myself. When I arrived at the appeal I was slightly unnerved to be faced with three councillors, a solicitor for the Education Department, a teacher from the chosen school (who was there to tell the panel the school was full) and the education officer representing the council's education department. Using my newly acquired skills I had prepared 'my case'. I had listed various questions I wanted to ask and a brief presentation explaining my preferences for the school. I produced a doctor's letter and my son's junior school report. The other side opened the appeal and I was able to pick up various important issues which I addressed in my response. When I presented my case I felt very confident. I spoke clearly and I asked the panel to use a common sense approach ... I was successful in my appeal and my son has settled down well in his new school. The Law in Action course gave me the courage to attend the appeal and represent myself (I could have sent a letter) and the confidence to believe that I could represent myself well. Thank you . . .

Inevitably in skills courses there are aspects of the curriculum which seem 'common sense' to students. This underlines the case for discussing different contexts and exploring underlying ambiguities in different models and criteria. One student wrote:

. . . over the year many students argued that parts of the course were wasted because they were learning things they had already learned from their adult lives . . . on the whole I would disagree with them. The course did cover some skills I had previously acquired but in doing this it has helped me to realise how those skills can be better applied to serve more use in the future. I would therefore recommend that such a point be made to future students and then re-emphasised over the year as those students develop their skills . . .

Other students identified previously unrecognised problems in the way in which they approached existing tasks and resolved to adapt their behaviour:

. . . This aspect of the course was for many evening students a case of adapting what they have learnt in their work to a new environment. This does not mean that it was less valuable for us but it does imply a different process and a greater need to approach it with an open mind. My job involves dealing with people most of the day, frequently in negotiations. Consequently I have found the course helpful in encouraging me to analyse my approach to this side of my work. I now try to appear more positive, even if I feel totally negative!

Skills courses can be a catalyst for students to consider their motivations in studying law. Some full-time day students said that the course had shattered their illusions about what being a lawyer might involve and that they now doubted what had previously been a career choice. Many evening students, however, suggested that 'Lawyers' Skills' had affected their career planning:

This was the first time in my life at any level of education that I have been asked to perform any sort of formal self-critique. Of course, I have been told that this is a good idea, but without the spur of actually having to hand in anything of this type for formal assessment very few students will bother. The self-critiques we have had to write served to force us to analyse our whole motivation for doing the course. For many this will be purely the achievement of one step towards qualification as a lawyer. But for others, such as myself, who are not sure what they want from their law degree the process is even more useful, if perhaps more difficult. I began by really only being interested in the academic study of law, without thinking too much about any practical applications. The academic interest is now being matched by an interest in the process of education and training, both professional and otherwise . . .

Other students benefited from the experience of structured reflection and, as a consequence, had resolved to continue the habit:

. . . I felt that the use of the log was valuable in assisting me to develop skills in critically appraising my own work, identifying areas of weakness and examining how these areas could be improved, thus paving the way towards self directed learning . . . Initially I was very apprehensive about the course and its heavy emphasis on practical work. Having completed the course I feel I have increased my theoretical knowledge and improved practice skills in the areas of interviewing, drafting and negotiation. I believe that the course has been valuable and one which will equip me well for the future . . .

Significant, though, was a recognition that both the substance of Lawyers' Skills, and what they were asked to do in the course, was different from what they typically did in other courses. Two extracts from a student log illustrate many of both the positive and negative themes of this paper. The first criticises the organisation of the course and the partial reliance on lectures. The second is concerned with the marginalisation of skills work, the resistance of students to content which is interdisciplinary in nature and methodology which is atypical, the importance of reflection and self direction and of the methods of stimulating and sustaining them and, finally, the ability constructively to criticise existing practice. The last of these is particularly important since it is a simple example of what Argyris and Schön (1974) call 'double loop learning', a disjunction between espoused theory and theory in use:

> ... less time should be spent in lectures and more experience could be gathered by more discussion-based learning and set tasks. This was where the majority of my learning came from through the research needed and then the trial and error of applying that research mixed with the self criticism which the course encourages ...

The second example widens the loop further to take a perspective on legal education generally:

> ... I must confess that I was initially sceptical, and remained so until well into the Law in Action course, about the potential or possible benefit of the apparently excessive requirement for self analysis and reflection upon performance. This scepticism has largely been dispelled since starting to write the log and to perform the tasks required. Analysis of the thought processes which went into formulation of plans of action, analysis of things which worked and things which didn't work, the recording of the same, and the viewing of assessments of performance in 'live' situations alongside self analysis I now see as a valuable learning aid which can be continued in almost all situations ... [However] unless the same techniques are applied in the other legal subjects, one academic year in one subject early in the degree course will probably have little residual benefit, with strategic learning, ie doing what is necessary to pass exams, dominating the learning process ...

Finally, I return to the issue of values and how the initial stage can contribute to the 'ethos' of the legal profession. The last example comes from a student's review of the course and the lessons learned from it. It demonstrates the integration of theory, ethics and experience in the personal perspective of the student:

> ... in the past, and perhaps still today, the lawyer was looked upon and also positioned himself in a place above others in society. Such an attitude can have severe consequences on the impression the young lawyer will make on others. Admittedly with his/her knowledge the lawyer is a powerful person in society but this should not lead to an abuse of such power. The lawyer is a servant of society and should act as such ... The

lawyer must always think of his client first taking into account confidentiality, compassion and fairness . . .

Skills and skills assessment in the undergraduate curriculum

Skills education at the initial stage addresses the concern that the time constrained pedagogy of the vocational courses, and their focus on the DRAIN skills, will encourage 'symbolic competence' rather than independent learning and critical reflection. According to Brayne, the discrete assessment of skills at the vocational stage encourages students to see their performance as something to 'get through' rather than a defining feature of their vocational education. They therefore have no responsibility for continued reflection on performance. It may also create a distorted perception that they have achieved 'competence'. There is:

> . . . no incentive to consider the part that a practising lawyer should play in society, and what legal skills are relevant to that part. The course [LPC] is therefore unlikely to create reflective, self critical practitioners.
>
> Brayne (1994)

Law degrees, in contrast, offer a sustained period of education and the possibility for the immersion of the learner in a 'practicum' in which such goals can be attempted (MacFarlane (1992)). Here, feedback need not represent competence judgments, but can adopt a more developmental focus using the learner's current stage of development as the starting point. This means that performance feedback can be more at a higher level of abstraction, avoiding the need for extensive behavioural checklists, modelling and repeat performances.

Because values have been absorbed over a longer period, and in an environment which encourages affective and perceptual change in the learner, there is a better prospect that students will develop 'robust ethical standards' and be less likely to sacrifice their values to the economic pressures of practice. However, one weakness of this kind of methodology is that affective and perceptual changes in students are less easy to observe than is symbolic or behavioural learning. How can we know that it has been achieved? The answer is that we cannot be sure in quite the same way that we can be sure that a student can demonstrate the behaviour of effective listening. However, assuming we have a suitable range of techniques we can ask that students attempt the task and then, at least, determine whether the failure to engage with our affective or perceptual goals is an issue of skill, attitude or motivation. Skills education which is spread throughout the curriculum is the best way of ensuring that these developmental goals are achieved without the undesired consequence that students use the skills gained inappropriately:

> The isolation of skills training in a special course which separates skill from legal content may risk the unintended consequence of reinforcing the tendency of some students and lawyers to think cynically of their craft, to regard it as the mastery of the arts of interpersonal manipulations. To the extent that this is a consequence, contemporary humanistic skills training may be at risk of backfiring, and contributing to the very self-aggrandising tendencies of lawyers which give rise to the desire to deprofessionalise.
>
> Carrington (1981)

A focus can, however, be provided by 'free standing' skills modules which introduce basic concepts and establish working practices which can be developed in other modules. This makes effective use of the limited resource of experienced skills teachers but increases the need for co-ordination in the curriculum. The course audit conducted as part of our CASEL research project (Boon and Humphreys (1994)), for example, showed that students were given ample opportunities to conduct independent research, through project work, but that methods were established in each subject and were therefore idiosyncratic. Further, there were relatively few examples of assessed group work or communication skills in the course programme.

Because lecturers are more likely to embrace ideas which reflect personal interests, the integration of skills in the curriculum is facilitated where the majority of staff are committed to such an approach. Staff must be prepared to compromise their 'ownership' of courses in the interests of the logical and sequential development of skills throughout the curriculum. They must also be able to, or be willing to be trained to, design and deliver material which allows them to adopt a facilitative role in relation to the teaching of their subject rather than to take a more familiar didactic role: see Allen (1991).

That achieved, staff must also be willing to take responsibility for the development and assessment of a particular skill in the context of their substantive subject.

Such developments are most likely to be successful if they are an organic development of the expertise and interests of staff and the needs of students; diversity and experimentation across the higher education system is valuable in itself. However, it is relatively uncontentious to suggest that a degree should attempt to develop students' intellectual skills, interpersonal skills and capacity for independent learning. A logical sequence is that skills are initially pervasive in the curriculum and yet increasingly focused as the degree programme progresses. It follows from the preceding section that 'integration' means both the integration of theory into skills-based courses and the integration of skills into substantive courses.

The assessment of skills is problematic when assessment must produce grades. While formal assessment is necessary for competence judgments at the vocational stage it can interfere with the developmental goals of skills education because formally assessed performance can negatively affect the confidence of those who are not rated in the top percentile range. While methods of delivery may preoccupy educationalists '. . . it is only relevant to the hassled student in so far as it matches the assessment . . .' (Brayne (1994)). A curriculum which uses self, peer and tutor review is more consistent with developmental goals (Allen (1994)). However, these forms of assessment rely on group work which, while having many advantages in terms of learning gains (Griffiths and Partington (1992)), gives rise to doubts about the validity and reliability of assessment.

A further problem is the increasing tendency of students to be strategic learners whose objectives are instrumental and who respond most effectively to the demands of formal assessment. Whatever the theoretical arguments, the fact of assessment both focuses the mind and improves both attendance and motivation (Wolstencroft and Van Zwanenburg (1989)). One answer to the problem is to adopt assessment profiles which indicate that students have achieved particular learning objectives but do not grade them (Assiter and Fenwick (1992)). However, profiles can be difficult to integrate with the demand to produce marks for classification and can lead to a diminution of effort if they are excluded from classification decisions.

A partial answer to this problem is to broaden the range of assessment evidence so that assessment marks are not only available for one or two 'events' in the course. The assessment of students' log books is an example of a way in which assessment evidence may be broadened, but this is problematic because these are, by their nature, idiosyncratic. Further, the aspiration that they be used as a vehicle for modifying and criticising one's own thinking is threatened by formal assessment (Boud (1991)). However, it is arguable that systems which do not provide the means for the development of students' evaluative expertise are also deficient both because they undermine the possibility that students will become 'self-directing' and because they set up 'false' performance ceilings for students (Sadler (1989)). In attempting to balance these considerations it is important that the criteria for the assessment of the learning log reflect the principle goals of the learning and assessment. The criteria published at the start of the course for assessment of the log were:

coherence of structure; clarity of expression; presentation of work; organisation; insightful reflection on performance; capacity for constructive criticism; grasp of practical and theoretical issues; ability to integrate perspectives.

In proposing a skills curriculum we must assume a system which insists on classifying students. In these circumstances it is argued that skills should ideally be dispersed in the curriculum, but possibly fanning out from core modules, with each stage systematically building on previous experience and increasing the demands of the tasks. They should be assessed by diverse methods which both provide new experiences for students and the incentive to take each activity seriously. The vocational stage would continue to assess competence according to whether students could behave in a certain way in a certain situation. However, vocational stage students would be more aware of the values underlying the particular behavioural requirements. An example of such a curriculum is shown overleaf (page 128).

Conclusion

Underlying the demand for a skills curriculum for the initial stage of legal education are a number of possible aims, each capable of influencing the design of that curriculum. These include:

● the valuing of artistry in the conduct of legal work;

Year	Activities	Assessment
1	Socio-legal perspectives: role of law, lawyers and legal profession.	Writing: case analysis, essays, problem analysis, report writing, research and referencing.
	Core skills: presentation, communication, problem solving, independent research, working in groups, reflection on performance and giving and receiving feedback.	Written analysis of student-led tutorials.
	An applied skill: eg interviewing.	Performance of core and applied skills.
	Cognitive skills: analysis, reasoning, synthesis etc in relation to legal materials.	Written and oral peer, tutor and self assessment of written and core skills.
2	Core skills: independent research.	Report writing, drafting of agreements and pleadings.
	Practical skills in context: Careers education.	Project.
	Fact handling, drafting, negotiation and advocacy.	Criteria based performance: self, peer and tutor evaluation.
	Analysis and reflection.	Learning logs.
3	Independent research.	Dissertation.
	Practice skills in clinic, work placement.	Staff, site supervisor and self evaluation.
	Analysis and reflection.	Learning log.

- the development of the ability for critical reflection;
- the increasing need for the initial stage to be 'transformative', that is, capable of changing values as well as changing behaviour.

Other aims relate to the changing needs of students and the increasing instrumentalism of some. These include:

- the adoption of more student-centred approaches to delivery of the curriculum;
- the development of a more diverse and interesting undergraduate curriculum; and
- the motivation of students by using materials which relate to the real world.

Finally, there are a group of reasons intrinsic to the study of law which may be the motivation for teaching skills. These include:

- the development of legally specific and transferable skills;
- the teaching of law in a practical context; and
- accessing that area of student consciousness which cannot imagine, for example, what making a decision with ethical implications may be like.

This paper has focused on the transformative function of skills teaching and learning. If the challenge facing higher education is to integrate the worlds of understanding and action, the challenge for legal education, given the transformative potential of lawyers' skills, is the management by academics and students of the interface of personal, professional and ethical values. The rationale for including skills in the curriculum of undergraduate legal education therefore rests on the ability of higher education, not only to use a skills curriculum to enhance an understanding of legal and professional contexts, but to establish a framework of personal and professional values.

In this paper I have argued for, and to some extent illustrated, a skills education which encourages students, not just to 'do' but to develop a perspective which enables them to ask why, given particular circumstances, lawyers should 'do' in a particular way. This must involve a scholarly enquiry into action, motivation and ethics, laying the foundation of an ability to reflect, not only on performance but on the underlying rationale for action. Finally it should inculcate an ability to question, challenge and transform conventional wisdom.

References

R Abel (1986) 'The Decline of Professionalism', 49 *Modern Law Review* 1.

R Abel (1989) 'Between Market and State: The Legal Profession in Turmoil', 52 *Modern Law Review* 285.

ACLEC (1994) *Review of Legal Education. Consultation Paper: The Initial Stage,* ACLEC, London.

M Allen (1991) *Improving the Personal Skills of Graduates,* Personal Skills Unit: University of Sheffield.

A Amsterdam (1984) 'Clinical Legal Education – a 21st Century Perspective', 34 *Journal of Legal Education* 612.

C Argyris and D Schön (1974) *Theory in Practice: Increasing Professional Effectiveness,* Jossey Bass, San Francisco.

A Assiter and A Fenwick (1992) *Profiling in Higher Education: An Interim Report,* CNAA/HMSO, London.

M J Atkins, J Beattie and W B Dockrell (1993) *Assessment Issues in Higher Education,* Employment Department Group, Sheffield.

A Bailey (1990) 'Personal Transferable Skills for Employment: The Role of Higher Education' in P W G Wright (ed) *Industry and Higher Education: Collaboration to Improve Students' Learning and Training,* SRHE/Open University Press, Milton Keynes.

R Barnett (1994) *The Limits of Competence: Knowledge, Higher Education and Society,* SRHE/Open University Press, Buckingham.

C Baume and D Baume (1986) 'Learner Know Thyself: Self Assessment and Self Determined Assessment in Education', 67 *The New Era* 65.

J Bennet (1990) 'Book review: Learning Lawyers' Skills', 24 *Law Teacher* 180.

A Boon and J Humphreys (1994) ' "Core" Communication and Interpersonal Skills' in Jones (ed) *Competences, Learning Outcomes and Legal Education,* Russell Press, Nottingham, p 71.

D Boud (1991) 'Three Principles for Good Assessment Practices', 1(1) *The New Academic* 4.

D Boud (1992) 'The Use of Self Assessment Schedules in Negotiated Learning', 17 *Studies in Higher Education* 185.

H Boyd and J Cowan (1985) 'A Case for Self Assessment Based on Recent Studies of Student Learning', 10 *Assessment and Evaluation in Higher Education* 225.

H Brayne (1994) 'LPC Skills Assessments – A Year's Experience', 28 *Law Teacher* 227.

D Bridges, (1993) 'Transferable Skills: A Philosophical Perspective', 18 *Studies in Higher Education* 43.

R Brownsword (1994) 'Teaching Quality Assessment in Law Schools: A Cause for Concern?', 21 *Journal of Law and Society* 529.

P D Carrington (1984) 'Civil Procedure and Alternative Dispute Resolution', 34 *Journal of Legal Education* 298.

D E Clement (1971) 'Learning and Retention in Student Led Discussion Groups', 84 *Journal of Social Psychology* 279.

L Cohen and L Mannion (1980) *Research Methods in Education*, Croom Helm, London.

P Cole (1993) 'Transferable Skills Teaching in the Humanities', 3(1) *The New Academic* 10.

R J Condlin (1983a) 'Clinical Education in the Seventies: An Appraisal of the Decade', 33 *Journal of Legal Education* 604.

R J Condlin (1983b) 'The Moral Failure of Clinical Legal Education' in D Luban (ed) *The Good Lawyer: Lawyer's Roles and Lawyers' Ethics*, Rowman & Allanheld, Totowa, NJ.

J J Costonis (1993) 'The MacCrate Report: Of Loaves, Fishes, and the Future of American Legal Education', 43 *Journal of Legal Education* 157.

D A Cruickshank (1994) 'Where "Show" Works Better Than Tell', 28 *Law Teacher* 13.

R A Docking (1986) 'Criterion-Referenced Grading Techniques', 12 *Studies in Educational Evaluation* 281.

K Economides and G Smallcombe (1991) *Preparatory Skills for Trainee Solicitors*, The Law Society, London.

Employment Department Group (1989) *Enterprise in Higher Education: Key Features of the Enterprise in Higher Education Proposals 1988–89*, Training Agency, Sheffield.

Employment Department Group (1994) *Competence and Assessment*, Issue 10, October 1994.

N Falchikov (1988) 'Self and Peer assessment of a Group Project Designed to Promote the Skills of Capability', 25 *Programmed Learning and Educational Technology* 327.

M F Fitzgerald (1993) 'Stirring the Pot of Legal Education', 27 *Law Teacher* 4.

C Glasser (1990) 'The Legal Profession in the 1990s – Images of Change', 10 *Legal Studies* 1.

N Gold (1989) 'Learning Lawyers' Skills: Research, Development and Evaluation – the Future Prospectus' in N Gold, K Mackie, and W Twining (eds) *Learning Legal Skills*, Butterworths, London.

L Gow and D Kember (1990) 'Does Higher Education Promote Independent Learning?', 19 *Higher Education* 307.

E H Greenebaum (1987) 'How Professionals (Including Legal Educators) "Treat" Their Clients', 37 *Journal of Legal Education* 554.

L E Greeson (1988) 'College Classroom Interaction as a Function of Teacher and Student Centred Instruction', 4 *Teaching and Teacher Education* 305.

S Griffiths and P Partington (1992) *Enabling Active Learning in Small Groups*, CVCP Universities' Staff Development and Training Unit.

R Grimes (1995) 'Reflections on Clinical Legal Education', 29 *Law Teacher* 169.

P Hager, Gonczi and J Athanasou (1994) 'General Issues about Assessment of Competence', 19 *Assessment and Evaluation in Higher Education* 3.

J Hannon (1991) *An Evaluation of the Personal Competences Demonstrated by Graduating Students and Graduate Recruits*, Newcastle Polytechnic, Newcastle.

O Hargie, C Saunders and D Dickson (1994) *Social Skills in Interpersonal Communication*, Routledge, New York.

C O Houle (1980) *Continuing Learning in the Professions,* Jossey Bass, San Francisco.

P A Jones (1994) *Competences, Learning Outcomes and Legal Education,* Institute of Advanced Legal Studies, London.

S Kemmis (1985) 'Action Research and the Politics of Reflection' in D Boud, R Keogh, and D Walker (eds) *Reflection: Turning Experience into Learning,* Kogan Page, London.

D A Kolb (1981) 'Learning Styles and Disciplinary Differences' in A Chickering (ed) *The Modern American College: Responding to the New Realities of Diverse Students and a Changing Society,* Jossey Bass, San Francisco and London.

D A Kolb (1984) *Experiential Learning: Experience as a Source of Learning and Development,* Prentice Hall, Englewood Cliffs, NJ.

D A Kolb (1976) *'The Learning Style Inventory': Technical Manual,* McBer, Boston.

D R Krathwohl, B S Bloom and B B Masia (1964) *Taxonomy of Educational Objectives: The Classification of Educational Goals – Handbook 2: Affective Domain,* McKay, New York.

R MacCrate (1992) *Legal Education and Professional Development – An Educational Continuum, Report of the Task Force on Law Schools and the Profession: Narrowing the Gap,* ABA, Chicago.

R MacCrate (1994) 'Preparing Lawyers to Participate Effectively in the Legal Profession', 44 *Journal of Legal Education* 89.

J Macfarlane (1992) 'Look Before You Leap: Knowledge and Learning in Legal Skills Education', 19 *Journal of Law and Society* 293.

K Mackie (1989) 'Lawyers' Skills: Educational Skills' in N Gold, K Mackie and W Twining (eds) *Learning Lawyers' Skills,* Butterworths, London.

Marre Committee (1988) *A Time for Change: Report of the Committee on the Future of the Legal Profession,* General Council of the Bar/The Law Society, London.

F Marton and R Saljo (1976) 'On Qualitative Differences in Learning: I Outcome and Process', 46 *British Journal of Educational Psychology* 4.

N M Maurer and L F Mischler (1994) 'Introduction to Lawyering: Teaching First Year Students to Think Like Professionals', 44 *Journal of Legal Education* 96.

G Miller (1994) 'Chess Strategies in Teaching Law', 28 *Law Teacher* 22.

R B Moberly (1984) 'A Pedagogy for Negotiation', 34 *Journal of Legal Education* 315.

J Murdoch (1994) 'Using Group Skills in Honours Teaching: The European Human Rights Project', 28 *Law Teacher* 258.

NAB – National Advisory Body for Local Authority Higher Education (1984) *A Strategy for Higher Education in the Late 1980s and Beyond*, NAB, London.

National Foundation for Educational Research (1995) *Westminster University: Course and Module Evaluation by Student Feedback*, NFER, Slough.

M Parlett and D Hamilton (1972) *Evaluation as Illumination: A New Approach to the Study of Innovatory Programmes*, Occasional Paper for the Centre for Research in the Educational Sciences, University of Edinburgh, Edinburgh.

W G Perry (1970) *Forms of Intellectual and Ethical Development in the College Years*, Holt, Rinehart and Wilson, New York.

A J Pirie (1987) 'Objectives in Legal Education: The Case for Systematic Instructional Design', 37 *Journal of Legal Education* 576.

Robbins Report (1963) *Higher Education*, Cmnd 2154, HMSO, London.

D Royce Sadler (1989) 'Formative Assessment and the Design of Instructional Systems', 18 *Instructional Science* 119.

A Sarat and R Felstiner (1992) 'Lawyers and Clients', 41 *Journal of Legal Education* 43.

C Saunders and O Hargie (1989) 'The Effect of Video Feedback on Students' Evaluation of Self', 15 *Journal of Educational Television* 143.

E Schneider (1989) 'Integration of Professional Skills into the Law School Curriculum: Where We've Been and Where We're Going', 19 *New Mexico Law Review* 111.

D Schön (1983) *The Reflective Practitioner: How Professionals Think in Action*, Basic Books, New York.

D Schön (1987) *Educating the Reflective Practitioner*, Jossey Bass, San Francisco.

W H Simon (1988) 'Ethical Discretion in Lawyering', 101 *Harvard Law Review* 1083.

C Stanley (1988) 'Training for the Hierarchy? Reflections on the British Experience of Legal Education', 22 *Law Teacher* 78.

C Stanley (1991) 'Enterprising Lawyers', 25 *Law Teacher* 44.

J H Stark, P D Tegeler and N L Channels (1987) 'The Effect of Student Values on Lawyering Performance: An Empirical Response to Professor Condlin', 37 *Journal of Legal Education* 409.

R Swain (1991) 'On the Teaching and Evaluation of Experiential Learning in a Conventional University Setting', 22 *British Journal of Educational Technology* 4.

M Taylor 'Learning for Self Direction in the Classroom: the Pattern of a Transition Process' (1986), 1 *Studies in Higher Education* 55.

S Thornbury (1991) 'Watching the Whites of Their Eyes: The Use of Teaching Practice Logs', 45 *English Language Teaching Journal* 140.

S Toddington (1994) 'Skills, Quality and the Ideologies of Managerialism', 28 *Law Teacher* 243.

M A Trow (1970) 'Methodological Problems in the Evaluation of Innovation' in M C Wittrock and D E Wiley (eds) *The Evaluation of Instruction*, Holt Rinehart and Winston, New York.

G Walker (1993) 'Mock Job Interviews and the Teaching of Oral Skills', 17 *Journal of Geography in Higher Education* 73.

J Webb (1996) 'Why theory matters', this collection.

E Williams (1992) 'Students' Attitudes Towards Approaches to Learning and Assessment', 17 *Assessment and Evaluation in Higher Education* 45.

A Wolf (1994) 'Assessing the Broad Skills within Occupational Competence', 25 *Competence and Assessment* 3.

T Wolstencroft and Van Zwanenburg (1989) *Broadening the Curriculum: A case study of non-law subjects in law degrees,* Development Services Briefing 19, CNAA, London.

A Zubrick (1985) 'Learning Through Writing: The Use of Reading Logs', 7(3) *HERDSA News* 11.

Chapter 5

The theory and practice of clinical legal education
Richard Grimes[1]

Introduction

The purpose of this paper is to look at what clinical legal education is and what it has to offer, both in terms of its theoretical and practical operation and implications. I shall also try to locate clinical developments within contemporary debates about the future of English legal education.

Before exploring the theoretical premises upon which clinical learning is founded, two questions need to be addressed:
- What do we mean by 'clinical legal education'?
- How does it operate?

What is clinical legal education?

Clinical legal education is a particular form of experiential learning. This latter term is itself used to describe a wide variety of learning approaches. Spiegelman (1988) defines it (p 257) as

> . . . a method of teaching in which students' performance of a task or role is the first step and the primary data in a process of discussion and analysis.

1   Thanks must go to Jo Larbie and Colleen Smith for sharing with me the demands and pleasures of the Law Clinic at Sheffield Hallam; to Hugh Brayne, Nigel Duncan, Keith Shelton and Julian Webb for their helpful comments on the drafts of this chapter; to Margaret Melluish for her patience, hard work and handwriting interpretation abilities and finally to the many students who have made my experience of clinical work so worthwhile.

By contrast, other commentators use it more broadly, to incorporate virtually all forms of active learning: see, for example, Schultz (1993), p 67. By this criterion, seminar work could be seen as 'experiential' where students were required to immerse themselves actively in the resolution of the problem. Drafting exercises, moots, etc, would all meet this wider definition. However, such approaches could not be described as clinical.

Rather, 'clinical' is used to describe a learning environment where students identify, research and apply knowledge in a setting which replicates, at least in part, the world where it is practised.[2] This might be in a court room or before a tribunal. It may be in correspondence between opposing sides in litigation, or it may occur during the course of a transaction. It almost inevitably means that the student takes on some aspect of a case and conducts this as it would (or ought to!) be conducted in the real world.

The origins of the law clinic

The clinical approach is not new. It has been practised in the study of other disciplines, for example medicine, for many years. In legal education, it has its origins in the law schools of the United States. The most prevalent form of clinic in the early period of development was the so-called 'legal aid clinic'. These were established to provide legal services to the poor, commonly supported by funding from private foundations, or through the public defender's office. The oldest clinics of long standing were those established at Harvard, Minnesota and Northwestern, all set up in 1913: see Johnstone (1951), p 541. A number of others were established in the 1920s and 1930s, at least to some degree influenced by American Realism and the Realists' discontent with the dominant Langdellian tradition of the American law schools of that period: see, for example, Frank (1933). By 1951, 28 law schools were providing legal aid clinics (Johnstone (1951), p 535). The educational value of the legal aid clinics was probably highly variable. They often offered little by way of skills training; the form and degree of supervision and credit-rating of clinical courses (if any) also varied widely.

---

2   Boon et al (1987) define clinical legal education thus (p 68):

> a curriculum-based learning experience, requiring students in role, interacting with others in role, to take responsibility for the resolution of a potentially dynamic problem.

Perhaps this is why others, more pragmatically, trace the modern clinical movement only as far back as the 1960s: see AALS (1990).

Either way, it was not really until the late 1960s that large scale expansion of the American clinical movement took place. By 1973, 125 out of 147 accredited US law schools had established clinical programmes (Zander (1973), p 181). This development arose in response both to professional pressures for more skills training, culminating in the Cramton Report of 1979 (see Spiegal (1987)), and to the realisation that clinics could provide a good environment for teaching professional ethics, with the result that clinical developments in the States received a significant (financial) shot in the arm in the form of funding from the Council on Legal Education for Professional Responsibility: see Zander (1973), p 183.

In the American context clinic has been seen to perform a number of more or less complementary functions. Perhaps, most obviously, it has long been closely connected with the idea of skills education: see Spiegal (1987), and Twining (1993), p 142. If skills can only be learned by performance, then clinic provides a logical environment in which to practise. But the clinical experience has also been defined in ways that take it beyond mere skills training. Bellow and Moulton (1978), for example, were instrumental in translating the Realist vision of clinic as a vehicle for sociological enquiry into the 'lawyering process' into some kind of reality. Other approaches chose to emphasise the humanistic and psychological dimensions of lawyering: see Goodpaster (1975); Meltsner & Schrag (1976).

To a much lesser extent clinical legal education has been around in British legal education for over 20 years. The earliest live-client clinical experiments were those at Kent, established in 1973: see Rees (1975) and Spjut (1977). These were followed by Warwick in 1975 (Sherr (1986), pp vii–ix). Also between the mid-1970s and early 1980s South Bank, Newcastle and Birmingham Polytechnics set up their own clinical programmes. Although a number of other institutions have experimented with clinical learning, following the final collapse of the Kent clinic in 1977, these four remained the only live-client clinics in the UK until the renaissance of interest in clinical education in the late 1980s and early 1990s.[3]

---

3   The fates of these founding clinics have been varied. South Bank has now ceased functioning; Warwick has dropped live client work in favour of simulation, while Kent has launched two new clinic-based options; Birmingham and Newcastle (now the Universities of Central England and Northumbria) continue.

Clinical legal education today

Clinical work today can take three main forms:
- live-client in-house clinics
- simulations
- placements

All have a common feature in that students take responsibility for cases under supervision. In the live-client clinics, advice and sometimes representation is provided for clients with real legal problems. As will be seen, the implications for the in-house clinic with a real clientele are considerable. It has been suggested, however, that by comparison with simulations and placements, the live-client approach offers the fullest and most intense learning experience: see, for example, Tarr (1993), p 36.

Simulations provide experiential learning in a more readily controlled environment, in which the material used can be carefully linked to the projected learning outcomes. The uncertainty of live-client demands can be effectively removed. This may sound attractive from a teaching viewpoint but it has been said that this may result in a loss of impact (Tarr). Role playing, unless performed by actors of a professional standard, does not have the real feel and does not place the same demands on the student. As McDiarmid (1990) argues, simulation also lacks the factual complexity and epistemological integrity of live-client work: 'we cannot be said to truly understand anything until we understand it in context and in complexity' (p 286). Nevertheless, case studies and simulation work do introduce students to experiential learning and have been developed to a sophisticated level, often linked with other, live-client, clinical programmes (University of Central England (1994); Sheffield Hallam University (1995)). In the USA some law schools make extensive use of simulation clinics (for example, at the University of California, Los Angeles).

Placements, being based in out-house venues, for example local solicitors' practices, the Crown Prosecution Service and local government, hold considerable potential in terms of clinical education. They also pose particular problems. Known as 'externships' in the USA, these work-based settings bring students face-to-face with real problems which have to be resolved against the legal, financial and logistical constraints of the court or office. They are very appealing from a resource perspective for, as compared with live-client and simulated work, they are relatively inexpensive. The main drawback of these programmes is that they are difficult to monitor, evaluate and control: see Tarr (1993), p 39 and Maher (1990). They are also problematic in terms of planning learning outcomes and assessment.

In a recent survey of skills and clinical education, it was found that of the 79 UK institutions of higher education offering a law degree, over a half use simulation as a method of tuition. Just under a quarter use some form of live-client clinic. Simulation is used more by the new universities than the old (69% and 56% respectively). Live-client clinics are predominantly based in new universities (23% and 5%). Clinical methods are used across all years of law undergraduate programmes, though most tend to be optional in the second and third years of the degree: see Grimes (1995).

How does clinic operate?

There are many different practices and operating styles within clinical teaching. The implications of some of these will be explored later in this chapter. The experience of one particular law school is examined by Hugh Brayne elsewhere in this collection.

Of the live-client variety, there appear to be three different but related approaches:

- the provision of advice only;
- advice, assistance and (in some cases) selective representation (arbitration/tribunals);
- legal services offered through an in-house solicitors' practice.

The first two do not require, as a matter of professional regulation, the services of an experienced and insured solicitor who holds a practising certificate. The third does (Solicitors' Practice Rules, 1990, rule 13; and Solicitors' Indemnity Rules, 1992; Solicitors Act 1974, s 1).

The client base for any live-client clinic can be selective (for example students or staff from that institution) or can be widely cast (members of the general public). The service may be open through drop-in sessions or by appointment or referral.

The clinic can be compulsory or run as an option. It may be assessed as part of the degree programme. If so, this can be on the basis of a pass/fail grade or through the allocation of a mark as for any other unit.

Some of the considerations and consequences of these models will be examined shortly.

The simulation clinics are equally varied in their approaches, with some offering case studies which are managed from initial interview to final disposal and others where a stage of a case is taken in isolation. The simulated exercise may be acted out by the students and/or staff or through the services of actors or practitioners.

Externships too operate in a variety of ways including short-term shadowing and longer-term sandwich placements: see, for example, Partington (1984).

With this overview of clinical education, the pedagogic, resource and professional implications can now be addressed; but before turning to this, it is necessary first to place clinical legal education in a theoretical framework, in terms of the process of learning that takes place.

Theories of learning

It is beyond the scope of this paper (and probably the author) to provide a detailed analysis of learning theories. It is important, however, given the claims made by those supportive of clinical education, to address, at least in outline, fundamental concepts of teaching and learning. These concepts are themselves the topic of current debate amongst educationalists.

The worth of the clinical experience is summed-up by a much quoted (but no less pertinent) proverb:

I hear and I forget
I see and I remember
I do and I understand
            (variously ascribed to Chinese philosophers and native
                American chiefs, but cited in Rogers (1989), p 39)

This places the emphasis squarely on the process of learning by doing – a more sophisticated variant of which can be found in Kolb's (1984) learning cycle: see also Maughan (1996). It is learning by doing, reflecting, applying and evaluating. This is widely viewed as alien to traditional teaching methods in law, being derided at best as more in the nature of vocational training than education fit for the university curriculum: see, for example, Bradney (1992).

Clinic as a learning process

It is the underlying theme of this chapter that clinical legal education not only represents an approach to learning that is effective, enjoyable and complementary to the rest of the law degree programme, but also is one that can be justified in terms of a sound methodology.

Macfarlane rightly asserts that:

Whilst realism is the hallmark of clinical work, it is insufficient as an explanation of the learning process which takes place.

Macfarlane (1988), p 176

What then is the explanation? Macfarlane suggests five characteristics which defined the distinctiveness of the learning method against which the learning process can be judged:

1   active participation;
2   interaction in role;
3   dynamic nature of the exercise;
4   student responsibility for the outcome;
5   integration within the curriculum.

ibid, pp 176–7

I suggest two more:

6   interactive, formative and possibly continual assessment with supportive feedback;
7   close interpersonal relationship between supervisor and student.

Perhaps the defining characteristic of the clinic is that it constitutes a *holistic* approach to learning. Learning through the clinical method enables the theoretical, practical and ethical to be studied side-by-side in an active learning environment. According to Dinerstein (admittedly talking of live-client clinics):

No other learning experience in law school combines the extraordinary varied and dramatic context of . . . cases and problems with the opportunity for intensive teaching, supervision, growth and reflection.

The experience of those who have embarked on clinical work in the UK is similarly reported very positively: see CLEO (1994). The implications of the clinical approach in terms of the delivery of the clinic and the rest of the law programme is explored later in this chapter; for now, however, we will start by considering its theoretical basis.

Towards a theoretical framework

BEHAVIOURIST AND COGNITIVE THEORY

In Macfarlane's work these important features are placed in the context of the behaviourist/cognitive debate in educational psychology. For many years student learning was perceived largely in behaviourist terms of stimulus–response: see Brown & Atkins (1988), p 150. In behaviourist models, knowledge is seen to be acquired largely mechanistically by processes of conditioning and the reinforcement of learned behaviours. The teaching of heuristics is not emphasised at all in such models.

Cognitive approaches recognise that students need to develop both 'learning for knowledge' and 'learning for understanding' orientations (Brown & Atkins (1988), p 156). Cognitivists stress the following characteristics of learning: see, for example, Brown & Atkins (1988), pp 151–3; Maughan & Webb (1995), pp 20–1:

- Learning is a highly individualised process, building on both theoretical ('scientific') and personal and heuristic knowledge.
- It is active rather than passive – individuals will seek out learning experiences, not just respond to external stimuli.
- Its quality is significantly affected by individual motivations. Students will be more likely to initiate, participate in and direct their learning if they believe success is determined more by their own efforts than by external factors (such as the quality of teaching, etc).
- Learning is purposive. The point is neatly summarised by Jerome Bruner who says: 'It matters not *what* we have learned. What we can *do* with what we have learned; that is the issue.' (Bruner (1979), quoted in Macfarlane (1988), p 191.)

As Macfarlane (1988) notes (p 193), legal education, historically, has been highly susceptible to a behaviourist approach, with an emphasis on content-based learning assessed by summative examinations. This tendency has not been helped by the historical pressure from the professional bodies to control (to varying degrees) the form, content and assessment of law degrees. Macfarlane goes on to suggest that cognitive theory and methods take the providers of education away from 'the formal information-based syllabus' and towards 'skills' teaching (p 196). Skills here include research, analysis, problem solving and interpersonal skills.

SURFACE AND DEEP LEARNING

One of the major contributions of the cognitive approach has been the recognition that students (and teachers) can adopt one of two primary orientations to learning. These are referred to as 'surface' or 'shallow' and 'deep' learning: see Gibbs (1992).

Surface learning concentrates on the external representations of a task. Students adopting a surface approach tend to focus on the reproduction of information in a manner largely driven by assessment requirements. They treat facts and concepts unreflectively and fail to distinguish the underlying principles of the task. Deep learning, by contrast, involves the student in attempting to make sense of the learning experience by integrating and applying knowledge rather than simply repeating it. Gibbs (pp 2–4) sees surface learning as all too common in higher education, and disastrous in terms of its lack of lasting impact on the student's learning experience. As Ramsden (1992) points out (p 44), the thing which we, as teachers, often forget is that deep or surface learning is the product of the learning experience, it is not an innate characteristic of the individual student. It is therefore up to us to create an environment that supports deep approaches to learning. The pay-off is that, as many research studies have shown, deep approaches foster better quality outcomes and higher grades.

Gibbs (pp 12–17) cites strategies for fostering a deep approach including independent learning, personal development, problem-based learning, reflection, group work, skills assessment and, significantly, learning by doing. The last is seen to involve simulations, role-plays, practical work and work experience.

When this is translated to legal education, it is suggested that the clinical experience offers a supportive environment which empowers and encourages a student to move towards a deeper learning approach, based on the understanding and not just the acquisition of knowledge. The clinic is – or should be – about deep learning.

Clinic as part of the curriculum

Either the clinic is part of a degree or vocational programme with a rationale behind its development and a place in the educational scheme, or it runs the risk of being seen as an enjoyable diversion with limited learning relevance. This is not to say that extracurricular activity is not valuable, far from it, but the full educational value of the clinical approach cannot be appreciated and realised without curricular integration. Without it, those delivering clinical programmes can be easily and readily marginalised: see Tarr (1993), p 41. Clinics can be ostracised as resource-intensive irrelevances or derisorily seen as just 'training workshops'.

But the problem goes beyond the issue of perceived relevance. As Macfarlane (1988) states (p 182):

> Experience unrelated to curriculum goals may add little or nothing to the student's understanding.

So, what are the benefits of a clinical approach within an undergraduate or vocational course and how do these relate to the aims and objectives of the programme?

Learning the law

The clinical method, whether through simulation or for real, offers students a tripartite learning opportunity in terms of advancing their understanding of law and the legal system.

First, it challenges the students' ability to conduct an analysis of the case before them. This necessitates discovering 'the facts', formulating the relevant questions, researching the law (and probably more facts) and defining strategies for problem resolution. It is suggested that this is properly part of the intellectual process essential to the study of law both as a discipline and as a set of rules governing a particular transaction or occurrence. Learning the law is about developing legal method. With case simulations this element can be closely structured and can operate very selectively. Live-client contact brings a qualitatively different challenge.

Secondly, clinical work provides material through which the substantive rules can be studied in action. In live-client work this frequently involves the 'core' subjects as well as the more specialised options. It is a common experience in clinical programmes for the clientele to bring problems of housing, social security, consumer issues and employment. A dispute between a disgruntled tenant and his or her landlord may require the student to consider principles of contract and land law, as well as the specific rules regulating the landlord/tenant relationship.

Thirdly, clinic also opens up the work of the legal system and the profession itself to critical examination. Thus, for example, the clinical experience at Kent was described as 'the experimental study of the legal process as a specific type of social control in its social matrix': cited in Rees (1975), p 132.

In clinic the students are, therefore, exposed to legal problems that relate specifically to other aspects of their study. It is suggested that the one necessarily complements the other. The learning of law through practical experience results in knowledge being redefined in terms of the processes involved rather than just the content: see Macfarlane (1992), p 301.

Developing skills

Undoubtedly clinical methods introduce students to skills and build on skills that students have already started to develop.

Some skills may be seen as law specific, for example research and advocacy. Research is obviously a key feature in the study of law. The identification of relevant problems and the formulation of research questions are central to an understanding of the concepts of law. In clinic students often have only limited subject expertise, little of which operates at a tacit level. The pressures of engaging with real-life problems force students to research in a way that is almost impossible to expect in more traditional academic environments. Students must be able to take these questions and utilise all available resources in finding the answers, so far as these exist.

Advocacy, in the sense of courtroom technique, is perhaps less obviously a skill developed as part of legal study, at least at the academic stage. Looked at more broadly, however, if advocacy is taken to mean persuasive communication, then this too is a skill law students should be encouraged to develop. It is a skill that can be directly addressed in the context of the clinic.

Other skills are seen as more practice-specific, practice being here the practice of law. Interviewing clients and witnesses, drafting legal documents and negotiating a possible settlement on behalf of a client are all examples of such skills. Understandably these skills are more often seen as 'training' and relevant to vocational rather than to undergraduate study.

Students also encounter skills that can be broadly termed as transferable. These include problem solving, team work, time and study management, and general communication skills.

The nature of the relationship between skills and clinical education is at present one feature of clinical legal education which is underdeveloped. Indeed many of the older clinical programmes in the USA and the UK did not initially place much emphasis on the need for formal skills education, relying far more on the supervisor functioning as a role-model: see, for example, Johnstone (1951), Rees (1975), and Brayne (1996). This apparent undervaluing of skills has prompted criticism elsewhere. Hoffman (1994), for example, argues that there is a general absence of 'skills theories' in American clinical programmes (p 105). It should be explained that the importance attached to 'lawyering skills' is a particular feature of American law schools (and something increasingly evident in the UK). The prominence of skills in the American law school programmes is a necessary adjunct of their vocational function. Successful students go from graduation via the State Bar examinations into practice without having to undergo any form of apprenticeship. This arguably renders the American clinical experience different from that of the UK.

Although this difference does not negate the need for a greater understanding and intellectualisation of skills teaching, it is important to locate skills education clearly within the undergraduate law curriculum as a means to more effective study, rather than as an end in itself. On the vocational courses a much stronger argument can be made for the incorporation of skills training as an objective of the course.

Having stressed the nature of the role of skills at an undergraduate level, weight should be given to some of the important spin-off benefits that skills encountered in the clinic have. If skills prove useful in another context (for example, when included on a student's CV or when put into practice in pupillage or during a training contract) this is to be welcomed. Their inclusion on a clinical programme, however, has to be for sound pedagogic reasons – as an aid to learning concepts and, where relevant, substantive rules of law. In a prophetic piece on law teaching in the 21st Century, Amsterdam reflects that it was:

> the assumption that the job of law schools was to impart to students a self-contained body of instruction in the law. In the 21st Century we realise, of course, that a major function of law schools is to give students systematic training in effective techniques for learning law from the experience of practising law.
>
> Amsterdam (1984), p 613

Whilst I would take issue over the word 'training', the point is clear. Clinical learning is more about understanding concepts and principles and less about amassing knowledge of legal rules or skills competences in themselves. Skills aid the process of understanding and the clinic fosters the acquisition of skills.

Active learning

If clinic is about learning law and acquiring skills to learn law, it also challenges, as part of its ethos, the extent to which the student becomes involved in the learning process. As Twining (1994) argues, law is at its heart a 'participant-oriented discipline' (pp 128–9), but this is not always reflected in the expository traditions and practices of law teachers.

Evidence of activity per se does not necessarily equate to active learning, however. Activity needs to be focused in such a way as to enable students to create their own knowledge – their own mental structures. Meyers & Jones (1993) stress (pp 20–1) that active learning requires that students engage in the key cognitive activities of talking and listening, writing, reading and reflecting within the context of well structured, participatory, learning strategies. Such strategies include case study techniques, simulation, group work and journal writing. While active learning can be developed in environments other than the law clinic, clinic clearly can enable students to become actively involved in their learning through a variety of processes with a range of aims and outcomes.

Depending on the type of clinic used, student involvement in the learning process can be, for example, in interaction with a 'real' client. It may also be in the preparation of the case or in the appearance before a court of tribunal. The active involvement of the student is often required in group work (as with the use of 'firms' in the Northumbria and Sheffield solicitors' practice clinics, and in the simulations at UWE, Bristol). It will almost certainly be in discussions with the tutor and in submitting an assignment or portfolio of work. It can be in the form of commentary on letters or draft pleadings and the student's response to this feedback.

The involvement of the students in their learning experience also provides 'the opportunity . . . for multiple emphases and goals' (Dinerstein et al (1990), p 16). The goals in the case of clinical legal education may be many and varied, from a better understanding of legal concepts to the opportunity for the student to tell a prospective employer that he or she has represented a real client before a court or tribunal.

Personal development

Education is a process that develops over a period of time that can be measured in terms of the learning outcomes for that particular unit, or level of course. It is suggested that this progression relates not simply to the student's acquisition and comprehension of substantive knowledge, but to the growth of the individual student in terms of self-confidence, maturity and general intellect. Through student participation in the learning process, to coin expressions, we are talking not only of active but of student-centred learning based on the needs of the learner: see Rogers (1965), (1969); Harris and Bell (1994). Student-centred learning, according to Rogers's model, is a form of learning that enables students to take full responsibility for their decisions, actions and their consequences. The teacher's role becomes facilitative, helping students to develop their potential as self-directed, responsible and autonomous individuals.

Clinical programmes are well based to facilitate and nurture a student's personal development. Feedback and assessment leans towards the personal and formative. The assumption of responsibility for clients and cases fosters a sense of loyalty, commitment and professionalism. Regular and structured opportunities to discuss and debate the educational experience improves the students' own image of their progress and ability. A levelling of power between tutor and student comes through the intense nature of clinical supervision and gives space for personal development.

As Rogers (1965) has noted (p 389):

> I know I cannot teach anyone anything. I can only provide an environment in which he (sic) can learn.

The provision of this environment through the clinical method enhances the personal development of the student.

Professional responsibility and ethics

The relevance of the ethical and moral are not, of course, the exclusive preserve of clinical programmes. They are recognised and dealt with in other parts of the curriculum. Their importance, however, should not be understated here and this point has been identified by the professional bodies as well as academics.

In its report on the structure and content of American legal education, the MacCrate Commission (1992) draws attention to the importance of what it terms 'fundamental lawyering skills and values'. In so doing it expressly includes the recognition and resolution of ethical dilemmas and the promotion of justice, fairness and morality (pp 140–1) as proper objectives of legal education. In the UK, the *Consultation Paper* issued by the Lord Chancellor's Advisory Committee, ACLEC, (1994) formally signals for the first time that legal ethics should play a significant part in undergraduate legal education.

It has already been suggested that those involved in clinical programmes develop a strong sense of personal pride and professionalism in their work. This is particularly noticeable in live-client clinics. But there is another dimension within clinical practice that stems from the students' attitude to their work encouraged by what is the central thrust of clinical pedagogy. Clinics encourage and enable students to reflect on their experiences. This process includes the detail of the case-work and wider issues of ethical practice and the role of law in society. Clinical students tend to recognise at an early stage that lawyers occupy a pivotal position in determining outcomes at crucial stages of other people's lives.

The clinic provides a forum within which students can look not just at the activity of lawyers, ethical or otherwise, but at the scope and function of the law in practice. Concepts of fairness and justice are of central importance to the study of law and are matters that regularly arise in clinical practice and related discussions. In this way clinic can inform debates about ethics, not just professional conduct.

The clinic is, through live-client work and/or simulation, able to focus realistically on these considerations and enables students to analyse them in an operational context, a context that has relevance and meaning to the student.

Assessment

It is often the case that the substance and delivery of a course is led by the means of assessment. Part of the reason for this is historical. In law at least, assessment has tended to be dominated by the three-hour unseen examination. This has traditionally been dictated by the professional bodies, through the validation of qualifying degrees. With the continuing relaxation of some of the formal rules relating to the content and assessment of undergraduate degrees in law, greater opportunities exist to re-examine assessment methodology and to clarify what it is that present assessment means achieve.

Clinical work is focused on student-centred learning and as part of this approach the means of assessment are tailored to be an integral part of the learning process. Whilst this has attracted criticism (Condlin (1986)) largely on the ground that the close supervision implicit in clinical programmes makes 'objective' assessment difficult, it begs the question of the efficacy and objectivity of the more traditional assessment methods.

According to Brandes and Ginnis (1986) student-centred learning includes student-centred assessment with 'testing' only used if it is formative and instructive in itself (p 65). This is problematic for the clinic for, if the clinic is to be taken seriously within the academy, it must have clearly-established learning objectives and outcomes, coupled with externally credible assessment criteria. Yet assessment that is not useful in terms of learning is credited with little importance by clinical staff. I do not suggest that formative assessment is peculiar to the clinic. Rather, it is the case that the clinic actively promotes and encourages such.

This presents both a challenge and an opportunity. The challenge is in overcoming the demands of designing assessment criteria that complement and support the learning outcomes of the unit. The opportunity is in the form of appraising assessment methodologies and, where necessary, departing from the more traditional and often summative means. Unseen examinations, or indeed any examinations that do not in themselves give a base for feedback, together with the rote learning that often precedes such assessment, are not part of the clinical ethos.

There is perhaps an argument to be made in favour of examinations, in so far as they require students to deliver under pressure and by a deadline. Other assessment methods can, however, do the same. Where the examination is little more than a memory test in which students can select (and avoid) topics and on which they receive little or no feedback, it has doubtful worth. Indeed, it can be seen as positively harmful to the extent that it may drive the content and structure of the programme itself.

A review of assessment, although difficult, is nonetheless valuable as it may bring into focus not just assessment in the clinic but assessment across the wider curriculum. Clinical education can provide, through its student-centred emphasis, the stimulus for such an exercise.

The consumers' choice?

It is not uncommon for clinical teachers to seek approval for their methods. Perhaps this is the consequence of being innovatory and in the limelight. Is the clinic really as good as we think and say it is? Without embarking on the evaluation of this approach to study of law (that is being worked on!) one answer to this question is to ask the students. The following is a sample of their responses:

> 'I learnt more than I did in the rest of the course put together.'
> 'Very enjoyable too – if frightening.'
> 'The best part of the course so far.'
> 'Easily the most worthwhile aspect of the course.'
> 'It's wonderful to do something useful.'
> 'It has enabled me to put the work we have done on the course into its true perspective.'
>
> Duncan (1994); see also Tarr (1993), p 41

Although these quotations (taken from actual student responses to a post-clinic experience questionnaire) are selective, they seem to represent the sort of response that clinic students regularly give and were the almost unanimous response of the students on one particular vocational course option.

The practice of clinical legal education

Doing clinical work presents challenges, problems and rewards. In this section the most important of these are noted. The implications of clinical practice are examined in general terms with specific reference being made to examples in existing clinical programmes.

Although the issues raised here can be related to many, if not all, aspects of clinical work, they are felt at their sharpest in live-client situations.

For whose benefit?

One of the first principles to be confronted in a clinical unit is who is the clinic for? The answer, at least initially, is straightforward. It is for the educational benefit of the student. Depending on the perceived course aims and learning outcomes, benefit may be defined as instruction in some combination of concepts, rules, skills and ethics. It may well involve all of these aspects.

The situation becomes more complex, however, if one introduces the real client with the real problem into the frame. A significant difficulty encountered by most, if not all, live-client programmes is that the clinic serves more than one set of objectives: its own educational aims and the client's needs. On one level this can be presented as unproblematic, so long as both student and client needs are defined in professional terms. For example, ethical standards (and for solicitors' practice clinics, professional practice rules) dictate that once one assumes responsibility for a client's problems, that obligation must be discharged in a satisfactory way that best serves the client's interests. The student need is achieved through the method of meeting the client need.

But not all cases will automatically meet the educational needs of the student. A case which is due to go to court the day after the client first consults the clinic may present little real opportunity for reflective learning (as well as being a quality control problem). A dispute or transaction very similar to cases already handled by students in the clinic may have limited learning potential. Demands of a particular case may clash with existing commitments of the students, for example, examinations or coursework requirements.

It becomes vastly more difficult when the clinic, through zealous staff, keen students and image- and resource-conscious managers, becomes driven by what is seen as the client's need. Having to turn away work because the educational needs of the student are not being advanced by that work is hard, especially when the client does have a problem with which the clinic could assist. Declining to act when a client could attract legal aid funding may also be hard.

This problem is particularly acute in clinics where unmet legal needs are targeted: see Lewis (1973), p 73. Many American law schools regard their clinical mission as being focused on providing services to the indigent community: see Tarr (1993), p 32. Indeed, many US clinics were and are funded with the specific brief of providing 'poor law' services. The temptation, for financial, political or altruistic reasons, to service the client's needs, without reference to the learning experience of the student, is at best foolhardy and at worst in danger of satisfying neither student nor client.

The message from this is clear: the clinic should be careful to take on *only* those cases that do enhance and reinforce the educational objectives whilst ensuring that the clients who are helped receive a proper, professional standard of service. In the solicitors' practice live-client programmes at Sheffield Hallam University and the University of Northumbria, clients are given written details of the purpose of the clinic and the nature and extent of the service provided. In this way the client is given a choice; if he or she wants to use the clinic (and the clinic feels able to take on the case) the basis of the retainer is understood. The service versus educational dimension of clinical work must be addressed if the programme is to deal realistically with both clients and teaching aims. Subject to professional ethics and responsibilities, cases must be assessed in terms of their educational value and if necessary passed over, or on elsewhere.

The tension between each set of demands may be manipulated, at least to a degree, by controlling the nature of the clinic's work (many concentrate on 'welfare' issues) or the source of the clinic's clientele (for example, staff or students from that institution).

Requirements of professional practice

Compliance with professional rules may be a legal requirement or it may be necessary because the clinic has adopted a model that offers good practice, or is replicating private practice in simulation.

Solicitors' practice clinics must comply with the Solicitors' Practice Rules and related legislation, codes of conduct and related requirements of practice (The Law Society (1993)).

Those rules that are of particular importance in the context of clinical practice include the supervision of the clinic (Solicitors' Practice Rules, rule 13), client care (rule 15), and waivers from the Practice Rules (rule 17).

In addition, solicitors running clinical practices within academic institutions must comply with the Employed Solicitors' Code 1990 (as amended) (rule 4) and in particular with rule 7, which affects law centres, charities and non-commercial advice services (The Law Society (1993), p 134). A waiver for solicitors' practice clinics will be required from rule 7(a)(i) to enable the clinic to be managed by its funder (the university/college). It is a requirement of rule 7 that no fees are charged, except under the legal aid scheme or where they are recovered from a third party.[4] Any fees recovered must be paid to the institution in which the clinic operates and the institution must carry indemnity insurance reasonably equivalent to that available to solicitors from the Solicitors' Indemnity Fund.

Live-client clinics that do not hold themselves out as solicitors' practices are not obliged to comply with the rules, unless a person who is a solicitor acts in that capacity in certain matters (eg advocacy). In such instances he or she must hold a practising certificate (The Law Society (1993), pp 21–3).

A live-client clinic that offers only advice, or representation before arbitration and tribunal hearings, does not fall under the practice rules, unless the client is represented by a solicitor in that capacity.

As a matter of good practice the supervision of students by suitable qualified staff and the provision of adequate indemnity insurance should be considered as essential.

These rules of practice can have a considerable impact on clinical work from both a professional compliance point of view and in terms of the selection of staff, and the financing of insurance and, where relevant, practising certificate fees. On the former, it is the author's experience that university insurers are willing to extend the university's third party cover to include the clinic's activity at little or no extra cost. On the latter it should be remembered that a reduced practising certificate fee is payable if the applicant's full income generated by his/her practice is below a specified limit, currently £5,000 (The Law Society (1993), p 24, and s 11(1) Solicitors' Act 1974).

Resourcing the clinic

It is important to acknowledge that both simulation and live-client clinics are resource intensive. What is certain is that they demand significant levels of staff input if the supervision, instruction, feedback

4   For some of the difficulties surrounding the interpretation of this, see Brayne (1994), p 20.

and assessment are carried out effectively. Depending on the type of clinical programme used, resourcing can also arise as an issue in terms of rooms, office space, library facilities, office equipment and clerical back-up.

CLEO has published model standards for live-client work that list the minimum and recommended levels of resourcing: see CLEO (1995).

The clinical experience does, therefore, come at a cost. But how is this cost to be measured? In an interesting response to a general enquiry on the cost-effectiveness of clinics, Professor Seibel of Cornell Law School rightly commented:

> The issue is not to make the non-clinical upper-class law school look useless, but rather to avoid having a witch hunt in the clinic just because it seems more expensive in terms of student/faculty ratio [and other resources]. It might be a good time to get . . . others . . . to try to identify what they think law students should be learning – don't . . . proceed on the basis of unexamined assumptions about what law students need to learn, much less on how best to teach those things. You can't have an evaluation or a cost/benefit analysis without explicitly agreed (sic) upon benefits that are being measured.[5]

The resource implication must therefore be gauged against the student's learning experience and the role that the clinic plays and can play in the whole of the education process.

Some of the benefits of clinical teaching that may be less obvious include: the generation of material for use in other subject areas (particularly for simulation and role-play); a control for reviewing teaching and learning methodologies and, in particular, means of assessment; and the research potential of the clinic in terms of a base for empirical research and scholarship.

Despite giving the initial impression that clinical work is resource intensive there is another longer-term view that can be taken. If one of the aims of clinical programmes is to produce self-reliant, confident, reflective and technically capable students, then such students might be expected to be able to take the clinical experience and use this in self-directed study. The student's capacity for autonomous

5 Unpublished e-mail response to law clinic list server enquiry about cost effectiveness of clinical programmes, July 1994.

learning is enhanced through what has been termed by Bezdek (1993) 'pedagogic diversity'.

If the clinic is resource hungry, what of sources of funding? Of course, if one extends the argument that the clinic is an integral part of the curriculum it should be funded from internal resourcing or 'hard money' as it has been coined by Tarr (1993), p 37.

Economic reality (and the particular position clinics occupy if doing live-client welfare work) means that external or 'soft money' becomes attractive. Grants to support innovative programmes such as clinics are not uncommon. Central government funds have long been used in the USA through the Title IX programme: see Tarr (1993), p 37, n 16. The rub here is that a service must be provided, in return, for clients on low incomes. In the context of the British legal system it does not take much imagination to foresee a time when legal aid as we have known it for over 40 years will disappear, with specialist agencies (whether in the guise of franchised private practice or other bodies) providing minimal cover. It would be very easy to advance an argument for a university law clinic to be one of these providers.

However attractive this might seem, danger bells ring at the approach of a client service-driven model of clinical education. (On another level the arguments for a major restructuring of legal services are well-documented in LAG (1992), ch 12).

Supervising the clinic

The professional practice obligations of supervising a live-client clinic have already been referred to. This section is concerned with the principles of supervision and the implications of this.

It is a central tenet of clinical education that students receive an adequate level of supervision that satisfies any professional rule or standard, that meets the needs of the client (if any) and that progresses the student's learning.

It is important to understand the nature of what is being supervised. The supervision of the student and the student's work can be seen from several perspectives.

First, supervision must be sufficiently 'hands-on' to ensure compliance with professional and self-imposed standards. Supervision, however, should not by its very imposition stifle that fundamental objective of clinical work – experiential learning. The student must be allowed and encouraged to make what he or she can of the task being addressed. This includes, in a qualified way, the right to make mistakes or, more properly put, the right to learn what was done and why, and if necessary what is now to be done. The qualification is the overriding need to ensure that clients remain unaffected by the process other than in the serving of their best interests.

Secondly, therefore, supervision needs to allow the space for learning whilst safeguarding the end product. It can be a difficult balance. Do you, for example, allow students to interview clients without the supervisor being present? Received wisdom seems to suggest that the learning experience is greater without a supervising presence. The safeguard is that the supervisor must approve the letter that is subsequently sent to a client which confirms the 'facts' as understood and the consequential advice.

Thirdly, as supervision is part of the student's learning experience, it must be designed, and put into effect, in such a way as to facilitate that process. Looking over a student's shoulder to check that he or she is on the right lines may be part of the safeguard mode but does little to aid the student's understanding.

The question to ask is *how* does the supervision relate to the learning? The use of standardised forms and procedures for giving detailed feedback arising from supervision may aid this process.

Supervision is also inextricably linked with assessment. The intensive nature of much clinical work gives the tutor and the student a rare opportunity to demonstrate to each other their roles in, and understanding of, the assessment process. Again the use of clearly established methods for recording the relevant content of supervision and the translation of this into a grade based on assessment criteria is essential.

The intricate and complex issues surrounding supervision are well-documented elsewhere: see, for example, Hoffman (1986). If supervision is regarded as another facet of learning, rather than a trouble-shooting role, it may provide an important stepping-stone to the improvement of understanding in legal education and the empowerment of students in the process.

Assessing performance in the clinic

It has been a constant and recurring theme in this chapter that the clinic offers refreshing opportunities to re-examine the techniques, approaches and methodologies used in many aspects of undergraduate and vocational legal education. Nowhere is this more markedly seen than in the assessment of clinical students.

With perhaps the notable exception of the four-year degree at the University of Northumbria (see ACLEC (1994), p 5), clinical education is not generally seen as a core element of instruction. Assessment appears not to be subject to the confines imposed in respect of other core units. The approach to assessment thus varies widely. Some institutions do not assess at all and others use a variety of methods including examinations, course-work, presentations and continuous assessment: see Grimes (1995); Grimes et al (1996), tables 12, 13, 19, 20 and 33.

Three observations should perhaps be made at this point.

First, students reportedly work extremely hard on clinical units. Whether this is fostered by staff enthusiasm, a professional sense of responsibility and/or the students' own enjoyment is debatable. Nonetheless, they do appear to put in the effort and therefore rightly expect to receive a grade commensurate with it. However, it is the amount and nature of the learning gained that has to be the measure of the students' progress.

Secondly, many clinical staff have developed sophisticated programmes in which their pedagogic objectives are clearly stated. It is suggested that the value of learning is both augmented and demonstrated by the existence of well-focused assessment criteria.

Thirdly, one of the aims of clinical education, as explained earlier in this chapter, is the development of reflection by the participating student. This desired consequence can be encouraged by giving the student an input into the assessment process as part of the established criteria.

Self and peer assessment is an important feature of this development. Tarr (1990) suggests (at p 967) that the implicit goal of self-assessment and critical observation is an important part of the learning process and as such should be made explicit to the student. Self-assessment is also a skill much needed by lawyers in their professional role.

One of the challenges in the re-examination of assessment, however, is that students (and staff), conscious of their new role, begin to question the basis upon which assessment is carried out elsewhere on their programmes! According to Webb ((1995), p 192) it:

> forces us to address the silences of liberal education on the predominance of content; on the justification for traditional assessment methods.

Conclusion

This chapter has attempted to describe what clinical legal education is and what it offers to our understanding and practice of educating lawyers. The extent to which experiential learning is founded on sustainable theoretical premises has also been explored.

The implications of clinical practice for the curriculum, whether through simulation or live-client work, have been examined. Where does this now leave the clinic?

In the introduction to this chapter it was suggested that legal education in the UK is at something of a cross-roads. Pressure is building from the providers of legal education, from the profession, from students and from the funders of education for a reappraisal of what legal education should do and how it should do it. Identifiable strands are appearing in the allied discussions. These talk of a better understanding of concepts, of less emphasis on bulk rule acquisition, of more relevance of the academic subject to the real world, and of the development of intellectual and transferable skills. Greater emphasis is being placed on quality and effective teaching and assessment methods.

The most recent reviews of the principles and content of legal education have concentrated on three main themes:

- the development of the students' intellectual capacity, including their ability to research, analyse and reason;
- a grounding in basic legal concepts;
- the application of knowledge including the use of legal and transferable skills and the recognition of practical and ethical issues.

It is the main thrust of this chapter that clinical legal education addresses these intellectual and substantive challenges on both undergraduate and vocational courses. It enables students to retain or take a degree of control over their own learning experience, and to become actively engaged in all aspects of the process, including the application of their knowledge, and in reflection on the learning process.

The value of the clinical approach is that it focuses on the issues of concern listed above and it tackles, very directly, the underlying objectives of quality. It uses teaching and learning methodologies that are specifically targeted at improving the students' experience and understanding.

Just as MacCrate has recognised and pushed forward the debate in the USA on the relevance of skills and clinical teaching, it is suggested that those responsible for overseeing legal education in the UK may soon formally acknowledge the contribution that clinical legal education has to offer. In the meantime, those engaged in clinical programmes will continue within their institutions, and collectively through CLEO and other forums, to develop this approach to learning. More in-depth evaluation needs to take place. A culture of greater clinical research and scholarship needs to be encouraged.

From a somewhat more established position within the USA, American clinicians are now being encouraged to contribute to both academic debates and research on the basis that vocational clinical law offices are now part of the academy of law: see Palm (1994), p 132. It is suggested that the clinic is beginning to make the same contribution to legal education in the UK.

References

AALS (American Association of Law Schools) (1990) *Final report on the future of the in-house clinic*, AALS.

ACLEC (Lord Chancellor's Advisory Committee on Legal Education & Conduct) (1994) *Review of Legal Education. Consultation Paper: The Initial Stage*, ACLEC, London.

A Amsterdam (1984) 'Clinical Legal Education – a 21st Century Perspective' 34 *Journal of Legal Education* 612.

G Bellow & B Moulton (1978) *The Lawyering Process: Materials for Clinical Instruction in Advocacy*, Foundation Press, Mineola, NY.

B Bezdek (1993) 'Legal theory and practice at the University of Maryland School of Law' 93(3) *AALS Newsletter* 13.

A Boon, M Jeeves & J Macfarlane (1987) 'Clinical Anatomy: Towards a Working Definition of Clinical Legal Education', 21 *Law Teacher* 61.

A Bradney (1992) 'Ivory Towers or Satanic Mills: Choices for University Law Schools', 17 *Studies in Higher Education* 5.

D Brandes & P Ginnis (1986) *A Guide to Student-Centred Learning*, Simon and Schuster, New York.

H Brayne (1994) 'Employed Solicitors and Inter Partes Costs' *Legal Action*, April, p 20.

H Brayne (1996) 'Law students as practitioners: developing an undergraduate clinical programme at Northumbria University', this collection.

G Brown & M Atkins (1988) *Effective Teaching in Higher Education*, Routledge, London.

CLEO (Clinical Legal Education Organisation) (1994) 'Response to the Lord Chancellor's Advisory Committee on Legal Education and Conduct's consultative paper', mimeo.

CLEO (1995) 'Model standards in clinical legal education – live-client clinics', mimeo.

R Condlin (1986) 'Tastes Good, Less Filling: The Law School Clinic and Political Critique' 36 *Journal of Legal Education* 45.

N Duncan (1994) 'Responses of students on the Free Representation Unit (FRU) of the Bar Vocational Course', mimeo.

J Frank (1933) 'Why Not A Clinical Lawyer School?', 81 *University of Pennsylvania Law Review* 907.

G Gibbs (1992) *Improving the Quality of Student Learning*, Technical and Education Services Ltd, Bristol.

G Goodpaster (1975) 'The Human Arts of Lawyering', 27 *Journal of Legal Education* 33.

R Grimes (1995) 'Legal Skills and Clinical Legal Education', *Web Journal of Current Legal Issues*, No 3.

R Grimes, J Klaff & C Smith (1996) 'Legal Skills and Clinical Legal Education – A Survey of Law School Practice', 30 *Law Teacher* (forthcoming).

D Harris & C Bell (1994) *Evaluating and Assessing for Learning*, Kogan Page, London.

P Hoffman (1986) 'The Stages of Clinical Supervisory Relationships', 4 *Antioch Law Review* 301.

P Hoffman (1994) 'Clinical Scholarship and Skills Training', 1 *Clinical Law Review* 93.

Q Johnstone (1951) 'Law School Legal Aid Clinics' 3 *Journal of Legal Education* 535.

D A Kolb (1984) *Experiential Learning: Experience as a Source of Learning and Development*, Prentice Hall, Englewood Cliffs, NJ.

Law Society (1993) *Guide to the Professional Conduct of Solicitors*, The Law Society, London.

Legal Action Group (1992) *A Strategy for Justice*, Legal Action Group, London.

P Lewis (1973) 'Unmet Legal Need' in P Morris, R White & P Lewis *Social Needs and Legal Action*, Martin Robertson, Oxford.

MacCrate Report (1992) *Legal Education and Professional Development – An Educational Continuum: Narrowing the Gap*, American Bar Association, Chicago.

M A McDiarmid (1990) 'What's Going On Down There In The Basement: In-House Clinics Expand Their Beachhead', 35 *New York University Law School Law Review* 239.

J Macfarlane (1988) *An Evaluation of the Role and Practice of Clinical Legal Education in the UK*, PhD thesis, CNAA BX 85358.

J Macfarlane (1992) 'Look Before You Leap: Knowledge and Learning in Legal Skills Education', 19 *Journal of Law & Society* 293.

S Maher (1990) 'The Praise of Folly: A Defence of Practice Supervision in Clinical Education', 69 *Nebraska Law Review* 537.

C Maughan (1996) 'Learning how to learn: the skills developer's guide to experiential learning', this collection.

C Maughan & J Webb (1995) *Lawyering Skills and the Legal Process*, Butterworths, London.

M Meltsner & P Schrag (1976) 'Reports from a CLEPR Colony', 76 *Columbia Law Review* 581.

C Meyers & T Jones (1993) *Promoting Active Learning: Strategies for the College Classroom*, Jossey-Bass, Chicago.

G Palm (1994) 'Reconceptualising Clinical Scholarship', 1 *Clinical Law Review* 127.

M Partington (1984) 'Academic and Practical Legal Education: The Contribution of the Sandwich System', 18 *Law Teacher* 110.

P Ramsden (1992) *Learning to Teach in Higher Education*, Routledge, London & New York.

W Rees (1975) 'Clinical Legal Education: An Analysis of the University of Kent Model', 12 *Law Teacher* 125.

C Rogers (1965) *Client-Centred Therapy*, Houghton Mifflin, Boston.

C Rogers (1969) *Freedom to Learn: A View of What Education Might Become*, Merrill, Columbus, Oh.

J Rogers (1979) *Adult Learning*, Open University Press, Milton Keynes.

N L Schultz (1992) 'How Do Lawyers Really Think?', 42 *Journal of Legal Education* 57.

Sheffield Hallam University (1995a) 'Legal skills course book', mimeo.

Sheffield Hallam University (1995b) 'Welfare Law Manual', mimeo.

A Sherr (1986) *Client Interviewing for Lawyers*, Sweet & Maxwell, London.

M Spiegal (1987) 'Theory and Practice in Legal Education: An Essay on Clinical Education', 34 *UCLA Law Review* 577.

P J Spiegelman (1988) 'Integrating Doctrine, Theory and Practice in the Law School Curriculum: The Logic of Jake's Ladder in the Context of Amy's Web', 38 *Journal of Legal Education* 243.

R Spjut (1977) '"Praxis" and Prudence: Reforming Clinical Legal Education at the University of Kent', 11 *Law Teacher* 89.

N Tarr (1990) 'The Skill of Evaluation as an Explicit Goal of Clinical Training', 21 *Pacific Law Journal* 967.

N Tarr (1993) 'Current Issues in Clinical Legal Education', 37 *Howard Law Journal* 31.

W Twining (1993) 'The Idea of Juristic Method: A Tribute to Karl Llewellyn', 48 *University of Miami Law Review* 119.

W Twining (1994) *Blackstone's Tower: The English Law School*, Sweet & Maxwell, London.

University of Central England (1994) 'Criminal and Civil Clinic Handbooks', mimeo.

J Webb (1995) 'Where the Action Is: Developing Artistry in Legal Education', 2 *International Journal of the Legal Profession* 187.

M Zander (1973) 'Clinical Legal Education', *New Law Journal* 181.

Chapter 6

Law students as practitioners: developing an undergraduate clinical programme at Northumbria University

Hugh Brayne[1]

Education: What is left after the facts are forgotten!
(G Gibbs 'Twenty Terrible Reasons for Lecturing')

This chapter is a personal viewpoint of one Law School's journey along the road to a better quality of education through a clinical approach.

The University of Northumbria and, in its earlier incarnation, New-castle Polytechnic, has had a clinical programme since 1981. Although not the first on the scene, our Clinic, I believe, is now the country's longest running live-client programme and certainly the largest.

How did we get here? Why? What have we learned on the way? Where are we heading? I hope you will have useful answers to these questions by the end of the chapter. But first, why us?

The University of Northumbria

The Law Clinic, from the start, was seen as a way of creating a distinctive undergraduate programme. The aim was not simply to provide a taste of practical experience, but to enable students to develop, apply and extend their academic skills through practical advice work.

There are undoubtedly features of this University that contributed to the nurturing of a clinical approach. As a new university with a long history of professional legal education (Part 2s, Law Society

1   This chapter is a case history from 1981–1995. It has not been possible to describe the most recent developments. For an analysis of theoretical issues in clinical legal education, please read the previous chapter by Richard Grimes. In writing this chapter I am particularly grateful to Pat Martin-Moran, who first developed the Clinic at Newcastle Polytechnic, to Aine Kelly for help with editing, to Ellen Vile for support in typing the several drafts, and Richard Grimes for suggestions on content.

Finals, and now the Legal Practice Course) we started out with a large number of professionally qualified and experienced staff. My own appointment in 1985 was typical. I had no postgraduate degree, or research profile, and came via an advertisement in the Gazette. I was recruited because I could teach on the Finals and short courses to solicitors, as well as degree students.

In terms of research, that approach to recruitment is now obsolete. But it helps explain why, in a School of 45 lecturers, it has not been difficult to find sufficient solicitors (currently 14) to obtain practising certificates and take part in supervising students. Until 1995 we have never needed to recruit specifically for clinical work. However, now we have taken on a half-time solicitor who co-ordinates all casework, including in vacations, as well as supervising students.

Northumbria University School of Law is probably one of the most stable in the country in terms of staff turnover. I personally imagined I would stay at Newcastle for two years. After ten I am still entrenched. We also have the longest serving Head of any Law School. This unusual staff stability has been a key ingredient in the survival and expansion of our Clinic. Live-client programmes can depend, at least at first, on particular individuals rather than particular structures. If these individuals move on, the programmes may collapse.

Several other factors have favoured the development of live-client work here. The School is large enough to have subject expertise in most areas that a client might present. This gives supervising staff extra confidence.

As we have expanded, two further factors have been important. Firstly, we have a highly developed continuing education programme. It is not big business, but it is a source of income which stays in the School and is not devoured by the University. Live-client work is, as I will discuss below, probably more expensive than traditional teaching. Our ability to invest extra cash has undoubtedly increased our confidence.

The second of these factors promoting recent expansion is the Northumbria four-year exempting degree. The first year enrolled in 1992. Instead of taking the Legal Practice Course as a one-year, postgraduate course, our degree students find LPC elements in all years of their degree, generally integrated into other degree work. As a result, we no longer suffer from what I believe is the sterile debate about whether legal skills are appropriate at undergraduate level. We explicitly develop professional and academic skills together.

I do not wish to imply that live client work has been universally popular or accepted by Northumbria staff. I was not around in 1981 when, I am told, the establishment of the Clinic caused enormous debate in staff meetings, even though the programme was modest by comparison with today's Law Office. The main staff concerns were whether the students were sufficiently trustworthy and responsible, and equipped with adequate skills to do the job; the quality of supervision; the School's liability should things go wrong; and the risk of souring relationships with the law profession. In the early years, I am informed, staff support, to the supervisor and to students, was patchy.

From Law Clinic to Law Office

The Clinic was originally just one part of a course called Legal Methods and Institutions. This was an activity in the second year of the three-year LLB where students had to do something practical. For example, they could do a short placement, generally with a solicitor, or they could follow and chart the progress of a piece of legislation, or they could carry out legal advice work. It was the last component which became the foundation of the live-client in-house clinical programme.

It was not easy, in those days, to set up a clinical programme. The old practice rules prevented employed solicitors from acting for members of the public. The Law Society was keen to protect private practice from encroachment on its client base. Fortunately the local Law Society was not hostile, and agreed that the Clinic could give advice, but only to the Polytechnic's own students. The Law Society appointed a monitor to keep an eye on the Clinic, meet the relevant staff each term and cast an eye over our activities.

We could not act, or go on the court record, we could not even contemplate recovering costs and using legal aid, instructing counsel or experts. It is noteworthy, with hindsight, how far this programme was removed from actual legal practice. But it got us started. A room in the School was labelled 'Law Clinic', an appointments book was opened, the Students' Union and counselling services were informed, and posters were sent around the Campus.

By the time I started, four years on, the profession's worries had clearly abated. The Law Society's appointed Big Brother had turned into our best friend, and continued to advise us long after he stopped reporting to the Law Society.

In my first year in 1985, I had 13 students who, in a year, saw 13 clients. These clients were generally despatched in one session. All ongoing paperwork was easily accommodated in one briefcase; I advised the students what to advise the clients, they advised them, and that was usually that.

Then we started to expand. Why? It was not the client demand, which remained fairly constant. Was it my own enthusiasm? Again, no. I had yet to become a convert to clinical legal education. The reason, I believe, was that more law students wanted to join in. Word was spreading from year to year that advising clients was hands on, good fun and relevant. They were exercising, before the concept had become educationally fashionable, customer choice.

As more students asked to join the programme I decided to take two steps. Firstly, I had to find more clients and, second, in the absence of more staff, I decided to limit student numbers so that all students got regular interviews. Of course, according to the law of supply and demand, imposing limits immediately made the activity more appealing, so student demand went up year by year.

The problem was, how to find more clients? The solution was to take the advice to where the clients were. From 1988 to 1992 appointments in the Law School were abandoned as not sufficiently accessible. Instead we started a drop-in advice session once a week in the Students' Union. This usually generated up to four client enquiries a week. The service now catered for about 30 student lawyers, working in pairs to advise some 50 student clients each year. The paperwork still fitted in a briefcase, and activity ceased from May to October.

Around this time I started to get personally excited by clinical legal education. The students' infectious enthusiasm had reached me. Equally important, my Head of School was supportive of new ideas. I was looking for new outlets for advice, and started negotiations with nearby Gateshead Law Centre. In fact it was unnecessary to negotiate with an organisation that responds, 'That's a really good idea, when can you start – and by the way, can you join our Management Committee?'

So from 1988, as part of the expansion of our client base, those same 30 students also advised at the Law Centre. For the first time, students could also handle the case work that resulted from the advice work. As we were in a Law Centre, we could have a retainer with clients, go to court, apply for legal aid, and begin to be real lawyers. Casework would offer students factual analysing, writing of relevant documents, a real relationship with a client, and a sense of personal responsibility.

Resource lessons

At this stage I began to learn the first of my lessons. Surprisingly it took me two or more years at the Law Centre to learn it. The simple lesson was this: If you offer a significant service to clients, whether via a Law Centre or otherwise, you have to be available to do the work. If you expect students to conduct the work, it must be made easy for them, otherwise you will end up doing it yourself. With hindsight, I recognise that I effectively seconded myself to the Law Centre for a significant part of my time to handle those cases that the Centre would not otherwise have taken on. Since the students were only scheduled to attend every four or five weeks, I became file monitor, case worker and messenger; and at the same time I dragged Law Centre staff into handling casework they would not otherwise have prioritised. We were running this rota and case work for 51 weeks a year in order to provide interviewing experience over only 25 weeks. The students, we found from experience, could rarely get to the Law Centre quickly or often enough to do useful follow-up work. When I complained that I was overstretched my Head of School reminded me that if I wanted to provide a year round legal service for the Law Centre that was up to me. (As I will describe below, the problem does not go away just by bringing the programme in-house. But there is a significant difference in psychology – it is the Law School's own programme, and not one individual's hobby. Also, the Law School can control the programme to suit its own, educational, requirements.)

The lesson was reinforced when I tried to share the burden of supervising weekly sessions with lecturing colleagues. By 1991 the clinical team had doubled in size – to two. My colleague took one look at the Gateshead set up and politely suggested we sort out those parts of the partnership which were relevant to educating students, and separate them from my desire to increase the availability of legal advice for the people of Gateshead. The latter was not the Poly-technic's priority, although the achievement of educational goals clearly requires clients to come. The Law Centre, quite reasonably, did not wish to invite clients for half the year and send them away unaided for the other half.

I needed ways of making the rota experience for students less expensive on my own time. The first was to renegotiate with the Law Centre, so that only advice work was undertaken. Any decision to take on a case was then one for the Centre, not the Polytechnic. The Centre would resource the case work, while liaising as far as possible with me and the students over its progress. But we were back to an advice only experience for students.

A second way of lightening the load evolved spontaneously. Every year one or two students asked if they could carry on advice work at the Law Centre over the summer period. Once a student starts seeing three or four clients a week, instead of every few months, their expertise develops rapidly, and the need for intense supervision declines. It became less onerous to attend advice sessions in the holidays, since I could get on with other work; it even became less necessary, as Law Centre staff were often willing to supervise on this basis.

Educational lessons

It is now hard to believe that I could have subjected myself to this, or believed it to be right, but for the first four years as a clinical supervisor I sat in on every student interview. I thought – in so far as I thought at all – that I had a professional responsibility to do so.

I was wrong. I seemed to be concerned with providing advice more than educating students. It meant sitting in cramped rooms with the pair of student advisers and the client, and sometimes the clients' friend(s), relations, baby or dog. It meant the client, and the students' turning to me to see if the advice was right. Often I would step in to correct or add to advice, with the result that the client might never speak to the student again during the interview. I believed that clients needed quick answers to legal problems, and that my presence was the way to ensure that.

In 1989, prompted by discussions with a number of clinical prac-titioners in the US, I had my eyes opened. I have almost never taken part in an interview since then. To avoid usurping the students' relationship with the client, I always try to have my discussions with the student in the client's absence. It is debatable whether the client even needs to meet the supervisor, so long as the client knows (in writing) what is the role and responsibility of the supervisor and how to complain if there is any problem. (I later learned that before I took over the Clinic it had never been the practice for staff to sit in on interviews. I had imposed the burden on myself through a failure to separate the two goals of legal service and student learning.)

I had not provided any training for the students before they started interviewing. A second educational shortcoming was corrected during this period. (Before I took over, there had been such a programme, but I had not been aware of this.) So I provided basic training in interviewing and the rules of professional responsibility, later adding, with the help of the Law Centre, legal aid, the basics of housing law and employment law, and how the Law Centre operates. The training programme was soon a whole term in length. Soon after this, we began to organise students into 'firms', and meet them to review their clinical work every week.

Surprisingly this added burden did not kill the students' willingness to do Law Clinic. We were now giving them 15 hours of lectures, perhaps 8–10 hours of client interviewing, a weekly meeting and a heavy sense of personal commitment and responsibility. Assessment was pass/fail only. The work still did not count towards the degree classification, and there were certainly easier activities available.

An important educational step forward was the use of 'firms' referred to above. We first started organising the rota sessions this way in 1989; the principal aim was to make the students themselves responsible for task allocation and to guarantee coverage of the rota. Students were divided into firms of five or six, each appearing on the Student Union rota and Law Centre rota about every five weeks. Students were required to meet in between rota sessions to discuss their cases.

We have continued with firms ever since, and for a staff supervisor I believe the close collaboration with a firm is one of the real perks of the job. Since they are smaller than traditional seminar groups, we get to work with each student at every meeting. Since they are larger than one-to-one or pair supervision (which is still necessary) there is a very significant student-to-student interaction. The tutor is just one member of this team. Year after year firms have taken on their own identities, friendships have been formed, and high quality legal discussions has taken place within these firms, as often as not in the absence of the tutor. Firms have worked well whether they have themselves chosen each other or we have told them who to be with, and even when (for one year only) we created firms of ten across two years of the LLB.

From Law Clinic to Student Law Office

We were struggling to offer students an experience going beyond advice and minimal assistance. At the Law Centre we had had some contact with casework. But students were still not responsible for their cases. We began to see the potential for ourselves providing the type of full legal service that a Law Centre can offer. This desire was accelerated by a visit to the University of Connecticut in 1990, when I was able to see what law students were capable of. There the students had rights of audience in state and federal courts, took almost total responsibility for big cases, including serious crime and appeal cases, and were clearly doing it well.

But when we first started to consider our own in-house American style Law Centre/Solicitors' Office for students to handle real cases in, we were hampered by Law Society practice rules. Employed solicitors were at that time not allowed to act for anyone other than their employer. Only Law Centre solicitors could get round this and act for the public. Even they, under the old rules, had no right to take on areas of work traditionally belonging to the High Street Solicitor – personal injury, conveyancing and family, for example.

At first we thought the answer might be to set up a fully fledged Law Centre of our own. This would require considerable funding, and, as it turned out, could not be approved by the Law Centres Federation, who required independent community management of any Law Centre, whereas we wanted the Polytechnic to have control of the service in order to ensure that the educational needs had priority.

But in 1990 the Rules changed. The new Code (Employed Solicitors' Code, rule 7) allows non-profit or charitable organisations to employ solicitors to act for the public. It was no longer necessary to be recognised as a Law Centre. Was there really nothing, apart from the resource implications, to prevent us just setting up our own Law Office?

It seemed too good to be true, and to make absolutely sure we wrote to the Law Society to enquire if we could therefore start a University Student Law Office. No, they replied, the Rules (Employed Solicitors' Code, rule 7) require the solicitor's employer and the provider of the funding for the service to be separate. We argued back that our funding would come from student fees, from the Department for Education and in due course from legal aid and recovered costs, and therefore from independent sources. The Society, however, insisted that the University was both the solicitor's employer and the service's funder. But the Society were obviously keen to let us go ahead. They also treated our letter of disagreement as an application for a waiver from this rule and granted the waiver.

So we were almost in business. The Employed Solicitors' Code requires that a solicitor giving advice to the public must have insurance equivalent to that required in private practice. The Municipal Mutual already insured the University, and would therefore have indemnified the institution; it agreed without hesitation to extend the existing cover of £15 million to any claim against individual students and lecturers involved in this legal work, at no extra premium. (This Company went out of business, but the University's new insurers (Zurich) have been happy to continue the arrangement.) No claim has yet had to be made.

The rules also require written advice to clients that we are not covered by the Solicitors' Indemnity Fund. We took this requirement as the opportunity to draw up a full Client Information Leaflet, setting out how we operate, the limits of a student's authority, and how to complain (to comply with Practice Rule 15, even though it does not apply to employed solicitors). Above all, the leaflet tries to make sure the client realises that we expect students to do the work, including looking up answers, and that it can take time. More recently we have also provided a short letter setting out the terms of our retainer, including our right to recover costs from the opponent, and our unavailability to represent the client at a hearing unless promised in writing. (This tempers any incautious enthusiasm of students that we have not managed to address in training.)

The present Student Law Office

We started in September 1991. We were no longer just a clinical programme, but a real legal office. The change of name, in 1992, was to recognise this. We had a secretary, two rooms, two clinical supervisors, a basic library, a box of toys, a kettle and mugs, dozens of blank legal aid forms, an empty diary, and several bottles of wine. The wine was the lubricant for the legal great and the good, plus the press, who were invited to the launch. Publicity, through the press and word of mouth, was highly effective, and clients – real members of the public, not just students – immediately started to book in to our twice-weekly lunchtime sessions. We reckoned at last we had no need to limit the numbers of student advisers, so numbers shot up from my limited intake of 30 to all those who volunteered – to 55, well over half the year group at the time.

We now had in fact more advisers than an average firm. We had taken on an enormous new responsibility. The students would be with us some 25 weeks a year, often preoccupied by other priorities (coursework and exams), and would be replaced the next year.

The demands placed on staff supervisors and other resources became a recurring theme from now on.

For the first year of the new office, we took new clients in at lunchtime sessions, offering four half-hour appointments twice a week.

These two sessions per week were very resource hungry. Four interviews over two hours during a lunch time session could generate a further four solid hours of discussion and paperwork, often more. We preferred not to let students leave the work room until every file met our critical satisfaction. We were asking higher standards than I had applied when in private practice, and the price was (and is) a high one. 'I'll make that attendance note tomorrow' was not acceptable.

What were the students getting back? Until 1994 when the third year of the Exempting Degree started, students were still not doing work that counted in their degree. But to ask the question only in terms of what tangible rewards a student gets misses the real point that underlies the clinical philosophy. What these law students were getting was an insight and depth of understanding of law that was its own reward, as well as giving context and meaning to their studies. I well remember a student drafting a particular claim for a personal injury and spontaneously shouting 'I've just realised what a cause of action is.' That student had studied Contract and Tort, had advised clients about problems in that area, and now the different parts of the jigsaw were beginning to fit. Students recognise real learning of this sort as highly valuable, they do not require assessments to become motivated, and they come back for more. Another reason for their lack of complaint, I believe, is that we had told them how hard it would be before they made their choice when Clinic was optional (until 1993). Genuine shirkers, presumably, did not join us, although some students with previous reputations as work shy came forward and excelled. It is a misconception that students do not like hard work. Once they recognise its relevance, students generally welcome it, and our task is often not to motivate so much as to direct and control the energy.

Another reason for commitment, of which we have received repeated anecdotal evidence over the years, is the value to students applying for placements or training contracts or pupillage of having real experience to talk about, both in the CV and in the interview. Indeed, in this region, some employers are known to ask of applicants 'why did you not take Law Clinic?'

In order to bolster this career advantage, and to develop personal insight into the clinical work, we offer students the chance to complete, and agree with the supervisor, a personal profile, which indicates progress made, lessons learned, skills improved, and experiences gained. As well as helping students to evaluate their work, profiling gives enormously useful feedback to the supervisors. As an example of feedback, in the first year I went through the profiling process, I was stunned to read in almost every case that students had described their role as passing on to the client the answers I had supplied to them. I had been a clinical supervisor for five years at that point, and had still not realised that most of the value comes from the students themselves formulating questions and researching answers. The supervisor's task is to be there as a safety net, for student and client. I now consider the need to give clients quick answers must be subordinated to the need of the student to gain understanding of legal content and method. I am not the only one who has to bite my tongue sometimes.

The strategy we now have, and emphasise very strongly in the training programme, is that no one gives advice, let alone answers, during initial interviews. This is spelled out to the client in the written retainer agreement, which the student goes through during the first moments of the interview. Students are encouraged to make a virtue of the fact that they are 'only' students, that the client's problem is helping them in their learning, that they are not allowed to advise without checking, and that this way of working will cause delay.

Delay! It can take four weeks just to draft a client statement exactly right, to the standards we aim to apply. Who ever saw a student do that in an assignment? What is more, we can help students every step of the way. When it comes to assessment, the student's ability to learn from the help given is part of that student's competence. We are as interested in rewarding the legal method used as the outcome. This is formative feedback and assessment. What a contrast with coursework and examinations on the rest of the degree programme!

On the question of delay, there is a potential conflict between the interest of the student in taking painstaking care and the interests of the client in having the problem solved quickly. We ensure that clients are told, orally and in writing, that students need time, and that the client should make clear if this is a problem for him or her. Having said that, we do not have problem files which fester in the cabinet unattended: we are not pursuing fees targets, and can turn work away to create time to work on present cases. Also students speed up during the course with no loss of quality.

Supervision in a student legal office requires a real commitment of resources. Cases that benefit students during their 25 weeks of availability often still have to be handled in June, December or August. Fortunately this school has many solicitors, nearly half of the staff in fact. Some already have practising certificates; many were willing to apply. So from 1991 to 1994 we went from two to 14 solicitor supervisors. But the problem of quality, year-round, coverage has now been addressed with the appointment of a dedicated solicitor.

With more supervisors, students have been able to specialise to an extent. While there is still initial diagnostic and advice/referral work to be done, often outside the area of specialisation, supervisors try to attract case work for their students in their own preferred area. Employment law has attracted students and clients, and fits the student year well, since cases are likely to be started and finished in a few months as well as affording rights of audience. Welfare, housing and small claims are other significant areas, but we also cover criminal appeals (referred from Liberty), family, child care, copyright, planning, and cases that do not fit any category.

I have mentioned more than once the resource commitment required. It is possible that this could put off any Law School that feels it is already stretched. What I, and colleagues here and elsewhere, recognise is that we are not only putting more in, we (students and staff) are getting more out. The research still needs to be done, but my hunch is that in terms of achieving objectives – real student learning – the clinical method may turn out to be cheaper than traditional teaching. Regrettably achievement of objectives is not prominent on most universities' balance sheets. I believe one hour of my time with six students, generating ten times that amount of self-directed intense activity, may compare well with one hour of my time lecturing to 100 students, who manage on a good day 50% attention and may do little follow-up.

Student Law Office in an exempting degree

We now come to the present, the clinical work that is a compulsory part of the four-year Exempting Degree. The 1994/95 programme is the first time we have had two full years of students conducting advice and case work. The work in the third year is graded for degree classification, the assessment covering research, problem solving, interviewing, professional responsibility, and drafting. It is based on records and critical analysis prepared by the student.

The Law Office itself is a vibrant, noisy, overcrowded but, underneath it all, efficient place, where students keep good files (with much chasing), messages fly around but end up in the right places, quality decisions are made, and students are learning for themselves. Listen in to any conversation between students, and you will hear them developing their understanding of law, ethics and legal practice. You will hear students complaining, for once, not about the burden of assignments or boring lectures, but about the unfairness of a legal decision, or the tactics of an opponent.

200 students are queuing up to gain access to the computers, work space, staff advisers and the secretary. We have a dedicated Practice Library, but most work is confidential and can only be carried out in the Law Office itself.

Students are divided into firms to work jointly on cases. Over the past three years, the firm sizes have ranged from four to ten, and, staff resources permitting, I consider the ideal to be five. These firms meet once per week to review every case handled, and meticulous minutes are required. Far more meetings take place than that, though, since clients are interviewed, documents prepared, negotiations and, sometimes, hearings prepared for. All these activities require supervision. A half day in court takes days of preparatory work.

The way we organise our operating systems is changing all the time. To allow for specialisation by students, we tried abandoning advice rotas, and allocating new clients to firms after a diagnostic conversation on the phone. This was administratively too complex, and rotas have been re-established.

Rotas are particularly important during the autumn, in order to attract sufficient work for 200 students to have something to work on. We have even had to advertise (once). We are advising over 500 clients a year, though the number of cases taken on is much lower.

Now where?

Supervisors are largely positive about their Law Office work. Some would even like to devote more time to it, and one direction is to reduce the numbers of supervisors by taking them off some traditional teaching and making Law Office teaching a specialisation. For we have learned that it is hard to dabble. The need to supervise interrupts concentration, and the need to avoid complaints to the Solicitors' Complaints Bureau interrupts sleep. Not all lecturers are comfortable combining academic work with this legal practice. But clinical specialisation may have dangerous implications for career development, and the problems caused by hiving off the clinic from the regular faculty is well documented in the States.

We are learning that there is no point being so busy that there is inadequate time for supervisors and students to reflect in depth on the work, the law, the procedure, and the social and moral issues. Just doing the work well misses the educational value. So we are planning to reduce the number of cases a student handles in their first clinical year, focusing on the training, on shadowing, and learning to reflect critically on the work their colleagues in their second year are handling. Practical legal research method, based on live client work, will be emphasised more strongly.

Should we apply for a legal aid franchise? We have so far in the Law Office resisted any process that would prioritise legal service ahead of educational provision. We do not – at least at present – want to have to take on cases where there is no student benefiting. I do not want us to become an advice factory. Students need time on each case to learn to be thorough and professional. The rush can come later.

Should we make it optional not compulsory? As we are offering at Northumbria a combined academic and vocational course, it is hard to imagine a student not wishing to be involved. For those who realise they are no longer interested in practice as a solicitor, we offer an honours degree at three years, so those students need not be compelled to do two years of clinical work. The main clinical work has, in fact, been postponed until Year 4 for this reason.

Issues in clinical legal education

In this chapter I have concentrated on the history. I have omitted many topics which might be of interest and relevance. There are huge numbers of issues worth discussing when setting up any kind of real client programme. Readers are invited to join the Clinical Legal Education Organisation, where debate on questions of this type is continuous. (CLEO can be contacted via the School of Law, University of Northumbria, Newcastle upon Tyne NE1 8ST.)

Here is the à la carte menu of just a few other issues on offer for discussion.

Is a clinic entitled to recover costs from opponents?

If you hold yourselves out as a solicitor clinic, on the Northumbria or Sheffield Hallam model, I believe the answer is yes: see May [1994] *Legal Action* 10. Don't count on huge earnings. A large number of our clients do not qualify for green form advice and we take on many cases where legal aid certificates are hard or impossible to get. We make enough to buy tea and coffee for clients, and to contribute towards computers, books and stationery.

Should the Student Law Office go on the record in proceedings?

If the client is legally aided, of course we must. But from having gone onto the record without thinking in every case when this was first possible, we have retreated to a more cautious position where, generally, the client goes on the record and we advise and assist. In this way we are making it plain that our commitment is not necessarily for the entire lifetime of the case. We require students to explain this to clients. (In practice we rarely drop a case until its conclusion.)

What about assessment of live-client work?

We work closely with students. Much of what they finally produce has been shaped under our guidance. (But isn't that what we want from education?) Each client poses a different challenge, and tasks cannot be moderated. It is also found by clinicians that students get higher grades than elsewhere in their studies, which can lead to unpopularity or a suggestion of lack of rigour. Clinical students receive a great deal of support and feedback. They work very hard. They put in large numbers of hours. Is it any surprise that they do so well?

We are still feeling our way. However, at least we are attempting to assess those skills we value, not just those that can be demonstrated in an exam.

Can part time students get involved?

I have involved volunteer part time students for many years. I often end up, between meetings with the students, having to do much of the case work myself. I am now getting too old to maintain such martyrdom. I recommend part time students do advice work only, and other systems be established to handle casework arising out of such advice work (referral to other parts of the clinical programme, as to other agencies).

How does the profession like it?

Reactions range from the frequent 'I wish we'd had it in my day' to the opponent who whinges, 'It's not fair, you have more resources' or 'we don't want to deal with a student, give me your supervisor'. Mostly we encounter courtesy and encouragement from all quarters, including the professional bodies like the Legal Aid Board, judges, tribunals, court staff, and opponents. We have been careful to foster links with the Law Society, the Bar, and other agencies. An advisory committee meets twice a year and gives us great support, both inside and outside the meetings.

How does the University like it?

They like it, even though we constantly ask for extra resources. We have been generously treated, but clinical work is so resource hungry that it can, as resourced at present, only ever thrive on the enthusiasm of the staff. And it does. The University particularly likes it when the Funding Council or the Law Society visits and delivers accolades about this real student centred learning. And it helps to know that this is the sort of thing the Lord Chancellor is probably looking for after he finishes his consultations on the academic stage of legal education.

How important is specialisation?

All the clinical programmes I have heard of in America are special-ised. They have criminal appeal clinics, civil rights clinics and so on – not generic clinics. We started on a generic model, and still have a unified programme with only limited opportunities to specialise. In our experience specialisation works best where the student has chosen, and is simultaneously pursuing, an academic subject in that area. Surprisingly, students themselves are mixed in their own desire to specialise, and some can be resistant to specialising in an area they did not choose. Specialisation assists the supervisor, of course, but as a non-specialist I have been able to offer students interesting cases in many areas, and have found students hardly ever refuse interesting work. (All legal work can be interesting to a student since it is not routine.)

Is there any work we cannot do?

We avoid work, at present, that will peak outside term time (in so far as we can predict this). We decided, after lengthy debate, to avoid suing solicitors or making complaints against them. This limits our scope, as often the client who comes to this kind of agency is dissatis-fied with their previous solicitor. We advise such clients of their options, but believe for two reasons we should not (yet) undertake such work. Firstly, we do not wish to appear 'anti solicitor', and given that wish, might be unable to pursue cases with proper robust-ness. Secondly, it is an area of specialisation where a student might feel at a particular disadvantage. But this decision could be – indeed is – seen as a failure of confidence by some colleagues.

Students with proper supervision are probably capable of any work. For example, in America graduate students represent defendants in capital cases, and take cases to the Supreme Court. Should we take on such weighty cases? Our students, unlike US law students, are not graduates. Also the big cases are, currently, picked up by private practice. The demand is not yet there, and the educational value of small cases, where the student can take the major share of responsibility, is, at present, sufficiently clear. Complex cases demand very high quality supervision, which leads to important resourcing decisions. Big value cases have more obvious implications – if we get a big case wrong there is potentially more publicity and a big claim on insurance.

What about prioritising poor clients' needs, as Law Centres do? This is the approach of all American clinics that I am aware of. Again, this is a subject of debate at Northumbria. Many clients are in fact poor, and no dilemma arises. But some well-off clients have come to the Student Law Office, for advice and possibly representation, on a range of matters. So far, we have chosen to act for them, as with poor clients, if we can identify the educational value. But if we end up antagonising private practice, by taking on those whose motivation is only to save legal fees, we will need to think again. If by acting for one large landlord we have a conflict of interest with large numbers of potential tenant clients, we may lose a larger clientele whose cases are educationally useful. Also I believe it is satisfying for the University to make a contribution to the community – which supports it. What better way than meeting some unmet legal need?

What about long-term goals?

Becoming a doctor and qualifying as a solicitor both take the same time. Medical students are introduced to clinical practice at almost every stage of the course, and their education is usually at the same medical school from start to finish. (It is also grant aided throughout, but that is certainly a closed door for lawyers).

Is it possible to envisage a university law school emulating a medical school, and providing similar practical training? To do so on such a model we would need a large number of clients just like a teaching hospital needs patients. We would clearly need to become a service provider as well as an educational institution. This has major funding implications. The NHS underwrites teaching hospitals. The Law Office would require at least a franchise for legal aid, or direct reliable funding from another source. It would change the nature of law teaching and legal research at the University, which would become clinically driven. Instead of focusing on small cases, we could aim to deal with cases at the cutting edge of law development, combining practice with research.

Northumbria has put its foot in this water. We have already provided articles to an existing lecturer wishing to qualify. We will replace him with two more trainees who will assist with Law Office work and other skills or practice orientated workshops. We have also appointed a solicitor to co-ordinate our case work.

Summary and conclusion

The Northumbria Student Law Office has grown incrementally. Other clinical programmes have grown in other universities in different ways, driven by their own enthusiasms and resources. We have come to believe that this hands on, live legal office is the best vehicle for learning about the practice of law alongside students' academic pursuits. But we have also learned that this approach is resource hungry, and requires dedication. Any enthusiast who can offer the dedication is recommended to obtain a long-term commitment to provide these resources before launching a clinical office.

Our original goal, of providing a distinctive degree programme, has without doubt been met. There is no doubt that a place on Northumbria's Exempting Degree is highly coveted by potential lawyers.

Chapter 7

Problem-based learning in legal education
David A Cruickshank[1]

Introduction

Problem-based learning is a rapidly spreading learning strategy used
internationally in schools of management, medicine, nursing, agri-
culture and, in one or two cases, law.[2] Because claims made in
support of problem-based learning fit closely with the goals of professional legal education (see, eg, Cruickshank (1985); Tobin (1987))
and with some of the attributes of competent legal practitioners,
there is merit in considering the use of this learning method at all
stages of legal education. In this paper there will be an explanation
of problem-based learning and its uses in full curriculum or partial
curriculum settings. I will explore the advantages and disadvantages

---

1 The author wishes to acknowledge the work of Keith Winsor of the College of
   Law, Sydney, whose article 'Toe in the Bathwater: Testing the Temperature
   with Problem-Based Learning' (1989) was a fundamental starting point for this
   paper.
2 Problem-based learning across the full curriculum can be found at McMaster
   University (Hamilton, Ontario, Canada)(medicine, nursing, occupational
   health), the University of Newcastle (Newcastle, NSW, Australia) (medicine), the
   Royal Melbourne Institute of Technology (Melbourne, Victoria, Australia)
   (management), and Hawkesbury Agricultural College, (Hawkesbury, NSW,
   Australia). There is an optional stream of law studies at the South Western
   University School of Law (Los Angeles, California) known as the SCALE programme. It uses problems as the vehicle for learning legal concepts (ie, 'agency')
   rather than traditional legal subjects. The only full undergraduate curriculum in
   law structured on problem-based learning is at the University of Limburg
   (Maastricht, Netherlands), where medicine and other professional faculties use
   the same core approach. Since 1991 it has also provided the underlying model
   for curriculum design of the new Postgraduate Certificate of Laws (PCLL)
   course at the City Polytechnic of Hong Kong: see Macfarlane et al (1992).

of problem-based learning. In addition, it will be important to distinguish the skill of problem-solving and what the research literature tells us about its relationship to problem-based learning.

Problem-based learning has the potential to address some of the criticisms aimed at traditional law school learning, professional training course methods, and the delivery of typical continuing legal education programmes. Furthermore, problem-based learning may promote greater individual capacities for 'learning how to learn' in the context of legal practice. The paper will suggest concrete means for using this learning method to meet the criticisms.

Finally, there will be discussion of the delivery requirements for effective problem-based learning. What does it mean in terms of instructional skills, materials, learning resources, time, assessment methods, and cost? At the implementation stage, particularly in professional legal training, there are challenges of fitting an experiment in problem-based learning together with a course constrained by time and a full agenda of skills, legal subjects and assessments. Similar issues face a law school curriculum committee or continuing legal education (CLE) programme designers.

What is problem-based learning?

Problem-based learning is a learning method more than a teaching method. The student or participant is presented with a problem situation before any subject-matter knowledge is acquired. The students, in small groups usually, analyse the problem and identify resources for learning how to solve it. Next, they independently pursue those resources and bring their new knowledge back to the groups and apply it to the problem.

Although the students are meant to solve the problem, the skill of problem-solving is only one objective of the learning method. More importantly, the participants learn how to use a variety of resources, beyond a library or textbook. In so doing, they 'learn how to learn' with guidance from an instructor who acts as a facilitator.

The detailed steps in a problem-based learning course or exercise have been described by Barrows and Tamblyn (1980), pp 191–2, who pioneered the method at the McMaster University Medical School:

1. The problem is encountered first in the learning sequence, before any preparation or study has occurred.

2. The problem situation is presented to the student in the same way it would present in reality.
3. The student works with the problem in a manner that permits his ability to reason and apply knowledge to be challenged and evaluated, appropriate to his level of learning.
4. Needed areas of learning are identified in the process of work with the problem and used as a guide to individualised study.
5. The skills and knowledge acquired by this study are applied back to the problem, to evaluate the effectiveness of learning and to reinforce learning.
6. The learning that has occurred in work with the problem and in individualised study is summarised and integrated into the student's existing knowledge and skills.

Boud (1985) has compiled a list of other key characteristics of problem-based learning (pp 15–16):

1. An acknowledgement of the base of experience of learners. At any level students make an important contribution to learning by drawing upon their own experience: see, for example, Evans (1981) and Keeton (1977).
2. An emphasis on students taking responsibility for their own learning. Students are expected to take an active part in planning, organising and evaluating their own learning. They are not simply subjected to activities designed and controlled by others. This issue is discussed in detail in Boud (1981).
3. They are multidisciplinary or transdisciplinary. If problems are the focus of learning then courses cannot fit into the well-defined categories of existing subject divisions. They necessarily cross established boundaries between disciplines. Staff are thus drawn into areas which fall outside their recognised academic expertise.
4. Theory and practice are inextricably intertwined. There is no pre-established division between concepts and applications. Theory is drawn naturally into knowledge through the demands of problem-solutions: see Argyris & Schön (1974); Argyris (1982).
5. There is a focus on the processes of knowledge acquisition rather than the products of such processes. Students are confronted with the need to know how to approach a problem and acquire new knowledge (Woods (1983)), and how to process their experiences through various forms of reflection: see Boud, Keogh and Walker (1985); Schön (1983).

6. The role of staff changes from that of instructor to that of facilitator. Less emphasis is placed on the presentation of information, more on assisting students to acquire skills of learning and problem-solution: see Knowles (1975).
7. The focus of student assessment changes from staff assessment of outcomes of learning to student self and peer assessment. Students must learn how to assess their own learning rather than to rely on others for this: see Boud and Lublin (1983).
8. Often explicit attention is given to communications and human relations skills even in highly technical areas. Students learn that in order to acquire knowledge and to communicate their understanding they need skills which go beyond the technical areas in which they are involved: Jaques (1984).

Problem-based learning must be contrasted with teacher-based learning and text or media-based learning. Most of us are familiar with teacher-based learning at all levels of legal education. Woods (1985) has described the pattern (pp 15–16):

> In 'teacher-based' learning the teacher selects the knowledge, creates the learning environment, develops and uses the evaluation materials, presents the knowledge and the problems, and provides a personal image of a professional. The students are locked into the pacing and sequencing used by the teacher. They have little control over the situation.

Teaching most often amounts to didactic instruction, whereas problem-based learning focuses on the student's learning.

Professional legal training and some CLE courses use text or media-based learning, in addition to teacher-based training. Although the teacher selects the material, the student can control what is to be read and applied. For example, there may be self-tests or assignments. The student can 'shop around' in assigned practice materials, casebooks, or statutes in order to meet a standard prescribed by the expert teacher. Unlike teacher-based learning, it is more difficult to see the professional expert in action.

A frequent response of teachers to problem-based learning is: 'But I use problems in class all the time; my students are learning through problems.' In fact, most teachers use problems to test, or promote application of, previously acquired knowledge. The problem is not posed first in the learning sequence. There is no independent inquiry outside of the assigned materials or resources. The teacher remains the expert who eventually provides a solution to the problem. Students may learn, by imitating the expert's steps, some problem-solving skills. Nevertheless, the use of problems in this way does not meet the criteria for problem-based learning.

Barrows (1986) has developed a taxonomy of problem-based learning methods that can help to understand how problems are now used by educators. Only the last two of his methods represent problem-based learning that meet the criteria described at the beginning of this paper. Barrows's taxonomy appears to be organised from 'least learner-oriented' to 'most learner-oriented':

1. *Lecture-based cases* The teacher presents information, then speaks about one or two written problems to illustrate the application of the information.

2. *Case-based lecture* Here the students receive a written problem in advance. The problem touches on the key material to be covered in the lecture.

3. *Case method* This is the method familiar to some business schools and most law school teachers. Students study written problem materials in preparation for a class discussion. The teacher through question-and-answer dialogue will extract the key principles from the problem, rather than necessarily solve the problem.

4. *Modified case-based* The students receive a written problem, but it contains limited facts. The students must analyse the problem and list information to be gathered. In a second class period, the student may apply the new information. In a computer assisted learning context, the student could make limited inquiries, thus interacting with the problem. However, the method is still structured around the written case and the teacher's analysis of the case.

5. *Problem-based* The problem is presented to the student as a simulated client. Through a real interview and investigation of facts, guided by a facilitator, the student meets the problem as in reality. Instead of a simulated client, there could be other 'trigger material'[3] to launch the inquiries. The students later take up a proposed solution.

---

3 The 'trigger materials', discussed below at p 210, can be patient histories, videotapes, lab reports, etc in the medical context. In legal problems they could be telephone messages, discovery (deposition) transcripts, written contracts, etc.

6.   *Closed loop or reiterative problem-based*   This method goes beyond the problem analysis and inquiry stages. There is a follow-up process for students to review and evaluate the reasoning process they used to solve the problem. This reflective stage encourages skill development in 'learning how to learn' for future problems.

Problems v exercises

Another issue arises from the teacher's proclamation that 'I use problems'. Woods (1985) has argued that most problems used by teachers are 'exercises' masquerading as 'problems' (p 20). In an exercise, the student has seen something similar before. An analytical method or previous approach suggests itself immediately. The student has an idea about how to solve it and the effort ahead involves only time and care in working through the exercise. In the context of law school classroom settings, the use of a 'problem' that falls between two lines of cases in an upper year course is a good example. Students by this time know how to reconcile conflicting cases and how to construct arguments that will solve the 'problem' in favour of one shade of grey or the other. In the lexicon of problem-based learning writers, this is solving an 'exercise', not a problem.

A true problem is something the student has never seen before. It throws up no clear pathways to a solution. Instead of just the basic knowledge, comprehension and application skills called for in the 'exercise', the student must use new means of analysis and synthesis (see Bloom (1956)) and find new resources even to tackle the problem. It is a struggle and many students find it upsetting. In professional legal training, the British Columbia course[4] uses a true problem in conveyancing. With very little prior instruction and some materials, the students are asked to complete a statement of adjustments following the closing of the hypothetical residential conveyance they have

---

4   The Professional Legal Training Course in British Columbia, Canada has been operating as a 10-week, residential full-time bar admission course since 1984. It is one of the first of modern practical training courses that focus on legal skills and transactions more than on lectures on practice, procedure and substance; see further Cruickshank (1985); Jones (1989). The conveyancing transaction is used to teach legal writing and the statement of adjustments is part of the report to the client. In more recent offerings of the course, instructors have given more initial guidance on the assignment, thus reducing student anxiety, but also diminishing the 'problem' value of the assignment.

studied. Many students return to class, after four or five hours of work, with no solution. They have not been able to use application, analysis and synthesis skills to correct the concepts of sale and purchase to the mathematical balance that must be reported to the client. They would agree with Woods (1985) that 'Problems are challenging! Exercises are straight work' (p 23).

Contrast the statement of adjustments problem to an exercise in drafting a statement of claim.[5] After prior instruction, readings, guidance from the Rules of Court, and several model statements of claim, the students are given a set of facts. They draft a statement of claim reasonably quickly. They demonstrate sound application of most substantive requirements and procedural rules. They struggle with drafting skills, but they produce a reasonable product. In the main, the students have solved an exercise, not a problem.

Donald Schön (1987), an articulate critic of current education for the professions, has suggested that practitioners need to learn how to handle the 'indeterminate zones' of practice. These are the true problems, which cannot be solved by the mere application of stored knowledge. Schön prescribes a practice-centred form of learning and calls for students and experienced practitioners to develop a new skill of 'reflection in action'. His preferred educational setting would be a 'reflective practicum'. Without delving into Schön's work in detail, it can be said that it resonates in the same frequency as that of problem-based learning advocates. Both point out the failure of traditional professional education to fuse theory and practice and to ground learning in actual or very realistic experiences. Both point to the challenges, and the learning potential, created by indeterminate problems. For the educator, the challenge becomes one of designing experience-based problems, not just exercises.

When we apply an understanding of 'problems v exercises' to the spectrum of legal education, the factor of ever-increasing professional experience must be taken into account. Early in university education, most new situations are true problems. With new learning and skills, the later problems become exercises. Fewer situations are true problems. At professional entry, the problem barrier is high once again. But over time practice problems, too, become exercises. One researcher in the medical field has estimated that an experienced

5 This exercise is part of a civil litigation transaction in the British Columbia Professional Legal Training Course.

medical doctor only encounters about 5% of problems in his or her practice (Norman, cited in Woods (1985), p 20). The rest of the cases represent something seen before. Woods (1985) has illustrated the diminishing confrontation of true problems as practice experience grows (p 21):

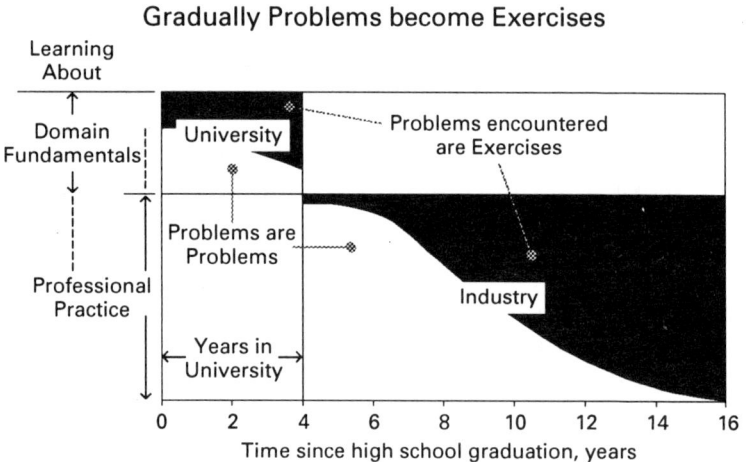

Gradually Problems become Exercises

Learning About

Domain Fundamentals

University — Problems encountered are Exercises

Problems are Problems

Professional Practice

Industry

Years in University

0   2   4   6   8   10   12   14   16
Time since high school graduation, years

In the legal education context, the proper design and use of problems will have to be adjusted to the typical experience level of the participants. Senior law students should be challenged with new research dilemmas. Professional training students should learn about the many resources available to an entry-level lawyer for solving problems. Continuing legal education (CLE) participants will want their experience recognised: they will have to meet a realistic problem that cannot be solved with well-known strategies.

Problem-based learning and problem-solving

These terms are too often presented as synonymous or as having a hand-in-glove relationship. Neither description is accurate. By way of review, here is a good summary definition of problem-based learning:

Problem-based learning is a process of acquiring understanding, knowledge, skills and attitudes in the context of an unfamiliar situation, and applying such learning to that situation. The process is designed to provide relevance and thus stimulus for learning. It should offer opportunities for application of what has been learned and, therefore, rapid feedback to the learner about the success or otherwise of his studies. Over and above all this, problem-based learning should provide continuous practice in logical analytical thinking and practice in structuring one's own learning.

Engel

The same author contrasts the skill of problem-solving:

Problem solving, to me, is an intellectual approach to making decisions in the face of a situation in which the nature and interplay of its components are not immediately obvious or fully identified.

The intellectual process, or cognitive skill, used in problem-solving may vary with subject content and a variety of associated skills. Woods (1985) defines problem-solving (p 23) as:

The process whereby a 'best' value is determined for some objective or unknown subject to a specific set of constraints and criteria.

He provides a more helpful list of apparent components at work in effective problem-solving (p 24):

- an organised approach or 'strategy';
- skill with such thinking abilities as creativity, analysis, generalisation, simplification, and broadening perspectives;
- skill with adjusting and controlling our attitudes;
- an ability to apply a wide variety of hints or heuristics that help in problem-solving;
- skill at evaluation;
- a range of prerequisite skills.

Could we take these components and develop a teaching strategy in law, so that everyone could learn an explicit problem-solving skill? Some legal scholars have recommended a method and a teaching strategy: see Nathanson (1989), (1992); Freund (1979). But the empirical researchers are not so confident. Researchers in science education taught one group explicit general problem-solving skills and compared their performance on specific physics problems to those who did not receive problem-solving lessons. There was no clear demonstration that the explicitly taught students were faster in solving problems. Although the results of the experiments would not transfer to large numbers, the researchers did find that explicit teaching goals aimed at cognitive skills were helpful to students: see Larkin & Reif (1976).

In medical education, the profession which has the longest experience with problem-based learning, there is doubt arising from experiments on problem-solving effectiveness. Reviewing the research some years ago, Nu Viet Vu (1980) declared (p 454):

> Although the general processes and skills of medical problem-solving have been assessed, it has not been clearly established how stable they are within an individual, or how they influence the effectiveness of problem-solving. Such results would provide answers concerning how to predict problem-solving more accurately. For example, if content is one factor which may affect problem-solving performance, is it necessary to measure the skills of incoming students independently of their knowledge? On the other hand, if skills are also a factor, it is important to determine how they affect performance and how they interact with other factors.

More recent research at McMaster University Medical School has questioned whether problem-solving has the characteristics of a skill (ie, independent of knowledge, transferable, amenable to instruction). One conclusion was:

> General problem-solving skills may exist. However, they do not appear to be assessed by any of the measures of problem-solving we have used in medical education. Furthermore, studies in a variety of disciplines suggest that even if these skills do exist, they do not go far in explaining the acquisition of expertise.
>
> Norman (1988), p 281

In short, we are not sure how the experts got their skills, whether they are independent of specialist knowledge, and whether they are transferable skills.

The overall conclusion about problem-solving skills is that there is no one model for learning them. We all have different learning styles and preferred strategies. Novices and experts operate quite differently, for example. Novices work backwards from a goal, trying to find an equation or pattern that will lead to the goal. This 'means–ends analysis' has been contrasted with the 'schemas' used by experts. The experts work forward from the givens. They have a structure, or 'schema' for placing the new problem against many previously-learned categories of problems. Then the experts follow the solution mode suggested by previously successful modes in the problem category: see Sweller (1985), pp 230–1. Another strength of experts is that they generate better hypotheses: see Norman (1988), p 280. Furthermore, when they draw a principle from memory, they do so with 'chunks' of associated principles, unlike novices who store principles individually: see, for example, Greenfield (1987).

If we could bottle up these expert characteristics and teach them, surely we could bridge the gap between novices and experts? Unfortunately, cognitive learning studies suggest that it takes about ten years to acquire expertise in problem-solving. Moreover, expert reasoning patterns are specific to a context and do not transfer easily to another area: see Hayes (1981). This does not suggest that we give up on bridging the gap. It means that we cannot expect great gains towards sophisticated expertise in the short time periods allocated to formal, conventional, legal education. A long-range approach, involving new educational methods at all levels and the teaching of problem-solving in continuing legal education, could bring lawyers from novices to experts more effectively and more quickly.

On the whole, the teaching of problem-solving skills is a very complex issue that must be separated from the learning method of problem-based learning. One could be pessimistic about extracting any worthwhile teaching approaches that would be supported by research data yielding better problem-solving skill outcomes. Nevertheless, there is a strong consensus in the literature that problem-solving strategies (not a single 'model' skill) can and should be taught.

These problem-solving strategies and hints (or 'heuristics' as they are labelled by the writers) have been summarised by Rubinstein (1975), (1980):

1. *Total picture* Before you attempt a solution to a problem, avoid getting lost in detail. Go over the elements of the problem rapidly several times until a pattern or a total picture emerges. Try to get the picture of the forest before you get lost in the trees.

2. *Withhold your judgment* Do not commit yourself too early to a course of action. You may find it hard to break away from the path, if it turns out to be the wrong one. Search for a number of paths simultaneously and use signs of progress to guide you to the path that appears most plausible.

3. *Models* Verbalise; use language to simplify the statement of the problem; write it down. Use mathematical or graphical pictorial models. Use abstract models such as symbols and equations, or use concrete models in the form of objects. A

model is a similar representation of the real world problem: it is supposed to help you.

4. *Change in representation*   Problem-solving can also be viewed as a change in representation. The solutions of many problems in algebra and mathematics in general consist of transformations of the given information so as to make the solution, which is obscure, become transparent in a new form of representation. Most mathematical derivations follow this route.

5. *Asking the right questions*   Language in all its forms is a most powerful tool in problem-solving. Asking the right question, uttering the correct word, or hearing it, may direct your processing unit to the appropriate region in your long-term storage to retrieve complete blocks of information that will guide you to a successful solution.

6. *Will to doubt*   Have a will to doubt. Accept premises as tentative to varying degrees, but be flexible and ready to question their credibility, and, if necessary, prise yourself loose from fixed convictions and reject them. Rejection may take the form of innovation, because to innovate is, psychologically at least, to overcome or discard the old if not always to reject it outright.

7. *Working backwards*   Do not start at the beginning and follow systematically step by step to the end goal. The solution path is as important as the answer and, in problems where the goal is specified, the path is the solution.

8. *Stable substructures*   In complex problems it helps to proceed in a way that permits you to return to your partial solution after interruptions. Stable substructures that do not collapse or disappear when you do not tend to them will serve this purpose.

9. *Analogies and metaphors*   Use an analogy whenever you can think of one. An analogy provides a model which serves as a guide to identify the elements of a problem as parts of a more complete structure. It also helps recognise phases as elements of a complete process.

10. *Talk*   When you are stuck after an intensive effort to solve a problem, it is wise to take a break and do something else. It is also helpful to talk about your problem at various stages in your search for a solution. Talking to someone may help you prise yourself loose from the constraints we mentioned, because your colleague may have a different world view and he may direct you to new avenues of search when he utters a word or asks a question.

The only drawback to these strategies is that there is no unifying theory about how and when to use them in particular fields of knowledge or on particular problems. Some inroads towards a general theory have been made, but the conclusion is that the mental process in solving a problem depends both on the characteristics of the problem and the knowledge of the problem-solver: see Greeno (1980), p 18. This is not the kind of uncertainty that legal educators or learners would like to endure in the course of curriculum reform.

It is submitted that our goals must be less ambitious. We cannot guarantee that problem-based learning will make everyone better at solving problems, nor that problem-solving skills can be taught the way that we teach advocacy skills. We should use problem-based learning to expose students to a variety of problem-solving strategies, like those suggested by Rubinstein or those used by expert lawyers. In problem-based learning, the instructor facilitates reflection on the learning process. Unlike other learning methods, this step alone may accomplish these more limited goals:

1. a basis for trial-and-error use of problem-solving strategies and hints;
2. a connection for the individual between the specific knowledge base and best personal approaches to typical problems;
3. an exposure to how others, peers and experts, solve the same problems;
4. a potential for learning and articulating an individualised method of problem-solving that will shorten the time span between novice and expert skill attainment.

Advantages of problem-based learning

Reviewing the literature and reflecting on a law school course experiment,[6] it is possible to list advantages claimed for problem-based

---

6 In 1990 in an Administrative Law course for second and third year students at the University of British Columbia, the author conducted two experiments in problem-based learning. A full-class experiment, using background readings and problems for application in class, ran for two months. The more 'pure' form of problem-based learning was conducted with a volunteer small group who were presented with a unique problem on regulation of aquaculture. They discussed the issues at the first session, researched the problem over three weeks, and returned for a follow-up discussion of their research products. All participants reported that it was a highly motivating experience, realistic, and contrary to the norm of their legal education.

learning. As with conventional instruction, there is not much empirical evidence to support the asserted advantages. But as an alternative model of designing instruction, it clearly will appeal to those who want to address a range of learning styles.

Motivation

There is great agreement among the writers that participants enjoy their learning more. They are excited about their work because they are pursuing individual learning objectives and producing a product of their own rather than a required essay or a knowledge-based test.

Testing problem-solving strategies

Although earlier writers such as Barrows & Tamblyn (1980) claimed that students would develop problem-solving skills (p 13), a more modest advantage should be claimed, as discussed above. Through explicit learning of problem-solving strategies and the provision of an immediate environment for applying them, students should have a superior 'test track' for developing individualised 'best' strategies.

Recall information in context

Knowledge can be recalled much better in the context in which it was learned. If we learned something in a courtroom setting, for example, we may recall it better in that same environment. There is some empirical evidence in medical education that students in a problem-based learning curriculum are better at recalling knowledge in the context of real patient problems, compared to students from a conventional curriculum school: see Norman (1988), p 283. That finding has critical implications for the diagnostic skills of the doctor, since they spring from a rapid scan of information. It is not known whether these results would hold true for a young lawyer recalling information for the purpose of 'diagnosing' a client's problem.

Relevance of knowledge to tasks

Students working with realistic problems can see the importance of legal concepts and knowledge because the tasks required to attack the problem call upon that base immediately. This relates to the motivation factor. When students can translate successful research, reading and comprehension into a practical solution, they will see the knowledge base as highly relevant. This in turn motivates them to be open to all kinds of potentially useful concepts and knowledge.

Expansion of learning resources

By pushing the student beyond prescribed materials, indeed, beyond the law library, the method expands the student's notion of where to obtain knowledge or skills. In the second phase of problem-based learning, the student considers whether telephone contacts, video-tapes, court observations, simulated client interviews, or other resources would be most helpful. Experienced lawyers know well that the answers are not always in the law reports.

Problem-based learning has the advantage of teaching this lesson through personal discovery.[7]

Interdisciplinary learning

Problems are frequently designed to cut across traditional subjects and disciplines. The student has ample scope to pursue a learning objective outside the disciplinary 'box'. For example, a personal injury problem could lead to medical textbooks, charts, and models which help the student understand a soft-tissue injury. It could require research in contract law or consumer protection statutes. This can be accomplished in conventional instruction, but the teacher's choice of 'appropriate' interdisciplinary input is more limiting for individual learning.

Perception of entry-level preparedness

Do graduates of problem-based learning institutions see themselves as skilled problem-solvers and self-learners? Although personal per-ception is not a measure of how graduates will actually perform, it

---

7   In the experiment at the University of British Columbia described above, one student spent two days looking for judicial review decisions on aquaculture. He found nothing and felt let down because his normal thoroughness in case law research had failed. During self-assessment of his learning, he reported that the problem had taught him to try many other strategies besides case research. In future, he suggested, he would spend little time on case research until he first attempted other problem-solving and research strategies.

does reflect on the professional preparatory education that they have just experienced. McMaster medical school graduates, surveyed at periods of two years or five years after graduation, reported that they felt 'well prepared' or 'prepared' for their first postgraduate year in the following areas (Woodward & Ferrier (1983), p 55):
- preparation for independent learning (96%);
- problem-solving (94%);
- self-evaluation techniques (89.2%).

More than half of the graduates reported that they felt 'better prepared' in each of the three categories than their fellow trainees. If these findings were replicated for other problem-based learning graduates, we could expect those graduates to feel confident in the very skills and learning attitudes to which their education was directed.

The perception of others supports the competence felt by graduates. McMaster has had a higher rate of 'first match' (77%) of its graduates and internship employers compared to other medical schools: see Neufeld & Sibley (1989). Furthermore, clinical supervisors rated interns from McMaster quite highly. Compared to a control group from other medical schools, clinical supervisors rated McMaster graduates as 'much better' 26.1% of the time and 'better' 38.3% of the time (combined 64.4%) in their clinical work: see Woodward & McAuley (1983).

Self-directed not teacher-centred learning

The use of problem-based learning facilitates the skill of 'learning how to learn'. It puts the focus of responsibility for learning on the student instead of the teacher. The teacher's time goes into problem design, resource building and facilitating group discussions, rather than lecture preparation. The teacher promotes student abilities in self-reflection and self-evaluation, rather than ability to mirror the teacher's processes. The advantage is that students will be able to apply these skills to on-the-job learning and continuing professional education opportunities. As an additional benefit, teachers will be able to concentrate on creating problem challenges for students' own learning instead of on repetitive modes of transmitting knowledge.

Self-directed learning also draws on the students' own experiences and encourages the use and sharing of those experiences. This is highly consistent with the principles of adult education.

The value of self-directed learning will only be esteemed if the assessment system also rewards it. Therefore, the advantage of problem-based learning will be realised if the instructor and peers assess the learning skills of the individual, not just the product of his or her work.

Small group skills

Problem-based learning works best in groups of six to eight students, although some institutions have attempted group sizes of up to 25.[8] Students learn interaction skills, peer evaluation techniques, and the necessity of co-operation. In addition, they can test their ideas and receive immediate feedback. Other forms of tutorial instruction have these advantages, but they do not pick up the learning issues as PBL instruction does in its last phase.

Disadvantages of problem-based learning

Most disadvantages of the method have been asserted in the health sciences literature: see Hamilton (1976). There are responses to these disadvantages, but the counter-arguments will not be emphasised here.

Basic theory and knowledge are lacking

The PBL method, in health sciences, stresses patient evaluation and case management at the expense of learning in basic sciences. In law, this would translate to gaps in knowledge about substantive law subjects. Problem-based learning could be very effective for learning concepts (ie 'intention'), as it is in the Los Angeles SCALE programme (Johnson (1982)), where the teaching of concepts is done through problems that cut across doctrinal subjects. But, as a full-curriculum approach, it may leave students short of rule-oriented knowledge in many subjects.

---

8   Ryan and Little (1989) report ratios of 1:25 for first year and 1:12 for upper year classes in the School of Nursing and Health Sciences at Macarthur Institute, Australia.

Inefficiency

To solve many problems, especially early in a curriculum, the student will have to explore many subjects and skills, often missing the mark. In time, the bits of knowledge may help with other problems, but they could be discarded when they do not assist with the problem at hand. Acquired knowledge is not organised by the teacher into a coherent system. The student is responsible for organisation; this is thought to be inefficient.

Recall for certifying examinations

Students will not do as well on first-level certifying exams (ie with true-false, multiple choice questions) because they are not trained to recall knowledge and facts in the context of subject-oriented learning. This has proven true for McMaster medical school graduates, who score lower than the national aggregate on Medical Council examinations in Canada: see Woodward (1984).

Outside of Canada, comparative studies between medical schools, or between two curricular tracks in one school, consistently show that PBL students fall behind their counterparts in traditional schools in basic science tests. By graduation, they have caught up with them.[9]

In Canadian board examinations in specialist subjects conducted after postgraduate training and experience, PBL graduates have had a 95% first-time pass rate, 8% higher than the pass rate for all Canadian graduates: see Neufeld & Sibley (1989). This result could not be attributed solely to PBL training, but it does confirm that PBL graduates catch up with or surpass others in areas of specialist subject knowledge.

Generalist tutors

The tutors in problem-based learning sessions do not have to be experts in the particular problem field. They are meant to direct the students only through questions and suggested avenues of exploration. The disadvantage is that they may not be able to judge the

---

9   Studies reported in Schmidt et al (1989) compared University of Limburg students to other Dutch medical students, Sydney and Newcastle (PBL) students, and two curricular tracks at New Mexico (p 221–2). The 'catch-up' findings were similar in all three countries.

analytical rigour of the discussion for that particular problem. Likewise, they may not be able to reward innovative solutions during the take-up phase. This can result in a less challenging experience for the better students.

Student anxiety over assessment

Students are used to traditional examinations or papers. They judge where they stand by these measures. In a full-curriculum PBL system, they only receive feedback in small groups and written narrative reports which go into an assessment file. This produces anxiety about individual progress. Assessment can also be tainted by the tutor-student relationship becoming closer, thus leading to subjective evaluation. In the health sciences, these problems are being addressed by a return to devices like independent evaluators, multiple choice tests, criterion-referenced clinical assessment, and records of student progress through structured patient improvement exercises: see Hamilton (1976); Ryan (1989), p 157.

Teacher and student adjustment

Some teachers have trouble adjusting to being a facilitator, rather than a subject expert. The temptation is to answer the question and display the right approach, rather than let the student find it. Likewise, students raised on a diet of passive learning in large undergraduate classes have trouble adjusting to self-directed learning. Unless this dual transition is carefully managed through teacher training and student orientation and counselling, the aims of a PBL curriculum will be seriously undermined.

Inexperience of students

An advantage of PBL is that it draws on the experiences of learners. But what if the student is a 17-year old in the first year of undergraduate studies? Programmes like undergraduate law at the University of Limburg have found it necessary to adjust to the fact that the life experiences of undergraduates can be a slim resource. Postgraduate courses, such as law in North America, or professional legal training courses, should not have the same difficulties, since more and more students have on-the-job experience and a rich variety of educational backgrounds.

Administration of resources and PBL objectives

Full-curriculum PBL programmes usually have a full-time education department or consultants to articulate and implement the programme objectives: cf Macfarlane et al (1992). Their goals can sometimes conflict with those of an individual teacher or a subject-oriented department. Frequent faculty meetings and co-ordination efforts seem necessary to manage a PBL programme.

Furthermore, there must be an expansion of learning resources which are carefully administered. Libraries need multiple copies of some books. New technology, such as CD-ROM computer facilities or video disc machines, may have to be provided. There has to be controlled access to the resources without limiting unduly the student's independent search for knowledge. These difficulties can hamper a PBL programme unless administrators can address them.

Costs

Administration costs may go up, particularly during implementation of a new PBL programme.

Because faculty-student ratios are higher, faculty size may have to increase. Some faculties have responded by using volunteers.[10] It might also be possible to reorganise existing preparation and contact hours, since PBL can eliminate the need for many lecture preparation and delivery hours.

Problem-based learning in action

In reviewing the many experiments and established PBL programmes, it is clear that new institutions have the best chance to adopt problem-based learning wholly. Because there was no competing tradition, universities like McMaster and Limburg have been able to refine and develop their curricula without intra-faculty battles over 'territory'. Established institutions, such as the University of New Mexico (medicine) and Southwestern University in Los Angeles (law)

---

10   The British Columbia Professional Legal Training Course, with seven full-time faculty, used some 400 volunteer lawyers per year for substantive and procedural expertise. These volunteers could be used in a PBL setting to free up contact hours for full-time faculty.

have skirted that difficulty by developing a parallel, optional curriculum track that features problem-based learning. The teachers and students attracted to the parallel track do not have to interact much with those in the established curriculum pattern. Many legal educators will look for a third option that would integrate problem-based learning into a curriculum, without tearing down the established curriculum structure.

To classify the various curriculum reform choices, I will divide selected PBL programmes into the following categories:
- Full curriculum pure models.
- Full curriculum modified models.
- Partial curriculum models.

For each of these approaches and examples, it is helpful to reflect on the PBL method used in relation to the Barrows taxonomy and the advantages or disadvantages of PBL discussed earlier in the paper.

Full curriculum pure PBL models

The 'pure' approach in a full curriculum is best seen in the health sciences faculties at McMaster University and the University of Newcastle in New South Wales, Australia. Other medical schools, particularly in the United States, have also shifted to full curriculum PBL. Even Harvard, though using a 'modified' approach, has shifted to problem-based learning, a move hailed by President Derek Bok (1989), a former law dean, as 'Harvard's most impressive innovation of the 1980s' (p 17).

The McMaster curriculum, dating from 1968, is the old wine in the PBL cellar, though it was revised significantly in 1983: see Neufeld (1983). McMaster represents the pure approach because problems are the core for teaching, from beginning to end. Furthermore, the method is 'closed loop or reiterative problem based,' the top rung of the PBL taxonomy. Their curriculum runs for 33 months in a three-year time span, unlike the four-year curriculum at most Canadian medical schools. Newcastle, taking students from the secondary school level, has a five-year PBL curriculum. So time is not a critical dimension of a PBL curriculum; but structure and teaching methods are all-important.

The first unit of the McMaster curriculum is representative of the full curriculum PBL model.

Their calendar uses the following charts to illustrate the first curriculum unit:

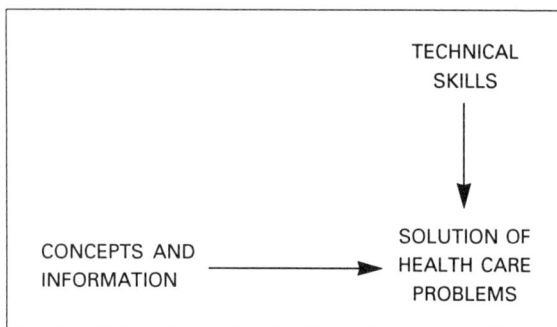

TECHNICAL
SKILLS

CONCEPTS AND
INFORMATION

SOLUTION OF
HEALTH CARE
PROBLEMS

	CRITICAL APPRAISAL SKILLS	CLINICAL SKILLS	SELF-DIRECTED LEARNING SKILLS
POPULATION PERSPECTIVE			
BEHAVIOURAL PERSPECTIVE			
BIOLOGICAL PERSPECTIVE			

TECHNICAL SKILLS

CONCEPTS AND INFORMATION

What one normally finds in a course subject list is found in one of the three perspectives. The skills agenda of the student features a well-known category of clinical skills (ie physical examination skills, interviewing skills) that were traditionally taught in the last year or two of medical studies. The two unique skills taught are critical appraisal (the ability to find and critically analyse literature, laboratory reports, etc) and self-directed learning (learning how to learn). What brings the concepts, information and skills together are the problems, which can cut across several of the boxes in the chart above. For example, early in unit one, a small group may choose to tackle the 'Mary Connell' problem, which is summarised in the calendar as follows:

> This 27-month-old child was playing in the kitchen as her mother prepared dinner. When mother left to answer the telephone, Mary wandered to the stove, reached for a pot and splashed potatoes and boiling water over her right arm, face, right posterior and anterior chest and neck. Mother called '911' for help.

This problem may be designed to emphasise the population perspective (ie home accident prevention strategies) and the biological perspective (ie burns and their treatment). It could also highlight a clinical skill (ie emergency treatment skills) and self-directed learning (ie how will students learn how to distinguish childhood accidents from parental neglect).

There are 18 problems in unit one, each designed to hit several of the boxes in the curriculum chart. The content of the curriculum, therefore, is defined by and found within the health care problems that students pursue. In order to catch all the content, the student needs a set of learning objectives, a tutor and established tutorial times, and a variety of learning resources. The learning objectives become a personal check list for progress through the curriculum unit. For example, an objective might be 'to identify the role for the physician in childhood burn accident prevention'. This objective might be achieved through self-directed learning in the Mary Connell problem. It could be reinforced through analysis of emergency clinical skills and primary prevention (population perspective) techniques in another health care problem.

Let's translate this curriculum plan into law school language for a moment. In her or his first year, a student might meet 'Jim Jordan', a car accident victim. Jim was a student driving a pizza delivery vehicle as a part-time job (employment contract). The vehicle, unknown to Jim, had faulty brakes, but Jim was also driving too fast for the wet conditions (tort law). He injured the driver of another vehicle and he has been charged with careless driving (criminal law). There is a witness who can describe what the other driver did (interviewing skills). A small group using self-directed learning would explore the issues identified here and report back in a take-up session. An important goal then will be to discover how they learned their new knowledge and skills. Through a series of these realistic problems, the student would use problem-based learning to attain the objectives of the first year curriculum.

McMaster would teach a problem like Mary Connell (or Jim Jordan) in three phases. First, there would be a two-hour tutorial to meet the problem and determine the issues, the lines of inquiry and student objectives. Second, the self-directed learning phase is used to explore the problem. This is normally a week long, or two weeks at most. Finally, the take-up phase occurs in a two-hour tutorial. About two-thirds of the tutorial is devoted to discussion of problem solutions. The rest of the time goes into peer evaluation of the learning skills each student developed during the self-directed phase.

The PBL writers often talk about 'interaction with the problem'. This is accomplished through what they call 'trigger material' or the stimulus material that is used in the first tutorial phase: see Neame (1989). In health sciences, trigger material can include a videotape, a simulated patient, a physical examination report, a patient history, laboratory slides, or a brief written case description. Sometimes the trigger material is presented in sequence, so that the broadest hypotheses are generated first, followed by a sharper focus in response to new trigger material information. The students request new information as they identify their learning needs in discussion of the problem.

The Newcastle medical school found some difficulties with the McMaster model and, while retaining the three phases of problem-based learning, the faculty has changed some elements of the McMaster full curriculum model. Nevertheless, Newcastle remains a 'pure' PBL faculty. They have taken detail out of their trigger material at Newcastle because it was leading students to narrow diagnosis too early. The trigger material now tends to lead students to inquire about 'basic pathophysiological and psychosocial mechanisms of disease' (Neame, op cit, p 125) rather than a specific condition. Next, Newcastle has substituted broader 'goals' for learning instead of objectives which were thought to be 'too prescriptive and restricting' (ibid, p 125–6). A goal is a functional issue to be resolved, not a specific learning prescription. An example goal statement is: 'How do proteins enter and leave the interstitial fluid?' (ibid, p 126). The handout material that follows problem analysis has been reduced from the previous 'lecture notes' format to brief goal overviews that give only enough information to guide further inquiry.

Newcastle made two other modifications that should be considered by legal educators. They found that using trigger material in a lock-step sequence inhibited real development of reasoning skills because students sat back and waited for the next handout. This is the experience in professional legal education, when students discover that there is an 'answer sheet' or 'model precedent' waiting for them at the end of class discussion. The Newcastle solution has been to make the tutor an 'information broker' (Neame, op cit, p 127). New information is kept on separate pages and released only when students identify the need for it and request it. The second change has been the development of an explicit model of the problem-based learning and reasoning process. Tutors are expected to be experts in the implementation of the model as well as in the conceptual basis of the problems they handle in class.

The pure PBL model is specific to medical problem analysis and management, but a parallel one could be developed for legal education. The medical model leads to a diagnostic decision after the problem identification phase. The next phase, called 'problem resolution', follows a model of patient management decisions and actions. Attached to both phases there are learning steps driven by the need to know more about the patient or the solution. Students must also set learning goals. In legal education, we would substitute fact investigation, issue identification and legal theory development for the first phase. After self-directed learning, there would be a case management phase involving law office management issues, procedural law, narrowing of issues and options and implementation of the best options.

One of the greatest contributions of the full curriculum pure PBL models has been in the field of assessment. PBL developers recognised that examinations based on disciplinary knowledge would undermine the goals of PBL. In response, they have developed an impressive array of instruments for self-assessment and formal assessment. In summary form, they include:[11]

1 PATIENT MANAGEMENT PROBLEMS (PMP)

There is a written case presentation; the student chooses from a list of possible actions and can get further information on an action by using a felt marker to reveal invisible ink. The student continues to select actions, patient management choices and data. Each choice is

---

11 Unless otherwise indicated, these tools are all described in M Verwijuen et al (1989), pp 180–95.

scored by a positive or negative number and an overall score is computed. Further feedback is provided through discussion with content experts or reading an expert's written description of how to handle the case. In legal education, we have a parallel example in some computer-assisted instruction programs, where branching is used to lead the student to a successful or unsuccessful handling of a hypothetical problem.

2   MODIFIED ESSAY QUESTIONS (MEQ)

Information is presented in sequence. At each stage, the student writes a very concise essay answer to a question about the developing biomedical problem. Unlike the PMP, answers to later questions in the sequence do not depend upon earlier answers. Scoring is done by answer sheets.

3   PROBLEM BOXES (PB)

Material related to a biomedical problem (ie audiotape of patient interview, photographs, x-rays, patient history, correspondence) is put into a box. The student must decide how and when to use the information in developing a patient management plan. There are open-ended questions posed by a written sheet or tutor to guide the student. There are scoring sheets, reference materials, and written expert protocols to assist in self-evaluation.

4   PORTABLE PATIENT PROBLEM PACK (P4-DECK)

The P4-Deck is a deck of several hundred cards, colour coded according to action categories that a doctor might employ for a patient (ie conduct physical examination, obtain lab test, etc). There are 'situation cards' to initiate a particular problem within the deck. That 'situation card' should cause the student to pursue only the handful of correct action cards in the larger deck. Each action card has standard questions on the front to stimulate clinical reasoning. On the back there are responses, physical examination findings, treatment results and the like. When the student feels s/he is finished with the patient, a 'closure card' can be drawn. This reports the result of the course of action taken (eg, patient deceased!). Scoring is done by numerical weights attached to each card chosen (as with

PMPs). Further feedback is available as reference material, a list of the P4 sequence chosen by experts and summaries of treatment by experts.

5   TRIPLE JUMP EXERCISE (TJE)

This is the PBL version of the oral examination. Within a single day, the student goes through three 'jumps'. First, in a meeting with the tutor (20–30 minutes) the student is presented with a problem and formulates hypotheses and key issues for learning. Next, the student studies individually using a variety of learning resources (two hours). Lastly, the student returns to the tutor and presents a précis of findings and discusses his or her learning insights. The tutor has a rating form, a list of references and a list of key issues to help in scoring. The triple jump exercise parallels the PBL method of learning and it can be used successfully in a full-day format as a teaching method rather than an assessment.[12]

6   MULTIPLE CHOICE AND TRUE–FALSE QUESTIONS

These tests have been reintroduced to PBL curricula to deal with student anxiety about how much they know. They may be conducted at the end of a curriculum block or held as a progress test, up to four times a year. Some schools make these tests part of formal evaluation. Others use them for student counselling only.

7   SKILL TESTS – THE OBJECTIVE STRUCTURED CLINICAL EXAMINATION (OSCE) AND SIMULATED PATIENT ENCOUNTERS (SPE)

In addition to clinical skill tests and tests in interviewing, PBL faculties have invented more integrated skill tests. The OSCE originated by Harden and his colleagues at Dundee, Scotland, is the most comprehensive: see Harden et al (1975). It is described in summary form as follows:

> To provide evaluation for students in their clinical terms, he sets up 18 stations. In two of the stations, the student is required to

---

12   The author participated in a full-day triple jump exercise at McMaster University during a training programme for new faculty. Although it was a medical problem, it had legal aspects of occupational health and safety and zoning law. The experience was highly motivating and the knowledge generated by the small group in a single day was vast.

take a brief history in a specified area from the simulated patient. At the station following each of these stations where there is a simulated patient, the student has to answer objective questions concerning the information he has obtained. At another station the student has to inspect a coloured transparency and at the following station answer multiple-choice questions concerning his observations. At five stations, the technique of examination is observed and scored, as performed on normal subjects who provided information concerning the student's technique. These examinations are in specific areas of the body, such as the abdomen or the lower extremities. In this manner, Harden is able to set up an examination procedure that can be reproduced in a number of locations and can survey, in a fairly objective and reliable manner, a wide range of student skills in the clinical setting.

Barrows & Tamblyn (1980), p 140

The performance of students on an OSCE is rated by trained observers using standardised checklists. The legal education equivalent of this test would be a transaction-based exercise combining videotapes, documents, transcripts, statutes, cases and correspondence. The test could be graded on the responses to questions at some stations or on the lists of 'information needed' or 'applicable legal theories' generated by the student at other stations.

The simulated patient encounter (SPE) is the legal education equivalent of a role-played interviewing and counselling test. In the SPE, the student interviews a role-played patient, uses a patient history file, and makes treatment and management decisions. The evaluator grades the interviewing performance and the quality of the decision-making. Because the content of the patient's problems can be scripted, controlled, and repeated for new students, this method is thought to be more reliable than the structured oral examinations that are traditionally given by hospital-based teachers during a clinical training phase.

All of the above assessment methods could be adapted for legal education purposes. Even outside of a problem-based curriculum they should be attractive because they get away from one-shot knowledge testing. Furthermore, the health sciences faculties have scrutinised their assessment tools for reliability, validity, and fidelity: see Barrows & Tamblyn (1980), pp 110–55. These are standard measures of whether a test actually achieves its intended purpose.

Unfortunately, these are terms rarely uttered in the process of creating law school examinations or tests of any kind: cf Josephson (1980).

Having outlined the important features of 'pure' full curriculum PBL faculties, it must be admitted that no law schools or legal education experiments will fit into these categories. The full curriculum 'modified' law school experiments, to be considered next, use the basic tutorial structure and self-directed study, but they do not meet other criteria of problem-based learning.

Full curriculum modified PBL model

The two most established models in this category are at Maastricht (University of Limburg) law school in the Netherlands and the Southwestern University law school (Los Angeles).

MAASTRICHT

The Maastricht model was taken from the medical school at the same university and has been revised since the founding of the law faculty in 1982: see Cohen (1987). Like the pure models, there is training in skills (writing, drafting, negotiating, etc) and subject content is delivered through problems in weekly tutorials (12 per week of 2–3 hours each). But the Maastricht curriculum is organised around theme or subject headings. The headings range from very broad themes ('unlawful behaviour') to subjects ('housing', 'traffic') or skills ('moot court', 'legal drafting'). Therefore the student, coming into the first tutorial, has a theme or subject box into which to place the problem. This is more limiting than the McMaster model because it forecloses potential avenues of inquiry. However, the law school teachers found it necessary to give more guidance to their students. In Holland, law is a first degree taken in a four-year curriculum. Although younger students may need more direction to make PBL function, it is curious that the upper years at Maastricht feature more specific course headings (ie Property, Evidence, Consumer Law), not the broader themes that one might expect more mature students to accommodate.

The curriculum is taught in six-week blocks. The skill courses are staged throughout the four years.[13] Most of them (eg Legal Writing

---

13 The PCLL Course at the City Polytechnic of Hong Kong, though far shorter, similarly runs skills sessions parallel to the PBL sessions.

in the first year, Negotiation or Legal Clinics in the fourth year) would not be out of place in a conventional North American law school. This contrasts with the medical model where a skill objective is pursued *after* the need for it is identified through a problem, not as a self-standing course.

Despite the modification, the core of the Maastricht curriculum is still problems. They teach a problem-solving model in a first year course and this is carried forward in the twice-weekly tutorials on themes or subjects. There is a significant variation in the way tutors handle the problems:[14] some use the take-up tutorial as a platform for mini-lectures on the 'answers' to the problem. Others draw the solutions from the students, which is how PBL is intended to work; they also devote time to the learning skills of the students.

The other main modification of the pure model is in the area of assessment. They do not use peer assessment or continuous assessment of small group participation, nor do they use adaptations of the inventive assessment tools from their medical school. On the other hand, they do not use course-based examinations either. There are three tests per year, each posing about 150 questions (multiple choice, short answer) from all the courses in the curriculum block. These tests do require students to keep up regular attendance and to integrate their knowledge, but no credit is given to improvements in learning skills. The remaining part of assessment at Maastricht involves skill tests in writing and the other skill courses. Overall, therefore, assessment at Maastricht has been anchored in examination methods and has not wholly reflected the PBL approach of the curriculum.

SOUTHWESTERN *SCALE* PROGRAMME

The SCALE programme, a full curriculum option at Southwestern University Law School (Los Angeles), has a modified PBL approach. For students who want a fast track through law school, the option is attractive because it can be completed in two years through full-time attendance for 47 weeks per year: see Johnson (1982). The SCALE curriculum uses problems within four main curriculum block headings: Perspectives (sources of law, economics and law, etc); Concepts (capacity, intent, jurisdiction, etc); Skills (oral communication, writing,

14   See Moust & Nuy (1987). The faculty acknowledges differences in styles of the tutors. The differences reported here were also observed by the author during classroom visits at Limburg in May 1990.

etc); and Transactions (within substantive areas like administrative law, business organisations, etc). Perspectives, Concepts and Skills are co-ordinated through materials and the problems in the first year; at the end of the year a review phase called Transitions is used to present material in a restructured doctrinal outline.

In the second year, the Transactions block takes most of the time. One third of the transactions studied require totally independent research, as a pure PBL approach would demand. In the remainder, the faculty provide introductions to the issues.

The last curriculum block is titled Externships. These are external placements which begin for brief periods in the first year and culminate in an eight-week externship at the end of the second year. Under supervision, students get to apply the skills and knowledge from previous curriculum blocks to experiences in judicial clerkships or law offices.

The SCALE programme was not developed by reference to the health sciences models for problem-based learning. Therefore, there have not been the explicit goals of (1) putting the problem first in the learning sequence and (2) reflecting on learning skills. In relation to the taxonomy of PBL methods, most SCALE methods would be classified as 'case method' or 'modified case-based'. Some of the skill problems and second-year transactions would rank as 'problem-based'. Because the written materials are often reviewed in advance of the problem and because students do not often set their own learning objectives, the SCALE programme is a significantly modified PBL approach. Nevertheless, it has succeeded in cutting across doctrinal lines, especially in the first year, and it has also shown the way for other law schools to integrate perspectives, knowledge and skills.[15]

Even with modifications giving more guidance and doctrinal structure for students, the SCALE faculty report the kind of student adjustment problems raised earlier in this paper:

> For many students, the shortened period of instruction, with its intensive workload and the amount of individual participation

---

15 Many law schools (eg Calgary, Toronto, University of British Columbia, University of Victoria) now have courses or first year curriculum blocks of a week or two, titled 'perspectives'. There has been a greater move to organise skills training in law schools on a coherent, step-by-step basis. Some schools also have mandatory externships (eg, Calgary). Few have taken up the idea of a 'concepts' block, but the SCALE programme can take credit for leadership in many of these other teaching blocks.

and skills performance called for by the program, requires a marked adjustment from the lesser demands of their previous educational experiences. For some, the inability to make this adjustment causes an emotional or intellectual trauma that results in disaffection, failure or withdrawal from SCALE . . .

It may be fairly stated that the program is most effective for students who have developed independent standards for performance and have been motivated by those standards to a consistent pattern of successes in other academic and life experiences before entering law school. In addition, many students who quickly adjust to the SCALE program have had experience in independently organising and managing the use of their time.

Johnson (1982), p 564

The health science PBL programmes do not report any significant numbers of withdrawals or failures. Perhaps the explicit attention to learning skills and the support of the tutors makes a difference. If the SCALE programme were to follow the criteria for the 'pure' PBL curriculum approaches, would students adjust with less trauma? One could speculate that the adjustment would be easier because the students would explicitly pursue the learning skills they require, rather than be expected to have them from previous work or educational experiences.

Partial curriculum PBL models

It has been said that the barriers to adopting problem-based learning in established institutions are so great that only new schools or programmes can handle the challenge successfully: see Newble (1989); Thompson & Williams (1985). One response has been to take a part of the curriculum, or a single course, and convert to problem-based learning. These approaches can be taken without broad faculty consensus or commitment. Alternatively, they may attract institutional support as a first step experiment on the road to a full curriculum model.

The course model has been attempted in medical school, in courses like physiology: see Mitchell (1988). Two modifications of pure PBL methods are apparent in reviewing the course model. Firstly, it is nearly impossible to cut across subjects or disciplines when the problems all arise under the course title. The advantage of promoting lateral thinking is lost. Secondly, course designers tend to restrict the scope of self-directed inquiry in order to focus on specific course goals. At Witwatersrand Medical School, for example, the physiology course uses a PBL method but it excludes clinical data gathering and treatment steps from the problem-solving process. Data is provided in the problems. They want students to become skilled at diagnosis from a physiology perspective.

The modifications, in this case, do not defeat the major goals of problem-based learning. Students receive explicit training in problem-solving. They encounter the problems first in the learning sequence. There is continuous assessment, using multiple choice testing and patient management problems (PMPs). There is feedback on learning skills. The complexity of the problems increases as the course progresses. These benefits could all be realised in a legal education course setting. However, like the established medical school, there would be a question mark about the ability of students to absorb and transfer the PBL skills from the single course setting to their broader educational and practical experiences. There is no research on learning outcomes or effectiveness in practice that would help to decide whether the course model achieves any of the longer range goals of problem-based learning.

Curriculum reform in an established institution could also be accomplished with what I will label the 'dispersion model'. In this model, several courses or curriculum blocks are chosen for PBL. The challenge of PBL is built up as the student progresses through the entire curriculum. The model would work best where all PBL-designated segments of the curriculum were mandatory. Something like this model has been used at the University of Adelaide, Australia, in the fifth year of a six-year medical programme: see Newble (1989). However, even this is such a concentrated exposure to problem-based learning that it is closer to the course model.

Professional legal training courses or CLE curricula may be the best homes for a dispersion model in law. In the modern professional legal training courses, there are not traditional course subjects because content, skills and transactions are woven together. Furthermore, most of the course is mandatory. Thus the advocates of a PBL approach do not have to fight the course boundaries that one finds in a law school; nor do they have to deal with a curriculum that can be up to two-thirds optional.

Continuing legal education planners are market-driven, but they can also create markets for new skills. The explosion in advocacy and dispute settlement skill courses attests to the latter point. It would be possible to design a series of one-day courses using a PBL approach. The courses would be grouped in one field of practice (eg corporate and commercial) and offered over one or two years. As part of the marketing, the CLE planners could announce problem-based learning objectives that would run parallel to the skill and knowledge content of the courses.

The prospects for a dispersion model in a law school are not as bright. There would have to be a commitment from faculty members in several first-year courses as well as highly subscribed courses in the upper years. The planning and sequencing of PBL objectives would require a team approach with assistance from adult education experts. Finally, the innovative PBL approaches to assessment would have to be incorporated in some traditional courses. Unfortunately, the 'academic credit' rewards for course design and teaching innovations may not be enough to attract a committed group of faculty to a dispersion model of problem-based learning.

Critiques of legal education

The critical literature on legal education leaves no doubt that there is widespread dissatisfaction with both the content and methods of law school education and postgraduate (professional) training. These criticisms are sufficiently well known (and, in many cases have been raised elsewhere in this collection) not to require detailed repetition here. Problem-based learning cannot cure all of these ills, but it may address some of the difficulties we experience in legal education. What follows therefore is a list of specific criticisms based on my own experience as a legal educator and administrator: each is accompanied by a suggestion of how problem-based learning could meet the criticism.

Law schools are instructor-centred, not learner-oriented

Law school objectives, to the extent that they are articulated in annual calendars and course descriptions, rarely say anything about what learning outcomes will be achieved. Instead, they speak of the instructor's goals, philosophies, and intended topic coverage. Instructor-centred courses also mean that students are rarely sent to the library unless it is a research paper seminar. The student has no choice about the pace of learning, the steps, and the content selected.

In the classroom, the questions that interest the professor tend to come first, particularly for those who still use a form of Socratic method. Student questions are usually directed to confusion about issues raised by the professor rather than new lines of inquiry. It must be acknowledged, however, that most law teachers welcome truly new areas of inquiry, even though their classes are not structured to promote this activity. Control of the teaching agenda is primarily the professor's; where lectures dominate, this is entirely the case.

Even discussion-based or problem-oriented classes are very instructor-oriented. Large class sizes mean that only a minority can participate. The goal of teaching and testing thinking processes is accomplished only through sporadic snapshots of the thoughts of a few volunteers in the classroom dialogue. Because the discussion or problem is meant to be a test of the assigned reading or its applications, the teacher cannot expect contributions to come from outside that reading. These classes call for more active learning, but there is often insufficient attention to the desired learning outcomes for the students.

Problem-based learning deals with the issues in three ways. First, the student uses the problem not only to identify issues and avenues for solution, but to define his or her learning objective. With some general guidance on how to formulate (behaviourally-oriented) learning objectives, the student defines the intended outcome of the inquiry that lies ahead: compare Winsor (1989). For example, presented with a problem in an environmental law course, the student may state that he or she 'will be able to describe the legal remedies that address the field of the problem and identify the remedy most likely to assist the client in this case.' The student might then research the law of remedies and consult experts on the most practical and viable remedy. The important point is that the student has chosen the learning objective.

Secondly, all students participate equally and all are expected to expose their thinking and learning processes. This happens through the initial analysis of the problem in small groups, and then again when they bring back the results of their research work. The professor and other students measure the contributions against the student's stated learning objective. In addition to feedback on the product (short paper, lists, charts, research summary, etc) that addresses the problem, the student receives comments on the learning steps he or she has taken. Even in other small group settings in law schools, the class rarely achieves these goals of equal participation and learning process review.

Finally, it is inevitable that the students will go beyond the learning sources found in an edited casebook or a reading list. They will be motivated by their own objectives and by explicit freedom and encouragement to look beyond the textbook and syllabus. In the take-up session, the professor will highlight the breadth of learning resources that students drew upon. This reinforces the importance of the 'learning how to learn' objective for the next problem.

Law school and bar admission courses test primarily examination-oriented knowledge

The 100% written final examination is well entrenched from the first year of law school onwards. Although some schools lighten the final burden with weight attached to mid-year assessments, the main testing of all course knowledge and thinking processes is in a three-hour, essay-style examination. Here, sometimes for the first time in a course, the student meets a problem to which he or she must reply by a written analytical formula. There is no time to consult outside sources, even if the examination is open book. More imaginative examinations also test theoretical perspectives. While the questions purport to seek the students' views or opinions, the professor is also looking for a sound knowledge of the assigned theoretical readings. In all the final examinations, the only feedback is a mark. The student receives no personal feedback on improving his or her presentation of knowledge.

Traditional bar admission examinations in Canada and the United States vary only in format, not in the objective of knowledge testing. In order to achieve more rapid marking and more reliable results, these examinations more often use multiple choice, true–false, and short answer questions. These examinations are even less capable of testing the steps in analytical thinking, since they call for a result of that thinking. As with law school, the testing of a well-organised, rapidly recalled body of subject knowledge is the goal. There are exceptions to these formats. Many law schools have one required research paper (dissertation) course. Most have courses with mid-term examination options. Others have optional or required clinical terms with broad evaluation objectives that are reported as pass or fail grades.

Law schools have optional skill courses with skill tests as the assessment. A few bar admission courses or examinations have moved significantly towards the assessment of knowledge, skills and attitudes.[16] But the mainstream assessment device is still the 100% examination. This is partly due to large class sizes, underfunding in law schools and bar admission courses, and competing pressures of research or practice engaged in by the teachers. It is submitted that the model also flourishes because legal educators have not asked themselves about the range of abilities their graduates ought to have and how those abilities could be assessed. However, it may be fairer to say that they have declared many of the attributes they hope for, but tested few. The message received by students is that last-minute knowledge is what counts – not classroom contributions, independent reading, research skills, writing skills, synthesis of interdisciplinary knowledge, or co-operative learning.

Problem-based learning gives credit to all of these attributes and more because of its assessment system. The assessment is continuous throughout the course or curriculum term. The instructor regularly assesses the work products, the verbal contributions, the skills and attitudes of the student. Peer assessment is also taken into account. There is a narrative record kept for each student and the instructor provides regular feedback on whether the student is operating at a passing level.

As noted earlier, there is a creative range of assessment devices in health sciences that could be adapted for law. Most PBL curricula or courses operate on a pass–fail system, but it is entirely possible to

16 The New Zealand bar admission course, at the Institute of Professional Legal Studies, has no knowledge examination, but tests knowledge through assignments. The main assessment focus is on legal skills. The British Columbia Professional Legal Training Course has a system that uses a narrative assessment, four skills tests (two-thirds of the overall assessment weight) and two knowledge exams (one-third of the assessment weight). Except for the California Bar, which uses 'performance tests' to test analytical and organisational skill together with writing and drafting, the US jurisdictions rely heavily on bar examination testing (multiple choice) for pre-admission licensing. The new Legal Practice Course in England assesses by a mixture of pass/fail skills assessments and written knowledge-based examinations, which may be open book.

have a grade point or letter grade system. The challenge is to avoid the accusation of subjectivity; this is done through the setting of specific criteria for skill performance and products of research. The student, in preparing his or her own learning objective, will incorporate these criteria and be measured against them and the overall objective. A course like this requires favourable faculty–student ratios and a good administrative support system for record-keeping, appeals, and individual student counselling.

Student acceptance of existing methods

Before we castigate legal educators, it must be said that most students have elected the conditions they find themselves in. In the upper years, optional courses with lecture methods and 100% final examinations remain popular. A choice involving too much independent research or cumulative assessment is regarded as a time burden during the semester. Students budget time allocations to a course according to the credit weight of the course and a norm of weekly preparation. In this mainstream context, it is difficult for a professor to sell the idea of fluctuating time demands, independent objective-setting, and continuous assessment.

For those who complain of third-year boredom, there is a variety of seminars, clinical options, and directed research to stimulate independent inquiry. Yet many students confine their choice to 'bread and butter' large classes. They accept the boredom as an inevitable by-product of the main law school teaching methods and the reward system. Law school becomes a filling station of knowledge that must be visited en route to a practising certificate.

It is submitted that this attitude has been encouraged by a message from the employer law firms, and fellow students, that subject content and numerical grades are what count in a law degree. Skills in independent thinking, researching, and learning are assumed to be represented by good grades in so-called 'fundamental' courses. The employers are later surprised to discover that graduates have few skills in practical legal research and problem-solving.

Problem-based learning offers a better solution to the dilemmas of self-inflicted boredom and the skills gap. If potential employers and faculty counselled students to look for challenge, for problem-solving skills, and learning skills in course selection, there would be some incentive for choices in those directions. Furthermore, there should be some problem-based learning in the mandatory final year curriculum in law school, so that all students discover the motivational boost of the learning method and relate it to a fundamental purpose of their education – the ability to pursue independent learning.

Students' motivation and their need for relevance will be enhanced by the fact that well-designed problems are realistic. They are situations that actually confront clients or groups in society. The extent to which legal solutions are helpful is a matter for student inquiry and critique. The realism of a problem does not mean that it must have a practitioner's 'answer': the problem can be a platform for exploring broad theoretical issues, legal skills, and interdisciplinary questions. To get beyond the current student acceptance of didactic methods and knowledge testing, there will have to be enough stimulation across the law school curriculum to avoid the marginalisation of PBL or other challenging learning methods.

The relentless structure of professional legal training

In the modern professional legal training courses, the curriculum is highly structured around a combination of transactions, skills, legal content, and professional responsibility. The integration of these elements depends upon detailed lesson plans, explicit learning objectives, mandatory attendance and building blocks of skill and knowledge. These factors ensure that a consistent educational product is being received across many small groups, in several sessions per year and in different locations. The legal profession can be assured that all graduates have achieved basic entry-level standards of knowledge and skill performance.

These same virtues have a negative side. Students are not able to set their own learning pace. If they fall behind or jump ahead, the classroom pace remains the same, every hour of the course is programmed and there is little time for diverted learning events or review of difficult areas. Some students rebel when faced with this adjustment from university structures and it affects their motivation. Student evaluation surveys in British Columbia in the late 1980s, for example, revealed a high degree of satisfaction with learning outcomes, but unhappiness with course workload and a perceived inflexibility in curriculum structure: see Cruickshank (1989).

Another difficulty, for those courses that operate in shorter semesters of 10–12 weeks, is that the structure allows little time for the recapture of law school theory. Because the acquisition of new skills and practice knowledge requires repeat performances and considerable pre-class reading, there is not much room to discuss what values underlie the current practice of law. When a student personally understands the procedures, costs, and adversarial nature of a personal injury lawsuit, that may be the best time to ask whether legislative schemes of accident compensation would serve clients better. But the structured timetable does not encourage such a pursuit.

The structure of professional legal training thus perpetuates the 'theory stage' then 'vocational stage' paradigm of professional education that has been attacked by Donald Schön (1983) as one of 'technical rationality'. In his view, the model of learning principles of science (or law) divorced from a practice context is seriously flawed. Schön calls for a structure that brings theory into play during actual performance of a professional. His mission statement is:

> Let us then reconsider the question of professional knowledge; let us stand the question on its head. If the model of Technical Rationality is incomplete, in that it fails to account for practical competence in 'divergent' situations, so much the worse for the model. Let us search, instead, for an epistemology of practice implicit in the artistic, intuitive processes which some practitioners do bring to situations of uncertainty, instability, uniqueness, and value conflict.
>
> Donald Schön (1983), p 49

Schön develops a learning model of 'reflection-in-action' that calls for professionals to reflect and theorise immediately during or after their performances. The questions he suggests we ask ourselves are precisely the 'learning issues' that a problem-based learning method focuses upon:

> both ordinary people and professional practitioners often think about what they are doing, sometimes even while doing it ... They may ask themselves, for example, 'What features do I notice when I recognise this thing? What are the criteria by which I make this judgment? What procedures am I enacting when I perform this skill? How am I framing the problem that I am trying to solve?' Usually reflection on knowing-in-action goes together with reflection on the stuff at hand. There is some puzzling, or troubling, or interesting phenomenon with which the individual is trying to deal. As he tries to make sense

of it, he also reflects on the understandings which have been implicit in his action, understandings which he surfaces, criticises, restructures, and embodies in further action.

It is this entire process of reflection-in-action which is central to the 'art' by which practitioners sometimes deal well with situations of uncertainty, instability, uniqueness, and value conflict.

op cit, p 50

Professional legal training courses could benefit from the infusion of the PBL method as a significant curriculum element. Problem-based learning would vary the relentless structure in favour of more independent inquiry. It would serve as a respite from the predominant skill-learning cycle of theory–practice–feedback. Students with different learning styles would find it appealing, although students with less self-motivation might struggle. Using this method would place a value on the individuality of the student's problem-solving, research and learning skills, contrasted to the dominant expectation of conforming to a skill performance standard. Finally, problem-based learning, in the hands of a trained facilitator, would promote a reunification of theory, skill knowledge, and practice knowledge.

Talking heads in continuing legal education

The primary method for delivering continuing legal education is still the 'talking head'. From a panel, experts speak to their written papers in sequence. Audiences of up to 200 have little input except for a handful of questions at the conclusion of each panel. In some courses, this goes on for two days, seven hours a day. It is well known from research on human memory that no one can retain a significant percentage of the information that has been verbally delivered. Nevertheless, lawyers attend these courses in large numbers, give them good evaluations (cf Nelson (1993), pp 87–8), and are satisfied with one or two new practical insights that can be applied on the job. But the course format may be what lawyers are used to, not necessarily what they want or need.

Many jurisdictions have designed successful alternatives to the 'talking head' format. There have been workshops using small groups to analyse a case study. Skill courses now use videotaping, critique and demonstrations to improve lawyers' performances. Even large audience courses can be stimulating where presenters use brainstorming, small group break-outs, or 'roving interviewer' tcchniques. These alternative formats are well-received, particularly by more senior lawyers, who have experience to contribute to everyone's learning. The better continuing legal education organisations are always experimenting with new formats, but they also know that the large audience, 'talking head' courses pay many of the bills.

There will always be a place for intensive, yet entertaining, lecture-oriented courses in continuing legal education. They work well for new legislative developments, refresher courses, and fundamental coverage for junior lawyers. But the format is overworked or unsuitable for a number of audiences, some of them untapped by CLE organisations. Attendance analysis in British Columbia, Canada, reveals that 50% of all lawyers attend CLE courses, attending an average of 2.26 courses per year: see Bognar (1990). Of lawyers with less than four years' experience, 64% attend at least one course a year; this drops to 52% of lawyers with ten years' experience and 35% of lawyers with 18 years' experience or more. British Columbia is not a mandatory CLE jurisdiction. It has one of the highest voluntary participation rates in North America. Yet 50% of the lawyers attend no CLE courses at all, even when there are exciting alternatives to the standard format.

I suggest that the missing audiences are specialists, more senior general practitioners, and lawyers working across disciplinary and professional boundaries. In some cases, they are the experts, so who can they learn from? In other cases, they opt out because they prefer to learn from CLE course materials or audiotapes, when they have a particular problem to solve. The specialists and cross-boundary lawyers may want to know how other professionals think and what works best for them, without having to become immersed in the language and knowledge of that profession. Even CLE courses with multi-disciplinary panels have trouble accomplishing this latter objective because they focus on the current useful knowledge of the non-lawyer, not his or her professional thinking or behaviour.

Problem-based learning could reach some or all of these audiences. It is suited to an audience that probably won't read much in advance, but will commit itself enthusiastically to a day or two of hard work in a course. It can appeal to the specialists, because the course leader is not publicised as a superior expert. If anything, problem-based learning gives the specialists a chance to display their expertise and have it improved through a high-level exchange of solutions to a problem. However, the one deterrent to specialist participation in PBL may be competitive attitudes. They may be reluctant to share their 'trade secrets' with others who are competing for the same sophisticated clients. The senior generalist will have to be convinced that PBL is different from the panel format and that there is a payoff in his or her daily practice. This could be done by inviting participants to bring hard-to-solve problems to a PBL course and dedicating some small groups to the analysis of those problems.

Problem-based learning courses, as an additional part of CLE curriculum offerings, could also meet a criticism that is related to the learning outcomes of traditional formats. Most CLE organisations see themselves as instrumental in the lifelong learning needs of lawyers. In existing course formats, however, the skill of learning how to learn is not on the agenda. The legal skill courses come close because they provide a model for learning similar skills; but the question 'How did I learn this?' is never taken up with each individual. The next step, if we really want to get at the lifelong learning needs and skills of lawyers, should be to make that question an explicit educational objective in CLE.

It is a sensitive issue, because volunteer participants may feel that they are paying for legal knowledge, not personal analysis. Well-designed problem-based learning would not make the learning skills question stick out so baldly. Since CLE participants do not have to be evaluated on their learning skills, the facilitator can always relate those skills to more efficient future problem-solving and call for peer comments on the learning skills of participants. From my experience, these comments will be constructive, largely positive, and well-received by the participants.

Implementing problem-based learning in legal education

Law school

Established law schools have two opportune curriculum slots for problem-based learning in the first year. If the school has a 'perspectives' teaching block or course, problem-based learning would be an ideal method for getting students to take responsibility for their learning. Furthermore, it would expose them to cross-disciplinary research and the value of their peers' contributions. The other place for problem-based learning could be in the first year Legal Writing or Legal Methods programmes. Here, the goal has always been to learn to think and write 'like a lawyer'. The use of PBL could add explicit teaching of problem-solving strategies to that thinking repertoire. Although the products of the self-directed learning would continue to be prescribed (eg, case brief, letter), they would be more meaningful to the student if they arose from a realistic problem. In addition, we could broaden the students' notion of what it means to 'think like a lawyer'. By doing this at an early stage, in small groups, law schools may change more student attitudes towards upper year legal education and the importance of lifelong learning skills.

For the upper years, I have discussed earlier the potential for a 'course model' or 'dispersion model' introduction of problem-based learning. One of the problems with these models is that there is reluctance to make specific courses mandatory in the upper years. Although a faculty might agree on the value of self-directed learning in small groups for all students, there are other values or themes competing for attention in the upper years.

One solution is to create curriculum groups in the upper years and to require one mandatory selection from within the group. For example, 'research seminars' may be a designated group and every course in that group would have a substantial piece of research and writing as the main assessment product. All upper year students would have to select a seminar from that group. Another designated group would be 'workshops', indicating a handful of courses which aim at integration of skills, knowledge and theory through exercises rather than lecture-oriented coverage of knowledge. The workshop group would be the place to put problem-based learning in a substantial number of courses. Since one selection from the workshops group would be mandatory, many students would get to build upon the learning skills they encountered in the PBL programme in first year.

In order to tie the curriculum together in a course model or dispersion model, there should be a set of PBL objectives for students to pursue throughout law school. The McMaster University objectives are an example to follow, although the law school list would be more modest. Ideally, where students had completed the objectives, they could advance to a stream of professional legal training that would enhance their learning skills using PBL methods.

Professional legal training

In the United States, there would have to be a significant change in thinking about postgraduate, pre-admission training before one could contemplate PBL at this stage. At the moment, the bar admission process is viewed as an examination-setting exercise, not a responsibility for training new lawyers to become competent at an entry level. Even the most promising experiments in competency-based training are post admission programmes.[17] As a result, law firms or individual lawyers must absorb the costs and responsibilities of learning to practice competently. A tremendous growth in in-house training for medium and larger sized firms has met some of these needs. Ironically, it is the sole practitioner who needs the learning skills from PBL programmes and who has the least time and resources to attain these skills. Therefore, American law schools have a particular responsibility to those graduates who will have to count on their own problem-solving and learning skills.

In Canada, Australia, New Zealand, England, Ireland and most other Common Law jurisdictions there is a professional training stage which, combined with a training contract or pupillage, can last up to three years. In this stage, there are exciting opportunities to introduce problem-based learning, though that opportunity was not taken by the universities and the solicitors' profession in England following the reformed vocational training proposed in 1990 and launched in 1993. The modern professional legal training courses, in jurisdictions like Canada and New Zealand, are densely packed with integrated training in skills, knowledge and transactions. They would have to make room for problem-based learning by deleting some teaching units or reformulating existing teaching. As the PCLL course at the City Polytechnic of Hong Kong shows (Macfarlane et al (1992)), these courses lend themselves to a modified PBL approach across the curriculum, or to a dispersion model. The criteria for where to locate PBL lesson plans might be to:
– create early exposure to student-centred learning;

<hr>

17 Washington and New Jersey have bridge-the-gap programmes that occur within the first year or two of admission. Unlike other bridge-the-gap courses, which are really condensed CLE courses by a different name, these two states focus on skills through supervised exercises or assignments. These two states have the closest thing to professional training courses but they are still far short of the time and resources that go into the courses elsewhere in the Common Law world.

- find substantive areas that have a large gap between law school course knowledge and practice knowledge (the problems will be challenging;
- create legal skill knowledge, and learning skill objectives for PBL (not just knowledge objectives);
- use PBL in areas where practice is very diverse (so students can benefit from a variety of peer solutions to problems);
- choose areas where students perceive their existing learning outcomes to be less than what is required for entry-level competence;
- find connections between the professional legal training lesson plans chosen for PBL and a follow-up curriculum path in continuing legal education.

Applying these criteria to the British Columbia Professional Legal Training Course (PLTC), the modified curriculum would look something like this:

(a) *Early exposure to PBL* In the first week of the Course, PLTC uses videotapes and written problems to target Professional Responsibility. With minor modification, the current learning resources could be used for a 'triple jump exercise' based on the Maastricht and McMaster models. They would start with 'trigger material' in the form of a videotape or written problem. During the two-hour research phase, the small groups would pursue a variety of learning resources, including senior lawyers who could be used to test out trial solutions. In the take-up phase, an instructor and a guest senior lawyer would address the solutions and the learning skills.

(b) *Bridging the law school–practice gap* Our experience suggests that the greatest gaps are in Real Estate, Corporate and Commercial law, and Administrative law. At present, the teaching in Real Estate through a transaction and associated writing skills seems to be working well. The current assignment, involving a statement of adjustments, might be used as the platform for the explicit teaching of problem-solving strategies. However, it is a technically-oriented problem, and it may not be perceived as typical enough for students to transfer their learning to other problems. The other three substantive areas are good candidates for PBL treatment.

(c) *Skill objectives* There is a temptation to use PBL for knowledge objectives only, particularly in a professional training course that has a highly effective established method for teaching

skills. However, skills such as Writing, Drafting and Negotiation are less susceptible to a formula for teaching because there is a variety of acceptable competent performance.

In PLTC, we might consider Drafting for an experiment with PBL. We have had a 'trial run' assignment that is similar to the assessment that students must complete. We could work backwards from the assignment instructions and create a more skeletal problem. The problem should have substantive and procedural challenge as well as a demand for drafting skills. In place of the written assignment instructions, we would have to build in a 90-minute discussion of the assignment problem, followed by self-directed learning in drafting skill materials, precedents, and substantive issues. The product would still be the drafting assignment. In a 90-minute take-up session, held after the assignments were submitted, the instructor could focus on the substantive solutions, the drafting skills observed on the assignments, and the learning skills. These adjustments would mean finding at least two hours in the timetable that do not now exist.

(d) *Areas of diverse practice* The Administrative law field is one where the law school–practice gap is great because law schools focus heavily on judicial review, whereas most practitioners work before a handful of specialised tribunals and they rarely seek judicial review. The tribunals are so unique that it is difficult to define, much less teach, a generic 'practice of Administrative law'. Given a limited time in PLTC, it may be preferable to use a PBL 'triple jump exercise', in order to convey the importance of self-directed learning skills for areas that have very diverse solutions to problems.

In order to prevent excess demand on learning resources, there would have to be one unique problem for every eight students. For an enrolment of 126, we would require 16 problems. The problems might be organised around three or four themes (ie skills of the administrative lawyer, statutory research and analysis, administrative v judicial dispute settlement, administrative rules and procedure) so that each class hears about more than one theme.

The triple jump schedule for the instructor and students in one class might be organised as follows:

9:00–10:00 am   Group A discusses Problem 1 with instructor.

10:00–10:30 am	Group A organises its learning objectives and internal assignments; no instructor present.
10:30–1:30 pm	Group A does self-directed learning.
10:30–11:30 am	Group B discusses Problem 2 with instructor.
11:30–12:00 pm	Group B organises its learning objectives and internal assignments; no instructor present.
12:00–3:00 pm	Group B does self-directed learning.
1:30–3:00 pm	Take-up phase with instructor and Group A: 30 minutes on learning skills.
3:15–5:15 pm	Take-up phase with instructor and Group B: 30 minutes on learning skills.

The instructor time commitment is five hours during the day, but keep in mind that it is a facilitator's role, which may be less demanding than the intensity of skills teaching. If another half-hour of instructional time could be devoted to take-up the following day, a spokesperson for each group of eight could outline the problem and solutions for the students who have not seen that problem. In this way, there will be greater exposure to the diverse problems and solutions in Administrative law. In order to follow up with assessment, the instructor and peer evaluation in the take-up phase should be recorded for later inclusion in the PLTC Narrative Assessment.

(e)   *Areas where perceived outcomes are less than needed* In PLTC student evaluations at the end of the course, we ask students to rank their perceived knowledge or competence achieved as a result of PLTC training. We also ask about time allocated to substantive subjects; although most skill and knowledge areas are ranked surprisingly high (ie adequate competence, enough time), the following received consistently low rankings between 1988–90:

Administrative law;
Professional Responsibility;
Drafting Skills;
Legal Research.

If PBL was used for some of these areas, it is submitted that students would feel more confident about their ability to face a practice problem in the field. With problem-based learning, students will not have 'coverage' of the field (which we cannot achieve in any event) but they will know how to ask the right questions, what the learning resources are, what typical solutions look like, and what learning skills they must apply. Since Administrative law, Commercial Transactions and Professional Responsibility fit other criteria I have suggested, they could be considered for PBL curriculum reform.

Continuing legal education

Earlier the potential audiences and the curriculum pathway ideas for problem-based learning in CLE were discussed. But what would an individual course look like? Two structures should be considered. The one-day course model would look like a triple jump exercise, similar to the structure suggested for Administrative law in PLTC. The other structure would have the three phases of PBL spread over two weeks:

Week 1
Monday   Meet with instructor,
8:00–9:30 am   discuss problem.

Weeks 1, 2
Own time   Use learning resources.

Week 2
Friday   Take-up phase
8:00 - 9:30 am   with instructor.

In order to have good faculty-student ratios, instructors would meet with two to four small groups in sequence, on the first and last day of the course.

Materials would be in two packages. First, there would be generic material on problem-based learning and problem-solving. Secondly, CLE would use an existing recent CLE publication, such as the Family Practice Manual, as the substantive learning resource. The 'draw' for the course would be problems that use the substantive materials but push beyond them. The materials are a 'bonus' on top of the learning in the class sessions.

My experience using a problem on aquaculture in Administrative law was grounded on a CLE publication titled 'Aquaculture' (1988). It provided enough information to address the framework issues in the problem, but further work was necessary to come up with solutions. The combination of volunteer instructors with repeat sessions, short in-class commitments, and the use of already-produced materials would mean that PBL in continuing legal education could be economical as well as successful.

References

H S Barrows (1986) 'A Taxonomy of Problem-based Learning Methods', 20 *Medical Education* 481.

H S Barrows & R M Tamblyn (1980) *Problem-Based Learning: An Approach to Medical Education*, Springer Verlag, New York.

B S Bloom (ed) (1956) *Taxonomy of Educational Objectives. Book 1: Cognitive Domain*, David McKay Inc, New York.

C Bognar (1990) *Characteristics of Law Society Members Participating in CLE Programs*, CLE Society of British Columbia, Vancouver.

D Bok (1989) 'Needed: A New Way to Train Doctors' in H G Schmidt, M Lipkin, M de Vries, and J M Greep (eds) *New Directions for Medical Education: Problem-based Learning and Community-oriented Medical Education*, Springer-Verlag, New York, p 17.

D Boud (1985) 'Problem-based Learning in Perspective' in D Boud (ed) *Problem-based Learning in Education for the Professions*, Higher Education Research and Development Society of Australasia, Sydney.

M J Cohen et al (1987) 'Skills Training at the Limburg University Faculty of Law', 5 *Journal of Professional Legal Education* 135.

D A Cruickshank (1985) 'The Professional Legal Training Course in British Columbia, Canada', 3 *Journal of Professional Legal Education* 111.

D A Cruickshank (1989) *Annual Report on the Professional Legal Training Course*, Law Society of British Columbia, Vancouver.

C E Engel 'Problem-solving, Problem-based, Problem centred and all that . . .' *Newsletter, Centre for Medical Education, Research and Development*, University of New South Wales, Sydney.

J C Freund (1979) *Lawyering: A Realistic Approach to Legal Practice*, New York.

L B Greenfield (1987) 'Teaching Thinking Through Problem Solving' in James E Stice (ed) *Developing Critical Thinking and Problem-Solving Abilities*, Jossey Bass, San Francisco, p 5.

J G Greeno (1980) 'Trends in the Theory of Knowledge for Problem Solving' in D T Tuma & F Reif (eds) *Problem Solving and Education: Issues in Teaching and Research*, Erlbaum, Hillsdale, NJ.

J D Hamilton (1976) 'The McMaster Curriculum: A Critique', 1 *British Medical Journal* 1191.

R Harden, M Stevenson, W Downie & G M Wilson (1975) 'Assessment of Clinical Competence Using Objective Structured Examination', 1 *British Medical Journal* 447.

J R Hayes (1981) *The Complete Problem Solver*, Erlbaum, Hillsdale, NJ.

N Johnson (1982) 'SCALE: An Educational Alternative', 68 *American Bar Association Journal* 558.

P A Jones (1989) 'A Skills-Based Approach to Professional Legal Education', 23 *Law Teacher* 173.

M Josephson (1980) 'Grading and Testing in Law Schools', unpublished paper, Loyola Law School, Los Angeles, USA.

J Larkin and F Reif (1976) 'Analysis and Teaching of a General Skill for Studying Scientific Text', 4 *Journal of Educational Psychology* 68.

J Macfarlane et al (1992) 'Designing New Legal Practice Courses: The Hong Kong Plan', 26 *Law Teacher* 84.

G Mitchell (1988) 'Problem-based Learning in Medical Schools: A New Approach', 10 *Medical Teacher* 57.

J C Moust & H J Nuy (1987) 'Preparing Teachers for a Problem-Based Student-Centred Law Course', 5 *Journal of Professional Legal Education* 16.

S Nathanson (1989) 'The Role of Problem-Solving in Legal Education', 39 *Journal of Legal Education* 167.

S Nathanson (1992) 'Creating Problems for Law Students: The Key to Teaching Legal Problem-Solving?', 10 *Journal of Professional Legal Education* 1.

R L Neame (1989) 'Problem-based Medical Education: The Newcastle Approach' in H G Schmidt et al *New Directions for Medical Education: Problem-based Learning and Community-Oriented Medical Education*, Springer-Verlag, New York, p 123.

J W Nelson (1993) *A Study of the Continuing Legal Education Needs of Beginning Solicitors*, Centre for Legal Education, Sydney.

V R Neufeld (1983) 'Adventures of an Adolescent: Curriculum Changes at McMaster University' in C Friedman and E S Purcell (eds) *New Biology and Medical Education*, Josiah Macy Jr Foundation, New York, p 256.

V R Neufeld and J C Sibley (1989) 'Evaluation of Health Sciences Education Programs: Program and (Student) Assessment at McMaster University' in H G Schmidt et al (eds) *New Directions for Medical Education: Problem-based Learning and Community-Oriented Medical Education*, Springer-Verlag, New York, p 177.

D Newble (1989) 'Introducing Problem-based Learning into a Conventional Curriculum' in H G Schmidt et al (eds) *New Directions for Medical Education: Problem-based Learning and Community-Oriented Medical Education*, Springer-Verlag, New York, p 271.

G R Norman (1988) 'Problem-Solving Skills, Solving Problems and Problem-Based Learning', 22 *Medical Education* 279.

Nu Viet Vu (1980) 'Describing, Teaching and Predicting Medical Problem-Solving: A Review', 3 *Evaluation and the Health Professions* 435.

M F Rubinstein (1975) *Patterns of Problem Solving*, Prentice-Hall, Englewood Cliffs, NJ.

M F Rubinstein (1980) 'A Decade of Experience in Teaching an Interdisciplinary Problem-Solving Course' in D T Tuma and F Reif (eds) *Problem Solving and Education: Issues in Teaching and Research*, Erlbaum, Hillsdale, NJ.

G Ryan (1989) 'Problem-Based Learning – Some Practical Issues', 11 *Research and Development in Higher Education* 155.

G Ryan and P Little (1989) 'Problem-based Learning Within the School of Nursing and Health Sciences at Macarthur Institute of Higher Education', University of Western Sydney, unpublished paper.

D A Schön (1987) *Educating the Reflective Practitioner*, Jossey-Bass, San Francisco.

J Sweller (1985) 'Learning Through Problem-Solving: Some Doubts' in D Boud (ed) *Problem-based Learning in Education for the Professions*, Higher Education Research and Development Society of Australasia, Sydney, p 229.

D G Thompson and R G Williams (1985) 'Barriers to the Acceptance of Problem-based Learning in Medical Schools', 10 *Studies in Higher Education* 199.

A G V Tobin (1987) 'Criteria for Design of Legal Training Programmes', 5 *Journal of Professional Legal Education* 55.

M Verwijuen et al (1989) 'The Evaluation System at the Maastricht Medical School' in H G Schmidt et al *New Directions for Medical Education: Problem-based Learning and Community-Oriented Medical Education*, Springer-Verlag, New York, p 180.

K Winsor (1989) 'Toe in the Bathwater: Testing the Temperature with Problem-Based Learning', 7 *Journal of Professional Legal Education* 1.

C A Woodward (1984) 'Summary of McMaster Medical Graduates' Performance on the Medical Council of Canada Examinations', McMaster University Faculty of Health Sciences, Hamilton.

C A Woodward & B M Ferrier (1983) 'The Content of the Medical Curriculum at McMaster University: Graduates' Evaluation of their Preparation for Postgraduate Training', 17 *Medical Education* 54.

C A Woodward & R G McAuley (1983) 'Can the Academic Background of Medical Graduates Be Detected During Internship?', 129 *Canadian Medical Association Journal* 567.

D Woods (1985) 'Problem-based Learning and Problem-Solving' in D Boud (ed) *Problem-based Learning in Education for the Professions*, Higher Education Research and Development Society of Australasia, Sydney.

Chapter 8

Skills teaching on the Legal Practice Course
Peter Kilpin

Introduction

My intention is to consider skills teaching on the Legal Practice Course from the perspective of someone who is neither legally qualified, nor a lecturer teaching Law. Writing from this frame of reference may appear unusual or, at worst, downright dangerous!

However, I can claim some relevant experience. I have worked in a law firm; taught legal skills to both trainee and qualified solicitors; run staff development programmes with academic staff teaching the LPC at four universities; taught skills to LPC students and helped devise skills teaching exercises.

This examination of skills teaching will focus on three main areas:
1. General issues relating to skills teaching.
2. Tutor and student viewpoints on skills teaching.
3. The development of skills teaching.

To address the second topic, I carried out a small scale research project to establish a body of data and opinion on skills teaching from academics and past LPC students.

Central to this chapter is a desire to explore several questions:
- How have the attitudes of tutors and students to the LPC influenced skills teaching?
- How has the requirement to assess skills on a competent/non-competent basis influenced skills teaching?
- Which of the essential DRAIN skills (drafting and writing; research; advocacy; interviewing; and negotiation) have proved easier, or harder, to teach and learn and why?
- How might the experience of teaching skills on the LPC help other providers?

General issues relating to skills teaching on the LPC

This section will look back at the challenge presented by the introduction of the LPC and reflect on how effectively staff development programmes have prepared law faculty staff to meet the demands of the new course.

The challenge of the LPC

The Law Society's new Legal Practice Course was launched in September 1993. Unlike the previous Law Society Final Course (LSF), which it replaced, this left provider institutions relatively free to determine how to deliver the course, provided that their schemes were consistent with the criteria prescribed by the Law Society. These required the teaching of four compulsory subject areas: Business Law and Practice; Conveyancing; Litigation; and Wills and Probate – together with four pervasive subjects that were to be integrated across the curriculum: Professional Conduct, European Union Law, Financial Services and Revenue Law. In addition, providers were obliged to incorporate the five DRAIN skills within the curriculum, and to offer such options as they chose. The Law Society took responsibility, through its Legal Practice Course Board, for the validation and subsequent annual monitoring of all approved courses.

It is already easy to forget how great the change from Law Society Finals to the Legal Practice Course was. Slorach & Nathanson (1995) resorted to the architectural analogy of a design and build project to try to describe (p 76) the demands of combining:

> curriculum, materials, financial plans, physical plant, library, pastoral care facilities, administrative procedures, teacher training, printing facilities . . . into a complex whole that would effectively prepare students for practice.

The new course required major changes in teaching methods and the provision of staffing and physical resources that would turn high expectations into reality. These demands tested the leadership and management skills of staff given responsibility for the introduction and direction of the new course. In particular they had to help colleagues, with attitudes ranging from enthusiastic embrace to fear and rejection, to come to terms with the change.

The content of teaching programmes was altered. To the tangible, well documented domain of 'black letter law' were added the less tangible interpersonal and communication skills, and with them a greater focus on what the student could *do*, rather than just what the student should *know*: cf Jones (1993), p 99. This also affected teaching methods. Institutions had to move away from the well-established lecture/seminar style of the LSF towards the small group 'workshop' style of teaching, much of which would involve skills-based simulation.

For many, the adoption of new methods meant a major initiative to create new teaching material for teaching and assessing skills. The requirement to assess skills brought with it a whole set of problems around judgment, fairness, how to handle appeals, how to organise and administer the assessment sessions, criteria and other issues.

The new course, in common with skills training in general, is heavily resource dependent. Teaching in small groups requires facilities and teaching staff in prodigious quantity; such demands lead, inevitably, to compromises between the ideal and the economically viable.

The LPC made enormous demands on staff, testing their ability to work together as a team, to devise new and creative ways of teaching, and to reach agreement on assessment issues such as a common view on what is a competent, or non-competent, performance of a skill.

Preparation and staff development

Looking back over the experience of working with law faculties on staff development programmes, it is easy to see the critical issues. How to teach skills was the essential element; the skill itself (eg negotiating) was felt to be of lower priority. A proposal for a programme of staff development, written in early 1994, included the following objectives:

1.   To provide an awareness of the major practical considerations involved in teaching legal skills, ie working with groups, preparing suitable teaching material, etc.
2.   To create an understanding of the 'shift' required to teach legal skills effectively, ie from 'lecturer' to 'trainer'.
3.   To provide experience in dealing with the issue of competent/ non-competent assessment and how to develop skills through developmental feedback.

The client was assured that the programme would be:

> practical in style – a workshop rather than a seminar – with a minimum of theoretical input and your staff having the opportunity for practical experience of workshop techniques, small group management, feedback for development and formal skills assessment. To achieve this . . . using a number of role plays and other exercises.

Implicit in such programmes was a need to:

- introduce a range of teaching methods and techniques familiar to the 'trainer';
- enable staff to test and understand how to apply the various skills criteria adopted by their institution;
- provide confidence and reassurance to staff (as part of a hidden agenda).

It is difficult to assess the benefits of such programmes, but these are potentially sixfold:

1. Displaying the skills and techniques used by the 'trainer' and in doing so prove that teaching staff could do likewise.
2. Encouraging teaching staff to focus on the skill rather than legal elements of the LPC.
3. Providing, in a safe environment, experience of running groups, giving feedback etc.
4. Exposing any existing teaching material (eg role plays, case studies etc) to critical evaluation, providing ideas for improvement and encouraging teamwork in the preparation of teaching material.
5. Encouraging a greater uniformity of approach to assessment issues (eg pass/fail, competence, or otherwise).
6. Enabling staff concerned with managing the LPC team to enjoy an opportunity to discuss with their team a range of issues such as establishing teaching standards, the preparation of teaching material, etc.

Given the wisdom of hindsight, the weakness of such programmes was a lack of integration between the skill, the best methods of teaching it, the delivery of feedback for development of competence and the demands of pass/fail assessment. The approach to staff development was dictated by topic, eg 'feedback for development', or 'running workshops'. The programmes should have addressed how to teach the DRAIN skills within each of the core legal subjects and how to ensure the highest level of competence for the maximum number of LPC students.

A second weakness may have been concentrating too much on interpersonal skills and not balancing this with issues important to the teaching of drafting and legal research. Ideally, a staff development programme should focus on the integrated development of the whole set of DRAIN skills.

It is interesting to note that for one institution with two years' experience of teaching LPC, the key issues nominated by staff for the content of a Development Workshop were: giving feedback, teaching negotiation skills and managing small groups. From this Workshop came a clearer understanding of the concept of competence, ie the amalgam of skill, knowledge and attitude that together is a 'competent' performance of the skill: see Ayling & Costanzo (1984). The Workshop also demonstrated the importance of the tutor giving feedback in ways that help motivate the students to improve their performance, rather than just being aware of their shortcomings.

Staff development is vitally important at the start of a major teaching initiative such as the LPC, and it should, thereafter, be an ongoing exercise. There is considerable value in bringing together the team, challenging preconceptions, sharing experience and setting new directions in teaching practice.

Tutor and student viewpoints on skills teaching

This section seeks to compare and contrast the experience of skills teaching from tutor and student viewpoints and to highlight issues specific to one or other group. The section also draws, with caution, general inferences from the results of the two surveys.

The questionnaires

To gain a 'snapshot' of the experience of staff teaching the LPC, 70 questionnaires were sent to four institutions. The questionnaire was completed on the basis that it would be anonymous for both the individual respondent and the institution. A total of 20 questionnaires was returned (a 21% return), and while it is accepted that this 'snapshot' is selective and not sufficiently randomised to be representative, the results are nevertheless interesting.

To gain a comparative, student, viewpoint on the teaching of skills on the LPC, all first year trainees at the Norton Rose M5 Group and the LawNet Group were also sent a questionnaire. A total of 70 forms were returned, representing nearly half the sample group. The 70 respondents had been students at 15 institutions providing the LPC. All attended on a full-time basis the 1993–94 Course, with two exceptions. As with the tutor survey, respondents remained anonymous.

A considerable amount of data and comment was collected, although it is worth underlining that most of the trainees sampled had been students in the first year of the LPC and the institutions have, by now, probably addressed many of the concerns raised.

The comparison will deal with seven main topics:
–   Tutor expectations of teaching on the LPC.
–   Student reactions to LPC foundation programmes.
–   The teaching of DRAIN skills and the balance of teaching between skills and 'law'.
–   Teaching methods, teaching materials and resources.
–   Feedback of skills performance.
–   Pass/fail assessment.
–   The ideal class size for skills teaching.

Tutor expectations of teaching on the LPC

When asked to comment on the difference between expectation and reality, many tutors felt that it was '. . . easier', '. . . more interesting' and '. . . less daunting'. This view is reinforced by the responses to a question about the effect of skills teaching on teaching core subjects (Business, Probate, etc). Respondents commented on how their teaching had changed to accommodate more skills based, 'practical' exercises etc.

Student reaction to LPC foundation programmes

When asked about the introduction to legal skills, 93% of trainees said that there was a foundation programme; 50% that they were asked to complete pre-reading and 80% that they felt they were clear from the outset on the part skills teaching was to play during the LPC.

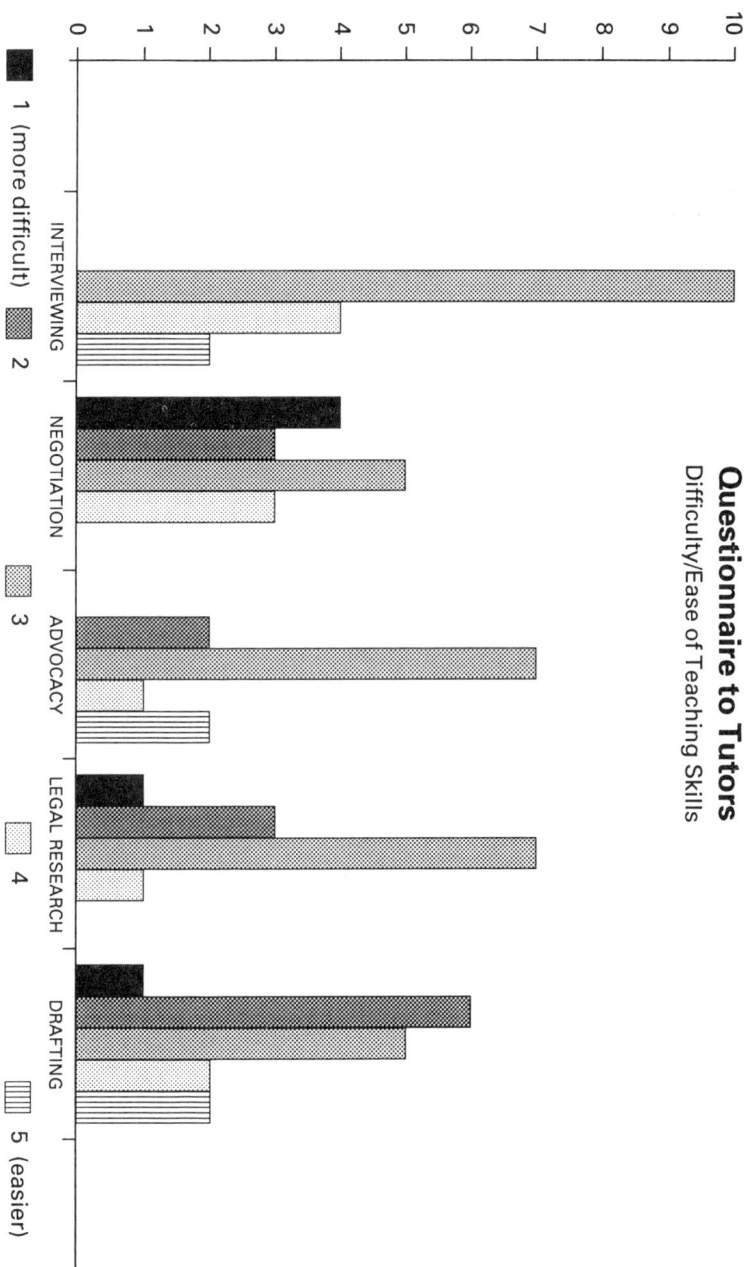

Questionnaire to Tutors
Difficulty/Ease of Teaching Skills

Comments about foundation programmes were very mixed, with many strongly expressed negatives, for example 'a complete waste of time'. Some respondents, however, were clear on the benefits of their Foundation Course as a 'scene setter', 'an introduction to LPC and skills teaching' and 'as a means of settling in'. Trainees were asked to comment on pre-reading. Roughly half those who replied, recorded (remembered!) doing any, with generally negative or, at best, neutral comments.

The teaching of DRAIN skills

Analysis of the response by tutors on the difficulty/ease of teaching the DRAIN skills reveals an interesting, but perhaps not surprising picture (see graph on page 247). As for difficulty, negotiation skills head the list; while on the other hand interviewing and advocacy were 'easier'. The perspective on legal research and drafting is more evenly balanced although, as we shall see, this view of teaching legal research contrasts strongly with the student perception.

An interesting viewpoint on the issue of teaching legal research came from one tutor who said, 'In my view, I started from the basis that students should be more capable than they are at both research and drafting from their past educational experiences; but it appears that undergraduate legal training inculcates little or no research ability, to the extent that many students are incapable of organising and analysing facts, while those who can research the law have no confidence that they have found the *right* answer – an assumption being that there must be a right answer rather than a range of answers.'

Trainees were asked to rate the quality of teaching against each of the DRAIN skills. The skills rated between 'satisfactory' and 'very good' were: Interviewing (Av 3.77), Advocacy (Av 3.64) and Drafting (Av 3.06). Those rated between 'satisfactory' and 'very poor': Negotiating (Av 2.97) and Legal Research (Av 2.62). A graphical representation of the responses to Question Six is shown opposite.

Teaching methods, teaching materials and resources

Tutors were given the opportunity to respond to a number of open questions on these issues. Unfortunately, only a few responded to the question on teaching methods. Comments were made on the necessity of gaining the full co-operation of all students in the group

Questionnaire to Students

How well were the main skills taught?

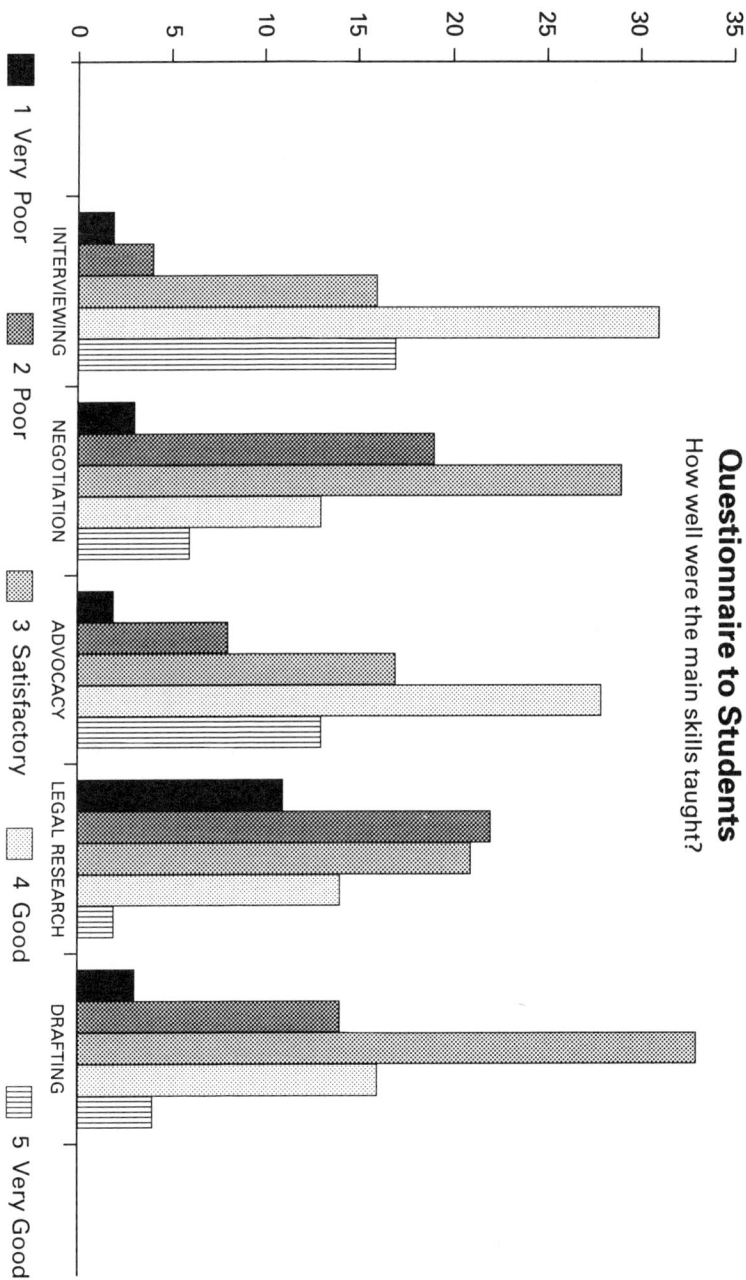

and the need to ensure greater variety in teaching methods to combat an overdependence on one method (typically role plays).

Students were asked to rate the effectiveness of teaching methods and to comment. Six teaching methods were rated. The most effective were: video recording and playback (Av 3.86); role plays (Av 3.64); case studies (Av 3.56); small group work (Av 3.51); video demonstration (Av 3.14); and, below average: legal research assignments (Av 2.62).

Perhaps not surprisingly, many comments concerned the teaching of legal research and all were negative. In summary, the skill was considered to be very important, and one that should have been given more time and been better taught. Mention was also made of the frustrations of working in groups caused by, for example, poor preparation by colleagues; or by being asked to complete a task on a group basis, when it would have been better to do it alone (for example, drafting a letter). Students also objected to having to watch others perform in role. The teaching of negotiation skills through written assignment, rather than by role play, came in for critical mention.

Comment was also made on the need for greater variety in methods, with less reliance on role play; this despite the relatively high score given to its effectiveness as a method of teaching.

Students did comment on the high quality of teaching materials. The many positive comments were tempered by some negative remarks on the lack of challenge; poor clarity of purpose in exercises; and the number of (non-deliberate) errors. The question of variety was mentioned with, again, 'too many' role plays being cited.

The research into resources for the LPC was tackled in different ways. Tutors, asked about the availability of commercial resources, commented that there were enough skills guides available, but felt that it would be useful to have video recordings that had been 'tailored' to support the teaching of specific aspects of legal skills: for example, a video of an interview for the purpose of gathering information in the preparation of a will; on aspects of advocacy; or the 'perfect' interview as an aid to assessment.

Students were asked to comment on the availability of resources within their institution. The lack of library space, the limited availability of reference books and computers/printers all came in for criticism. Those institutions with dedicated LPC facilities, or Resource Centres, received favourable mention.

Feedback

A range of concerns were highlighted by tutors in their comments on giving feedback for developing skills performance. Comments included the problems of working with large groups, not having enough time, and doubts about how best to cope with the reaction of students to this form of learning. Of particular note were the observations that students were only interested in the result (ie, 'was it good'), and were reluctant to analyse their performance, rather confirming thereby Hugh Brayne's (1994) concern that assessment has, at least for students, become the tail that wags the skills competence dog (pp 227, 239). A number of tutors commented that there was insufficient time to help the 'competent' students develop their skills.

The issue of self-appraisal by students brought a wide range of comments from tutors, ranging from '. . . very good' to '. . . does not work'. A similar response met the related question on peer appraisal, with comments ranging from '. . . too nice' to '. . . very tough on each other'.

Students were asked to rate the quality of feedback they received and to give views. The overall rating of the quality of feedback was satisfactory (Av 3.19). With regard to how feedback was provided, 80% received feedback from self-appraisal; 87% from peer appraisal and 97% from tutor appraisal. The comments elicited a range of views, stressing the difficulty of getting feedback beyond the pass/fail point; the failure to use video recordings to help with feedback; and a lack of continuity of method throughout a course. Tutors were considered not critical enough in the feedback they gave. However, pre-assessment mock exercises with tutors were felt to be very effective. Peer appraisal was considered by the majority of respondents to be of questionable value. As an afterthought, it would have been interesting to have found out more on how effective self-appraisal was thought to have been. From the author's experience of teaching post-LPC students, they are no better than their LSF colleagues at critical self-appraisal, or critical observation of skills exercises.

Taken as a whole, the comments on giving feedback raise serious questions about the effectiveness of these methods for reinforcing the learning and development of skills in the LPC context. This issue will be returned to later in the chapter.

Pass/fail assessment

The area of pass/fail assessment was explored in the tutor questionnaire. While there was general agreement that pass/fail assessment was better than grading, several replies raised the more fundamental question about whether one was assessing competence, or 'the performance'. The importance of dealing with failure through a second chance and giving one-to-one coaching where needed was highlighted.

I sought also to examine the impact of pass/fail assessments on students. The general view of staff was that students coped very well with this perhaps, in their experience, novel form of assessment. The majority of respondents commented that pass/fail assessment of skills was essential to ensure that students took legal skills seriously.

The student response to questions on pass/fail assessment brought many comments, with a clear divergence of view between those who felt it mattered ('. . . as important as core', '. . . passing gave me confidence to build on skills') and those who did not ('. . . since it was impossible to fail, it was not taken seriously', '. . . thought of it as a bit of a joke'). Several interesting points were made about the need to develop skills rather than just pass/fail, about uncertainty as to what standard of skills performance was expected, and what 'competence' meant: compare Brayne (1994), pp 232–4.

Ideal class size and other comments

Tutors were in agreement that the group should contain between eight and 12 students. There was similar agreement from students, who felt that small groups of 12 or less were good for skills teaching (the analysis of their replies gave an average of 10.7 as the ideal group size). The reasons students gave were the increased likelihood of receiving feedback from tutors and a reduction in the inhibitions resulting from working in large groups.

Respondents were also asked to comment on the balance of time spent on the course between skills and core subjects. This highlighted a difference of view between the majority of tutors, who thought it about right, and others who commented that skills were being taught 'at the expense of law'. Student views were divided between those who would have liked to spend more time on learning skills, against those who commented that more time was needed for core legal subjects. Several respondents felt that more ground could be covered in the year and that the LPC could include the Accounts Course and certain aspects of the Professional Skills Course. A few replies expressed concern that the course content was not relevant to the needs of those going into commercial firms.

Only a few tutors responded to a question about using practitioners to help with skills teaching; those who did emphasised how useful it had been, particularly with the preparation of case studies and advocacy exercises.

Summary

For the majority of tutors, the experience of teaching skills has been a positive one and certainly better than their expectations. The 'new' style of teaching has had a significant impact on the teaching of law at vocational level and there is evidence that tutors, with growing confidence, have sought to use the techniques of skills teaching in core area teaching.

The teaching of negotiation skills has proved most difficult and interviewing skills the easiest. The response to 'feedback', in all its forms, is mixed and highlights an area of concern for the course. On balance, pass/fail assessment was accepted and preferred to any grading of skills performance. Interesting points were made at both ends of the pass/fail spectrum. On the one hand, students assessed as competent were not encouraged to develop further. On the other, the importance of providing support to those who have failed, or are likely to fail was stressed.

Interestingly, while the use of external practitioners was seen to be very useful, few had used this resource. Finally, there was consensus that the ideal class size is between eight and 12 students per tutor.

Students were generally unimpressed by the Foundation element of their LPC and averse to pre-reading, particularly on the more abstract legal skills subjects. The teaching and resourcing of legal research came in for the heaviest criticism. The teaching of this important skill will need to be improved if it is to meet the realities of preparation for legal practice and to match the positive view on the teaching of other skills such as interviewing and advocacy. Curiously, this concern about legal research is not reflected in the opinion of tutors, who generally considered the teaching to be satisfactory. However, there is anecdotal evidence that a number of providers have since been engaged in substantially reviewing their research training.

Students had very mixed views on the quality of feedback, but were clear that the tutor is the primary source of feedback. Other methods, such as peer feedback, were considered to be far less influential and accordingly of limited value to skills development. How far this reflects a passivity inculcated by prior learning, or a lack of training in the objectives of such assessment techniques, or some combination of effects, remains to be seen. Attitudes to pass/fail assessment were polarised between those who thought it mattered, and those who did not. This division reflected, largely, the attitude of the institution. Some institutions appear to have been very successful in creating an attitude that skills were very important, while others had (for whatever reason) failed to get this message across.

Resources, or more particularly the lack of them, were heavily criticised, adding to the relatively poor performance of legal research teaching. The ideal group size was under 12 students per tutor.

The development of skills teaching

This section seeks to comment on skills teaching on the LPC and offer suggestions for the improvement and development of the course.

Skills – Cinderella or Prince Charming?

In his preface to *Lawyers' Skills*, Philip Jones (1994/5) writes:

> ... in the LPC, as in the early years of working as a lawyer, the concern is not with greatness, but competence. You may not emerge [from the LPC] as an artist, but you will be proficient.

The concept of competence involves a balance of the knowledge, attitudes and skills required to be a proficient lawyer. However, a fundamental problem facing the LPC is for all institutions to ensure that the 'skills' element of their course is treated and perceived by students as important and equal to 'the knowledge'. The comment from one trainee solicitor that pass/fail assessment was considered a 'bit of a joke' is a serious indictment of the institution and, indirectly, the status of the LPC.

To lift skills from the status of a Cinderella subject it is important not to isolate 'skills' from the practice of being a lawyer. Legal skills and legal knowledge are both sides of the same coin and both are vital to the competent, proficient lawyer of Jones's statement. I doubt if the lawyer sees a forthcoming interview with a client as an end in itself, but rather a part of the stream of legal process that makes up the job.

The introduction of the LPC has brought legal skills into sharp focus, but, in doing so, perhaps runs the risk of divorcing in the mind of the student the skill from the reality of legal life. For example, it is convenient to teach certain DRAIN skills within defined core areas, eg interviewing within Wills and Probate. However, this approach may serve to 'ring-fence' the skill and confine it unnecessarily: see Hogan (1983). If the question of where and how to teach skills were reversed (ie when teaching this aspect of the law, how should, or will, it be applied and what skills will be used in the process), then we would hope that the problem highlighted above will disappear. The DRAIN skills should, as far as possible, be integrated within the teaching of each core subject and not be separated, or seen as secondary.

A contrary argument sometimes presented is that it is often necessary to isolate a skill to teach it and in doing so provide opportunities for feedback. For example the teaching of interviewing skills requires the understanding of questioning techniques that can be taught in the abstract and do not necessarily require a legal context to achieve understanding. The need to understand skills at a basic level has been the rationale behind foundation courses where students were introduced to the DRAIN skills within a limited legal context.

To achieve the best of both worlds (ie integration of skills within the core legal subjects and isolation of certain skills to enhance learning), the option may be to fragment mainstream sessions with short excursions into skills to highlight important issues, get practice and gain feedback on the specific skills used to solve the legal problem or task. The pre-reading for sessions of this kind could cover both legal knowledge and skill, thus integrating the two.

The integrated approach outlined above would, I hope, serve to reduce the impact of negative attitudes towards skill teaching and, by underlining the notion of transferability of skills, help the student realise the importance of skills in their work as a lawyer.

The integrated approach has positive implications for changing the perception of pass/fail assessments. It is possible that the way pass/fail assessment has been organised may have contributed to further isolating skills. Assessments should not be labelled as 'skills assessment': if competence is the objective, then the ability to blend knowledge, attitude and skill in a proficient performance is what should be judged. The assessments should be a means of judging competence and be seen by students as a means of assessing how well they can apply the knowledge and skills they have learnt in a proficient and professional way, not as a low-level test of whether or not they can meet or greet a client.

Foundation courses – a waste of time, or time well spent?

The weight of evidence seems to point away from the foundation course as having major significance to the student. However, it is worth examining the objectives of such introductory sessions. The argument above against separating skills would, on the face of it, go against using the foundation course to introduce skills. In my view, the foundation course is useful for orienting students to the new course, eg explaining something about feedback and assessments; settling in; introducing small group work and workshops; and introducing 'skills' topics like client care, information handling, problem solving and information technology.

Feedback – lip-service, or service to the student?

The ability of tutors to provide high quality feedback is critical to the success of the LPC. The evidence from students is that they welcome and expect the feedback from tutors and value what they hear. However, giving feedback is not an easy skill and tutors should be helped in this task by regular staff development and review of performance.

The value of feedback is related directly to a belief in the value of skills training. Raising the profile of skills, within the context of total competence, is therefore essential. The higher profile will, in turn, make it easier for the tutor to give feedback that motivates the student to change or modify their behaviour; after all, that is what feedback is ultimately all about.

The process of feedback can be enhanced in several ways and many institutions already use observer and self-appraisal methods. It may be worth examining these to ensure that they serve a useful purpose and that they are being followed up by the tutor. For the individual student, reflection and self-appraisal should be encouraged. One suggestion, more commonly adopted on undergraduate courses, is that each student be given a personal learning log and asked to complete this at regular intervals. The log could also be used to contain reading lists, references etc. The student should review their log with a Personal Tutor, who would expect its completion and encourage reflection and further development. Conversations with the tutor would have benefit to both the able and less able student and be a good discipline for the Training Contract that will be followed in the near future. In the case of able students, the tutor should aim to stimulate and encourage further reading and development, over and beyond the pass/fail benchmark.

Legal research – neglected skill, or impossible criterion?

It is evident that students felt that this skill was badly taught and furnished with inadequate resources. A suggested way to approach the teaching of legal research is through a closer focus on problem-solving methods and techniques. The skills of defining objectives, sorting information, looking at the problem from different angles, inventing options etc could usefully be applied to problem solving in the legal context and in particular to legal research. A clear exposition of these skills is offered by Margot Costanzo (1995).

Negotiating skills – lose/lose, or win/win?

One danger of teaching negotiation skills is expecting too much of students too soon. The skill is a complex one, requiring considerable experience and further development to achieve mastery. However, the LPC is certainly the place to lay down the basics of good negotiating practice and to go further than certain institutions who have confined teaching to a written assessment of strategy. In teaching face-to-face negotiating skills, tutors need to be aware of the many facets of behaviour involved in a negotiation: for example, the difficulty of behaving in an assertive way, or in not being too aggressive. Although I cannot support my view with fact, I suspect that student reaction to the teaching of negotiating skills is largely dependent on how well, or otherwise, they have fared in face-to-face role plays.

The successful teaching of the skill requires particularly careful exercise design and feedback. For students with particular 'problems', feedback should be given on a one-to-one basis. The teaching of negotiation skills would, I believe, benefit from further staff development and training. The greater use of self reflection and tutor support would also prove helpful in this difficult area of teaching.

Conclusions

Through its emphasis on teaching skills within the traditional legal disciplines of the old Law Society Finals, the Legal Practice Course has achieved a significant breakthrough in the professional training of lawyers in England and Wales. Based on the evidence gathered from the first and probably most critical year of the course, the skills element is generally popular with tutors and students. The teaching of legal research and negotiating skills should be modified to ensure that they complement the needs of students and the profession. The most important issue is how to manage the perception of legal skills; whilst most acknowledge the importance of legal skills to the modern practitioner, the message is lost on some. This position must be changed to ensure that the value of the LPC as a measure of excellence is maintained.

The future development of the course should include attention to the issue of feedback and this area may benefit from further research into students' needs. Tutors at present are the key to the feedback process and need to ensure the feedback they give motivates as well as informs. Students, with support from tutors, should be encouraged to consolidate learning through reflection and self-appraisal far more than at present.

References

R Ayling & M Costanzo (1984) 'Toward a Model of Education for Competent Practice', 2 *Journal of Professional Legal Education* 99.

H Brayne (1994) 'LPC Skills Assessments – A Year's Experience', (1994) 28 *Law Teacher* 227.

M Costanzo (1995) *Problem Solving*, Cavendish, London.

A Hogan (1983) 'The Foundation and Development of the Australian Capital Territory Legal Workshop', 1 *Journal of Professional Legal Education* 1.

P A Jones (1993) 'Skills Teaching in Legal Education – the Legal Practice Course and Beyond' in P Birks (ed) *Examining the Law Syllabus: Beyond the Core*, Oxford University Press, Oxford.

P A Jones (1994) *Lawyers' Skills*, 1994/5 Edition, Blackstone Press, London.

S Slorach & S Nathanson (1995) 'Design and Build: The Legal Practice Course at Nottingham Law School', 4 *Nottingham Law Journal* 75.

Chapter 9

Taking reflection seriously:
How was it for us?
Caroline Maughan and Julian Webb

How did we get here?

Julian: I had been involved with skills teaching since the mid-1980s, but had been unable to get a coherent lawyering skills course off the ground, for a variety of reasons I suppose. I was still relatively new to law teaching, and had not really marked out my own territory. I was teaching across quite a range of subjects then, so there were real time constraints. I suppose I did not feel that confident about going it alone. At that stage, there were not many colleagues who were interested in trying to develop an 'academic' approach to skills teaching. In 1989, after moving to Bristol, I had floated a paper version of the course I wanted, but that was about all. The catalyst came when Caroline joined the Faculty in 1990.

Caroline: I started teaching languages in Essex in the early seventies but got fed up some years later because (a) hardly anyone in Dagenham wanted to learn German, and (b) I ran up against the 'conceptualisation' problem: students could use and manipulate structures and meanings correctly when we practised in class, but found it difficult or impossible to generate the rules correctly in new, unpredictable situations. (I have to say that I had never heard of Kolb at that stage – the psychology of learning element of my teacher training course had focused almost entirely on rats.)

I decided I wanted to exchange skills for a good dose of 'content' and went to study law.

My attitude to teaching substantive law was inevitably influenced by my language teaching experience. When preparing 'content' it was therefore natural for me to think about how to put it across, using a variety of learning methods which were as interactive as possible.

When Julian met Caroline: instant empathy! We both felt that skills had an important place in undergraduate legal education and that a lot of the early work on legal skills was lacking something.

Julian: I was interested in legal theory and the sociology of the legal profession as well as skills; I had done some research on legal education and from that I was aware of some of the American work on clinical legal education, and also of what Avrom Sherr and Roger Burridge were doing at Warwick, and Diana Tribe at Huddersfield, and then Hertfordshire. I had a fairly strong feeling that knowledge (in a wide sense of the term) and skills could not be separated, and by the early 1990s I had started to explore these ideas through some of the more general educational literature. Taken together, these influences encouraged me to try to link theory and practice in legal education through a course which took the DRAIN skills as a starting point but then used students' experiences as a vehicle for analysis and critique of the legal process. This element of critique I felt was vital in creating the academic dimension of such a course. Students had to be encouraged to relate what they had learnt to the wider questions about the role of law – and lawyers – in society.

Caroline: I felt that what was lacking in the early skills work was a coherent teaching methodology. The vocational materials that were coming out, though revolutionary in content, appeared to take a didactic approach, suggesting that students should 'learn' the DRAIN skills by being told how to do them. None of them provided any guidelines on teaching method.

I shared Julian's views on legal education and so was in sympathy with his 'academic' approach to the course.

When we began to plan it I concentrated on constructing exercises in which the skills could be practised and
developed. My past experience gave me a fairly sound
methodological basis on which to experiment.

Initially, we both invented and borrowed materials on a fairly ad hoc
basis. In fact we had a tacit theory, based on a mixture of experience, intuition and learning theory, though we probably could not
have articulated it as a developed model for teaching and learning –
that came later (are we there yet?). Looking back on it, the course
was developed experientially. We tried things out because they
seemed to fit what we were trying to do and then revised or dropped
them, as necessary, and increasingly sought to rationalise the programme as a whole. Two key aspects of our methodology emerged
very early on – using team teaching and reflection:

Caroline: We planned the team teaching really meticulously at
first – which of us should introduce a topic, lead/sum up
a discussion, role play the client in a demonstration, etc,
and what the other one needed to be doing while this
was going on. However, as we became more experienced and confident we would often change, even
abandon, some of these plans and play it by ear, taking
cues from each other. Similarly, as our relationship with
the group developed, we became more receptive to
what they could teach us. Again, we might spontaneously alter our plans at times and let the group dictate
the agenda.

It's not that our approach to planning and delivery
became more cavalier, it's just that we learned to value
the unintended and unplanned outcomes of learning.
This could sometimes be far more insightful than the
teaching we had planned.

Julian: Our other key idea (though it was not an original one)
was that we wanted to build a deeper element of student
reflection into the learning process rather than just rely
on the usual performance/feedback approach of skills
courses. To this end we tried to encourage our students
to distinguish between reflection on skills and reflection
on the wider professional 'context'. This was quite difficult for us and the students. They in particular tended to

divorce Legal Process, as a skills course, from everything else on the degree. It wasn't 'academic'; it wasn't about 'knowledge' but skills. It has taken us a long time to get away from that image. I think we are finally succeeding, but only by making the academic objectives increasingly explicit in both the workshops and the assessments.

We launched the Legal Process course in September 1991 as a year-long combined second and third year option on the full-time LLB at the University of the West of England.

The Legal Process course

What is it?

In its first year of operation, it is probably fair to say that it was little more than a course on the DRAIN skills with a few academic frills. We ran the course as a series of weekly three-hour workshops. These explored experientially the basics of fact management, interviewing, writing, drafting, negotiation and advocacy. The students then applied these skills through two case simulations. One case study was a personal injury claim (which was constructed so as to encourage the students to settle before trial), the other an indictable offence, which was carried through to trial in the Crown Court. The students divided into 'firms' of four for the casework, and remained in those firms for the year. They were assessed by three methods: an individual interview or negotiation exercise; a group oral presentation (on each firm's experiences of running the civil case) and a document file and set of reflective essays from each firm on the criminal case (we discuss these elements in more detail below).

The course has grown and developed organically, but this has remained the basic framework for what we do. The present module objectives are expressed as follows:

1. to enable students to show basic competence in the practical skills of legal research and problem-solving, interviewing and counselling, simple drafting, letter writing and negotiation;
2. to enable students to acquire the capacity for effective group working and case management;
3. to encourage students to develop a greater awareness of the ethical dimensions of legal practice and of the role of the lawyer in society;

4.   to enable students to develop the capacity for independent and reflective learning.

How has it evolved?

We have made four major adjustments to the programme since its launch.

First, we have increasingly made our learning methodology explicit. Since 1993, we have committed the first two workshops in the sequence to encouraging students to reflect, critically, on their experience of (legal) education; helping them to think about their strengths and weaknesses as learners and introducing them to the methods of experiential learning and reflective practice. The rationale and impact of this change we discuss in the next section of this paper.

Second, we have gradually increased the range of techniques we use to try and improve the quality of the students' independent learning, particularly learning through the case simulations. Students are deliberately launched 'in at the deep end' with these. We give them no additional tuition on the substantive law[1] and only some very basic guidance on adjectival law and procedure; nor do we offer instruction on group working. To that extent our methodology is problem-based in the true sense of that term: see Cruickshank (1996). Although all the assessment events are tied in to the case-work, this does not enable us easily to monitor the whole process, rather than the outcome, of their learning. We have therefore implemented a number of (formally) non-assessed process checks, involving (1) on-going reviews of letter and document drafting; (2) progress reviews of casework with each firm; and (3) a requirement (though one that is not strictly policed) that all students maintain 'learning diaries' in which they record their experiences and their reflections on those experiences.

Third, we introduced a formal element on legal ethics into the programme in 1994. Prior to that, ethics and conduct had been a background issue, but not one that we had been able to get the students to address to our satisfaction. As our workshop programme

---

1   Students on our programme will have studied Criminal Law in their first year and Torts in the second. Inevitably, one of the greatest shocks they receive is the realisation of how little of this substance they actually *know* in the sense of being able to understand and apply it to a 'real-life' situation.

was already crowded, we had only introduced the issue of ethics briefly in specific applied contexts (eg, interviewing and client care; negotiation strategies; advocacy and adversarialism in the court-room). In 1994 we supported this by presenting students with some basic theories explaining professional legal ethics (lawyer as hired gun, lawyer as moral agent, and so on), and outlines of the rules of conduct, through a set of materials and questions which mostly took the form of various hypothetical and ethics/conduct scenarios. The students were then told to go away and write up answers to the questions raised.[2] This certainly increased students' awareness of the ethical context of practice, but we still felt generally dissatisfied with the quality of ethical awareness and reflection students were show-ing. Accordingly, for 1996 we intend to formalise this element into a modified 'Keller', or self-paced learning, package in which students will get worksheets and materials at the start of the course and be expected to work through these (with small group mini-tutorials out-side of the normal workshop sessions) during the first six weeks of the course.

Lastly, we have also discontinued our original practice of allowing students to remain in the same firm for the whole year. The rationale behind this change needs to be considered within the wider context of the learning environment we have attempted to create for the course as a whole.

Creating the learning environment

We believe that the kind of experiential learning we are trying to foster can only be achieved in an appropriate learning environ-ment. We have put a lot of thought into this and developed a model which borrows quite heavily from theories of action learning: see Revans (1980); McGill & Beaty (1992). Action learning describes:

> a continuous process of learning and reflection, supported by colleagues, with an intention of getting things done. Through action learning individuals learn with and from each other by working on real problems and reflecting on their own experi-ences. The process helps us to take an active stance towards life

2   These materials formed the basis for Maughan & Webb (1995), ch 4.

and helps to overcome the tendency to think, feel and be passive towards the pressures of life.

McGill & Beaty (1992), p 17

Accordingly, we have identified three learning contexts within the programme, which we term the learning community, learning sets and activity groups.

THE LEARNING COMMUNITY

This is a formal term for the whole group following the course, including us, the facilitators. It is the focal point for much of the workshop activity, and particularly for reflection and discussion, and for community-wide decision-making on the progress of the course. Most of the work we do in the learning community is undertaken 'in the round'. This layout is important. Students do not have the security of a desk between them and us. Indeed, the whole spatial divide between teacher and student disappears. No one can hide at the back, or dominate from the front. There is also an open space in our midst for demonstrations and activities. For most of our students, working in this sort of environment is the first culture shock. They do feel exposed and uncertain to start with. But they seem to get used to it, particularly once it becomes apparent that the public space it gives us is not going to be used in a threatening way. Most also come to recognise the obvious benefits of working through problems in this environment:

> You're watching other people learning as well, and you are almost hearing them thinking through the process, and you learn with them by watching their mistakes as well as your own.
>
> [T4/93][3]

The learning community approach has its implications for us as teachers. The context demands that we try and subsume our roles within the community. To do that, we try to share our learning and our own uncertainties with the group. We stress from the start of the course that we do not see our functions didactically; that generally

---

3   The student quotes incorporated in this paper are drawn from action research data we have gathered on the course, either from taped interviews with students on the course, or from the students' own learning diaries (used with permission). Our research into the course is continuing.

our roles are guiding and participative rather than directive. To some extent this is illusory, however, as our own reflections show:

Julian: I always find this [facilitative] aspect of my role the hardest to manage. I find it difficult sometimes not to be didactic – giving students the answer, or at least pushing them in the 'right direction', is a lot more painless and less frustrating than watching them groping in the dark, though ultimately it is less rewarding than seeing their confidence and abilities grow when they realise they can work things out for themselves. At the same time I think some degree of teacher direction and control is inevitable, given our present conception of the course. This is for the following reasons. (1) We need to establish some basic parameters if our learning objectives are to be met. We have not gone so far down the capability road as to allow students to define their own learning objectives and, unless or until we do, we cannot legitimately call for our own redundancy! (2) The bottom line is that, in some respects, we *are* the experts, and some elements of our coaching role demand that we show or tell of our expertise. That is part of the sharing of experience. (3) Ultimately I doubt whether the students can forget our traditional status and role any more than we can. To suggest we are other than what we are is an ideological con trick.

For me, the knack is to use our authority constructively. I suppose I tend to see my function in broadly counselling terms. I've long been influenced by John Heron's work:[4] as he points out, a good counsellor will use their expertise and distance from the problem to create positive interventions which are supportive of the individual's development and growth but which, at times, may be directive or confrontational. This is the effect I try to achieve.

THE LEARNING SET

In a full action learning environment, the learning set serves as a group environment for individual learning. The theory is that individuals

4   See, for example, Heron (1989), (1990).

bring problems or 'projects' before colleagues in their set, – for example, problems relating to their feelings about a particular organisational environment, interpersonal relationship, task, etc. The learning set provides an environment for reflection within what should be a supportive group, though not a support group. The function is to facilitate learning, not just make people feel better! Set members encourage reflection by asking questions that help the individual concerned explore the issues involved in the problem and by challenging the problem-solver's assumptions.

At present, our model falls some way short of this ideal, and this is possibly because of a flaw in our methodology. We have attempted to combine our learning sets with the main problem-solving groups used in the course – the students' firms. These have been self-selecting, thereby ensuring the broadly voluntary constitution of our sets. Nevertheless, we have found that there is often a certain tension between the problem-solving/learning set functions of the firms.

The group work is one aspect that the students always find difficult. Many of the problems they encounter with the civil case arise more out of their limited capacity to work together, than out of dealing with the law and procedure involved. By the time the firms start the criminal case (in early February) they have normally sorted out their strategies for group working, which is why we then disband those firms and require them to reconstitute with at least 50% different personnel! This forces individuals to renegotiate at least some of their working relationships, which we hope they will do by building on their experiences first time around. One of our students has described this process:

> The reorganisation of the groups at the outset of the criminal case came as a surprise. As [a firm] we had made a concerted effort to air our 'grievances' so that the problems that had arisen during the running of the civil case would *not* haunt us during the criminal case. Nevertheless, the reorganisation gave us all an opportunity for a new, 'fresh' start.
>
> Thus 'Locke Tuppe and Dunnover' was born. I believe we all had learnt a great deal about the logistics of group work from the first term. We *immediately*
> – devised a basic plan as to each group member's area of responsibility;
> – sorted out convenient meeting times;

exchanged contact numbers and addresses and established
a link person to facilitate communication.

[D3/94]

However, the difficulties students encounter in working within their
firms (difficulties which, in a sense, we *want* them to encounter) – ie,
of task-allocation, time-management and interpersonal relations – do
not always make for harmonious and supportive firms. These groups
may then function less than efficiently as supportive learning sets.
The obvious solution would be to separate these functions. But it is
doubtful whether the students could cope effectively with managing
two distinct sets of group relationships outside of the allocated workshop time. Confidentiality within firms might also be compromised
if learning sets were to cut across firm boundaries. This problem is
one we have yet to resolve.

THE ACTIVITY GROUPS

These are sometimes selected, but mostly self-selecting, groups of
between two and six students which function in the workshops. The
activity groups are the main environment in which students practice
their skills and other activities. As a matter of practice we normally
divide the whole community into activity groups to undertake exercises in tandem, rather than rely extensively on demonstrations. This
is one practical reason why we rely heavily on team teaching, since,
in our view, effective supervision of and feedback from (normally)
six to 12 activity groups cannot be undertaken by one person.
Experimentation and feedback on specific tasks and exercises is
undertaken within these smaller groups, though it may also be reinforced by further reflection and review within the learning
community as a whole.

The role of reflection

As the course developed, so did our concept of reflection. We knew
that teachers were interested in Donald Schön's theory of the reflective practitioner, but at that time we were not aware of any skills
courses which put the theory into practice. We both felt Schön's theories could work on our course. His rejection of the knowledge/skills
divide in favour of an integrated model of professional education

reflected our own concerns and feelings about legal education. Moreover, his concept of the 'reflective practicum' fitted well with the experiential learning methodology we were developing. We therefore decided to experiment with Schön's ideas.

Briefly, these ideas can be summarised as follows. Professional education is in crisis because it has been dominated by the 'technical rational', or 'high ground' approach to professional knowledge. This approach distinguishes knowledge from action by claiming that professional practice is simply the application of a body of propositional knowledge to a practical situation. This approach, however, does not reflect the reality of professional practice. Established textbook theory and techniques are inadequate to deal with the complexity of practice (the 'swamp') in which the practitioner will meet situations of uncertainty, uniqueness and value-conflict:

> The problems of real world practice do not present themselves to practitioners as well-formed structures. Indeed, they tend not to present themselves as problems at all but as messy, indeterminate situations.
>
> Schön (1987), p 4

The competent professional uses a combination of knowledge, intuition and action to deal with these 'messes'. Searching through her repertoire of past experience helps her to identify, or frame, the problem. She will then improvise to find the solution – selecting and adapting strategies which she has used successfully, and trying them out in the new situation.

This 'art of problem framing, an art of implementation, and an art of improvisation' (p 13) relies on intuitive processes which Schön (1987) calls *knowing in action*. This is the capacity to perform tasks and respond to situations spontaneously and unconsciously. This tacit knowledge gets us through our routine daily tasks. However, to expand our repertoire of responses to the novel, unpredictable problems of the swamp we need to bring our knowing in action to the surface, ie consciously confront and assess our tacit theories of action, norms and attitudes.

This process of articulating tacit knowledge relies on two kinds of reflection. *Reflection in action* is an interaction with the problem as it unfolds. It involves matching the situation with similar ones in the practitioner's experience. If the two do not match, she must reframe the problem and try another approach.

Reflection on action takes place after the event. Here the practitioner makes the theories of action she used to solve the problem explicit. In other words, she uncovers and works through the 'reflective conversation' she had with herself while in the middle of the problem.

Much of what Schön says is not new. For example, the notion that learning involves reflection which should lead to the exploration and modification of theories of action is well-established in experiential learning and other cognitive theories, as is the integration of knowing and doing.[5] However, what we found particularly interesting about Schön's work was his emphasis on professional *practice* as a valid and rigorous learning experience. He aims to reproduce this experience in the 'reflective practicum'. Here, students are encouraged to develop their repertoire of practical and experiential knowledge in a closely supervised environment – a 'virtual world' in which they perform tasks which resemble professional practice as closely as possible. The job of the teacher, or 'coach', is to guide the learner, through reflection, to discover the reasoning and decision-making processes which informed her actions.

To make these discoveries, the learner must articulate her reflection in action. If she fails to do so, reflection on action may be simply a rationalisation after the event of intuitive action, in which the reasoning processes remain undetected. The result is *single loop* learning: achieving intentions without re-examining the values and habits which shape her behaviour. Moreover:

> We strive to organise our individual and organisational lives by decomposing them into single loop problems because these are easier to solve and to monitor. Unfortunately, we get increasingly better at the routine and increasingly more frightened about questioning the program that makes the routine possible. So we may be good at accomplishing the routine, but only with increasing costs, one of which is an unquestioning acceptance of the routine that appears to get the job done. As a result, we may produce something for today but lose control of tomorrow.
>
> Argyris (1989), p xii

Reflective practitioners, on the other hand, use their reflective conversations to confront and challenge their responses to problems and

---

5   This notion is discussed in Maughan (1996), in this collection.

the action theories which govern those responses. Argyris (1989) and Schön (1987) call this *double loop* learning. It involves recognising that the theories underlying our knowing in action may be dubious, particularly when based on deeply embedded attitudes and values. It involves uncovering the processes of discrepant reasoning.

Discrepant reasoning occurs when we act inconsistently with our avowed values and beliefs. It happens easily and often in the difficult practical situations of the swamp. Argyris and Schön identify two kinds of action theories. Our *espoused theories* are what we say we believe in. *Theories in use* are implicit in what we actually do. They are usually tacit, and often conflict with our espoused theories. Because we may not be aware of a theory in use, we may not realise why we respond as we do in an unpredictable or threatening situation. This can lead to 'distancing'; in a situation which is not resolved success-fully we may attribute the unsatisfactory outcome to some external cause, failing to question and analyse the values and assumptions that influenced our behaviour.

For example, in the context of legal negotiation we use the Red–Blue game[6] to highlight processes of discrepant reasoning. It demon-strates very clearly how our deep-seated beliefs and values can conflict with those we *claim* to operate by. By the time we play it the students have already practised different negotiating styles. Before the game, we ask the students to consider and identify the character-istics and behaviour of an effective negotiator. Then they play the game, the object of which is to obtain the highest possible score for their team. The way to do this is to use a win/win strategy. Invari-ably, the teams end up with minus scores, some having consciously adopted a strategy we call 'lose/lose': they become so competitive that they think they have won the game because they haven't lost as much as the other side! At some stage they have decided that the main task is to outdo the opposing team, even if it results in an unsat-isfactory outcome for their own.

During feedback, various discrepant reasoning processes are identi-fied. Before the game, most students had favoured problem-solving and co-operative negotiating styles for the majority of legal contexts. When these students become aware of their discrepant behaviour,

---

6 A variant of the well-known Prisoner's Dilemma game. See Axelrod (1984); Johnson & Johnson (1991). For our version of the Red–Blue game, see Maughan and Webb (1995), pp 288–90.

some will put it down to the fact that they were playing a game. They strongly maintain that they would not behave like this in a real negotiation. This is a classic example of distancing yourself from your espoused theory. Or a student may say that she wanted to co-operate with and trust the other side, but felt pressured by the team into playing competitively. In this instance the student disconnects herself from her espoused theory, either because she lacks confidence in her reasoning processes, or her ability to convince her colleagues, or because she is not really sure what theory she espouses: see Argyris (1989), Schön (1987).

We find that using reflection to surface these discrepant reasoning processes as they occur excites and challenges our students. However, we have learnt not to push it. Red–Blue feedback stimulates lively, though sometimes uncomfortable, and occasionally angry, debate. Which is espoused theory and which theory in use? Some students can't always tell the difference. To what extent has the idea 'thinking like a lawyer = thinking adversarially' become part of their tacit knowledge and modified their attitudes and values? If to a large extent, are they comfortable with this? Does it fit with 'non-law' areas of their experience, such as family relationships? Confronting inconsistencies in your values and belief systems can be disturbing or threatening.

Constructing tasks and exercises which allow students sufficient opportunity to engage in this kind of reflection can pose other problems. For a start, there is the practical problem of time: reflection is never done.

Caroline: I find this one of the most frustrating aspects of the course. Our course content and methodology dictates that we facilitate a number of activities in each three-hour session. I hardly ever feel that we have explored an area thoroughly enough before we run out of time. It's like those infuriating television discussions that finish before they've barely scratched the surface. I want to make sure everybody gets everything out, and then have time for synthesis and summary. Because you know you've got a limited time for feedback, it's tempting to jump in with 'answers', or push the discussion in a certain direction, so as to speed up consciousness-raising.

Perhaps a five- or six-hour block, say, every three

weeks, would suit our purposes better. A further hour a
week could be timetabled for the learning sets to meet.
Between blocks there would be more time for further
reflection, further reading and preparation of materials
for the next block.

This brings us to the second problem. A student may not reach the
point where she can surface her action theories and conceptualise
until some time after the event – perhaps weeks. Such insights may
get lost, particularly if she is not in the habit of recording her learning. Moreover, she may not get the chance to test out modifications
to her theory if the class has moved on to another topic or activity.

Thirdly, as we suggested above, not every student will be able to
articulate their reasoning processes, even after lengthy reflection
and feedback. We give them extra guidance on managing their
learning and the techniques of self-assessment, but accept that on a
one-year course the most we can probably do is introduce them to
this kind of thinking and provide them with the tools to develop it
for themselves.

We thought that some of these problems would be alleviated if the
learning community were absolutely clear about what it was being
asked to do, and why. There is no point in asking students to engage
in this kind of reflection if they don't understand its purpose. We
therefore decided that once we had clarified what learning theories
we were going to use, we should make the students aware of them.

Making learning theory explicit

Post-hoc (or hic?) reflection: January 1993

Caroline: I need a drink – badly.
Julian: Really? I thought the session went quite well. The Red–
            Blue Exercise brought out some very interesting contra-
            dictions . . .
Caroline: I'm depressed. I can't go on.
Julian: What are you so miserable about?
Caroline: I just have the feeling that some of these students – X
            and Y, for example – only took our course because
            there's no exam. Do they think no exam means the
            course is a doddle? Their capacity for self-assessment is
            poor . . .

Julian: Well, what do you expect when we don't give them any idea how to do it?

Caroline: *(now in full flow)* . . . their complacency is breathtaking. They seem to blindly accept all the assumptions about law and lawyers that we encourage them to question, without providing any rational arguments to support them. Have they learnt anything at all?

Julian: Oh, so just the usual crisis then. To be fair, I must admit I felt very frustrated today when X insisted that his group had 'won' the game because they ended with a lower minus score than their opponents! I'm not sure I'd want him negotiating for me.

Caroline: He still didn't get the point when the rest of his group spelled it out in words of one syllable; he just argued it was all a game anyway.

Julian: Come on, let's get this in perspective. Everyone else seemed to get the point without too much prompting. Perhaps X will when he thinks about it a little more. I shall be interested to see his learning diary entry. Maybe we can take up some of the points with him again then. That is, if he makes an entry. He hasn't been too conscientious about it in the past.

Caroline: Why doesn't X keep a diary? Doesn't he see the point of it? Mind you, some of the other diary entries seem very perfunctory, don't they? As if they're just going through the motions.

Julian: Yes, I agree. Either there's not a lot of deep reflection going on, or if it is, it's not being recorded. We can't have got the message across. You know, I've been thinking about this whole problem quite a lot lately. Do you remember telling me about your problems in getting students to accept different teaching methods when you were teaching English as a Foreign Language? Because they didn't understand why you were using them and what they were for?[7]

Caroline: Right. We've got a similar situation. It's been nagging me for weeks. Our brief introduction to experiential

7   See Maughan (1996), in this collection.

	learning in week one is useless. We've got to think about going the whole hog.
Julian:	We've fallen victim to discrepant reasoning ourselves. We sing the praises of experiential learning and devise a whole programme based on its principles. Yet at the beginning of that programme we briefly tell the students what those principles are, rather than let them discover them by going through the learning cycle. What a pair of prats! No wonder they don't get the point.
Caroline:	Just like when I was having the problems with my English class – at the time all their other classes were taught in the traditional way. How could I expect the students to divine the purpose of a new method? You have to spell it out, work through it, discuss the reasons for it, make them feel secure using it.
Julian:	Do you know what this means? For the course? *(Laughs nervously)*
Caroline:	Oh God! We've got to make the learning theory explicit – all of it, experientially. We'll need six weeks, at least.
Julian:	I need a drink – badly.

Why did we think we had got it so very wrong?[8]

It was only around the time of this discussion that we were in a position to articulate our learning theories fully, let alone share them in detail with others. Also, we took the view that the traditional law student is not remotely interested in anything which is not law. Educational theory, if not handled carefully, could be a big turn-off.

Nevertheless, both of us had been aware for some time that sooner or later the nettle would have to be grasped . . .

Grasping the nettle

Many of our students join the course (at least partly) to get familiar with the DRAIN skills before enrolling on the vocational courses. Our course helps some of them make up their minds finally whether they want to practise or not and, if so, in which branch of the profession. We therefore felt there was a risk that our students could lose motivation if confronted with such a large chunk of theory at the

---

8 How many people do you know who double loop easily and often?

beginning of the course. Furthermore, some students wilt at the very
mention of the word 'theory'. Trying to convince them that theory is
good for them goes down about as well as a dose of salts, and twice
as fast.[9]

Nonetheless, we decided to take the risk. There was no question of
dealing with the theory later, or in selected bits during the course;
we had to make our students familiar and comfortable with it as
soon as possible. In order to learn, they had to know how they were
learning.

The following year we devoted the first two workshops (six hours)
to learning theory. It seemed natural to introduce it in the legal context, using the students' experiences with legal education as our
starting point. We invited them to reflect on their legal studies to
date, and then to extend their analyses to broader perspectives:

● the separation of theory and practice in traditional legal education;
● the nature of legal professional knowledge;
● their perceptions of the lawyer's social role.

Defining the context in this way allowed us to introduce the students
to Schön's concepts of artistry and reflective practice. We designed
exercises to get them thinking about knowledge, skills, attitudes and
values in lawyering. Some were structured, while others encouraged
open-ended discussion. This was the subject-matter of the first workshop.

Reflecting on the event, however, we were not satisfied that it had
been a valid learning experience. This was the first time the group
had met and so some students did not feel confident enough to contribute to the discussions. We needed to do more to break the ice.[10]

Furthermore, despite our efforts to deepen the discussion, it
remained superficial some of the time. We had deliberately set out to
use some element of surprise – the shock tactic of putting people 'in
the swamp'. But we hit them with too many new and complex ideas

9   You will probably begin to see that at this point we were in danger of losing
    sight of our real objectives. We had started to adopt the vocational aims of our
    students and, perhaps, unconsciously we were accepting the view that learning
    theory is just not 'done' on law courses (although we were well aware that it is
    an important part of the learning process in other disciplines).
10 Breaking the ice was something we had always been concerned about when we
    began the course with skills, and we had found it easy to set up ice-breaker
    exercises. However, we discovered it is not so easy when you start with theory.

with insufficient introduction, and no real opportunity to grasp the concepts involved, or to make links with their experience in advance of the workshop.

We think the way to get round this difficulty in the future is to ask the students to read selected texts and to summarise and critique the main ideas in writing before they attend the first workshop. This would give them a much stronger foundation on which to reflect as we discuss and develop the ideas in the first workshop.

In the second workshop we introduced the group to the theory of experiential learning. There was a large amount of content here, and we had serious doubts as to whether we could cover everything satisfactorily in three hours. In fact, we found we needed at least four.

We set the scene for the workshop as follows:

> This workshop will introduce you to the concept of experiential learning. This demands that you take charge of your own learning and practise critical self-assessment. We will ask you to begin recording your learning in a personal journal and to make an assessment of your preferred learning style. Experiential learning processes enable you to develop a flexible repertoire of responses and techniques which you will continuously refine through new experiences and reflection. This is how you acquire artistry.

Objectives

To:
- examine Schön's concept of reflection;
- outline behaviourist and cognitive learning theories;
- explain the principles and techniques of experiential learning;
- enable you to explore and apply these principles and techniques;
- examine the concept of discrepant reasoning;
- discuss and assess techniques for self-assessment, in particular the learning diary and learning styles questionnaire.

It was important the students grasped quickly that the 'reflective practitioner' was not simply someone who considered thoughtfully and carefully before taking action! We therefore used 'swampy' role playing exercises which forced the 'lawyers' to improvise on the spot when something unexpected happened. During feedback we attempted to elicit their 'reflective conversations'.

In a demonstration, for example, a student played the role of a law student on work experience in a solicitor's firm. A furious client (played by the tutor) storms into the office, demanding to see her solicitor. Both the solicitor and her trainee are unavailable. The receptionist passes the client on to the law student. The client is extremely abusive at the start of interview, and may remain so, depending on how the 'lawyer' handles it. After the the role play, the 'lawyer' was asked to describe his thoughts and feelings at two points in the scene:

(a)   when he is asked down to reception to meet the client, and

(b)   when the client hurls abuse at him.

A lively discussion ensued, in which the 'lawyer' started by articulating his internal dialogue. This revealed the two action theories he had chosen to use:

1.   After letting off steam the client would probably cool down, as long as he stayed calm and polite, yet looked her clearly in the eye to show he was genuinely interested in her problem, and that he was not intimidated by her behaviour.

2.   A person in this state would probably calm down more quickly if he could get some information from her, thereby interrupting the flow and momentum of abuse. This would also enable him to find her case file and perhaps solve the problem.

Then other group members described various action theories for dealing with rude and angry clients, and whinging, obnoxious people in general. Some students had experience of the problem while working on helplines or in 'customer complaint' departments. The group also seemed to grasp the concepts of knowing-in-action, reflection-in-action and reflection-on-action and how they are linked in Schön's model. However, some couldn't recognise when they were actually involved in these processes, and how these enabled them to learn.

We put this down partly to lack of familiarity with the techniques of role playing. By the second week of the course everybody had done only one role-playing exercise. Some group members had found it difficult to take that exercise seriously, let alone put themselves into a role sufficiently to act, feel and think it. Others had role-played with the 'script' in front of them – in some cases clipped into a large, open file!

Later in the session, when we had introduced and discussed Kolb's learning cycle (1984), we asked each individual to reflect on a recent problematic or threatening experience and record their reflective conversation. Primarily, this was to enable them to experience the processes of *knowing in action, reflection in action* and *reflection on action*. It was further designed to reinforce the learning cycle concepts (*experience, reflection, rule-making, planning and testing*), and to introduce them to the learning diary and the techniques of recording. To prompt their reflection, we listed some of the standard feedback questions they should ask themselves: compare Maughan (1996).

This exercise helped individuals discover and analyse how their reflective processes worked to enable them to learn. However, it is an artificial exercise because in some cases reflection may be so long after the event that individuals may find it difficult to remember their reflection-in-action in any detail. This can lead to large amounts of fabrication! We therefore encourage each person to select a recent event which has had such a profound effect as to be fresh in their memory.

The lack of realism has one major advantage, however. Many of our students are reflector/theorists[11] at the start of the course: see Honey & Mumford (1992). It therefore suits them to think out how the processes work from a position of detachment rather than whilst in the thick of it.

Recording the learning experience

We ask the students to keep a learning journal as soon as we are satisfied that they have understood how they learn – ie how the learning cycle works. However, some find it difficult putting the theory into practice. The very idea of 'letting it all hang out' can put off a theorist/reflector, even though we impress upon them that they can keep the details confidential. Some get hung up on the headings

---

11 Honey and Mumford's learning styles – Activist, Reflector, Theorist, Pragmatist – correspond to the four stages of the learning cycle. In our experience, the majority of our students are theorists or reflectors (or a combination of the two) when they arrive on the course. People with these learning preferences tend to feel uncomfortable with the open-ended participatory activities of experiential learning.

– 'Should this point go under "Reflection" or "Rule-Making"?' We don't think it matters ultimately, as long as cycles are completed. These problems can be resolved fairly easily with practice, guidance and encouragement.

A more serious issue is the failure to conceptualise. As we said earlier, not everybody can do it all of the time, or even some of the time. Another major problem is the assumption made by some that great changes will take place after one trip round the cycle and, once this is done, learning is finished. We therefore feel it necessary sometimes to read the journals to see whether any individual needs extra help. Infringing their rights of ownership and confidentiality in this way is a dilemma we have yet to resolve.

Analysing learning preferences

When emphasising the role of self-assessment in personal and professional development, we think the starting point should be an analysis of your learning styles and preferences.[12] We say a starting point because it is tempting to view the findings as an answer to all learning problems – 'I'm an activist, so that's why I can't stand going to lectures. End of story'. However, the analysis does help our students understand more clearly how they learn. Most have one or two preferred styles. Once they have identified these, we encourage them to consider ways of developing all four. This means that a person's preferences (and questionnaire results) are unlikely to remain the same throughout the course.

Our students fill in Honey and Mumford's (1992) questionnaire and plot their results on a graph. It is of course possible that respondents will not answer the questions honestly and accurately. We ask our students to check their results carefully against their own preconceived ideas about their preferences, and also to compare them with a friend's view of their preferences. We finish off the Learning Theory sessions with a discussion of the merits and drawbacks of each style and draw some conclusions about the learning process in general. By then, or after further reflection, we hope the activist will not only know why she can't tolerate lectures, but have some idea of what to do to improve her learning in that situation.

12   Kolb's Learning Styles Inventory and Honey and Mumford's Learning Styles Questionnaire are discussed in detail in Maughan (1996), in this collection.

Assessing reflection

What we assess

In our assessment programme we assess a range of skills and attributes. These incorporate both the intellectual skills of the law degree (eg ability to do independent legal research; the ability to analyse and apply legal rules) and wider transferable skills (of oral and written communication, of group working and group presentation) as well as the applied or DRAIN skills.[13] We also attempt to assess some elements of student performance within the affective domain – notably, the decisions students make at a strategic level in their casework, and their awareness of 'ethical' as opposed to 'conduct' constraints on courses of action.

These skills and attributes are assessed in three contexts: an individual oral communication exercise (each student must do an individually assessed client interview or negotiation); a group video presentation from each firm on aspects of the civil case; and a document file and set of essays from each firm on aspects of the criminal case. The correspondence between the range of skills we assess and each assessment event is shown in the Table on page 285.

We specifically seek to develop and assess not just our students' performance, but their capacity for reflection in all of these events. To this end we have distinguished broadly between three kinds of reflection in our course.

- Reflection on the specific skills, attributes or behaviours displayed in the performance of a task.
- Reflection on practical legal knowledge (ie substantive law and procedures).
- Reflection on 'law in context' and theories about the legal process. Our aim here is to enable students to become more reflective critics of the system, with the capacity for what Henderson (1989) calls (p 12) *illuminative achievement*: the ability

---

13 Though we teach basic advocacy, we have considered it inappropriate to assess advocacy skills. We have reservations about obliging students to be assessed in a skills area where they often feel the least confident of their abilities. Also, at the late stage of the course at which it is taught, we are not convinced that students have sufficient opportunity to practise their advocacy skills to bring them up to a level where meaningful assessment is possible.

through personal experience to define 'new positions for one-self and perhaps for one's culture'.[14]

How we assess it

Our approach to assessment appears, relative to some skills-based courses, fairly casual. While we have identified assessment guidelines and criteria, these are not based on detailed written standards or competencies. This is deliberate. In our view competency-based assessment is problematic, especially in the context of a course that seeks to assess not just a range of skills and attributes, but also elements of the knowledge underpinning them. Competence standards are inadequate in our view because they:

- over-simplify performance, creating what Tribe and Parry term 'two-dimensional models for what are essentially three-dimensional activities': Jones (1994), p 86;
- attempt to assess both underlying knowledge and changes within the affective domain by reference only to behaviours exhibited in the assessment event;
- do not, in any event, 'objectify' assessment in the way that is sometimes assumed. Standards may identify what sub-skills go to construct a competent performance. But where an activity involves higher level cognitive skills, they cannot tell us *how* those sub-skills need to be combined to constitute competence. The 'quality' of the overall performance remains, ultimately, a matter for subjective evaluation.

As one of our aims is to assess the students' capacity for reflection, we assess each student's feedback on their performance. This is essential, we believe, if we are to assess their *learning from doing* rather than just their *doing*, and to maintain thereby a close link between our objectives and our assessment methods. This obviously also creates an obligation on us to create assessments that are capable of eliciting our students' reflection-in- and -on-action. In so doing we have tended to focus on the importance of 'surprise' as a way of generating learning.

---

14   It thus requires an element of self-reflection, of considering one's own position relative to the received wisdom about (say) the lawyer–client relationship, as well as the capacity to work through the practical implications of the academic debates about the lawyer's role.

Opportunities for assessment in the Legal Process course

	1a	1b	2	3
ORAL SKILLS				
Presentation			•	
Interview	•			
Negotiation		•		
Advocacy				f*
WRITTEN SKILLS				
Essay				•
Letter			f	•
Drafting			f	•
PROBLEM-SOLVING				
Critical thinking	•	•	•	•
Research		•	o	•
Strategy/Ethics	•	•	o	o
GROUP SKILLS				
Management			•	o
Participation			•	o
REFLECTION				
Legal knowledge	•	•	o	•
Skills	•	•	•	•
Context			o	•

Key: *Assessment Events:*   1a = Individual interviewing exercise
    1b = Individual negotiating exercise
    2 = Group oral presentation
    3 = Group written presentations and document file
   Assessment requirements: • = normally assessed in that event
    o = optional criterion (ie, if group objective)
    f = formative feedback only; does not 'count'
Note: advocacy skills are not assessed directly on the course; advocates may obtain formative feedback which they can use to reflect on their advocacy in the final, written, assessment.

A good example of this is the kind of exercise we set up for the client interview in the criminal case. We teach interviewing technique as an aspect of client-centred practice. Most of the exercises and roles we use are based on lawyer–client interviews that take place in the lawyer's office, though we also discuss the territorial and 'political' dimensions of interviewing in the police station. Most of the full role plays we use also have some sort of twist in the tail: information the client will not volunteer, an ethical problem, etc, so students are used to being surprised and thereby forced to 'think on their feet'. The scenario for the case study varies, but usually around the following themes: the client has already seen – and been poorly advised by – a duty solicitor. He has had an initial application for bail refused, with the result that he is being held in custody. The interview thus takes place on alien territory (the prison), with a client who is not that impressed with the legal profession, and whose primary concern is not so much any forthcoming trial, but when he can get out on bail. Inevitably this creates a number of indeterminate problems of practice for our students and quite a demanding test of their interpersonal skills and professional knowledge. Reflection often focuses on how students tried to deal with the unexpected aspects of the situation – the client's initial lack of confidence in them and his short-term objectives, which may be very different from those they anticipated. They need to be able to talk clearly (and reasonably confidently) about bail procedures rather than substantive criminal law.

These kinds of ploys are not unusual in skills assessments. What may seem unusual, particularly for teachers on the English vocational courses, is the idea of assessing the student's reflections on how she dealt with the situation. We will want to know whether or not the student can identify the strengths and weaknesses of her performance, and the strategies that she might implement in the future. We encourage students to enter into a reflective conversation with us and their 'client'[15] (out of role) to facilitate feedback, rather than just expecting them to offer a monologue at the end of their performance.

15   In negotiation assessments, feedback is shared between the two participants, both of whom are being assessed on their negotiating. We have been very pleasantly surprised how well this has worked. The students have tended to be frank, but also very supportive of each other in their feedback, rather than using the time for reflection as an opportunity for competitive point-scoring against each other.

This emphasis on reflection not only gives us some insight into cognitive and affective processes underpinning performance, but also may help the student who has an 'off-day' pick up some marks on reflection that they lost on the performance itself.

However, our approach to reflection has a number of limitations.

Firstly, we can only assess the capacity for reflection at a fairly crude level. To assess individualised learning would really require some form of 'before' and 'after' assessment of each student – ie a measure of their capacity for reflection at the start of the relevant skill or transaction and at the end. We do not have the time and resources to make that feasible.Therefore we measure reflective capacity by reference to various triggers:

- the depth or superficiality of the performer's feedback;
- their capacity to recognise discrepant reasoning and inappropriate theories of action, or behaviour;
- their ability to identify new techniques or strategies for the future, and how these might improve on those used in the assessment.

Secondly, our dependence on simulations as the basis for some assessment is, arguably, problematic. Clinicians have often suggested that the emotional investment is less in simulated learning than in live casework, resulting in less motivation and a lower level of learning: see, for example, Laser (1993). Our own students' views are mixed. Some do not seem to find the 'artificiality' of the environment a problem, others have certainly used it as a device for distancing themselves from their 'failure' to handle a particular situation effectively. We are not wholly convinced that simulation is inferior in this respect. Our own feeling is that in live casework the motivation is directed towards the client and their problem. Our primary focus is not on teaching our students how to be effective *lawyers*, it is on helping them to become reflective *learners*,[16] and that simulation may actually be a better vehicle for this. However, it is not always easy to get this difference in objectives across to our students.

Thirdly, our approach creates some difficulties when it comes to assessing the casework, particularly in respect of the second (group) assessment. We have tried to avoid being too prescriptive about what we require for this assessment and, as a result, we have had some extremely innovative work from our students. We have had

16   Though we think the first objective should flow from the second.

presentations which include video reconstructions of the events leading up to the case, showing the different possible interpretations of
the facts that the evidence discloses. We have had a firm present
their experiences in a quiz show format, which they used particularly
to emphasise what they had learned about the law and procedure.
Other groups have presented a video diary of their work on the case,
thereby emphasising the group dynamics and research elements of
their work. This enabling approach is difficult to incorporate into
assessment criteria that are flexible enough to reflect what are often
very diverse presentations from across the same year group.

Also, in encouraging students to reflect frankly and critically about
their experiences, we have to be careful that we do not then use their
criticisms as a basis for penalising them for their (mis)management of
the case or poor analysis of the problem, etc!

Where do we go from here?

Caroline: I get a lot of satisfaction out of this course because by
the end of it our students seem so much more confident
than when they started, both intellectually and personally. They have learned to work collaboratively. Active
learning has sharpened their intellectual skills. The
value we all put on experience has brought us closer to
being all-round, holistic learners.

I would like law students to have acquired this
amount of confidence and these learning skills by the
end of their first year. How about a two-year course,
compulsory for first and second years? The trouble is,
for those who want to practise law, so much of the
degree is compulsory already, now we have virtually
seven core subjects. It isn't feasible to make anything
else obligatory.

Julian: A year isn't long enough to make the changes in learning style that we have talked about but, like you, I
would be reluctant to see more of the curriculum
become compulsory. I've always wanted to develop the
course the other way, leading from simulation to live
client work. I don't think clinical methods in this
country have generally put enough emphasis on reflection in the learning process – I would like to give that a

try. And what about incorporating some of these methods and objectives into the substantive law subjects? Isn't that really the way to overcome the knowledge/ skills divide?

Caroline: I have always been interested in problem-based learning and have experimented with it in a piecemeal sort of way. Unfortunately, it's so easy to overdose on content when designing and teaching your syllabus, and not build in time and opportunity for proper reflection. What's more, it encourages students to cut corners and 'learn' only for the assessments. It's no wonder so many of them get worried in Legal Process when they find they can remember hardly any law. Do you remember last week in the interview when the client said she'd sold a child a toy which injured him and she'd been told she might be prosecuted? The lawyer told us afterwards that his first thought was: 'What does this come under? Negligence? Criminal Law? Sale of Goods?' And then he panicked. I'm sure that the law they deal with in their Legal Process casework becomes part of their tacit knowledge much more swiftly. It therefore makes sense, surely, to give our students the tools to find and use the law in as realistic a context as possible. In this way they have to think for themselves rather than relying on what we and the other 'authorities' tell them.

References

C Argyris (1989) *Reasoning, Learning and Action,* Jossey-Bass, San Francisco.

R Axelrod (1984) *The Evolution of Co-operation,* Basic Books, New York.

D A Cruickshank (1996) 'Problem-based learning in legal education', this collection.

J G Henderson (1989) 'Positioned Reflective Practice: A Curriculum Discussion', *Journal of Teacher Education,* March/April 1989, p 10.

J Heron (1989) *The Facilitator's Handbook,* Kogan Page, London.

J Heron (1990) *Helping the Client*, Sage, London.

P Honey & A Mumford (1992) *The Manual of Learning Styles*, Honey, Maidenhead.

D W and F P Johnson (1991) *Joining Together: Group Theory and Group Skills*, Prentice Hall, Englewood Cliffs, NJ.

P A Jones (1994) *Competences, Learning Outcomes and Legal Education*, Institute of Advanced Legal Studies, London.

D A Kolb (1984) *Experiential Learning: Experience as the Source of Learning and Development*, Prentice Hall, Englewood Cliffs, NJ.

G Laser (1993) 'Educating for Professional Competence in the Twenty-First Century: Educational Reform at Chicago–Kent College of Law', 68 *Chicago–Kent Law Review* 243.

I McGill & L Beaty (1992) *Action Learning: A Practitioner's Guide*, Kogan Page, London.

C Maughan (1996) 'Learning how to learn: the skills developer's guide to experiential learning', this collection.

C Maughan & J Webb (1995) *Lawyering Skills and the Legal Process*, Butterworths, London.

R Revans (1980) *Action Learning*, Blond & Briggs, London.

D Schön (1987) *Educating the Reflective Practitioner*, Jossey-Bass, San Francisco.

Chapter 10

We're all reflective practitioners now: reflections on professional education
Philip A Jones

Introduction

The idea of reflective practice and the concept of the reflective practitioner have emerged as key terms in debates about the future of
professional education. They have an immediate appeal, providing
an image of the open-minded professional who stands back and
thinks both before and after acting. The reflective practitioner is
thoughtful, wise and contemplative, not just 'skilful' or 'competent'
but one whose work involves intuition, insight and 'artistry'. The
reflective practitioner works not just in the world of predefined rules
and checklists, and is not just a technically proficient problem
solver. He or she works instead with a repertoire of richly refined
exemplars, constantly framing and reframing a problem, testing out
interpretations of the problem and reviewing his or her interventions at the very moment of the action.

The concept of the reflective practitioner invokes this set of images
but it involves much more. It refers to a transformation in thinking
about the structure of professional education as a whole. This transformation involves a challenge to both traditional and 'technocratic'
forms of professional education.

Traditional forms of education were centred around models of
apprenticeship. The apprentice learnt through observation and
doing, on the job. Apprenticeship worked well when a varied pattern of work was provided and when the 'master' provided a
structured work experience, guidance, supervision and inspiration.
Even then it provided little or no formal introduction to the theories
and principles that underpin professional practice. It provided

unsatisfactory training when the apprentice was exposed to only a limited set of experiences and when supervision was poor. In most professions, including law, apprenticeship has been replaced or supplemented by technocratic or academic forms of professional education.

Technocratic or academic forms of professional education

The technocratic model is characterised by the division of professional education into three main elements: see Schein (1972), Schön (1983), (1987), Bines (1992). The first element involves the development of a knowledge base drawn largely from the academic disciplines. The second element involves the interpretation and application of that knowledge base to practice. The third involves supervised practice in a sheltered environment before the emerging professional is fully exposed to the full range of clients and problems.

Legal education since Ormrod has been informed by a version of the technocratic model. The first stage, the academic or initial stage, provides students with a knowledge of legal institutions and substantive law and, one hopes, an understanding of the social context within which law operates. Although substantive law underlies professional practice, considerations of practice are remote at the academic stage, which aims to provide not just a legal education but a liberal or academic form of education, albeit in the discipline of law. The second stage, the vocational stage, provides an introduction to the steps and procedures that inform professional practice. It introduces the student to a set of typical case studies of the kind they will encounter in the early years of practice. It provides in addition an introduction to those skills that underpin professional practice: legal research, interviewing, writing and drafting, negotiation and advocacy. The final stage, pupillage or the training contract, provides supervised and limited practice. It is at this stage that the lawyer-to-be experiences legal practice for real. It is then that he or she acquires the personal and practical knowledge that is involved in working as a lawyer.

There are a number of problems with the technocratic model. It can lead to a separation between each phase, with a particularly sharply drawn distinction between theory and practice, and between academics and practitioners. The emphasis in education is on propositional knowledge, formal academic knowledge, knowledge about the content that underpins professional action. The practice element is effectively marginalised and under-theorised. Implicit in this academic view of professional education is a view of professional knowledge as hierarchically organised. General principles, theory, occupy the highest level; 'concrete problem solving' in practice occupies the lowest. The difficulty with this hierarchy, according to the critics of the technocratic model, is that while the problems of the high ground provide the greatest intellectual and technical challenge, it is the problems of the low ground that are particularly pressing for clients and society. The real action is to be found in the swampy lowlands, where problems present themselves as 'messes', which cannot be resolved by technical solutions. These are the crucial areas of professional practice, the problems of greatest concern, the areas in which experience, trial and error, intuition and 'muddling through', provide the method.

It is easy to apply this critique to legal education. The Lord Chancellor's Advisory Committee on Legal Education and Conduct (ACLEC) has argued, for example, that the three-stage approach leads to artificial divisions between the 'academic' and 'vocational' study of law, and between specifically vocational training and practical training under supervision. This creates the false impression that there is a sharp difference between the university study of law and the needs of practitioners. The division leads to a focus on content at the academic stage, which is organised around the internal imperatives of subjects. This in turn encourages students, and perhaps some teachers, to see the aim of the process as being *training* through mastery of a body of knowledge, often at low levels of rigour (ACLEC 1994). While the new skills-based courses, the Bar Vocational Course and the Legal Practice Course, represent a considerable improvement on their predecessors, each of the vocational elements would benefit from a more rigorous intellectual approach (ACLEC 1995).

Alternatives to the post-technocratic academic model of professional education

What then is the alternative? This, according to the critics of the technocratic model, is provided by structures designed to develop the 'reflective practitioner', the post-technocratic model of professional education. This model is characterised by a focus on *knowledge for practice*, the acquisition of professional competencies and the development of systematic reflection on practice: see Bines (1993).

The focus has shifted from an emphasis on propositional knowledge, content, structured around academic prerogatives, to a focus on knowledge for practice structured around the ways in which personal and practical knowledge is used in practice. There is a growing concern to identify the competencies involved in professional work, though some critics juxtapose a crude model of competence-based education with a more holistic approach that is structured around the concerns of 'professional artistry': see Elliott (1993), Fish (1995). As professional practice is seen to draw on particular combinations of propositional knowledge, process knowledge and personal knowledge, so the focus in professional education has shifted to a concern with the personal and critical skills involved in the systematic reflection on practical situations that lie at the heart of professional practice. At the same time the 'practicum' emerges as the key site of professional learning. This should provide a carefully structured environment organised around a set of tasks, activities and experiences in which the student is supported by a 'mentor' or practitioner-educator. This in turn requires new partnerships between the profession and the institutions of higher education and a much greater degree of integration between the different elements of professional education. It also requires a commitment to the principles of 'lifelong learning'. This shifts the focus from learning at the initial stage as a foundation for practice to a more fluid process according to which the reflective practitioner engages in a continuing process of professional development.

The exact structure and institutional forms of the post-technocratic alternative have yet to be constructed. To date the theorists of the new order have proved to be more adept at constructing critiques than constructing alternatives. This chapter provides a review of theoretical underpinnings of the post-technocratic order. It starts inevitably with the work of Donald Schön (1983), (1987). His contribution is pivotal but partial. He provides a particular perspective on professional education and a distinctive view of reflective practice. The reflective practitioner's work is characterised less by the application of rules and more through interpretation of images, vignettes, and exemplars. Reflective practice is a process of 'artistry'. This concept of reflective practice will be examined along with two other complementary conceptions.

The first integrates a post-Schönian conception of professional knowledge with an elaborated model of competency-based education. It juxtaposes propositional knowledge and knowledge-in-use, but provides a much more balanced picture of the different forms of knowledge that inform professional practice. In this analysis, which is articulated in the work of Michael Eraut, reflective practice loses its pivotal role and the concept of reflective practice is seen as just one form of practical reasoning, not the only form.

The second seeks to build upon Schön's conception of reflective practice, but it seeks to argue that reflective practice is a concept that has universal validity throughout all the stages of professional education. Reflection, according to this perspective, provides a process of critical emancipation enabling students to identify the social, political and cultural constraints that impede understanding. Reflection is less a process of *self*-reflection, an exclusively internal dialogue, and more a process of *critical* reflection informed by the student's acquired conceptual apparatus and knowledge. This second perspective on reflective practice is articulated most clearly in the work of Ronald Barnett (1990), (1992), (1994).

Reflective practice as professional artistry: the work of Donald Schön

The theory of reflective practice

Analysis of reflective practice and the reflective practitioner has to start with the work of Schön. His work has been extraordinarily influential. It provides a unique synthesis that draws on the work of theorists such as Gilbert Ryle, Polanyi, Piaget and Vygotsky and which combines their insights with a critique of the positivist social science which so dominates American discussions of professional work and professional education. Schön's work combines a rigorous critique of the technocratic model of professional education with a celebration of the artistry of the reflective practitioner. His analysis is constructed around two critiques. The first is a critique of technical rationality and its prioritisation of propositional knowledge. The second is a critique of the soulless technical and mechanical problem solver. Both critiques are informed by Schön's attempt to construct an alternative epistemology of professional action. This 'epistemology' is constructed around a number of concepts that have informed attempts to construct an alternative post-reflective model of professional education: the concepts of reflective practice, knowledge-in-use, reflection-in-action, the artistry of reflective practice, the ladder of reflection, the reflective conversation, and the practicum. It is not, however, clear that Schön achieves his stated intention of articulating an alternative epistemology of professional action, nor is it clear that he provides a coherent alternative model of professional education.

Schön's alternative epistemology of professional practice is constructed around a particular conceptualisation of tacit knowledge. Tacit knowledge or, in Schön's terminology, knowing-in-action is that body of personal knowledge that is implicit in a professional's patterns of action and their 'feel' for the 'stuff' with which they deal. It is expressed in the recognition of phenomena – families of symptoms associated with a particular disease, peculiarities of a certain building, irregularities of materials or structures, idiosyncrasies of a particular set of cases. It is found in the innumerable judgments of quality that professionals make but for which they cannot state adequate criteria, and in the skills for which they cannot state the rules and procedures: see Schön (1983), p 49.

The centrality of reflection-in-action

Reflection-in-action is central to this process. It is the process that arises when people, stimulated by surprise, turn thought back on action and on the knowing that is implicit in action. As the professional works on a problem, something puzzling, troubling or interesting will prompt reflections on the understandings which are implicit in the action, understandings which the professional brings to the surface, criticises, restructures and embodies in further action: see Schön (1983), p 50.

This process of reflection-in-action is central to the 'art' which practitioners bring to situations of uncertainty, instability, uniqueness and value conflict. It is implicit in the jazz musicians' 'feel for their materials', in a football player's 'feel for the ball', in a lawyer's 'feel for a case'. Practitioners develop this 'feel' by building up a repertoire of examples, images, understandings and actions. The professional does not solve problems through the application of rules, he 'sets', 'frames' and 'constructs' problems; the professional 'sees' it as part of a repertoire, something that has some features of a previous case, but not others. To see a problem in that light is not to subsume it under a familiar category or a rule. It is, rather, to see the unfamiliar, unique situations as both similar to and different from the familiar one, without at first being able to say similar or different with respect to what: see Schön (1983), pp 51, 138.

Design exemplifies the process of reflection-in-action. It is a process in which professionals learn to 'frame' problems, impose a kind of coherence on 'messy' situations and through which they discover the consequences and implications of their chosen frames. These attempts to impose order provoke unexpected outcomes – 'back talk' that gives the situation a new meaning. They listen and reframe the problem. The internal reflective conversation is made up of this process of problem framing, on-the-spot experimentation, detection of consequences and implications, back talk and response to back talk. It is this which provides the design-like artistry of professional practice: see Schön (1986), pp 156–60.

Schön uses design to support the argument that reflection-in-action is learnable and coachable, but not teachable. First, the rules that are used in design cannot be applied. When working with rules the designer does not apply them to a static situation, but engages in a process of experimentation, a thoughtful invention of new rules based on an appreciation of the results of earlier interventions. Design, moreover, is a holistic skill that can only be acquired in its totality. It cannot be broken down into its constituent parts: it must be grasped as a whole. This is because design requires the ability to recognise and appreciate desirable and undesirable qualities, qualities that cannot be expressed through verbal descriptions, which can only be grasped through a reflective dialogue with a coach, who can ground these qualities through action. Design, finally, is a creative process in which a designer aims to see and do things in new ways. No prior description of design can take the place of learning by doing: see Schön (1986), pp 157–62.

All professional work is conceived in the same manner, all professionals have to deal with uncertainty, uniqueness and conflict, all professionals have to 'build', 'design', and 'construct'. Lawyers, for example, build cases, construct arguments and make agreements, while physicians construct diagnoses and regimes of treatment: see Schön (1986), p 157. The design studio functions in a similar fashion, to provide a model of reflection-in-action and education for artistry. It becomes the prototype for the *reflective practicum* in which students learn, mainly by doing, with the help of coaching. The practicum is 'reflective' in a double sense: it helps students become proficient in a kind of reflection-in-action and, when it works well, it involves a dialogue of coach and student that takes the form of reciprocal reflection-in-action.

Problems with the theory of reflective practice

Programmes based on notions of reflective practice proliferate: courses that cross interdisciplinary boundaries and integrate theory and practice; courses that seek to develop a specific model of the reflective process; and courses that promote specific reflective strategies, such as action research, a reflective journal, or reflective coaching. Most of these initiatives are based in some way on the work of Schön, but this energy does not disguise debate and disagreement. All agree that Schön's work is inspirational, but many agree further that it is very difficult to put Schön's ideas about reflective practice into action, while some agree the conceptual model is itself flawed.

Practical dilemmas

The practical problems involved in implementing ideas of reflective practice have come to the surface most readily in the field of teacher education, a field imbued with conceptions of reflective practice. Calderhead and Gates (1993) provide an excellent summary of questions and dilemmas that have a much broader application; see also Russell (1993), Calderhead (1992), Grimmett (1988).

The first set of dilemmas involve questions about the relationship between public knowledge and personal knowledge. What, for example, is the relationship between a body of knowledge and personal knowledge? What, for example, is the relationship between the body of knowledge developed in the professional curriculum and the knowledge developed in practice? How can the personal knowledge developed through reflection-in-action be linked to theoretical knowledge and empirical research evidence? This leads to further questions about the relationship between professional growth and personal development. Schön's practicum envisages a collaborative relationship between coach and student, but it is difficult to reconcile the demands of openness, autonomy and responsibility required by such a facilitative relationship with the more didactic relationship implied in the development of particular areas of knowledge and skill. It is even more difficult to reconcile with the assessment and certification demands of professional validated courses and with the organisation of work in a professional setting. Professional settings often put a premium on immediate unreflective action which makes it difficult to set aside the time required for analysis and deliberation.

A further set of problems arise in the area of personal growth. Professionals approach work in different ways. These differences reflect their personal learning styles, their background experiences, their beliefs about professional work, and the culture of their particular professional environment. It is difficult to reconcile these differences in courses that seek to promote reflective practice. Should the course favour the weak reflective practitioner over the strong unreflective practitioner? How can an observer recognise a reflective practitioner? Does being reflective mean thinking about one's practice or does it also require doing something about one's practice (Calderhead & Gates (1993), pp 2–5)? This leads to an even bigger question. Does reflection require a process of personal and professional growth? Can practitioners immediately reflect on their practice or do they require a phase within practice when they use routines which can later be analysed? If so, by exploring reflections with the student professional, are we aiming too high?

Conceptual problems

These dilemmas are very real. Many have emerged in a practical context as professionals have struggled to develop reflective practitioner programmes; many, though, are embedded in conceptual weaknesses in Schön's contribution. Particular problems are caused by the sharp distinction between technical relationality and formal knowledge on the one hand and professional artistry and tacit knowledge on the other, and by the lack of clarity in thinking about reflection-in-action. These problems are compounded by Schön's refusal to distinguish the different orientations of experts and novices.

THE SHARP DISTINCTION BETWEEN FORMAL KNOWLEDGE AND REFLECTION-IN-ACTION

Schön's analysis of professional action is informed by a series of distinctions and dichotomies; between the high ground, where the situation and goals are clear, and the swampy lowlands where 'complexity, instability, uniqueness and conflict abound'. Fenstermacher (1988) argues that this provides an *either–or* description of a situation that is actually a *both–and*. Schön has nothing to say about those situations that are in between, situations that are complex but stable, or simple, stable and routine but in situations of conflict or, finally, situations in which complexity and instability are routine. Such situations call for a mix of strategies, some of which are systemic, some of which are ideographic. Schön's analysis focuses only on the latter.

The problems are compounded by Schön's commitment to a constructivist epistemology, according to which all acts, including acts of perception, 'create' the reality of which they are a part. This is not problematic in itself but, as Selman (1988) argues, if all actions create the reality of which they are a part, then there is nothing distinctive about professional action. The use of design as a metaphor is doubly problematic. If all human action involves design, creation and construction, then these are not the distinctive processes that characterise professional action: they are the processes common to all forms of human action.

Schön's commitment to a constructivist epistemology builds upon the often cited dictums of Gilbert Ryle. Ryle argued that there were not two separate entities, mind and body: 'When I do something intelligently, ie thinking what I am doing, I am doing one thing and not two'; see Ryle (1949), quoted in Schön (1983), p 51. Ryle is right that there is knowing-how and knowing-that, but he proceeds as if there is nothing but intelligent knowing-how. Knowing-how cannot be reduced to knowing-that and, equally, knowing-that cannot at the same time be reduced to knowing-how: see Barnett (1994), p 176. Ryle and Schön get close to this position. Ryle is used by Schön to support the argument that thought is implicit in the action, in the footballer's 'feel' for the ball, in the lawyer's 'feel' for the case. Schön argues that although we think before acting, it is also true that in much of the spontaneous behaviour of skilful practice there is a kind of knowing which does not stem from a prior intellectual operation. Schön then seems to dismiss the prior intellectual operations in his valourisation of the kinds of knowing that are implicit in the action. He gets dangerously close to arguing that there is no point teaching such operations or skills both in his analysis of design and his account of the *reflective practicum.*

Schön's distinction between formal propositional knowledge and 'knowing-in-action' is constructed in a similar either–or fashion. It is either one or the other with no space for other kinds of knowing in between. Schön tends therefore to underplay the role of *formal propositional knowledge*, which provides some of the language through which professionals 'frame' the situation; he tends to underplay the importance of the *technical skills* that are involved in working as a professional; he neglects the role of theorising at a *practical level* about the nature of professional work, the process used in it, and the values that inform it, and he neglects the importance of *critical emancipatory reasoning* which provides an insight into the wider ethical, social and political forces that provide the context within which professionals work: see McIntyre (1993).

THE LACK OF CLARITY IN THINKING ABOUT REFLECTION

A focus on reflection in the analysis of practical problem solving and experiential learning is not new. Dewey (1993), for example, argued that reflection arose from a directly experienced situation which creates a state of doubt, perplexity or mental hesitation. Reflection provides a means of transforming a situation characterised by doubt into a situation that is clear, coherent, settled and harmonious. Reflection leads to inquiry, the development of possible courses of action and then to a tentative resolution of the problem. Reflection, though, was only a part of Dewey's analysis, which included deliberation, inquiry and contemplation.

Kolb (1984) worked with a similar experimental cycle in his analysis of experimental learning; see also Maughan (1996). Schön moves beyond both accounts, of what he would call reflection-on-action – reflection as a means of reviewing action while at a distance from the event – to provide an analysis of reflection-in-action, practical reasoning during the event. There are two problems with his analysis. First it assumes, or at least implies, that reflection-in-action is always the appropriate response to a practical situation; and it treats reflection-in-action as the principal or essential form of practical reasoning when it could be better seen as a particular form of practical reasoning. Reflective practice is consequently always a goal for professional educators, never a means to other ends.

It makes more sense to construct formal analytical thinking and tacit practical reasoning on a continuum rather than as dichotomies.

Hammond (1980), for example, argues that most thinking is neither purely intuitive nor purely analytical but has 'quasi-rational' characteristics. When the action is fast and poorly structured, quasi-rational modes of thinking might include peer-aided judgment and system-aided judgment. When the action is slow and well-structured, surveys and formal experiments may be more appropriate. Hammond argues further that tasks can be placed on a continuum which takes account of the complexity of the task, the ambiguity of the context of the task, and the form in which the task presents itself. Practitioner's reasoning, he argues, is more effective when the mode of thinking adopted is constructed around central features of the task.

One of the missing dimensions in Schön's analysis is the time-frame within which practitioners are engaged in a task. This emphasis is provided by Eraut (1994), (1990), who introduces the notion of a 'performance period', the period which it takes to complete a task from initiation to completion, to explore the impact of time on practitioner's reasoning. A performance period may last a matter of minutes as in a client interview, or a distinct part of a day when drafting a relatively complex document, or it may extend over a period of days or even months when a case is being prepared. Reflection-in-action describes the thinking processes that are a distinctive feature of interaction during a rapid time period. Reflection, though, takes a different form when the action takes place over a period of days or months and there is time for reflection on the action either after the event or in the pauses during the action. Schön's distinction between reflection-in-action and reflection-on-action fails to take account of the temporal context of action. The distinction is valid when the action is rapid, but the form of reflection does not seem any different whether it is described as *in* or *on* the action, when the action is slow and deliberative: Eraut (1994), pp 145, 154.

This points to real ambiguities in the analysis of reflection. Reflection, Eraut argues, is used by Schön to conflate two different forms of reflection and as a metaphor for a variety of forms of thinking of which reflection is only a part. The first meaning of the term, Schön's *reflection-on-action*, refers to reflection as a form of deliberation; the second meaning of the term, *reflection-in-action*, refers to reflection as a form of metacognition. In both cases the term *reflection* is being over-stretched. It should be seen as a sub-set of theorising in general, rather than a synonym or metaphor for different kinds of theorising.

(a)   Reflection as a deliberative process

Reflection as a deliberative process is emphasised where practition-ers seek to interpret or understand cases or situations by reflecting upon what is known about them. Reflection in such cases may be informed by personal knowledge or it may be informed by any available public knowledge. Reflection, though, is only one aspect of deliberative thinking, which may include planning, problem-solving, analysing and decision-making. Deliberative thinking, in whatever form, is characterised by knowledge of the context, situation or problem, and conceptions of practical courses of action or decision options. When acquiring knowledge of a situation, professionals need to be able to draw upon a wide repertoire of potentially rel-evant theories and ideas. The formulation of a range of options depends both upon knowledge of existing practice and the ability to invent or search for alternatives. Deliberation may include 'strategic thinking', the ability to conceptualise and look at an organisation, a policy or a programme of work from several different perspectives. These abilities are interactive processes and often a result of the kind of teamwork that brings different kinds of thinkers together: see Eraut (1994), pp 126–8, 149–57. Reflection is only one, perhaps minor, element in this and other deliberative processes; the other processes are distinctive and have their own characteristics.

(b)   Reflection-in-action as a form of metacognition

Reflection-in-action, on the other hand, is best seen as a form of metacognition, the process by which individuals think about their own mental processes, the processes through which the individual becomes aware of and directs her own behaviour. It involves learn-ing how to learn, learning how to learn from experience, planning, the organisation of time, the allocation of tasks and the management of thinking. Reflection is a critical component of metacognition: it expresses itself in the form of mini-conversations about action and the subject's role in it; it provides a means of checking engagement with a problem as the problem emerges; it also provides a means of watching plans unfold, and of reviewing plans as obstacles emerge. Reflection-in-action is a good term to describe those intuitive pro-cesses of self-direction used when the action is rapid; but in longer time periods when there is time for deliberation, metacognition involves the overall control of an individual's thinking and the ongoing evaluation of progress.

When the concept of reflection is used to describe all these processes it functions not as a theoretical concept but as a metaphor, but it is a metaphor that has to work too hard. Reflection is an important aspect of practical theorising, but is only part, not the whole.

THE DISTINCTION BETWEEN NOVICES AND EXPERTS

Schön's distinction between technical rationality and reflection-in-action evokes another distinction, that between experts and novices. One of the most famous studies of expertise is that conducted by the Dreyfus brothers (1986). Their analysis of the novice, who applies rules and plans rigidly, who has little situational understanding, and who has no judgment of a situation, recalls Schön's technically rational problem-solver. Their analysis of the expert, on the other hand, who no longer relies on rules, who has an intuitive grasp of situations based on deep tacit understanding, and who has a vision of the whole, recalls Schön's reflective practitioner. Dreyfus & Dreyfus provide a five-level model of expertise which moves from novice, advanced beginner and competent practitioner, to proficient practitioner and expert. Proficiency marks the shift from routinised behaviour to a semi-automatic approach, characterised by a more holistic approach to situational understanding.

The Dreyfus model suggests that Schön's critique of the technical rule-based problem-solver conflates two categories: the rigid professional who adheres to a rule-based approach, and the novice who moves uncertainly and tentatively into the world of professional work. The Dreyfus model is itself problematic; it is based almost entirely on learning from experience with only occasional references to theoretical learning or the development of fluency in standard tasks: see Eraut (1994), p 125. The model assumes a linear progress from level to level. The analysis does, however, suggest that novices may in fact encounter very real difficulties as they first experience professional work and that reflection-in-action is perhaps an over-ambitious goal. This view is supported by Elliott (1993), who argues that at the early stages of development theoretical concepts and ideas may be used to illuminate aspects of situations that might otherwise remain hidden. It is only at the higher levels that learners can begin to view their professional situation as a whole and that reflection on experience becomes a meaningful goal.

McIntyre (1993) agrees (p 43). Reflection should indeed be a central aspect of experimental learning for experienced professionals whose practice is automated and intuitive, and depends on tacit understandings. They have extensive repertoires of past experiences which they can use to frame and reframe problems. They have rich capacities for thinking through reflection in and on their experience. Novices, on the other hand, achieve competence through conscious control: their action is not embedded in fluent, well learned professional practices. Novices have few experiences; they need to develop ways of construing situations and possibilities for action. Ideas from outside the professional's own expertise are most likely to provide the necessary stimulus. Reflection-in-action can only be of limited importance, but learning to reflect-on-action is an important starting point in developing the skills needed to continue learning from accumulated experience.

Further support for these propositions can be found in research on the development of expertise in medical practice. Schmidt, Norman & Boshuizen (1990) suggest that propositional knowledge has a key role to play in providing the elaborated mental networks that provide a conceptual perspective on disease. At the early stages the knowledge provided is prototypical with only a limited understanding of the variability with which normal and abnormal conditions manifest themselves in reality. Clinical experience sees a restructuring of these mental networks so that they manifest themselves as high-level, simplified causal models. Formal knowledge is activated more selectively and exposure to real patients provides an opportunity for short cuts in reasoning. As experience accumulates, so practitioners give increased attention to contextual factors. Representations of cases become increasingly rich, idiosyncratic and bear only a superficial relationship to the 'prototypical' cases which are found in textbooks. Formal knowledge does not, however, disappear as experience develops; it provides an anchor to support decision-making if needed. This may happen when the expert is confronted with a new problem or if previous cases are too dissimilar for use in the instant case.

Problems with Schön's analysis

Schön's critique of technical rationality informed a broader critique of the technocratic structure of professional education. It informed an argument for a more integrated approach and provided a model, the reflective practicum, that was to be a prototype for new forms of professional education. The prototype took reflective coaching as the norm and flowed from the assumption that design could work as a metaphor for all forms of professional education. It assumed further that the 'skills' involved in professional work were unteachable, only coachable.

Elements of Schön's analysis have been shown to be problematic. It is fraught with practical difficulties and there are real conceptual weaknesses in his work. It provides too stark an opposition between formal and academic knowledge and personal tacit knowledge; it constructs reflection-in-action as the paradigmatic form of practical reasoning, when it is best seen as one particular form of practical reasoning; and it constructs an argument for an approach to professional education in general from an analysis of the narratives of experts in a particular professional domain.

Schön's account does not, then, in itself provide a complete foundation for the development of emerging forms of professional education. It does, however, provide a starting point, one that has been adapted by other theorists. Two will be considered here. The work of the first reformats Schön's analysis of the relationship between the different kinds of knowledge at work in professional practice; the second emphasises a particular conception of reflective practice: that involved in critical reflective practice.

Towards an integrated map of professional knowledge as a foundation for competence-based education

While a focus on reflective practice provides a key element of the post-technocratic challenge to contemporary forms of professional education, further elements are provided by the analysis of different forms of professional knowledge and by the attempt to produce an interpretative non-behaviourist conception of competence. Michael Eraut's work explores both of these elements. He starts with an attempt to map the forms of knowledge that are used in professional work and uses this to challenge existing conceptions of competence-based education and the structure of contemporary educational practice.

The mapping of professional knowledge

Eraut's project builds explicitly upon Schön's work, but it resists the conceptual flaws that obstruct his analysis. Resisting Schön's dichotomies, he explores the interrelationships between three conceptions of knowledge – propositional knowledge, personal knowledge and process knowledge – and considers the different modes in which they are used in practice.

Propositional knowledge is the most public form of knowledge: it is that body of knowledge that can be expressed in the form of explicit statements. Three forms of propositional knowledge are identified: systematic, coherent discipline-based theories and concepts; generalisations and practical principles; and specific propositions about particular cases, decisions and actions: see Eraut (1994), p 43.

Whilst most academics think of propositional knowledge in the form of discipline-based theories, practitioners work with a mixture of the three with a preponderance of specific propositions derived from experience. These experiences may be generalised into practical principles or related to theoretical ideas, but both of the latter are at least one step removed from practice. They are rarely applied in any simple fashion, but used in a variety of different ways.

Eraut (1948) distinguishes (p 49) four modes in which knowledge is used: replication, application, interpretative and associative. The replicative and applicative modes are associated with technical forms of vocational education: the knowledge learnt is translated without much change from the form in which it is learnt to the form in which it is used. The interpretative mode of knowing involves adapting knowledge to suit the particular demands of each situation. It involves selecting one aspect of a situation from another and it involves selecting one version of a principle from another. The associative mode of knowledge involves the use of metaphors or images: it involves that intuitive balancing of alternatives that is at the heart of Schön's analysis of knowing-in-action. The interpretative and associative modes provide a means of thinking about the understanding and judgment that are an essential part of higher forms of professional education.

Propositional knowledge in this sense moves towards *personal knowledge*. This is the knowledge embodied in personal impressions from experience. Much of this knowledge exists in the form of fleeting ideas, a collection of experiences, much of which it is hard to express in the form of propositions. Personal knowledge may, however, include elements of propositional knowledge: theories that are remembered from formal courses, theories that provide a working language in professional encounters, and theories that provide a cognitive framework when constructing situations and making decisions. Experiential learning provides a means of stopping the professional, in the context of his or her work, and trying to provide a language within which personal knowledge can be understood, reflection at a later date providing a means of working on such personal experiences away from the immediate setting of the action.

Process knowledge is the term used to describe the various processes that contribute to professional action. It incorporates skills, practical procedures and know-how, but it is deliberately defined as 'knowledge', to emphasise the point that professional processes encompass distinctive ways of knowing as well as the action that is at the heart of professional work.

Eraut (1994) identifies five kinds of process for extended discussion: acquiring information, skilled behaviour, deliberative processes, giving information, and the metaprocesses involved in directing and controlling one's behaviour (p 107).

The concept of process knowledge incorporates skilled behaviour but Eraut (1994) suggests that skills are a subordinate element of professional practice. Skilled behaviour is defined (p 111) as a complex sequence of actions which have become so routinised through practice and experience that they are performed almost automatically. It is hard to apply this definition to professional work because professional skills tend to involve a significant amount of rapid decision-making. The decisions are not deliberative in character but are based upon rapid readings of the situation made in response to the interaction and its overall purpose. It might be necessary to develop routinised skills as a means of coping with the onrush of experience but, because professional work is imbued with tacit knowledge and intuition, the skills rapidly become dysfunctional.

Information acquisition typically combines formal knowledge and professional processes: knowing that and knowing how. Information is acquired in most professions in a number of ways: interviewing, observing, listening, formal and informal research, scientific and quasi-scientific observations. Propositional knowledge is vital in each but is never sufficient; it always needs to be combined with the ability to select and implement appropriate methods of inquiry. Information acquisition requires at least four types of knowledge (Eraut (1994), p 108):

- an existing knowledge base in the area concerned;
- some kind of conceptual framework to guide one's inquiry;
- skills in collecting information; and
- skills in interpreting information.

Interpretation has a particularly important role to play. Interpretation can take different forms. It can be rapid, as in the middle of an interview, or deliberative, when there is time for thought and discussion. Rapid interpretation is particularly hard to teach; so too is pattern recognition, which involves making comparisons between apparently different cases. Reflection after the event can be helpful, particularly where a tutor is available to note the significant points.

Academic study uses processes that provide a parallel with information-gathering processes. It provides practice in processes which expose the student to a particular body of knowledge: formulating questions, collecting evidence, discovering principles, listening. It also provides practice in processes which allow the student to extract meaning from the body of knowledge: analysing, reorganising, integrating. Finally, it provides practice in processes which enable the learner to make the knowledge significant: inferring generalisations, relating to other situations, and reconstructing the knowledge. Students learn through such processes to acquire information, extract meaning and think about the status of conclusions drawn from the knowledge.

Competence-based forms of professional education

Eraut broadly supports a competence-based approach to education and training in professional qualifications. He argues that its adoption at professional level would correct the current overemphasis on propositional knowledge and give more attention to the processes which determine the quality of professional action. He suggests (1994), though, that the current methodology is problematic (p 118).

First, the current system of functional analysis breaks a job down into small functional units and creates a qualification defined in terms of elements of performance, each with their associated performance criteria. This creates a complex qualification structure expressed in a long document with an enormous assessment burden. It works with a narrow construction of underpinning knowledge and understanding that restricts the specification of knowledge to that which directly underpins practice. This in turn leads to all sorts of attempts to avoid the limitations of a performance-based assessment system by incorporating other assessments. Many of these work by interpreting 'performance' broadly, perhaps even including 'performance' in an examination. This undermines the credibility of the qualification. Finally, the qualification is inflexible: it is defined in 'binary' terms to mean a person is either 'competent' or 'not competent'. No gradations, such as 'just competent' or 'highly competent' are permitted. This implies both that the only way to progress is to become competent in something new, and that further learning after competence has been attained is a waste of time: see Eraut (1994), pp 118 and 298–320.

The model of professional processes, identified by Eraut, could be used as a different methodology for analysing work at the professional level. This would provide a more economical structure of the qualification: it would provide links to the modes of knowing and use of knowledge as well as attending to the thinking which underpins a professional's capacity to perform in a wide variety of contexts and situations.

Introducing the notion of 'capability' could provide another means of refining the methodology of competence-based education. Capability has both a present and a future orientation. It refers both to the capacity to do current work and it provides a basis for developing future competence, including the possession of knowledge and skills to do future professional work. Capability in the latter sense could include foundation knowledge: the critical understanding of concepts, theories and principles that is needed to 'go beyond the information given', the conceptual, perceptual and ethical knowledge needed to continue to learn, to grow professionally and to respond flexibly to future, yet unforeseen, challenges and circumstances. It could also include interpersonal skills, the ability to work in teams and the cognitive skills such as problem-solving. For many professionals it is not possible to demonstrate these skills in practice – they simply aren't exposed to the full range of practical situations – but they could provide evidence of their capability. Capability evidence could therefore be used to supplement performance evidence, without undermining the integrity of the latter.

A more flexible approach to the design of qualifications could differentiate between basic competence, at which point a person might only be able to practise under limited conditions, and subsequent specialist qualifications allowing for later additions after qualification. In most professions this model of progression should take into account the following kinds of progress: extending competence over a wider range of situations and contexts; becoming more independent of support and advice; routinisation of certain tasks; coping with a heavier workload and getting more done; becoming competent in further roles and activities; extending professional capability; and improving the quality of some aspects of one's work: see Eraut (1994), pp 218–19. This would lead to an agreed model of progression which begins before qualification and continues after qualification, and which develops habits of self-assessment, target-setting and planned learning, all of which are important for continuing professional development.

A critique of contemporary forms of educational practice

Eraut's analysis of the different forms of knowledge used in professional work is also used to inform a critique of educational practice. The dual qualification system is seen to be problematic. The higher education element is particularly problematic because it ignores the problem of developing and using propositional knowledge in professional contexts. The practice setting is little better, for the processes involved are rarely analysed, learning goals are rarely clarified, and the appropriate support is rarely given. Because the processes analysed characterise the actions of experienced professionals who use thinking skills of a certain level, it points to a need to provide an integrated system of continuing professional development. This too should focus not just on knowledge in the abstract but it should provide support for the acquisition and development of the processes involved in professional work.

The professional curriculum should be designed to achieve a significant interaction between formal teaching and professional practice. Significant parts of the initial qualification should be performance-based, with process knowledge providing the focus. Propositional knowledge should not be neglected, as it plays a key role in process knowledge, but initial blocks of propositional knowledge should be kept as short as possible, unless there are opportunities to use that knowledge in practice-related processes. The volume of propositional knowledge taught in the early stage of professional education should be drastically pruned: unless it is used in practice it is rapidly forgotten. It does not, moreover, become professional knowledge just because it is relevant to professional practice. It is only when it is used in a professional context in which it will be interpreted and tested that it becomes professional knowledge in any meaningful sense. The time that is currently given to comprehension and reproduction should therefore be shortened, leaving more time for the considerable intellectual effort involved in using propositional knowledge in context: Eraut (1994), p 120.

Eraut's analysis

Eraut's work builds upon Schön's analysis. It is less polemical in form and more analytical. While Schön selects his examples to support his analysis, Eraut refines his concepts through an interrogation of examples. Like Schön, though, his analysis suffers from its experiential focus and its emphasis on education in the workplace. Like Schön too, he rejects the dual qualification system in favour of a more integrated approach. The analysis is sharp but some sense of perspective is missing.

It is all very well to adapt the standpoint of professional development when considering continuing professional development, or when clarifying the goals of coaching during the initial practical stage of professional development. In these situations the professional standpoint is already clear. Career routes, however, tend to be diverse and varied, and at the initial stage subsequent choices have yet to be made. Eraut recognises this. He rejects the notion of full professional accreditation defined on the basis of a heavily knowledge-based initial curriculum. He argues instead for provisional accreditation with multiple sites of reaccreditation, as the professional moves through different career transitions. The professional, he argues, should not be assumed to be universally competent within the professional domain, but competent only in those areas where she is demonstrably competent. Much of his analysis is concerned to develop means of evaluating competence at relatively advanced stages of career development.

There are, though, real advantages in dual accreditation systems. Such systems provide a degree of front-loading which enables the professional to acquire a foundation in the requisite knowledge before subsequent specialisation and immersion in practice. Propositional knowledge will inevitably dominate, partly because it is hard to develop process knowledge outside of the context provided by experience, and partly because it provides a foundation upon which subsequent specialist forms of knowledge can be developed. This is critical. The knowledge that directly underpins performance at the higher level is often underpinned itself by a conceptual infrastructure which requires time to learn. A dual accreditation system provides the young professional with an opportunity to experiment with different aspects of a career before subsequently developing the more specialist knowledge that can and will be acquired in practice. It is true that much of this knowledge will be forgotten, especially where it is learnt outside of the professional context, but it is also true that an understanding or interpretation of those concepts will remain, providing a structure of understanding expressed often in inchoate form at the level of personal impressions.

Reflective practice as critique

Reflection in Schön's account is a deeply personal process. It provides a means of constructing personal knowledge and it is informed by a self-reflective process that takes as its object a person's individual and idiosyncratic experience of professional work. Schön's account provides a means of theorising those personal interpretative understandings that inform professional experience. Aspects of this model were considered earlier and found to be problematic. It was suggested that reflection is best seen as providing one form of practical reasoning, not a synonym or metaphor for different kinds of practical reasoning. Schön's account has been challenged from another, different, direction which provides a more radical critical form of reflection. Critical forms of reflection address more fundamental moral and ethical questions which provide an insight into the wider ethical, social and political forces that provide the context within which professionals work.

This critical or emancipatory conception of reflective practice is informed by the work of the critical theorist Jürgen Habermas. Habermas, like Schön, provides a critique of the positivist assumptions that underpin 'technical' and 'rational' forms of reasoning and he elaborates an alternative emancipatory social scene. Critical social science seeks to provide for the emancipatory interest in freedom and autonomy. It accepts the interpretative insight that social life cannot be explained in terms of generalisations and predictions, but argues in turn that the source of subjective meanings lies outside the actions of individuals: rather, they are socially constructed or redefined by external manipulative agencies.

Carr and Kemmis have developed these ideas in the context of teacher education, challenging dominant ideas of reflective practice with a call for a critical educational science serving the emancipatory interests and promoting freedom and rational autonomy. Such a science would be based on forms of reflection, as embodied in the process of action research, but it would seek to transform education, providing teachers, students, parents and school administrators with the means of critically analysing their own situation in ways which will improve the educational conditions of students, teachers and society: see Carr & Kemmis (1986), pp 156–7.

Ronald Barnett argues a similar position in relation to both higher and professional forms of education. In contrast to Schön, the theorist of professional action, Barnett is a theorist seeking to articulate the ideologies at work in higher education. In a series of texts, *The Idea of Higher Education* (1990), *Improving Higher Education* (1992), and *The Limits of Competence* (1994), he has begun to construct a social philosophical analysis of higher education. This is a form of analysis that interweaves the philosophical and the sociological, the conceptual and the empirical, the descriptive with the recommendatory, and the what-is, with the what-might-be: (1994), p 3. It is a form of analysis that explores the unarticulated assumptions at work in debates about higher education, locates these debates within their social context, and seeks through an immanent critique to construct an alternative conception of higher education.

Barnett is at first sight an unlikely theorist to consider in a chapter on professional education. Professional education is thought to be, as Barnett himself observes, perhaps the most significant and complex feature of current developments in higher education. Theories about the values at work in higher education are particularly pertinent in discussions about professional education, Barnett's work doubly so. This is because, first, he argues that the idea of reflective practice has a general validity for higher education as a whole and, second, he seeks to contextualise the influence of vocational or more accurately operational conceptions of know-how, competence and skill in academic life.

Consider first the critique of operationalism. Barnett (1994), like Schön, constructs a critique both of academic conceptions of knowledge and education and of operational conceptions of competence (p 154). He argues that two versions of competence jockey for position in academe: one is an internal or *academic* form of competence, built around the student's sense of mastery within a discipline, the other – now being pressed robustly – is an *instrumental* conception of competence, essentially reproducing wider social interests in performance.

The two definitions of competence contain alternative clusters of related ideas, turning on different interpretations of transferability, skill, communication, situation, focus, orientation, critique and epistemology. Each defence is coherent in itself and both are inevitably narrow. Both have elements of closure in them. Disciplines are in fact more susceptible to closure than operational contexts precisely because they have a high degree of systematicity. Operational definitions are more open to influence from the world of economic performance, but in a truncated form, and only to improved versions of performance: see Barnett (1994), pp 168–70.

Both reveal their limitations in their language: within the operational conception of competence, terms like 'skill' and 'outcome' are relevant, while within the academic version of competence, terms like 'discipline' and 'objectivity' are used. Both sets of terms constrain both thought and action. The language of skills and outcomes is, Barnett (1994) argues, completely unable to handle the idea of understanding, while a concern with disciplines, objectivity, and truth is exclusively focused on thought and has nothing to say about action (pp 187–8).

A pervasive concept of reflective practice

What then of reflective practice? Barnett reads Schön in support of the proposition that the effective professional is a reflective practitioner, one who conducts a continuing reflective conversation. The conversation has a necessary critical edge, for the professional is always asking the question: 'what if . . . ?' The idea of the reflective practitioner implies, first, that the professional is able to create in her imagination different possibilities, without putting them into effect in the real world and, second, the professional is able to assess them in the imagination, weighing up alternative courses of action and evaluating them against criteria of different kinds. The effective professional is therefore continually self-critical or critically reflective: see Barnett (1992), p 183.

The concept of *critical* reflective practice builds upon Schön's analysis, which works through an internal dialogue in which the student is able to stand back from his or her offerings and accomplishments, to take a view of them by placing them in the context of a wider framework, to evaluate them and envisage practical possibilities. The student does not, though, evaluate them in the light of experience but on the basis of the student's acquired conceptual apparatus, knowledge and activities. Critical self-reflection is all about intellectual independence, in which the student is able to see through the apparent givenness of a proposition and its theoretical anchoring and so provides a sense of freedom from entrapment by any conceptual schema: see Barnett (1992).

This conception of critical self-reflection is developed further in an analysis of each of four key elements of professional education and in an evaluation of Schön's key concepts: action, interpersonal engagement, 'reflection-in-action', and 'knowing-in-use'.

The four areas of professional education

In Barnett's analysis of professional education, he discusses four areas in which the student's critical or reflective abilities are identified. Two, core knowledge and contextual knowledge, are in the cognitive domain and two, professional action and professional values, are in the professional domain.

Core knowledge is that body of knowledge that professionals claim as their own by virtue of being a professional. It includes knowledge that goes beyond the core subjects that are a prototypical feature of the law curriculum; but the history of the core subjects typifies the approach of the professional bodies who have a history of policing and prescribing the undergraduate core. Such prescription, Barnett argues, is counterproductive because it can unintentionally reduce the openness of the learning experience provided. For Barnett (1994), the corpus of knowledge that constitutes the core of a programme of professional education should receive the same degree of critical reflection as that normally expected of students in higher education (p 187).

Critical reflective thinking, however, plays a particular role in relation to contextual knowledge. Two forms of contextual knowledge are distinguished. Those operational forms of knowledge from outside the core discipline that are provided for instrumental reasons to make the practitioner more effective – forensic science, for example, in the law syllabus – are contrasted with liberal forms of knowledge, that are provided to illuminate the nature of professional practice. Barnett prioritises the liberal disciplines. It is through these disciplines that students are empowered to be critical observers of professional situations, in relation to both the wider social settings in which they occur and the internal character of the individual's role as defined by the relevant professional bodies: see Barnett (1994), p 188.

Barnett does not provide a detailed analysis of professional knowledge, nor does he provide too detailed an account of professional values; his purpose after all is not to design curricula in professional education but to provide an analysis of critical reflective practice.

Professional practice is conceived as providing a complex of possibilities which varies in terms of the client and the range and character of the knowledge fields on which the professional has to draw. Professional work is by definition imbued with a set of values, whether explicit and formulated in a code of practice, or implicit and revealed through action. It is this set of values that enables professionals to act in the world with some kind of predictability and to be recognised as a distinctive group.

Professional values provide a rich source of reflection for the critically reflective practitioner. Such issues are unlikely to be explored in the undergraduate curriculum but they should provide a focus of reflection in the early stage of professional education. One strand of critique should question the role of the profession in society: how does it see itself, what are its dominant motivations? Another focuses on the interests and assumptions embedded in the role of the profession as such. A third focuses on the role of the profession and its relationship to clients. Finally, there are questions about the internal structure and associated values within the profession itself: see Barnett (1992), pp 187–91.

The characteristics of reflection

This analysis of the domain of professional education identifies the areas in which the student should be critically reflective. The second level of analysis focuses on the processes involved in being critically reflective. It is expressed in an analysis of the relevance of Schön's key concepts: action, interpersonal engagement, reflection-in-action and knowledge-in-use, and a consideration of how these might be expressed in the context of higher education.

Barnett's analysis of *action* sets the scene. Students in higher education should be able to evaluate knowledge claims and these claims and evaluations should be supported by the student's use of reasoned argument or evidence. Making statements, forming arguments, putting forward ideas or expressions of understanding, and expecting to be taken seriously, become therefore forms of action. This is a particular orientation to action: it is one that derives from the forms of argument and analysis advanced through academic argument, but stripped of the constraints provided by the framework of an academic discipline. The theme is continued in the analysis of *interpersonal engagement*. The practice of giving reasons and sustaining arguments implies an audience. Interpersonal engagement expresses itself then in the ability to form ideas by and for oneself and the ability to offer them as public claims, along with supporting argument.

Greater problems are encountered in applying *reflection-in-action*. Barnett focuses entirely on the product of student work and a particular product is used as an example, the essay. The essay emerges as a statement that reflects the current stage of the student's internal dialogue. The essay, though, expresses a particular achievement, the engagement with knowledge. The engagement with knowledge is quite clearly different in academic and professional settings, but the boundaries between the two are not entirely distinct. *Knowledge-in-use* is the term used by Schön to describe the way in which professionals have to place knowledge in the context of a client's demands, to imagine alternative solutions, to evaluate them imaginatively. In an academic setting students have to work in a similar fashion: they have to make sense of the different voices around them, they have to identify the problem to hand and create possible solutions, and they have to work through the solution, ensuring that it leads to a satisfactory conclusion. Knowledge claims they have to learn are provisional, and theories only apply in a given context and within specific conditions. The intellectual strategies used in an academic context are not, he suggests, dissimilar from those used in a professional context, even if they do not have the manifold complexities and demands of the immediacy experienced by professionals: see Barnett (1992), pp 195–6.

Barnett does not provide a structure or a model for a professional curriculum, though he advocates interdisciplinarity, the integration of theory and practice and a partnership between higher education and the professions. He provides a refreshing challenge to closed definitions of knowledge, whether the closure is imposed externally by professional bodies or internally through the demands of a discipline. His analysis is indeed frustratingly elliptic. He has nothing to say about professional action and nothing really to say about which kinds of knowledge should be the subject of critical reflection. He promotes a conception of reflective knowing, a stance that is relaxed about all forms of knowing. Science is not given any special status, nor is know-how. His own objective is to promote forms of knowing that lead to the development of minds engaging with the world and searching collaboratively for wisdom: see Barnett (1994), p 186.

This enables him to escape from the really difficult questions of how to integrate different conceptions of a curriculum. He does, though, present a timely challenge to operationalist conceptions of knowledge and articulates a clear sense of the values that may need to be protected in the technocratic structure of the professional curriculum. This may lead to artificial barriers between the academic and vocational aspects of professional education, but the barriers may have been constructed around values that are worth protecting.

Conclusion

This chapter has sought to review the concepts at work in the terms 'reflective practice' and 'the reflective practitioner'. These are terms that are frequently used uncritically to describe the humane, responsive, open and thoughtful practitioner. A term is not, though, just a symbol: it is a concept that is underpinned by a further set of related theoretical concepts. These concepts are open to different sets of readings but they share a critique of the technocratic three-stage model of professional education.

The first two interpretations adopted the standpoint of the professional educator. Both were concerned to overcome the gap between theoretical learning and practical performance, both take seriously the argument that college-based studies, although valuable and interesting in their own right, provide little preparation for the 'real' learning that takes place in the work place. They both assume that learning *about* professional work is essentially different from learning *to* work as a professional and both therefore seek to construct forms of analysis that facilitate learning in the workplace.

Schön's analysis is inspirational. It has provided the point of departure for much innovative and practical work but it is beset by theoretical and practical problems. It works with too sharp a distinction between formal propositional knowledge and knowledge-in-action; it elevates reflection as *the* form of practical reasoning when it is best seen as one particular aspect of practical reasoning; and it is constructed upon an analysis of the thinking processes and styles of work exhibited by experts, without properly considering how such concepts might be appropriate for the rather different set of experiences encountered by novices. Michael Eraut's work, which builds upon Schön's analyses, provides a more subtle account of professional knowledge and provides a sound foundation upon which to construct a post-technocratic alternative.

Eraut and the other critics of Schön suggest that such a post-technocratic alternative would have the following characteristics:

- A significant part of the initial qualification must be performance-based.
- Initial blocks of propositional knowledge should be kept as short as possible, unless there are many opportunities to use that knowledge in practice-related processes.
- Process knowledge of all kinds should be accorded central importance.
- There should be a clearly articulated approach to professional learning and development, linked to a system of initial and advanced qualifications (Eraut (1994), p 121).

This model involves a positive rejection of the dual qualification system.

It is not easy to apply these principles in the context of legal education. Legal education is not designed as a coherent, deliberately structured route to a professional qualification. The degree provides a period of intellectual and personal growth that is a vital part of a professional's preparation without being directly tied to a particular route through the profession. It provides a broad background to practice in a range of positions in an increasingly fragmented profession. This is essential for professionals who are rarely in a position to predict which part of the profession they will move into as they begin to specialise. Finally, law as a field of practice appears to be heavily saturated by conceptual knowledge without which it would be difficult to 'see' in the early years of practice.

Degree studies in law provide a framework without which the professional could find it hard to 'frame' the problems presented. It is not easy to short-cut this process in which mental structures are constructed. Intensely practical subjects, like conveyancing and commercial law, are only given a context by a further set of concepts that are themselves embedded within the conceptual base of the foundation subjects.

The third approach, which treats reflective practice as a process of critique, would seem to be more relevant. It too is based on a critique of the dual qualification model, though its critique is based on the limitations of academic concepts of knowledge and education and operational concepts of competence. This position in itself provides no real alternative. It adopts the standpoint of higher education as a value system in its own right. It is not concerned with professional development in the world of work. Its concern is with the development of minds engaging with the world and seeking collaboratively for wisdom.

The ACLEC reports are clearly informed by some of the concepts associated with reflective practice, but it is an ambivalent association. The reflective practitioner appears to function more as rhetorical symbol and less as conceptual device. ACLEC (1994), like Barnett, provides a critique of narrowly academic approaches to education. It moves on to provide a critique of narrowly operational conceptions of skills training that, it argues, inform both the Legal Practice Course and the Bar Vocational Course: see ACLEC (1995).

The three approaches to the concept of reflective practice take the term seriously. It is not just a slogan or a symbol. It expresses something distinctive about each of the different stages of professional education, and implies a set of interrelated concepts about the processes involved in professional education. Each of the approaches is well constructed and each ultimately flawed. Further work could lead to a subtle combination of their distinctive approaches to reflective practice. This could provide a multi-layered approach to educating the reflective practitioner.

References

ACLEC (1994) *Consultation Paper: the Initial Stage of Legal Education*, ACLEC, London.

ACLEC (1995) *Consultation Paper: the Vocational Stage and Continuing Education*, ACLEC, London.

R A Barnett (1990) *The Idea of Higher Education*, Open University Press, Milton Keynes.

R A Barnett (1992) *Improving Higher Education*, Open University Press, Milton Keynes.

R A Barnett (1994) *The Limits of Competence*, Open University Press, Milton Keynes.

H Bines (1992) 'Issues in Course Design' in H Bines & D Watson, *Developing Professional Education*, Open University Press, Milton Keynes.

J Calderhead (1992) 'Dilemmas In Developing Reflective Teaching', *Teacher Education Quarterly*.

J Calderhead & P Gates (1993) 'Introduction' in J Calderhead & P Gates *Contemplating Reflection in Teacher Development*, Falmer Press, Lewes.

W Carr & S Kemmis (1986) *Becoming Critical: Education, Knowledge and Action Research*, Falmer Press, Lewes.

H L Dreyfus & S E Dreyfus *Mind Over Machine:The Power of Human Intuition and Expertise in the Era of the Computer*, Basil Blackwell, Oxford.

J Dewey (1993) *How We Think*, D C Heath & Co, Boston.

J Elliott (1993) *Reconstructing Teacher Education*, Falmer Press, Lewes.

M Eraut (1990) 'Identifying knowledge which underpins performance' in H Black and A Wolf (eds) *Knowledge and Competence: Current Issues in Training and Education*, Employment Department, Sheffield.

M Eraut (1994) *Developing Professional Knowledge and Competence*, Falmer Press, Lewes.

G Fenstermacher (1988) 'The Place of Science & Epistemology in Schön's Conception of Reflective Practice' in P Grimmett & G Erickson *Reflection in Teacher Education*, Pacific Educational Press, Vancouver.

D Fish (1995) *Quality Mentoring for Student Teachers*, David Fulton, London.

P Grimmett (1988) 'The Nature of Reflecting and Schön's Conception in Practice' in P Grimmett and G Erickson *Reflection in Teacher Education*, Pacific Educational Press, Vancouver.

K R Hammond et al (1980) *Human Judgement and Decision Making*, Hemisphere, New York.

D A Kolb (1984) *Experiential Learning*, Prentice Hall, Englewood Cliffs, NJ.

D McIntyre (1993) 'Theory, Theorising & Reflection in Initial Teacher Education' in J Calderhead & P Gates *Contemplating Reflection in Teacher Development*, Falmer Press, Lewes.

T Russell (1993) 'Critical Attributes of a Reflective Teacher: Is Agreement Possible?' in J Calderhead & P Gates *Contemplating Reflection in Teacher Development*, Falmer Press, Lewes.

G Ryle (1949) *The Concept of Mind*, Penguin, Harmondsworth.

E Schein (1973) *Professional Education*, McGraw-Hill, New York.

H G Schmidt, G R Norman & H P A Boshuizen (1990) 'A Cognitive Perspective on medical expertise: theory and implications', 65(10) *Academic Medicine* 611–21.

D A Schön (1983) *The Reflective Practitioner*, Avebury, Aldershot.

D A Schön (1987) *Educating the Reflective Practitioner*, Jossey Bass, San Francisco.

Part III

Competence, assessment and evaluation

In this final section we turn our attention to three closely interlinked aspects of the educational process: competence, assessment and evaluation.

The shift to skills-based learning begs important questions for the assessment and evaluation of courses. In particular it raises four major issues: (i) to what extent should we engage in a move from norm-referenced to criterion-referenced assessment; (ii) what sort of balance needs to be achieved between developmental or *formative* and *summative* assessment; (iii) how are we to manage the assessment pressures created by more skills-based and developmental assessment, and (iv) what systems do we need to monitor and evaluate the changes in our methods of teaching, learning and assessment?

Assessment traditionally relies on norm-referenced criteria, ie on a broadly consensual but impressionistic standard which defines the student's relative standing in each subject. In law norm-referenced assessment has formed the basic model adopted through the primary medium of written assessment – traditionally, the unseen examination, albeit increasingly supported by coursework requirements. The impact of this model on the learning process is now commonly defined in negative terms (see Tribe's paper which follows).

One implication of the growth in skills education of 'outcomes' or 'competence' models of curriculum design (discussed in the Introduction to this volume), has been the need to find new ways of assessing. It is, after all, axiomatic in educational theory and practice that assessment should closely reflect learning objectives. Once one moves away from the assessment of content-based knowledge, norm-referenced assessment is of far less application. A feature of skills courses, therefore, has been the shift towards criterion-referenced assessment. This involves the setting of predetermined and generally standardised assessment criteria which reflect the learning outcomes of the course of study.

A key approach to criterion-referenced assessment in the UK has been the 'standards methodology' of the National Council for Vocational Qualifications (NCVQ). Under this scheme, standards of competence are defined on the basis of both a statement of outcomes expected of a competent performer of the task at hand (a client interview, say), and performance criteria which define the expected behaviours to be displayed by the performer. These latter essentially constitute the measure used to judge performance. The NCVQ is already well down the path of creating National Vocational Qualifications (NVQs) at levels 4 and 5, which equate to degree level education and beyond. But is the standards methodology appropriate for degree and professional levels of education?

In assessment terms, the standards methodology involves a major shift in perspective. Our judgments of ability become far less based on 'knowledge' and more focused on what the student can do in a specific context. At one level, this might be seen as a valuable corrective. We can at least, it is argued, infer some degree of knowledge from appropriate action, whereas focusing on the capacity to *know* tells us little or nothing about the ability to *do*. However, we suggest that such behavioural measures of competence still leave a number of blanks: they tell us little about the individual's capacity to learn from a situation; they are of doubtful utility in developing the ethics and values consistent with professional action; they overlook the fact that one of the most important dimensions of professional competence is the ability to recognise what we do not know or cannot do.

The chapters by Richard Winter and Mike Maughan are instructive in offering ways in which we might develop competence approaches which move beyond the confines of the NVQ.

Richard Winter constructs a general theory of professional work involving a complex of knowledge and affect, skills and values which form the basis for constructing competences at degree and professional levels. While essentially competence based, this model goes beyond the generic, task-based, approach to competence which underpins the NVQ approach, to incorporate those cognitive competences inherent in the empathic, ethical and self-reflective dimensions of the professional role.

The changes to teaching and learning implicit in this model will inevitably create new assessment pressures on teachers. The ACLEC Consultation Paper on *The Initial Stage* ((1994), para 6.14) comments that:

> The emphasis on active learning will make greater demands on teachers as assessors. They will be expected to comment more frequently and in greater detail on oral and written work. Students need to know what they have to do to achieve the required levels of performance, and how far short they are of them in various areas, if they are to develop in a properly structured way.

Given the pressures already created by modularisation, increased student numbers, audit and assessment etc, it is important that we look for ways of mediating the impact of changing assessment priorities. The practical difficulty as always lies in maintaining, or even enhancing, the quality of learning while meeting the needs of teaching staff. Diana Tribe's paper in this section suggests that self and peer assessment present methodologies which can satisfy both pragmatic and educative criteria. Yet, as Richard Grimes pointed out earlier in this collection, they are techniques which have tended to be under-utilised in the law school. Tribe's paper offers both theoretical justifications and a practical example of peer assessment in skills-based learning at degree level. It suggests that peer and self-assessment provide mechanisms that are developmental and can satisfy demands for valid and reliable assessment processes. They also offer a means of ensuring that the lessons of student-centred and group-based learning are carried through into the assessment process.

Mike Maughan, like Winter, rejects a narrow functionalist approach to competence and its assessment. Rather, using the Legal Practice Course as an example, he argues for the development of a more rounded 'capability' approach to professional education. Capability, unlike competency, focuses on the individual's need to continue developing beyond the threshold of competence required of the new trainee. Maughan's paper also squarely identifies perhaps the greatest challenge for legal education, and its accreditation: the extent to which the logic of capability should lead us, and the profession, towards a far more developmental approach to assessment.

The balance to be achieved between developmental and summative assessment is a central question for all, not just skills, teachers. One of the underlying themes emerging from this collection, and one that is followed up in this part, is that we need to determine our focus. Is it to be on the *process* or the *outcomes* of learning? In an outcomes-dominated approach, developmental assessment remains primarily diagnostic; it enables students to develop the skills and knowledge which will enhance their performance in periodic assessment and examinations. But, if we are to emphasise the process of learning, then continuing developmental 'assessment' becomes, as Mike Maughan shows, an end in itself – a shift which he signals by his preference for the term 'evaluation' over assessment. Drawing on the established field of management learning, Maughan explores a range of evaluative techniques and processes geared to the development of individual capability. These too offer a significant challenge to our traditional assessment culture, but one that deserves to be taken seriously.

Finally, then, we turn to another dimension of evaluation – the student evaluation of courses. This now seems to have become a permanent feature of modern higher education. Of itself, that is not necessarily a bad thing. At the very least one might argue that student evaluation ought to be a logical concomitant of student-centred learning. But do we need to consider what constitutes effective student evaluation? Anecdotally (there is a dearth of subject-specific research on modes of course evaluation), it appears that there is a wide variation in practice, with some institutions taking student evaluation very seriously indeed and others paying little more than lip service to the idea. There is a danger here that poor student evaluation may be considerably worse than none at all. If student evaluation is to be taken seriously, it must be shown that it is not, as Diana Tribe noted in Chapter One, susceptible to measuring tutor popularity rather than the quality of learning.

Drawing primarily on the process of evaluating the new Bar Vocational Course, Joanna Shapland explores a range of methodological, resource and 'political' issues surrounding student evaluation. While there are clearly pitfalls to be avoided, the essence of Shapland's case is that, properly implemented and used, student evaluation does offer a powerful and empowering mechanism for educational change.

Chapter 11

Outline of a general theory of professional competences

Richard Winter[1]

Competence – broad or narrow definition

The problem to be addressed in this paper arises in part because almost all current examples of the analysis of vocational competences concern forms of employment involving relatively low status. This has provoked the question: how appropriate is the 'competence-based' approach in devising 'professional level' awards? This question tends to arise because of an assumption that the skills involved in lower status occupations are 'narrower' than in higher status occupations, and can thus be more easily identified as observable behaviours. This assumption (that the hierarchy from high status to low status skills corresponds to a hierarchy from abstract to concrete skills) is largely a cultural convention, and clearly open to challenge: there is an important sense in which hairdressers are aestheticians and brain-surgeons are manual operatives. Indeed, the

1   This paper was originally written as part of a development project, the ASSET Programme (Accreditation and Support for Specified Expertise and Training), funded by the Employment Department and carried out by Anglia Polytechnic University and Essex Social Services. The purpose of this paper was to present a general theory of professional work as a step towards formulating the nature of 'competences' at the level of 'professional' occupations. An earlier version of the paper was published in Winter & Maisch (1991) and was also presented at the 1990 annual conference of the British Educational Research Association. It is reprinted here with permission.
    I should like to acknowledge the valuable help received during the writing of this paper from Maire Maisch (co-worker on the ASSET Programme); Maggie MacLure and Nigel Norris (University of East Anglia); Susan Hart (Cambridge Institute of Education); and colleagues in Anglia Polytechnic University Faculty of Health Nursing and Social Work, Paul Stanton and Bryony Webb.

very distinction between 'abstract' and 'concrete' is itself problematic: see Wolf (1989), pp 42–4 and Leacock (1972).

In view of this, it is extremely helpful that the Training Agency
(now the Employment Department Training, Education, & Enterprise Directorate) consistently uses a *wide* definition of competence:

> Competence is a wide concept which embodies the ability to
> transfer skills and knowledge to new situations within the occu-
> pational area. It encompasses organisation and planning of
> work, innovation, and coping with non-routine activities. It
> includes those qualities of personal effectiveness that are
> required in the workplace to deal with co-workers, managers,
> and customers.
>
> T A Guidance Notes (1980), p 1

The breadth of the definition here allows us to be clear that competences do not simply refer to one narrowly determined skill
required by one aspect of a particular task and identifiable on the
basis of a single observed performance; on the contrary, competences cannot be *perceived*, they can only be *inferred*: see Wolf
(1989), pp 46, 48. This is of great practical significance. It means
that the assessment of competences must always be a complex judgment, not a simple 'reading' from a measurement scale. This in turn
is essential: if competences did not have this inherently generalised
quality, the lists of criteria would become endless: see McClelland
(1973), p 9; Wolf (1989), p 48.

To sum up: a competence is an 'externally defined standard'
(FEU (1989), p 16) which is created when a particular complex
employment role requires from incumbents of that role a particular
form of ability. This wide definition seems an appropriate starting
point: professional workers are apt to resist definitions of their practice in terms of precisely circumscribed task skills: see Douglas
(1990), pp 23–5. But before we consider further the implications of
this claim for the complexity of competences, we need to clarify the
way in which competences are derived.

Empirical or theoretical methods of derivation

The work of Richard Boyatzis (1982) is instructive as a starting point.
For Boyatzis (in marked contrast to the argument of the previous section) 'a job competency is an underlying characteristic of a person

which results in effective and/or superior performance in a job' (p 21). Now, although he had access to a large amount of data collected in previous studies sponsored by MacBer and Co, the outcomes of his extremely laborious method are very disappointing. For example, the competences listed are so general as to be unhelpful in specifying professional needs. For example, the 'leadership' cluster includes 'self-confidence', 'use of oral presentation', 'logical thought', and 'conceptualisation' (ibid, p 118). One of Boyatzis's problems is that he wishes to describe his approach as 'inductive' rather than 'a priori' (p 249) and he therefore constructs his 'integrated model of management competences' at the end of his analysis (p 194) as though it simply 'emerges' from his lists of separate competences. But this model then contains such inexplicable features as the following suggestions: only junior managers require the competence of 'developing others' and only middle level managers (*not* higher levels) require 'logical thought' (p 226). He makes no comment on these absurdities, presumably seeing them as 'facts' generated by his 'objective' method. But Boyatzis's 'inductive' method is also highly inconsistent: although he wishes to avoid 'imposing some arbitrary theoretical or value-based assumption as to what constitutes effectiveness as a manager' (p 44), he recognises that each measure used in his investigative procedure is 'a relatively subjective judgment (and) therefore ... based on a particular theory or set of values' (p 43). The source of the confusion is obvious: 'induction' can never be a complete methodological basis for inquiry, since the collection of examples can never proceed without a theory as to what would count as an example. (The work of Karl Popper is a widely accepted critique of the inadequacies of induction.) Boyatzis therefore illustrates the inadequacy of defining competences in terms of the characteristics of individuals without first of all defining a model of the occupational role in terms of which these characteristics are significant.

In contrast to Boyatzis's attempt to avoid starting from a theoretical model, the report *Classifying the Components of Management Competences* produced by the Training Agency Occupational Standards Branch (1988) explicitly starts from 'a model of a manager' (p 4) and uses a classificatory, subdividing logic to generate 'performance criteria'. But this only takes us one step forward: 'classification' is the most minimal form of model building, since it rests on a reductionist theory of thought processes. Classifications are widely used as the 'reconstructed logic' of a situation but they do not give us the 'logic-in-use' (ie the interpretative schemas) by which those involved in the situation make sense of it: see Kaplan (1964). The problem is as follows: phenomena can indeed be 'classified' in a nearly infinite variety of dimensions, but this only means that in order to guide the classification along more (rather than less) 'relevant' lines a prior model of the phenomenon will be needed. And this prior model may not itself be presented as a set of classificatory terms, otherwise we get an infinite regress. The model which guides a classification must be articulated as a description which encapsulates the essential dynamic processes of the phenomenon at issue (in this case: 'management').

This is where *Classifying the Components of Management Competences* is weak. It presents no argued grounds for the threefold distinction that they treat as their starting point: 'Managing Resources and Systems', 'Personal Effectiveness', 'Sensitivity to Environment and External Factors'. We do not know whether these categories are exhaustive, discrete, or at the same level of abstraction from the experiences to which they refer. The report asserts that the later sub-divisions are incomplete (p 5) but we cannot judge what it is that is lacking nor (therefore) what might be needed to make the analysis complete. Without a descriptive overall theory of what managers do, we cannot generate a usable classification of their various activities.

A further step forward in this respect is represented by the Training Agency 'Functional Analysis' approach. This creates a description in terms of the *purposes* of the occupation and the means by which the purpose is achieved. This addresses the question of the *relevance* of the classification, and its comprehensiveness is addressed by starting at the most general level: what is the *purpose* of 'management' (or any other occupational area)? The dynamic here is that of means/ends instrumental action, and the general approach is derived from a 'functionalist' theory of the relation of systems and subsystems. This is acceptable as far as it goes, but it is so abstract that it cannot inform any fine judgments. It articulates a simple and familiar generality (actions have purposes and are connected with one another) but it says nothing about the inevitable contradictions and complexities of any real situations, such as those of professional work.

Differentiation of levels of knowledge

How, then, can the mode of activity characteristic of a professional worker be specified? One conventional way of differentiating 'higher

strata' of occupations is by saying that they require 'more knowledge': see the Care Sector Consortium Steering Group (1989), p 11.
We could start to answer the question, therefore, by focusing on the
particular form and level of knowledge required. But the difficulties
of specifying different levels of knowledge are revealed by an examination of statements from the former Council for National
Academic Awards (CNAA) on the matter. Consider first of all the
following statement of the CNAA's 'general educational aims' (ie
aims which informed *all* CNAA programmes, including certificate,
diploma, honours degree and higher degree levels of work. These
general aims were:

> The development of students' intellectual and imaginative pow-
> ers; their understanding and judgment; their problem-solving
> skills; their ability to communicate; their ability to see relation-
> ships within what they have learned, and to perceive their field
> of study in a broader perspective ... an enquiring, analytical
> and creative approach, encouraging independent judgment and
> critical self-awareness.

CNAA (1989), p 52

But subsequently, in describing the intellectual requirements for honours degree work, CNAA merely used the phrases 'sustained
independent work at high level . . .' (ibid, p 59) and 'demonstrating
the ability to analyse, synthesise, and creatively apply what has been
learned . . .' (ibid, p 60). Clearly, the aims specified for the honours
degree were wholly subsumed (except for the question-begging
phrase 'at a high level') under the general aims, which included
levels of work both higher and lower than the honours degree, so
that we are not helped to specify what it is that an honours degree
will demand that other levels of award do not. To say that the higher
award will demand *more* of it does not help, since our task is to create
a description of competences which will be criterion-referenced, ie
where the criterion specifies the *level* of achievement, rather than the
dimension in which varying degrees of excellence are displayed.

Moreover, a line of argument which attempts to differentiate occupational levels in terms of a specific 'knowledge' component poses a
serious question to the NCVQ enterprise of assessing occupational
competences in terms of work-related performances. If, as John
Burke (1989) says (p 2), 'In essence an NVQ is conceived as a statement of competence clearly relevant to work', and if possession of a

body of theoretical knowledge is one of the defining characteristics of a professional worker, it might seem acceptable to include old-fashioned 'examinations' of theoretical knowledge in the assessment of professional competences.

The implications of this problem are considered in a recent collection of papers: see Black and Wolf (1990). The issue underlying the Black and Wolf collection is: does knowledge relevant to an occupation have to be assessed separately or can it be inferred from the ability to act appropriately and effectively in a *range* of different situations? Alison Wolf suggests that it must be assessed separately when occupations are characterised by situations which are unpredictable and/or enormously varied: see Wolf (1990), p 37. But this would (or could be said to) characterise all professional work. In contrast, Bob Mansfield (1990) is concerned to argue that knowledge can be tested directly in performance (p 20), but when he analyses the example of medical diagnosis, he argues that since problems can have 'an almost unlimited number of solutions at higher professional levels ... assessment ... would need to gather evidence about the processes by which the candidate came to the decision made' (ibid).

Given this problem, the way forward suggested by several writers in the collection is that: (a) the knowledge component can be included by specifying the *range* of situations in which effective action is expected; and (b) knowledge can be presented as 'supplementary' evidence (eg oral answers, written essays) which leaves 'performance evidence' as the primary form of assessment: see Jessup (1990), pp 40–4.

All this suggests that the key issue is: how is professional workers' knowledge related to their practice? Wolf begins to address this issue positively by stressing that knowledge is closely allied with experience, and that it cannot be treated out of context: see Wolf (1990), pp 32–3. Eraut (1990) pursues the argument further. He presents a classification of the ways in which knowledge can be utilised: replication, application, interpretation, and association (p 25). He also gives us a classification of *types* of knowledge (which he derives from studies of management, but which he believes 'can also be found in other occupations'): knowledge of people, knowledge of practice (facts, courses of action), conceptual knowledge (ie theoretical perspectives), process knowledge (eg interpersonal), and control knowledge (self-knowledge and understanding of the knowledge process itself): ibid, pp 26–7. This is helpful, but inconclusive and problematic: why, for example, the categorical distinction between 'knowledge of people', 'interpersonal knowledge', and 'self-knowledge', when they are clearly so interdependent? Nevertheless, what Eraut presents here is the beginnings of a model of the relationship between professional workers, professional work, and professional expertise, and this is the direction in which the argument will be pursued in the following section.

Towards a model of the experienced professional worker

This section contains four subsections. The first considers professional work in relation to its inherent values, the second considers the inherent emotional dimension of professional work, and the third and fourth consider two contrasted approaches to the relationship between professional work and professional knowledge.

Professions and values

Many would argue that professional work is defined by its involvement with moral issues, just as much as by its specialised knowledge. The point is clearly made, in respect of the teaching profession, by Wilfred Carr (1989), pp 3–4. He argues that teaching has its own *intrinsic* criteria, as opposed to *extrinsic* criteria such as cost-effectiveness, number of pupils achieving certain test grades, etc. The general argument is derived from Aristotle's emphasis on the importance of the category of 'Practical Wisdom', which is at the same time a virtue, a practical interpersonal skill, and a form of understanding – the ability to deliberate on 'what is conducive to the good life generally': see Aristotle (1976), p 209. Hence, the argument might run, each profession is *intrinsically* concerned with a particular practical aspect of 'the Good Life' – teachers with the realisation of the capacity for understanding, lawyers with the realisation of justice, medicine with physical health, nursing with the overall well-being of the sick, and social workers with the application of the principles of care, justice, autonomy, and well-being to the life situations of the vulnerable.

Now, it is essential to moral principles that their application to particular cases involves the exercise of complex judgments and, usually, the management of dilemmas, since actual situations bring different moral principles into conflict with each other, eg through the competing rights to well-being, care, and autonomy of different individuals. The ability to make these judgments in an equitable and effective way is a dimension of the practice of experienced professional workers; lay persons, in contrast, are concerned to pursue their own legitimate interests, not to adjudicate between the moral rights of others.

Furthermore, professional practice involves an obligation to avoid 'oppressive' judgments, ie judgments which make non-justifiable discriminations on the basis of age, gender, sexual orientation, race, cultural background, language, religion, political affiliation, disfigurement, physical or mental disability, etc. This value commitment is intrinsic to professional work because professional workers have an inherent responsibility to ensure that their services (whether they concern legal justice, medical care, social welfare, or educational progress) are equally available to all members of society. This principle of equity as applied to all clients (often expressed in official 'ethical codes') means that professional workers' specific skills are particularly required by vulnerable (disadvantaged, oppressed) citizens, who thus provide the real test of the profession's general effectiveness. In most societies there are processes which tend to reinforce patterns of privilege and disadvantage, including a widespread tendency to discriminate against the vulnerable: see, for example, Erving Goffman's well-known work on 'stigma' (1968). The ability to avoid oppressive discrimination is thus an element of a specifically professional understanding, and the ability to do so consistently, comprehensively, consciously, and effectively (albeit never finally or perfectly) will be a significant and complex competence of the experienced practitioner.

The emotional dimension of professional work

The role of the professional worker institutionalises the process whereby the problems of one person (or group) are submitted to the authoritative involvement of another person (or group): see Parsons (1954); Illich (1975). The basis for this authoritative involvement is the professional's specialised knowledge (see also the sections following), and one of its consequences is acceptance of the ethical and quasi-political responsibilities noted in the previous paragraphs.

There are a number of reasons why such relationships have an inherently emotional dimension. Firstly, the basis for professional work is that the client has a *problem* and therefore a range of anxieties concerning that problem. These anxieties in turn serve to extend and exacerbate the original difficulty. Secondly, in order to understand the client's problem, the professional needs both to empathise with the problem and its attendant anxieties and yet to preserve emotional distance from them, which creates a characteristic emotional tension in the worker, ie compassion versus guilt. Thirdly, there is a power dimension, created by (at the very least) the presupposition of the professional's authoritative expertise in relation to the client's problem, and this will activate some form of 'transference' effect: as an immediately present authority figure, the professional is someone whom the client can blame for their problem and thereby relieve part of their anxiety. (In many contexts this emotional pattern is magnified by the fact that the professional also has direct institutional power over the client.)

Professional work thus has an emotional dimension in the same way as it has cognitive and ethical dimensions: for professional workers, emotions (their own as well as their clients') are a topic, an obstacle, and a resource: see Salzberger-Wittenberg et al (1983). Experienced professional workers will be aware of this. They will recognise the emotions underlying clients' statements, and will respond in ways which address the emotions as well as the words; they will also recognise that their own emotions are likely to be 'hooked' by those of the client: see Harris (1973). Hence, they will have accepted that complex and apparently 'irrational' emotions are not an avoidable and regrettable indication of professional failure but an inherent aspect of the professional situation, which (like its other aspects) needs to be understood and effectively managed. *Inexperienced* workers, in contrast, will, like non-professional lay persons, find it difficult to maintain a practical and strategic awareness of the emotional structures with which they are inevitably involved, and are likely – as a result – firstly to ignore them, and subsequently to find themselves responding directly (ie non-strategically) with their own emotions to those of their clients.

Knowledge: the 'Expert Systems' model

As we have already seen, many aspects of a general theory of professional work will entail consideration of the role of knowledge.

The simplest type of theory here is that represented by the 'Expert Systems' approach. This characterises professional practice as a series of decision-making events, and professional expertise as a body of knowledge in the form of a system of general factual propositions which are applied in making professional decisions: see, for example, Takenouchi and Iwashita (1987).

If knowledge has this form it can be codified and computerised. There is no doubt that computerised programmes can, in certain contexts, be a useful support. For example, University College Swansea has constructed a system to 'assist hospital staff' with decisions involved in planning the discharge of geriatric patients (DISPLAN): Crystal (1989). Some, however, would go further than suggesting that such programmes may 'assist' staff and go on to claim: 'Expert Systems . . . simulate the behaviour and incorporate the knowledge of rational human experts': Oxman and Gero (1987), p 4. But this claim rests on a crucial proposition concerning the role of professional knowledge in professional practice: 'Transformational rules encode knowledge about how to generate a new state from a current state' (ibid, p 5). In other words, professional practice is taken to be a set of 'rule-generated operations' (ibid). This proposition relies on a metaphor from the manipulation of closed systems (grammar, mathematics), and it is in principle inappropriate for situations constituted by the open parameters of empirical experience. In the real world, rules can only guide decisions, not 'generate' them: an inevitable act of interpretation always intervenes. (The argument derives from Wittgenstein's *Philosophical Investigations*: every rule relies on another rule as to how the first rule should be applied in a particular case, in an infinite regress.)

It is significant that the first quotation from Oxman and Gero used the phrase 'the knowledge of rational human experts'. The general theme of the collection of papers on 'Decision-making' edited by McGrew and Wilson (1982) is that the model of rationality used by most decision-making theory is a logically derived ideal (based on a means/ends theory of action) which is unrealistic because it is always an oversimplification, ignoring the complex and contradictory demands which real human actors perceive in the situations where they must act. Decision-making in practice is never the following through of an objective algorithm but 'appropriate deliberation', seeking 'good' but not 'optimal' solutions (Simon (1982), pp 88–90) since there can be no consensus as to what the optimal solution is, except (perhaps) some time after the event! Expert systems, therefore, can assist but never 'simulate' the knowledge-processing activities of experts; they do not formulate a model of professional expertise.

The Implicit Expertise model

The critique of expert systems is the starting point for the influential work of the Dreyfus brothers. One of the Dreyfus brothers wrote a book called *What Computers Can't Do* (H Dreyfus (1979)). What his brother said they can't do is to model the relatively 'unstructured situations' which typify the world of professional work (S Dreyfus (1981), p 3). By 'unstructured' Dreyfus means those features of unpredictability and uniqueness which characterise the settings of the 'caring professions' just as much as those of the 'selling professions'. (But not, perhaps, the 'making professions': Dreyfus cites 'blending petroleum' as his example of the sort of 'objectively defined problem' which is amenable to what he calls 'systematic analysis' (op cit, p 3)). Thus, according to Dreyfus, experienced professionals do not possess and apply their professional knowledge in the form of systematic analysis based on universal rules and clear-cut factual propositions. On the contrary, he says, this is how *novices*, still dominated by recent book-learning, set about taking their first faltering steps into the practical world *before* they have built up the forms of proficiency and expertise which will enable them to do without it. In contrast, the fully proficient professional worker's knowledge is no longer in the form of rules and facts, but consists of rough guidelines, elliptical maxims, long-range goals which determine priorities, and a repertoire of typical examples which are available to be invoked as precedents. Dreyfus charts the stages of this process, and ends with a description of the 'expert' professional, whose knowledge has become largely 'intuitive', locked into the context-bound 'situational understanding' where it originated (S Dreyfus (1981), p 22) and thus almost inaccessible (either to themselves or others) except through the skilful practices which embody it: 'At the highest level of skill . . . understanding is created unconsciously from concrete experience, and cannot be verbalised' (ibid, p 38).

It has already been noted that the Dreyfus model of professional understanding arises from a critique of formal analytical models and of computer-based idealisations of rationality, and a celebration of the 'tacit' dimensions of 'personal knowledge'. ('The expert must be made aware of his (sic) own uniquely human capacities and of the inadequacies . . . of any formal model': ibid, pp 51–2). But this high-lights an important problem with the Dreyfus model. If the highest level of skill is 'intuitive' and cannot be verbalised, then Dreyfus is closing off the possibilities for facilitating the development of that skill. We may agree that expertise cannot be verbalised without being transformed, but Dreyfus's argument is only concerned with how verbalising interrupts the skilful flow of expert performance, and it strangely neglects the well-known argument that verbalisation is part of the creative development of understanding: see, for example, Vygotsky (1962). In other words, although he celebrates the achievements of expert experience, Dreyfus's argument makes it difficult to formulate how it is that experts can continue to learn from their experience, and tends to close off the formulation of methods for cognitive development by means of the 'critique' of knowledge-as-ideology.

It is for this reason that there is an important limitation in Pat Benner's (1984) widely acclaimed celebration of the expert knowl-edge of practising nurses. She uses the Dreyfus model of progression from 'novice' to 'expert' (from deliberate application of facts and rules to 'intuitive' interpretation). As with Dreyfus, the main point of her argument is the defence of practitioners' practical knowledge against the prescriptive claims of academic theory. However, she is less clear about the processes by which such practical knowledge can be the basis for further professional learning, except to say that pro-fessional colleagues should share it. Hence the title of her research project: 'AMICAE'.

To summarise, the Dreyfus/Benner model of professional knowl-edge shows the valuable learning resource which is present in practitioners' accumulated experience, and makes a strong case that professional work spontaneously *generates* knowledge: pro-fessional workers do not need to *be presented with* 'reconstructed' theories of their work. But what Benner and Dreyfus lack is a the-ory of the process whereby practitioners' knowledge is deepened and refined through the cognitive dimensions of work, ie interac-tion and communicative verbalisation. To invoke such notions as 'intuition' is to de-intellectualise professional practice, to deny its capacity for systematic, purposeful self-transformation. Further-more, their model makes it impossible to consider the very important question: how can professional expertise avoid becom-ing an entrenched and self-reproducing ideology? It is to this process of *learning* from professional experience that we now turn.

Professional work and the learning cycle

We have established that the analysis of the competences of professional workers will need to take into account the fact that professional knowledge develops through the accumulation of concrete experience. Hence, if we wish to describe such competences in such a way that they can form a framework of opportunities for professional development, we need a detailed model of how professional workers learn from their experience.

Experiential learning

This is a basic concept for any formulation of work-based competences. It is elaborated in Kolb (1984) and a convenient simplified version can be found in Gibbs (1988). The essence of it can be represented in the well-known diagram of 'The Experiential Learning Cycle' (Gibbs (1988), p 11): and see Caroline Maughan, this collection, p 71.

In principle one can use this model to describe the process by which proficient workers develop their abstract conceptualisation by active involvement with an ever-widening range of concrete situations. Clearly a key role in this model is played by the term 'reflective observation'. 'Observation' is awkward, since it suggests that withdrawal from involvement which Dreyfus sees as deskilling the expert practitioner, and thus as an unrealistic element in a model of the processes of professional expertise. But 'reflection' brings us to the important work of Donald Schön.

Donald Schön: 'The reflective practitioner'

Schön's work (1983), (1987) is concerned with the precise nature of the learning processes at work in professional practice:

> The process [of reflection-in-action] spirals through stages of appreciation [of a professional case], action, reappreciation. The unique and uncertain situation comes to be understood through the attempt to change it, and changed through the attempt to understand it.
>
> Schön (1983), p 132

Like Dreyfus, he contrasts the 'artistry' of the experienced practitioner (ibid, p 140) with 'technical problem-solving' (p 133). Thus, the professional worker does not acquire a set of validated rules or categories but a 'repertoire' of past examples as a set of possible 'precedents' or 'metaphors' (p 138). It is in terms of these that problems are 'reframed' so that solutions can be envisaged (p 134), and subsequently the unintended consequences of the reframing are 'appreciated' (p 135).

One basic criterion for this process is coherence, but another, equally important, is 'keeping the inquiry moving' (p 136). In other words, 'solutions' are not seen as permanent, because the practitioner's relation to the situation is 'transactional' (p 150): ie it has the form of a 'conversation' in which the search for an adequate interpretation 'shapes the situation but . . . [the practitioner's] own models and appreciations are shaped by it' (p 151). This involves a systematic recognition of the *client's* meanings in a *collaborative* dialogue where the professional's authority is always open to question (pp 295–6). This stance has a quasi-experimental form: the practitioner creates a 'virtual world' by means of exploratory discussion which rehearses hypothetical alternative courses of action (pp 157–62). S/he also attempts to maintain a consistent 'double vision', ie a recognition that the order which s/he has provisionally imposed on the events might always need to be changed later (p 164). 'Problem-solving' at one level is thus simultaneously (on a larger scale) 'problem-setting' (p 165).

In a later work (1987) one aspect of the learning process is presented in more detail. Schön presents a 'ladder of reflection' which suggests an ascending scale of explicit verbalisation of implicit understanding:

1) Practice.
2) Description of practice.
3) Reflection on description of practice.
4) Reflection on reflection on description of practice.

Schön (1987), pp 114–17

However, there is one fundamental weakness to Schön's work: it is *not* derived directly from sessions where practitioners are developing their own practice, but (obliquely, as it were) from sessions where experienced practitioners in a tutorial role are attempting to pass on their knowledge to novices. But if we take Dreyfus's argument seriously, we will not be surprised to learn that there is evidence (Benner (1984), pp 37–8) that experts do not actually follow (in practice) the instructions they use in instructing trainees! So Schön's work must be taken as suggestive, rather than as the last word on this issue.

Action-research

Another 'oblique' approach to the question of how professionals learn from experience is found in some of the literature on action-research. This also presents a cyclical format. Consider, for example, the following version by John Elliott (1981), p 3:

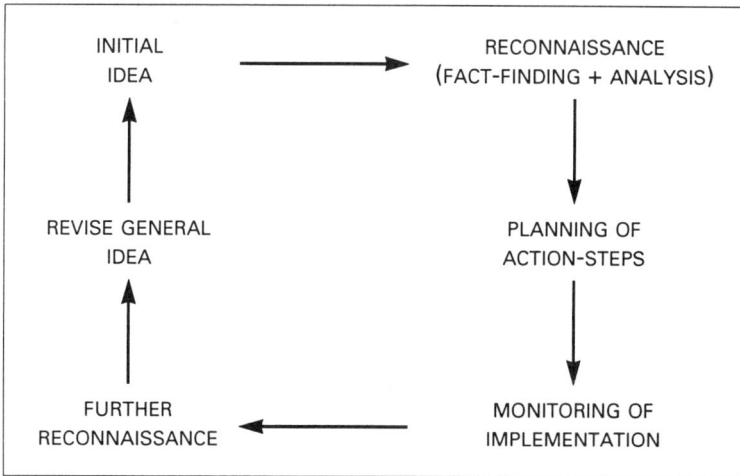

Recent work in this area has begun to address the question of the nature of the reflective process in this cycle: see Winter (1989). It is suggested that practitioners engaging in action-research into their own work situations need a specific set of cognitive principles. These will link together:
(a) a theory of knowledge based in experiential development;
(b) a collaborative stance towards practice and inquiry into practice;
(c) a commitment to the need for – and to the possibility of – learning from professional situations;
(d) a recognition of the validity of others' experience;
(e) a set of criteria for identifying relevant modes of analytical and interpretative reflection, namely: relating a situation to its contexts, seeking its contradictions and dilemmas, and understanding it within a process of change: Winter (1989), chs 3 & 4.

Furthermore, it has been argued that the above principles devised for action-research (ie for sustained inquiry which is relevant to but separate from professional practice itself) are in fact closely related to Schön's description of the forms of reflection which occur *within* professional practice as the process by which practice generates learning: see Evans (1990). Following this suggestion, the final section, below, includes a number of points which are attempts to translate principles originally presented in the context of practitioner action-research (Winter (1989)) into the context of professionals learning from their practice. It will be noted that, as Evans points out, many of them echo key points from Schön's argument, and that the basic notions of 'experiential learning' underlie both.

Conclusion – developmental reflection through professional experience: towards a general theory of professional competences

This section draws together the various suggestions from earlier parts of the argument into a statement of the forms of competence which might (in principle) be expected of a professional worker. It is intended as a sketch of a theory of professional work in the interpersonal professions, and thus a general framework which could provide a basis for selecting and analysing empirical data concerning occupational 'competences' contributed by practitioners. It will enable competences at the requisite 'level' (ie the level of a professionally qualified worker) to be differentiated from those more appropriate to other levels. The points are numbered for ease of reference, but they are intended to form the interdependent elements of a unified process which links professional practice and professional understanding, skills, commitments, and self-knowledge, as indicated, roughly, in the final diagram. (The main authors from which the various elements are derived are noted in brackets.)

1. The nature of professional work is that situations are unique and knowledge of those situations is therefore never complete. Good practice, therefore, for professional workers, is practice whereby knowledge is developed through the forms of reflection which practice itself requires. (Dreyfus, Schön.)

2. It follows that, for professional workers, a given state of reflective understanding will be transformed by further experience

of practice, and that (by the same token) future practice will be transformed by the reflection which arises from practice. (Schön, Winter.)

3. Professional work involves commitment to a specific set of moral purposes, and professional workers will recognise the inevitably complex and serious responsibilities which arise when attempting to apply ethical principles to particular cases.

4. The responsibility for equitable practice which characterises the professional role commits professional workers to the comprehensive, consistent, conscious, and effective implementation of 'anti-oppressive' non-discriminatory principles and practices.

5. Authoritative involvement in the problem areas of clients' lives inevitably creates a complex emotional dimension to all professional work, and professional workers therefore recognise that the role involves understanding and managing the relationship between their own feelings and those of clients.

6. Consequently, professional workers recognise that the understanding of others on which their interpersonal effectiveness depends is inseparable from self-knowledge, and consequently entails a sustained process of self-evaluation. (Training Agency, Eraut.)

7. The incompleteness of professional knowledge (see 1 & 2 above) entails that, for professional workers, relationships with others will be collaborative rather than simply hierarchical, so that the authoritative basis of judgments will always remain open to question. Professional workers are thus on principle willing to learn from others, and recognise that this involves a willingness to place their own prior assumptions and authoritative status (as 'experts') at risk. (Schön, Winter.)

8. Professional workers recognise that judgments are not simply empirical observations based on objective factual evidence, but always involve interpretations and theoretical, moral, and political assumptions, so that alternative judgments are always possible. (Schön, Winter.)

9. For professional workers, effective reflection upon a situation entails a grasp of:
   (a) its relation to its context (eg institutional, legal, and political constraints and opportunities) (Training Agency, Winter);
   (b) its contradictions and dilemmas (Winter);
   (c) its place within a change process (Winter).

10. Professional workers will have at their command a grasp of the relationships (similarities and contrasts) between a wide range of situations (different clients, different legal frameworks, and different practice settings). (Jessup, Dreyfus.)
11. The process of understanding which professional workers will bring to their practice will necessitate independent, critical thought, involving creative translation of meanings between contexts (see 11, above), analysis of problematic situations into constituent elements, and synthesis of varied elements into a unified overall pattern. (CNAA.)
12. Professional workers will be aware of available codified information – eg concerning legal provisions, organisational procedures, resources, and research findings, but they will recognise that the relevance of this information for particular situations always depends on their own resourceful interpretation.

A diagram linking these points is presented opposite.

References

Aristotle (1976) *Ethics*, Penguin, Harmondsworth.

P Benner (1984) *From Novice to Expert*, Addison Wesley, Menlo Park.

H Black & A Wolf (1990) *Knowledge and Competence*, HMSO, London.

R Boyatzis (1982) *The Competent Manager: A Model For Effective Performance*, John Wiley, New York.

J Burke (ed) (1989) *Competency-Based Education and Training*, Falmer Press, Lewes.

Care Sector Consortium Steering Group (1989) *The Residential, Domiciliary, and Day Care Project: Volume 1, Background Material*, HMSO, London.

W Carr (ed) (1989) *Quality in Teaching*, Falmer Press, Lewes.

CNAA (1989) *Handbook*, CNAA, London.

Crystal (1989) *Newsletter*, Issue No 5, April.

A general theory of professional work:
Developmental reflection through professional experience

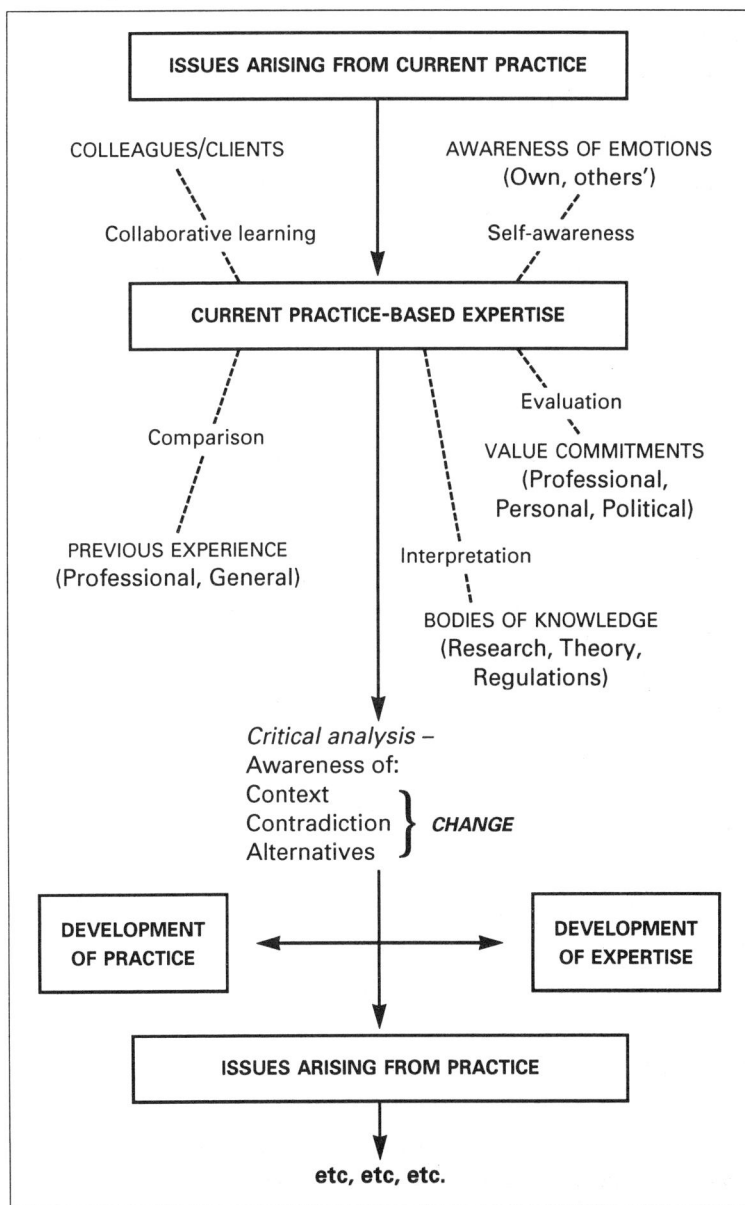

ISSUES ARISING FROM CURRENT PRACTICE

COLLEAGUES/CLIENTS

AWARENESS OF EMOTIONS
(Own, others')

Collaborative learning

Self-awareness

CURRENT PRACTICE-BASED EXPERTISE

Comparison

Evaluation

VALUE COMMITMENTS
(Professional,
Personal, Political)

PREVIOUS EXPERIENCE
(Professional, General)

Interpretation

BODIES OF KNOWLEDGE
(Research, Theory,
Regulations)

Critical analysis –
Awareness of:
Context
Contradiction } *CHANGE*
Alternatives

**DEVELOPMENT
OF PRACTICE**

**DEVELOPMENT
OF EXPERTISE**

ISSUES ARISING FROM PRACTICE

etc, etc, etc.

J Douglas (1990) 'The wholeness of care', *Community Care*, 5 April.

H Dreyfus (1979) *What Computers Can't Do*, Harper & Row, New York.

S Dreyfus (1981) *Formal models vs human situational understanding*, International Institute for Applied Systems Analysis, Schloss Laxenburg, Austria.

J Elliott (1981) *Action-Research: A Framework for Self-Evaluation in Schools*, University of East Anglia, Norwich.

M Eraut (1990) 'Identifying the knowledge which underpins performance', in H Black & A Wolf, op cit.

N Evans (1990) 'Systematic reflections', *Times Educational Supplement*, 23 March.

FEU (1989) *A Guide To Work-Based Learning Terms*, FEU, London.

G Gibbs (1988) *Learning By Doing*, FEU, London.

E Goffman (1968) *Stigma*, Penguin, Harmondsworth.

T Harris (1973) *I'm OK, You're OK*, Pan Books, London.

I Illich (1975) *Medical Nemesis: The Expropriation of Health*, Calder & Boyars, London.

G Jessup (1990) 'The evidence required to demonstrate competence', in H Black & A Wolf, op cit.

A Kaplan (1964) *The Conduct of Inquiry*, Chandler, San Francisco.

D Kolb (1984) *Experiential Learning*, Prentice Hall, Englewood Cliffs, NJ.

E Leacock (1972) 'Abstract vs concrete speech: a false dichotomy', in C Cazden et al (eds) *Functions of Language in the Classroom*, Teachers College Press, New York.

B Mansfield (1990) 'Knowledge, evidence, and assessment', in H Black & A Wolf, op cit.

D McClelland (1973) 'Testing for competence rather than for "intelligence"', *American Psychologist*, January.

A McGrew & M Wilson (eds) *Decision-Making: Approaches and Analysis*, Manchester University Press, Manchester.

R Oxman & J Gero (1987) 'Using an expert system for design diagnosis and design synthesis', 4 *Expert Systems* 1.

T Parsons (1954) 'The professions and social structure', in *Essays in Sociological Theory*, Collier-Macmillan, New York.

I Salzberger-Wittenberg et al (1983) *The Emotional Experience of Learning and Teaching*, RKP, London.

D Schön (1983) *The Reflective Practitioner*, Basic Books, New York.

D Schön (1987) *Educating The Reflective Practitioner*, Jossey Bass, San Francisco.

H Simon (1982) 'From substantive to procedural rationality', in A McGrew & M Wilson, op cit.

H Takenouchi & Y Iwashita (1987) 'An integrated knowledge representation scheme for expert systems', 4 *Expert Systems* 1.

Training Agency Occupational Standards Branch (1988) *Classifying the Components of Management Competence*, Training Agency, Sheffield.

L Vygotsky (1962) *Thought and Language*, John Wiley, New York.

R Winter (1989) *Learning From Experience: Principles and Practice in Action-Research*, Falmer Press, Lewes.

R Winter & M Maisch (1991) *The Development and Assessment of Professional Competences*, Essex Social Services Department & Anglia Polytechnic.

A Wolf (1989) 'Can competence and knowledge mix?', in J Burke, op cit.

A Wolf (1990) 'Defining the knowledge component', in H Black & A Wolf, op cit.

Chapter 12

DIY learning – self and peer assessment
Diana Tribe

The evaluation of one's own learning is one of the major means by which self initiated learning becomes also responsible learning. It is when the individual has to take responsibility for deciding what criteria are important to him, what goals are to be achieved, and the extent to which s/he has achieved those goals, that s/he truly learns to take responsibility for himself and his directions.

Carl Rogers

Traditional forms of assessment – the effect on law academic staff

Whilst there is an acknowledged lack of consensus about the aims of legal education in this country (see, for example, Leighton & Sheinman (1986) for an account of the differing models of the last decade), law lecturers, it would appear, do not aim for students simply to gain a rote knowledge of many detailed legal rules. Rather, aims are concerned with the acquisition of legal concepts, together with the ability to apply those concepts to problems and thereby solve them. Indeed,

> Legal education has always aimed at education rather than the simple imparting of information. It is less concerned with rules and techniques than it is with the principles and ideas which underlie them . . . it is less concerned with verbal precepts than with the legal concepts of which they are a reflection.

Grodecki (1977)

The Law Student Assessment Project reported that this apparent general agreement among law lecturers about the aims of legal education was reflected in the main forms of assessment employed by law lecturers in the (then) Polytechnic sector: see Tribe and Tribe (1989). Most assessment took the familiar form of three-hour examinations combined with in-course assessments (which were normally based on essays or hypothetical problems). In those days, these were easy forms of assessment for lecturers to use; student numbers were relatively low (at least by today's standards) and staff had the time to set, mark and double mark in time for the Boards of Examiners, which were normally held annually.

With the advent of the modular system in the 1990s, main Boards of Examiners are now held in some universities as often as three times a year with referred boards adding to this number. To this may be added the subject boards, which often sit before the main award boards. At the same time there has been an expansion (now mercifully capped) in higher education, which has produced an ever-increasing number of students to be assessed at an ever-increasing number of Examination Boards. As a result of these changes challenges are being made to the traditional forms of assessment, which are seen to place an increasingly heavy burden on those law staff responsible for the implementation of the assessment system. Typical comments from law staff interviewed for the Law Student Assessment project as early as 1989 were that: 'Examination marking is the worst part of my job: I simply dread it'; 'I don't feel confident that I have time to make my marking accurate enough'.

At the same time, with the increase in the number of students and the number of Boards of Examiners, the burden on the external examiner system has become heavier; indeed, the role of the external examiner has become (inevitably) one of 'moderator', concerned with a general auditing of examination procedures, assessment practices and cohort standards rather than as an additional or second marker primarily concerned with individual standards of student achievement. This is emphasised by the fact that in many Law Schools batches of 'sample' scripts rather than those of 'problem' students are now sent to the external examiner.

At a time when law lecturers are being encouraged to become active researchers, to participate in income-generating activities and to undertake responsibility for an increasing number of administrative duties, the current assessment burden promises to become the straw that will break the academic camel's back.

For the practical reasons given above, if for no others of more educational weight, law academics have for some time been contemplating changes in at least some of the assessment strategies used, so that students' work can be fairly and validly assessed, whilst at the same time relieving staff of the increasingly heavy burden imposed by traditional assessment strategies.

Traditional assessment strategies – the effect on law students

It is unfortunately rather easier to induce a surface rather than a deep approach ... It is very easy to make students anxious, cynical or simply over-worked – all excellent soil for surface strategies to flourish, but much more difficult to make them curious. A few excellent teachers can do this; (but) many more teachers find it easier, all too often with institutional help ... to create a context of 'busywork', so that students' top priorities (in self defence) are to meet the letter of the demands made on them ... Getting a presentable assignment in by the deadline date is institutionally more important than spending time on an excellent one.

Biggs (1992)

An investigation recently undertaken by Phil Harris and Steve Bellerby of Sheffield Hallam University (1993), in the Legal Education Research Project, indicates that the number of modules required to be studied on undergraduate law programmes in the UK varies considerably between universities, ranging from 30 modules in some universities to 18 in others. It is obvious that the higher the number of modules to be studied and assessed, the more likely it is that breadth rather than depth of study should be assessed. Despite this fact, however, it is apparent that in most universities the traditional forms of assessment, designed to assess depth of learning and understanding, continue to be used. This is undoubtedly to the detriment of students, who find the burden of regular formative assessments, followed by summative assessment at the end of each semester, a very heavy one.

The large number of in-course assessments to be marked by staff may lead to the possibility that the level and quality of feedback given to students on their work will be limited, and in some cases returned to students too late for them to take full advantage of it.

Students interviewed as part of the Law Student Assessment Project commented, 'I remember taking weeks to write an essay; my tutor just put "Fair" at the bottom'; 'When we got our coursework back it was long after I wrote it and the comments were just meaningless, I don't really understand where I went wrong'.

Similarly, the standard examination set at the end of ten, twelve or fourteen-week semesters leads the student into rapid last-minute learning, to be forgotten soon afterwards with no possibility of feedback from the markers apart from the final mark. Students commented, 'I just learn my lecture notes by heart, there's no point in reading cases or articles'; 'We never get to see our examination papers, so we never learn from our mistakes'. Such an examination system leads to a form of rote learning based on surface processing which produces undesirable consequences: see Ramsden and Entwistle (1983); Tribe (1996). Students have little time to reflect on their learning in this system but rather are driven to a regurgitation in examinations of information which is soon forgotten.

Indeed, there is anecdotal evidence that with the development of the modular degree spread over semesters or trimesters, there is an increasing number of referrals, outright failures and withdrawals in the system. These factors are picked up by the ever vigilant assessors from the Higher Education Funding and Quality Councils when making their assessment visits to institutions, to the undoubted disadvantage of the Law Schools in question.

Despite the aims of law lecturers to help their students to develop the ability to understand, critically analyse and evaluate legal rules, it would appear that in many cases the depressing conclusion reached by Gow and Kember in 1990 still remains true. As a result of the combination of the traditional assessment strategies currently in use and the reduction in staff resources, it is 'questionable whether typical higher education is succeeding in meeting the stated goals of independent learning which are espoused by both government and lecturers'.

New approaches to student learning

Over the centuries university education has been traditionally wedded to the assessment of individual written work; however, as indicated above, there are pragmatic reasons why there should be a change in this system of assessment with the aim of benefiting both marker and marked.

Quite separately from this practical analysis, recent psychological research points directly to the need for the inclusion of learning and assessment through small group activities. Investigations into student learning carried out from the interactional perspective have shown that where students work and are assessed in co-operative settings their learning is superior to that of students working in the traditional competitive and individualistic style. This would seem to indicate that there may be reasons other than the pragmatic for departing from traditional individual forms of assessment.

Moust et al (1987) have shown that the interaction variables which are most beneficial to the learning of students are those of 'giving help' and 'receiving help': both activities show a positive relation with achievement. Where the curriculum requires students to, for example, explain difficult subject matter to their peers, it would seem that they learn more than in settings where this is not required. The effect on achievement of receiving help depends upon whether the help is given in response to a student's need and whether the help involves explanation as well as the correct answer. What is clear, however, from the investigations published to date is that students who actively participate in small group work and discussion show superior learning to those who learn as individuals. Their participation can be interpreted as elaboration on prior knowledge which contributes to a richer cognitive appreciation of the topic under discussion.

The model for learning proposed and developed by D P Ausubel (1961), (1978) (discussed in Chapter 1) suggests that meaningful learning is a distinctive process with distinctive outcomes: it is qualitatively different from the rote learning of material that is short on meaning. Ausubel rejects this type of learning in favour of more active student participation with the aim of developing meaning.

The development of peer and self assessment in law

There is a literature on student peer and self assessment stretching back over the past 50 years, but it has only been fairly recently that the topic has begun to be seriously studied and self and peer assessment used systematically for both learning and grading purposes. It is now well accepted that the ability to to assess one's own work is an important element in most forms of learning and that it is an ability which must be cultivated if learners are to engage effectively in lifelong learning. There have been two main areas of applied research in peer and self assessment: firstly there have been studies on the reliability of student self grading taking lecturer marks as the independent variable. Comparisons have been made between the scores produced by teacher and students. The second area for research has focused on ways in which students can become more self critical and perceptive about their learning with the general goal of improving learning strategies.

Self assessment by students is thus becoming increasingly common in higher education and the educational merits of self assessment as a part of the learning process and of encouraging students to engage in self-monitoring activities have been firmly established: see Boud (1986), (1989). This is what Boud refers to as the 'educational argument', However, there is also a second argument based upon *expediency* which he describes as follows:

> If students can take a greater role in assessment there is a potential for the saving of staff time on the often tedious task of marking. Staff time is valuable, and that devoted to marking which does not result in feedback to students (such as for final projects or examinations) is time which is not devoted to facilitating learning. If students mark their own work, either with respect to specified standards (model answers) or their own self-established criteria, they not only release staff for more educationally worthwhile activities, but they are encouraged to reflect on their own work and the standards with which it is appropriate for them to be concerned.
>
> Boud (1989)

Empirical research studies have investigated the extent to which there is any systematic bias amongst students which leads them to give themselves or their peers systematically higher or lower marks than those awarded by staff. Although, as Boud points out, it is ironic that this should be a matter for such intense debate since the literature is full of well-documented variations between different staff markers, or the same marker over time: for an excellent summary, see Heywood (1977). The best evidence which can be deduced from the literature, however, suggests that so long as students are required to exclude the element of personal effort from consideration when grading themselves or their peers, most students will generate marks which are reasonably consistent with the marks that would have been given by academic staff. Whilst it is true that the literature suggests that weaker students do tend to overrate their work, this should not necessarily lead to abandoning the idea of student self and peer assessment. After all, many research studies exist which show the unreliability of staff marking and yet there has been no general call for this form of assessment to be abandoned.

With this research in mind, changes are now being implemented in some universities where students are now assessed not only on their individual work but also on their ability to learn together in groups and to solve legal problems; this type of group work assessment has obvious advantages for the staff involved in assessing the work; however, it does pose some difficulties since it presents problems for the marker in determining the relative contributions of individual students within the group. One way around this problem is for the marker to allocate a mark to the group product and then require the members of the group to allocate the mark amongst themselves on the basis of the contributions that individual members have made. This is a form of peer assessment which in its turn is based on self assessment.

The development of self assessment in undergraduate law programmes is by no means a new phenomenon: however, it is one that is not widely utilised. Fear has been expressed that the professional bodies who provide exempting qualifying status for law degrees will not 'approve' of these new forms of assessment. In the writer's experience, however, officers of the Law Society and the CLE have been both helpful and open to suggestions for the use of innovative forms of assessment and have shown a considerable degree of interest in the outcomes of these activities.

Expertise has already been gained in relation to using new forms of assessment for group learning activities in law, and the CNAA prior to its demise funded several research projects into self assessment. This has resulted in the development of a variety of activities in the new universities, including mock trials, interviewing and negotiating tasks, group presentations and group reports, many of which are assessed by the participants themselves.

Self assessment, probably the most novel form of assessment for lawyers, involves the individual student in (possibly) setting criteria for his own assessment and then (definitely) applying them to his own work: see Cowan (1986).

Students may at first find the setting and application of criteria difficult tasks to undertake, since this differs so much from the traditional educational approach where a student is assessed solely on the basis of a lecturer's professional judgment, possibly augmented by the second opinion of another professional colleague. It is argued, however, that if students are required to develop their own criteria for assessment, carry out the work and then apply those criteria, this will prove to be a more valuable learning experience with better learning outcomes. In theory, at least, it is quite possible for an individual or a group of students to determine the criteria for assessment in advance of carrying out an allocated task. This in itself should focus students' minds very clearly on the required outcomes for the work in question.

Suppose, for instance, that groups of first-year LLB students are required as part of a legal skills/legal method course to carry out field surveys on various aspects of the functioning of the legal system (eg the incidence of legal representation in magistrates' courts, county courts, rent tribunals, social security appeal tribunals and industrial tribunals). If one of the criteria for the assessment of such a group project set by the members of the groups is that every student should participate equally in the preparatory work and in the writing up of results, then it is likely that group pressure alone will be sufficient to ensure that this occurs. If, however, this is not a specific criterion for assessment, then it is more than likely that the group will contain one or two malingerers or malcontents who fail to participate, or who participate only marginally.

Formative and summative self/peer assessment

In so far as in-course (or formative) assessment is concerned, it is common enough to find schemes where students are involved in self-assessment strategies; in many subjects they are encouraged to monitor their own performance by completion of self-assessment questions. The stimulating work of the Law Courseware Consortium, currently being carried out under the leadership of Abdul Paliwala at the University of Warwick, is based on precisely this principle. Clearly, the effectiveness of such assessment strategies is to a large extent based upon the skill of the individual lecturer in setting the questions. Other mechanisms for self assessment used formatively include the use of logs, diaries, periodic reviews with a tutor and tutorial discussion.

Much more contentious is the use of self assessment as a part of formal assessment procedures, that is, as an activity which includes student-derived quantitative assessments as an element of officially recorded assessments. If self-generated student marks are to be used for this purpose it is necessary inter alia to demonstrate that students can produce marks that are acceptable to lecturers. This has meant that there is a very high probability that student marks will be the same as staff marks for a given assignment. It is also necessary to demonstrate that if students can produce acceptably similar marks when they are not being recorded for official purposes, the context of formal assessment does not distort their ratings so that students do not produce unacceptably dissimilar marks when they *are* used for this purpose.

An example of self/peer assessment in use

The use of self and peer assessment for summative purposes is more unusual, particularly when the mark achieved contributes directly to formal degree classification. In addition, there are some difficulties associated with its use. There are some examples, however, as for instance the assessment of the final year Legal Skills course at the University of Hertfordshire, the marks from which contribute towards students' final degree classification. A similar programme is also in use at Anglia Polytechnic University and no doubt at others.

Here students are required, as an integral part of their course, to assess their own contribution to a group project which is based on a personal injury exercise. In this exercise students are split into small groups or firms of about six. Each group interviews a 'client' who has been involved in an accident at work; following the interview each group is then provided with a file of information including pleadings, specialist and private investigators' reports and other background materials. Students draft correspondence to eg employer(s), the Health and Safety Executive, doctors, local hospitals and so on to acquire any additional information they need, which is provided by law staff. Following a further interview with the 'client' each group is required to carry out a fact analysis exercise culminating in the production of a case note book, a written 'Twining'-style analysis of evidence and a negotiated settlement which is recorded on video tape.

The course requires students to demonstrate skills of fact analysis, research, interviewing, negotiating, drafting and self management. Whilst it is possible for the lecturers who devised the course to mark the finished product in its entirety, it is not possible for them to identify the varying roles played by individual students within the groups. Thus, when completed, the work is handed in, together with a peer evaluation of the contribution of the various firm members which, in its turn, is based on a self evaluation by each student. Since the marks allocated are of some considerable significance, contributing as they do to the final assessment of the students, it was obviously important that care should be taken in the development of the self and peer assessment strategies employed.

The materials provided for the students include a model self/peer assessment schedule, and the first lecture of the session is devoted to a full discussion of this model. Whilst for convenience the format remains the same from year to year, different groups of students have negotiated with the staff different criteria for assessment. Once agreed, these criteria are then entered on the model and recirculated to students *before they commence work on the project* so that it is clear from the very outset what criteria for assessment will be applied by students in respect of themselves and their peers (see p 369 below for some details of this course and of its assessment).

This form of summative self/peer assessment is used alongside tutor assessment so that it complements it rather than acts as the sole form of measurement of a student's success. Thus, the tutor allocates a final mark for the case note book presented by the students and this final mark is allocated amongst the students on the basis of the pre-agreed criteria.

John Cowan, reporting on his experiments with self assessment at Heriot Watt University reported that:

> The old authoritarian strategies which had served me well when I controlled assessment . . . were rendered inappropriate. I now took authority only for the decision to pass authority to the learners, and then I had to devote time and effort to learning my role in this entirely new situation. For I still had responsibility to facilitate learning and developing.

This certainly mirrors the experience of the law staff at Hertfordshire who mark the final year Legal Skills project.

Other possible uses for self/peer assessment

Other possible uses of the technique will depend to a large extent on the context in which individual law lecturers work; in some cases students are asked to agree or to draw up criteria for marking a piece of coursework and are then returned their own piece of work and asked to mark it, without knowing the tutor's mark, in relation to those criteria. The student's self assessment may then be compared with the tutor's mark, together with a copy of the tutor's outline answer for the assignment. By this means, it is argued, students become familiar with the types of criteria by which they are assessed and are able to make a more realistic appraisal of the value of their own work. To those of us who at some time or another in the past have been faced with the law student who seems completely unable to understand why his work has received such a 'low mark', this might be a strategy worth trying.

Problems with self and peer assessment

The main problems that have been identified by commentators in applying self and peer assessment strategies include:
- the need for dependence upon the integrity of the students;
- the alleged natural tendency for students to overvalue their work;
- the need for summative self assessment to be carefully monitored to ensure credibility; and
- the fact that students normally lack the experience to carry out self assessment without prior instruction.

However, many of these problems can be avoided by adopting measures which are specifically designed to improve student marker reliability. These could include the establishment of explicit criteria for both satisfactory and for unsatisfactory student performance, in relation to a particular task. Other possibilities would include using marking scales in which categories are unambiguously defined, and training markers through practising the application of agreed criteria to examples of student work, with the resolution of differences between markers through discussion. It is interesting to note that all these strategies have been used by staff involved in the new task of assessing students' skills on the recently introduced

Legal Practice Course.

In phase II of the Law Student Assessment Project, lecturers and students at ten selected Law Schools were asked to identify their first choice of assessment criteria: see Tribe, Tribe and Fitzgerald (1989). The Table below shows the percentage of first choices of both lecturers and students, indicating a very strong relationship across the ten institutions between what lecturers and students chose as criteria of importance for assessment.

LECTURERS' AND STUDENTS' FIRST CHOICE OF ASSESSMENT CRITERIA (10 SELECTED INSTITUTIONS)		
	Lecturers	*Students*
Conceptual understanding	53.1	51.7
Application	13.1	22.0
Factual knowledge	13.8	11.6
Analysis	10.0	7.2
Evaluation	6.9	5.2
Synthesis	3.1	3.1

This evidence of agreement between students and lecturers about the criteria for assessment is important for the advocates of self and peer assessment, since it indicates that there are not wide differences between staff and student conceptions of what amounts to quality in student work.

Strategies for incorporating self and peer assessment into the curriculum

Self assessment schedules where the marks are subsequently moderated by staff

Students prepare a self assessment schedule in which they identify the objectives to be achieved in the particular piece of coursework and the extent to which they or their peers have in their opinion met those objectives. These documented achievements are then allotted a mark based upon the student's understanding of the marking strategies used in the department (which will have been explained and documented in advance). Where the staff mark and the student mark are within (say) 5% of each other, the student mark will be retained. Otherwise, if there is a greater discrepancy than this, discussion will take place in which justifications for the mark variance are explained and agreed. The 5% agreed variance has been selected since this is the percentage variation which is generally accepted by commentators as being the norm between staff markers.

Self marks moderated by peers

Another approach described by Boud (1989) is for one or more student peers to be required to confirm a student's self-generated mark; discrepancies between the two marks which are greater than 5% are remarked by staff. Students use staff-prepared model answers as a basis for this strategy and the peer assessment is carried out anonymously. In order to encourage students to take the exercise seriously, they are informed that random checking of the assessments will be carried out by staff. Even allowing for the time taken in preparing model answers, checking and remarking, a research study carried out by Boud and Holmes (1986) showed that considerable staff time could be saved with a class with more than 260 students. The disadvantage for staff with this strategy is that although they spend less time on marking, the time that they do spend is more challenging, and there is also the danger that unless the scheme is administered carefully, students may collude with each other and undermine its intentions.

Criteria generated by peers

One of the reasons that student marking is perceived as being unreliable is that students have less experience of the marking criteria which are used to judge their work, and even where they are provided by staff with the appropriate criteria they may still find it difficult to interpret these criteria correctly. A strategy which can be used to avoid this problem is to involve the whole class in the determination of the criteria for assessment, and then to use the common criteria which are developed through this exercise to form a checklist against which the work is marked. The Legal Skills module taught at the University of Hertfordshire, which was described earlier, uses this technique with some success. Hertfordshire staff have found that this approach is particularly effective when the student-generated criteria are then approved by staff before they are applied. The writer has been impressed by the thoroughness with which students generate relevant criteria and, where these criteria are used in conjunction with staff marking which is based on the same criteria, it appears that the assessment outcomes are reliable.

Use of learning contracts

This strategy can be used alone or in conjunction with the methods described above. Each student (or group of students) will write a contract which specifies the goal of a particular task and the criteria which will be used to judge success. This contract is approved by a staff member, and discussed if necessary, and then after any necessary modification it will form the basis for assessment of a given course. Students may also indicate at the outset what grade they hope to achieve and the criteria against which they will measure their achievement.

Boud concludes that the situations in which the use of student self or peer assessment may be legitimate are as follows:

–   there is a high trust, high integrity learning environment; students are rewarded for high integrity marking;
–   marks are moderated by staff so that deviations from staff marks need to be justified;
–   blind peer marking is used as a check;
–   random staff marking is used as a check;
–   students have had the opportunity to practise and develop the necessary skills;
–   the criteria against which assessment is to be carried out have been sufficiently unambiguously defined for there to be little scope for misinterpretation of grade boundaries;
–   student effort is explicitly excluded as a criterion.

To this could be added the requirements that this type of assessment is not used during students' first year of study when they are unfamiliar with staff marking conventions, and that where there are several staff members in a course team, great care is taken to ensure that all staff understand and agree with the strategies to be used. Finally, it is obviously of importance, in these days of student litigants, to be quite sure that both staff and students are aware of the relevant appeal procedures.

References

Ausubel et al (1961) 'The role of Discriminability in Meaningful Reception Learning', 56(6) *Journal of Educational Psychology* 266–74.

Ausubel et al (1978) *Educational Psychology: a Cognitive View*, Holt Rinehart and Winston, New York.

D Boud (1989) 'The role of Self Assessment in Student Grading', 14 *Assessment and Evaluation in Higher Education* 20–30.

D Boud & J N Falshikov (1989) 'Quantitative Studies of Students' Self Assessment: a Critical Analysis of Findings', 18 *Higher Education* 529–49.

D Boud & W H Holmes (1981) 'Self and Peer Marking in an Undergraduate Engineering Course', E–24 *IEE Transactions on Education* 267–74.

J B Biggs (1992) *Teaching: Design for Learning* quoted in N Entwistle (1992) *The Impact of Teaching on Learning Outcomes in Higher Education: A Literature Review*, University of Edinburgh Centre for Research on Learning & Instruction, Edinburgh.

J Cowan (1986) *32 Questions About Independent Learning*, SCED Occasional Paper.

N Entwistle & P Ramsden (1983) *Understanding Student Learning*, Croom Helm, London.

J Grodecki (1977) *Legal Education: Dilemmas and Opportunities*, Leicester University Press, Leicester.

L Gow and D Kember (1990) 'Does Higher Education promote Independent Learning?' 19 *Higher Education* 307–22.

P Harris & S Bellerby with P Leighton & J Hodgson (1993) *A Survey of Law Teaching 1993*, Sweet & Maxwell/Association of Law Teachers, London.

J Heywood (1977) *Assessment in Higher Education,* John Wiley, London.

Leighton P and Sheinman L (1986) 'Central Questions in Legal Education', 20 *Law Teacher* 3–11.

H C Moust, H G Schmidt, M L de Volder, J L Belien and W S de Grave (1987) 'Effects of Verbal Participation in Small Group Discussion' in Richardson, Eysenk and Piper (eds) *Student Learning: Research in Education and Cognitive Psychology*, Society for Research into Higher Education, London.

P Ramsden and N Entwistle (1981) 'Effects of Academic Departments on Students' Approaches to Studying', 51 *British Journal of Educational Psychology* 368–83.

D M R Tribe (1996) 'How Students Learn', this collection.

D M R Tribe & A J Tribe (1988) 'Assessing Law Lecturers' Attitudes and Practices', 13 *Assessment and Evaluation in Higher Education* 105–18.

D M R Tribe & A J Tribe (1986) 'Assessing Law Students', 20 *Law Teacher* 160–8.

D M R Tribe, A J Tribe & J Fitzgerald (1989) 'Law Students' Attitudes Towards Assessment', 14 *Assessment and Evaluation in Higher Education* 31–9.

Appendix

Example of materials designed to employ self and peer assessment strategies

Legal skills – fact investigation and analysis module

INTRODUCTION

Based largely on the study of appellate cases, legal education typically fosters the impression that the primary function of litigation is to understand legal rules and their policy underpinning, in order to construct appropriate legal arguments regarding the application of old rules, or the need to formulate new ones. Indeed traditional legal study inherently suggests that if one understands the relationships between values, social policies and the applications of legal principles, one fully understands the law and its operation.

Whilst this view may be useful, it certainly does not present a complete picture of how lawyers, clients and the legal system function. *Substantive rules are not self-activated* – they are triggered by evidence which proves, to the degree of certainty required, that certain facts exist, to which the rules in turn can then be applied. This triggering mechanism itself relies on lawyers to collect, organise, appraise and present facts in such a way as to render a given substantive rule applicable or inapplicable. Thus the *gathering and management of facts* is as essential to the operation of the law as is the application of rules once the facts are determined. 'Ferreting out facts may not be the most publicised or romanticised aspect of litigation, but in the main it is what lawyers actually do' (Binder and Bergman (1984)).

Fact management, therefore, is fundamental to all aspects of a lawyer's work and underlies other 'lawyerly' skills such as interviewing, negotiating, drafting and advocacy.

DESIGN OF THE MODULE

The module is designed to develop and practise each stage of fact management skills through lectures, seminars, groupwork and private study.

For some of the time students will work in groups of approximately six members; these groups will need to meet on a regular basis, and members will have to take full responsibility for organising and attending these meetings.

In addition, each group will:

- jointly prepare a case note book for assessment, and will finally arrive at a negotiated settlement, a report of the outcomes of which must also be included in the case notebook;
- carry out two interviews with the 'client' and will be required to assess, and record for inclusion in the case note book, an assessment of the interviewing skills employed by the interviewer;
- have the opportunity to operate self/peer assessment in respect of individual contributions to the case note book.

Aims

This module aims to develop skills which will assist students in thinking about facts, assessing their importance and organising them to construct a logical form of argument in order to achieve a client's objectives.

The module also aims to assist students to develop skills of self and group management and self and peer analysis.

Objectives

At the end of the course each student should be able to:

(i) organise information from a variety of sources;
(ii) distinguish between relevant and irrelevant facts;
(iii) identify gaps, ambiguities and contradictions in the information;
(iv) distinguish between fact and inference;
(v) construct an argument from the facts to support the client's case;
(vi) recognise the interaction between law and fact;
(vii) identify the legal issues raised by the facts;
(viii) select possible solutions to the client's problem;
(ix) understand and begin to develop an appraisal of the basic skills of client interviewing and negotiating;
(x) construct and agree criteria for assessment and apply them to self and peers.

ASSESSMENT – CRITERIA FOR THE CASE NOTE BOOK

Each case note book should:

(i) identify the client's legal objectives;
(ii) collect and order facts;
(iii) identify legal relevance of facts;

(iv) identify the factual issues;

(v) identify the legal issues;

(vi) identify any further information required;

(vii) show the strengths and weaknesses of the plaintiff's/defendant's case;

(viii) include a written account of the negotiated settlement of claim, together with an evaluation of the bargaining positions adopted by each side and the negotiating strategies utilised (making reference to the appropriate literature where relevant);

(ix) include a written assessment of the interviewing strategies employed in the two interviews (making reference to the appropriate literature where relevant);

(x) complete an Analysis of Evidence which will be based upon the case materials, outcome of interviews, replies to correspondence and information.

In preparing the case note book it will be necessary to identify fact omissions and appropriate source(s) from which to acquire further information. This will involve each group in writing letters to the identified source requesting the information sought. All these letters are to be sent to the Law Department Office IN SEALED ENVELOPES and addressed 'for the attention of Legal staff.'

REPLIES WILL BE RETURNED TO THE SENDER VIA THE STUDENT PIGEON HOLES. ALL LETTERS MUST IDENTIFY THE GROUP NUMBER AND THE PERSON TO WHOM REPLIES ARE TO BE SENT.

Letters sent will be returned with a reply and/or comments. The group case note book must contain the original copies of all correspondence, together with answers and any written comments.

LECTURES AND GROUP MEETINGS

Keynote lectures

Week

1. Introduction to the course; outline of case note book requirements; revision of interviewing skills; discussion of criteria for self and peer assessment and final agreement of criteria to be used for all students.

2. Preparing the case note book – question and answer session. Individual assignments – question and answer session.

3. Revision of interviewing skills.

4. Revision of negotiation skills prior to group negotiations.

5. Analysis of evidence – instructions for assessment.

Schedule of group meetings for case note book preparation

Week

1.   Introduction to the course.

2.   Allocate negotiating roles.

        Book studio for recording of negotiated settlement in week *.
        Arrange time, date and place for group to carry out the
        first interview with client. Following completion of the
        interview commence case note book and enter basic data.
        Collect additional case materials from staff immediately
        after the interview.

3.   Group discussion to consider factual outcomes of interview,
        identify fact omissions and develop general lines of enquiry.
        Allocate group tasks. Additional preparation of materials
        for case note book.

4.   Analysis and discussion of information acquired re injury
        and loss to client; assessment of quantum as at May 1995;
        insurance.

5.   Liability of defendant; analysis of information acquired re
        facts and legal issues; issues of remoteness/foreseeability/
        limitation/contributory negligence etc.

6.   Arrange time, date and place for group to complete the sec-
        ond client interview; confirm any fact omissions; group
        discussion of additional facts elicited and further legal issues
        (if any).

7.   Commence preparation of case note book.

8.   Negotiated settlement.

        In this exercise each firm will divide into two groups, one
        to represent the plaintiff and one to represent the defen-
        dant. The members of these two groups will then negotiate
        an agreed settlement on behalf of the two parties.

        Additional information will be made available to each side
        IMMEDIATELY PRECEDING the negotiation exercise. Notify
        staff of time and date and make arrangements to collect
        new materials.

9.   Completion of case note book, including written account
        of negotiated settlement.

        Each completed file must identify the group number, the
        names of its participating members and the individual con-
        tributions that they made. Students are also required to

complete the self/peer assessment forms in this session (see below) to be handed in with the case note book.

NOTE: supplementary materials will be made available to groups immediately prior to your negotiation sessions. Please inform staff in advance as to date and time of session, so that materials can be collected.

Negotiation exercise

The vast majority of civil actions are settled without the need for trial (approximately 98% of all personal injury actions commenced in the High Court reach a negotiated settlement).

These negotiations are often protracted and may either be conducted by correspondence or by the parties' solicitors meeting to negotiate a solution to the problem.

Effective negotiations are determined by the lawyers' ability to understand thoroughly the FACTUAL issues raised by the case. In addition, familiarity with the relevant law and information about the level of award that a judge might make if the case went to trial are also valuable.

The defendant's solicitor rarely offers a payment equal to the full valuation of the case – he invariably pitches his offer just short of this figure to allow for the risks involved in litigation, the uncertainty of what the judge may actually award and the equal uncertainty of what reduction, if any, might be made for contributory negligence.

By this stage of the course students have already had the opportunity to determine the facts of the case and their effect on such issues as causation, liability and quantum. Negotiations will take place between firms; a report of the negotiation process must be prepared for each pair of firms, and handed in no later than *. Reports should not exceed 1,000 words in length.

The object of the exercise will be to determine common ground between the parties, as well as issues which are contested. In the event that the negotiation does not lead to settlement, each side must identify what is offered by the other as regards a possible future settlement. Students representing the defendant may use the tactic of further payment into court to force the plaintiff to compromise the action. This is the most potent weapon that the defendant can use and requires great skill and judgment on the part of both plaintiff and defendant.

Self/peer assessment

GROUP CASE NOTE BOOK EXERCISE

STUDENT NAME .... 　　FIRM ....

NUMBER ....

Criteria for peer assessment

The following are the criteria which each firm will use as the basis for self/peer assessment of the individual contributions to the case note book; each firm must hand in a sheet for each firm member, indicating the total individual score for the case note book.

	Outstanding participation	Satisfactory participation	Poor participation	Nil participation
1. PLANNING THE NOTEBOOK Did the member usefully contribute to discussions on: overall strategy and organisation and mode of presentation? other?	+2	0	-2	-5
2. FACT FINDING Did the member identify: relevant facts from documentation and initial interview? follow up questions for the second interview? other?	+2	0	-2	-5
3. RESEARCH Did the member complete allocated research tasks in agreed time?	+2	0	-2	-5

	Outstanding participation	Satisfactory participation	Poor participation	Nil participation
4. ACCOMPLISHING TASK ALLOCATED Did the member successfully accomplish all other tasks allocated by the group?	+2	0	-2	-5
5. FEEDBACK TO THE GROUP Did the member: inform the group of the outcomes of the research? provide feedback to the group in a useful form and at the agreed time?	+2	0	-2	-5
6. PARTICIPATION IN PRESENTATION OF NOTE BOOK Did the member: contribute to the organisation and production of the case note book? participate effectively in determining its final form?	+2	0	-2	-5
TOTAL ADDITION/ DEDUCTION FOR STUDENT				

Chapter 13

A capability approach to assessing skills on the LPC: a strategy for developing effective future performance
Mike Maughan

Why change to a capability approach?

Introduction

The legal skills of Drafting and writing, Research, Advocacy, Interviewing, and Negotiation (the DRAIN skills) are firmly incorporated into the teaching and learning of substantive areas of the Legal Practice Course. They are tested, however, separately and discretely. This is surprising, since the LPC as a whole is avowedly developmental. To begin with, the course is part of an integrated framework of professional development. After completing the LPC, the student enters into a training contract, in which she practises under supervision. After successful completion of this stage, she enters into practice, subject to demonstrating continued professional development.

The developmental theme is also apparent from an examination of the Written Standards of the Law Society's Legal Practice Course Board.

The aims of the Written Standards include:
  (i)   to prepare the student for general practice;
  (ii) to provide a general foundation for subsequent practice.
The learning outcomes support this theme:
  (vi) make the most of the experience which follows and gain the confidence necessary for competence in practice;
  (vii) learn from the experience of the course and from future practice;
        . . . etc.

The fact that the aims and outcomes, as well as the standards for specific skills, emphasise future performance places the onus on the assessment process to achieve this. There are two ways in which assessment can do it:

1.   Through *summative* assessment: that is, by having recognised standards of performance against which each student is assessed before going on to the next developmental stage. These standards should ensure competence at a level that will enable the student to cope effectively with the demands of the next stage of professional development.

2.   Through *formative* (developmental) assessment: that is, by feeding back judgments on students' performance which enable them to identify their strengths and weaknesses, to learn from their experiences and consequently to improve their performance.

The concern is that the second of these is not being done, and the developmental intentions of the LPC are being thwarted as a result. There may be several reasons for this. Brayne (1994), for example, comments on the enormous assessment load of the LPC as well as the preoccupations of the students with summative assessment; that is, with passing and making it through to the next stage. Moreover, many law teachers are probably more familiar with summative assessment than with formative approaches. Some may not know the difference.

How, then, should we assess skills?

Skills development is incorporated into the Legal Practice Course so that students, once 'competent', will be able to enter a training contract and continue their development under appropriate supervision.

This notion of competence is not as clear cut as the normative assessment processes with which we are all familiar. Although the DRAIN skills have a set of standards and criteria against which students are assessed, it would be wrong to consider these standards as being predictive of future professional capability. Professional effectiveness, as I will argue, requires much more than technical mastery of a restricted set of behaviours.

The question for tutors, then, is what are the processes we can use to give us confidence that future performance will be effective? Clearly, they will differ from the summative 'end point' assessment I referred to above. There is no end point of developmental learning.

What we have to assess are the students' learning and reasoning processes. There are LPC standards for these, though because each individual experiences learning and carries out reasoning in individual ways, it is extremely difficult to write useful criteria against which they could be assessed. Nor would it be reasonable to compare one student with another in this respect. Therefore conventional issues of validity and reliability of assessment are replaced by questions about the evaluation of individual progress, the ability to challenge the student and to give useful feedback, and the ability to encourage the student to articulate aspects of her learning and reasoning processes.

Successful performance of the DRAIN skills inevitably requires a knowledge of the law applicable to the situation. This is why the skills are developed in an integrated context. So how are these skills learned and developed? How can we know when a student's satisfactory performance of those skills in the protected and largely predictable atmosphere of the law school will be transferred to effective practice in the outside world? How can teachers help to develop this transferability?

The notion of capability

I want to suggest to you an approach to skills assessment that is centred around the notion of 'capability'. Capability is related to one of the two principal 'competence' approaches. The first of these (of which capability is one strand) says that competence resides in the intellectual and affective qualities of the individual: see Boyatzis (1982); Pedler et al (1994). The second is a reductionist view which says that competence can be defined as a set of more or less complex behaviours as they are applied to a specified job or role. The latter approach is the one taken by the National Council for Vocational Qualifications (NCVQ), which is the body responsible for co-ordinating the development of national vocational qualifications (NVQs). The outcome of such an approach for any given occupation is the production of standards of performance and criteria of assessment against those standards. Assessment of competence against the standards is achieved principally by observation of performance. The Law Society's Written Standards for the LPC are clearly influenced by both approaches.

In so far as they describe learning outcomes in terms of performance, they owe some allegiance to the NCVQ model, though the descriptors of performance rely heavily on the judgment and experience of the assessor. For example, the standards for Interviewing and Advising say the student should be able to:

(v) elicit relevant information and distinguish between relevant and irrelevant information . . .

(ix) assist the client to make a decision regarding the best course of action . . .

(xii) establish a professional relationship with the client and deal with any ethical problems that may arise when advising the client . . .

In the first example the relevance or otherwise of information is highly context-specific and dependent on the sensitivity of the student to the events she is participating in and on the judgment of the assessor as to the appropriateness of her decision-making. In the second example the 'best' course of action is again a matter of judgment on the part both of assessor and student. And in the third the nature of the professional relationship or the ethical problems that arise will again be matters of contextual sensitivity as well as personal and professional values. It would be impossible to write specific criteria against which to assess these in any meaningful way.

Moreover, there are difficulties inherent in attempting to infer the complex intellectual and attitudinal processes purely from observing these behaviours: see Maughan et al (1995). When you observe competent performance you are not always observing a competent performer. The more open the context of performance, and the more variables there are outside the performer's control, the more experienced and capable the assessor needs to be.

Furthermore, the notion of a standard implies that learning has an end point, however difficult this may be to describe. Yet the Standards in this section also demand that:

> the student should be able to demonstrate an understanding of the principles and criteria of good interviewing and should be able to:
>
> . . .
>
> (iv) develop techniques for appraising and developing their own interviewing style.

Three issues arise from this. Firstly, a standard like this has no end point. That is, it is not possible to say at what point development is complete, because it never is. Secondly, the strong implication is that the students will take responsibility for developing their own interviewing styles. Thirdly, the student is being asked to develop techniques which are highly personal and are likely to be different from those developed by other students. All of these issues make the process of summative assessment problematic, if not impossible.

It is quite proper for the Standards to focus on these important personal and developmental issues. But I suggest we are not able, through summative assessment, to characterise a student as 'competent'. Are we really to have confidence in her ability to deal effectively with the complexity, open-endedness and uniqueness of the work that she will meet in professional practice? Although I would support Phil Jones's (1996) criticism that alternative 'reflective practice' models pay too little attention to the routine and systematic in professional practice, nevertheless, for a new practitioner, almost all of the work is non-routine. Although she is supervised during the training contract, the very 'realness' of the problems she deals with challenge her intellectual and emotional resilience. The new practitioner may be catapulted quite rapidly from the world of the hypothetical problem to the world where the outcomes of her decisions could have a serious and important impact on people who rely on her judgment.

The development of skills to cope with this transfer from the hypothetical to the real is consequently a serious business. It would be a pity to reduce it to the assessment of technical skill outputs without challenging the student to consider her own learning processes and the values and attitudes through which her reasoning is filtered.

The Standards themselves recognise this issue and require what I would call a 'capability' approach. Coming from the first of the approaches to competence that I mentioned above, it focuses on the individual qualities and values of the student. It is an approach which *gives both assessor and assessed confidence that future performance will be effective and that skill development will be part of continuing professional development.* It achieves this by looking not only at performance but by bringing to the surface the processes which bring about that performance. Moreover, it provides a vehicle for articulating, reflecting on and modifying theories of action which enables assessors to have confidence in the student's ability to cope in real-world practice and to continue developing.

This approach therefore requires a more sophisticated means of assessing students. It needs to:

1.   go beyond the summative function of current assessment processes *to give confidence in* effective future performance;
2.   enable assessment to be *developmental* and therefore *individualised*;
3.   provide for a *negotiation* between tutor and student of elements of assessment;
4.   encourage an *increasing responsibility* on the part of the student for her development.

The need for developing assessment processes in this way is clear. You have little knowledge of the job your students are going to be doing after qualification, beyond that they will be working in the field of legal practice. But this comes in many differing forms. Even if you have worked as a practising lawyer, and consequently have an understanding of what it is like to make your living in the profession, your experience, wide though it may be, will not even have scratched the surface of the variety, complexity and diversity of all the jobs available to your students.

Nevertheless, you are going to want to be sure that your assessment gives as reliable as possible an indication of the students' ability to use those skills appropriately, effectively and ethically, first of all during the Training Contract and subsequently in professional life. How can this be done? We have already seen that you are to some extent groping in the dark as to the type and context of the work that your student is going to be doing. So you cannot customise the assessment on the basis of the precise requirements of the job she is going to do.

This idea of assessment for future performance needs some amplification if we are to look at processes by which capability might be evaluated. The concept of capability is dealt with in John Stephenson's and Susan Weil's book, *Quality in Learning: A Capability Approach in Higher Education* (1992). Capability implies that students will need to continue to develop, refine and adapt their skills in contexts and environments that the law school cannot predict. Observation and assessment of skill performance, even on more than one occasion, will not give confidence that an individual can continue to develop and refine those skills in a complex and unpredictable climate and at a time of rapid professional change. At best it represents a kind of 'threshold' competence in the skill on which future development may be based.

Stephenson and Weil have identified other abilities to assist in the assessment and evaluation of capability:

> Capable people have confidence in their ability to
> (1)   take effective and appropriate action,
> (2)   explain what they are about,
> (3)   live and work effectively with others and
> (4)   continue to learn from their experiences, both as individuals and in association with others, in a diverse and changing society.
>
> (1992), p 2

These abilities are entirely consistent with the requirements of the Written Standards as well as with both theoretical and practical perspectives on capability. They go beyond a traditional outcomes model of learning in several particulars. Firstly, an outcomes model is the description of the outcomes of learning as defined by someone else. It is essentially a dependence model. The essence of a capability approach and, I would contend, the essence of effective professional performance, is the assumption of responsibility for one's own development. Secondly, an outcomes model emphasises a point reached through learning. It does not take account of the learning that is to take place after the outcome has been achieved. Thirdly, the incrementalism of most professional learning is difficult to encompass in the description of outcomes.

Learning only comes from what you make of experience. It does not come merely from *having* experience. The key to developing capability is therefore the capacity to reflect on experience, to adapt our theories of action into an ever-increasing repertoire of responses, to develop more sophisticated rules of behaviour as a result of our reflection and to test out modifications of behaviour in new contexts. The Written Standards make explicit reference to this process by requiring students to use the course and subsequent practice as learning opportunities.

TAKING EFFECTIVE AND APPROPRIATE ACTION

This is probably the one aspect of capability which all skills programmes would claim to address. Exercises and assessment will have been designed to develop and test a student's ability to grasp the issues involved in a situation, prepare to deal with them and to demonstrate the skills needed to achieve a satisfactory result. Yet while observed performance may give you a view on the effectiveness of the behaviour, does it also give you confidence in its appropriateness? The appropriateness of an action is the result of a number of decisions the actor makes about the situation they are dealing with. These decisions will take account of factors external to the student and also those factors relating to their own intellectual abilities, perceptual processes and values. The range of possibilities open to a student in this situation will therefore vary from individual to individual. To understand these possibilities is to begin to understand, and to help the student understand, their own capability.

SAYING WHAT YOU ARE ABOUT

Effective and appropriate action in the context of a law school skill assessment will inevitably lack some of the open-endedness of 'live' practice. Consequently, a satisfactory performance, while convincing the assessors that a student possesses the capacity to perform in this context, does little to give confidence that capacity is transferable into professional life. By encouraging the student to explain what they did and why they did it, and perhaps by challenging them to think through their response to possible (unexpected) variations to the situation, the tutor begins to explore the student's reasoning processes and the level at which those processes have been internalised.

Skills teachers, in any domain, have all met the phenomenon of discrepant reasoning. The discrepancy in question is that between what the actor *claims* are the principles guiding her actions and the principles she *actually* uses. Typically in the domain of professional development, it occurs when a particular theory of action is presented as the one which will achieve maximum professional benefit. Students interpret this as meaning that this is the theory that a competent professional uses in practice, and that they should do likewise. So, when asked, a student will in good faith say that this is the theory that they use. In practice, however, it may become clear that the student is in fact making use of quite a different theory of action. The latter is the student's 'theory in use', whilst the former is their 'espoused theory': see Schön (1987); Argyris (1989). The challenge for teachers is threefold: firstly, to ask the student to articulate her espoused theory; secondly, to bring her theory in use to the surface; and thirdly, to consider strategies for closing the gap.

This discrepancy is known to everyone engaged in the development of professional capability. Chris Argyris (1989) deals with the phenomenon at length. The more situationally complex, or emotionally charged, or politically sensitive a situation is, the more likely the practitioner is to fall back on habitual or conditioned responses, which may run counter to her espoused theory. The formation of capability, then, resides in the development of theories of action which are grounded *both* in formal learning *and* in experience. These theories can be articulated, modified in the light of new experience and put into operation when appropriate. In this way the student takes ownership of her theories of action and the likelihood of discrepant reasoning is minimised.

WORKING EFFECTIVELY WITH OTHERS

This aspect of capability highlights the social and ethical domains intrinsic to professional practice.

For the practising lawyer the social aspects of the work cover three areas: working with colleagues and other professionals; working as a member of a prestigious profession; and working with and on behalf of the client.

Much of the day-to-day work of the lawyer is carried out in some sort of contact with other lawyers. Because these colleagues will share broadly the same professional training and ethos of practice through a similar process of formation, interaction with other lawyers will normally be consistent with their expectations of such interactions. However, these norms and social processes of the profession as a whole do not preclude significant variations between and within different parts of the profession: see, for example, Greenebaum (1991); Laumann & Heinz (1977). Each firm will have a different 'feel' from any other. This is what is called in the discipline of organisational behaviour the 'culture' of the firm. It is often summed up in the phrase, '. . . the way we do things round here'. The culture of an organisation is difficult to describe adequately, but is influenced by such things as the formality between colleagues and between seniors and subordinates; the size of the organisation; its key activities; the nature of its leadership; the allocation of work; its history, etc.

Understanding this has important practical implications. It may, for example, influence the quality of supervision that the new trainee receives. It will determine many of the practices the trainee will be expected to adopt. These are some of the unpredictables of the job that a mere technical mastery of the DRAIN skills will not deal with, but which are, I would contend, at least as important for an effective and satisfying baptism into professional life. In the LPC as presently designed ignorance of the cultural dimension is reflected in at least three capability 'gaps'.

Firstly, the skills of group working do not in themselves form part of the LPC skills development programme. Indeed, the Standards assume that students are already able to do this effectively before beginning the course. This ignores the fact that those skills (if developed at all) will have evolved in response to a very different 'academic' culture.

Secondly, the skills outputs of lawyers, practising or trainee, are an integral part of the social activities of the profession. The DRAIN skills have all to be carried out with others in mind, or indeed in collaboration with others. If this aspect of professional life is not given the emphasis it deserves, then the application of skill risks being largely ineffective. It is therefore a pity that the DRAIN skills, the development of which is integrated into the core and pervasive topics, are not also assessed integratively. This would give greater context to their assessment and would enable the assessor to evaluate the processes underpinning the student's decisions and performance in a way which gave an indication of the student's sensitivity to context.

Thirdly, the demands and constraints imposed on an individual by the culture of an organisation are frequently the source of value conflict. You may have to work with clients you don't like, or whose activities you find yourself out of sympathy with. You may feel uncomfortable with the personal relationships in the organisation. There are a host of issues which could give rise to a clash in values between the individual and the organisation. Some of them are clearly dealt with in codes of professional conduct. Most are not. Even if the profession makes it clear what your duty is, it is difficult to do your best in a situation where you are not personally committed to what you are supposed to be doing. Under the present scheme of training, students are unlikely to face such value conflicts in a meaningful or realistic way before entering practice.

In addition, lawyers often find themselves working with other professionals. The norms and social processes of these professionals may differ widely from those of the lawyer. Sensitivity to such differences will be important in making the relationships work effectively, and consequently in serving the client's needs. Moreover, in many areas of work lawyers need to interact with a range of professionals in the context of a single case. Each of them will have a responsibility to achieve a particular end, which may well be at odds with that of the lawyer. The ability to negotiate this complex of relationships again requires a degree of skill that goes beyond a threshold technical competence.

The legal professions exist because they have clients who need their services. Serving the needs of the client is the core activity of the legal professions. The need to gain and give information, consult, advise, take instructions are all processes that need to be renegotiated afresh with each new client. Each will require a 'customised' approach depending on their needs. The capacity of a lawyer to be sensitive to different needs and to adapt appropriately is a critical element of her professional capability.

CONTINUING TO LEARN FROM EXPERIENCE

This is arguably the most crucial of the capability skills. It presupposes that the student is a capable learner able to recognise and exploit learning opportunities that arise in everyday situations. It also assumes an ability on the part of the student to modify and refine her skills as a practitioner. For the tutor it represents a move from student dependency to independence.

There are several models of experiential learning which will assist this development. The most well known is probably the Kolb learning cycle: see Kolb (1984); C Maughan (1996). The cycle makes clear that learning from experience is not a hit and miss process. It should be carried out systematically, with progressively more autonomy being handed over to the students as to the content, process and assessment.

I suggested earlier that a package of skills like the DRAIN skills, mastered as a set of technical behaviours, represents no more than a threshold level of performance. The student labouring under the impression that she now possesses the necessary skills to perform adequately in practice is in for a shock. I would therefore strongly contend that unless tutors enable students to move towards greater autonomy as learners during their formal learning programmes, their professional development will be slowed.

Challenges for the assessor in developing capability

I do not consider a move towards capability to be an easy option for the teacher any more than it is for the student. The notion of any programme or part of a programme being individualised is probably enough to make you move on to the next chapter immediately.

Resistance in the context of legal vocational education may take the form of arguments based on all or some of the following:
- large group sizes;
- resource constraints;
- too great a risk with students' futures;
- role confusion for tutors;
- unfamiliarity with techniques and processes;
- student resistance to greater independence.

These are real reservations, which I hope the following remarks and suggestions will address.

LARGE GROUP SIZES AND RESOURCE CONSTRAINTS

These are now a given throughout higher education. Yet the question needs to be posed as to whether the traditional approaches to teaching, learning and assessment are themselves capable of sustaining quality in this environment: see Centre for Legal Education (1994). I would argue that greater student autonomy, appropriately negotiated and facilitated, along with the collaborative approaches to learning which a capability programme would make use of, will actually enhance the quality of learning.

TOO GREAT A RISK WITH STUDENTS' FUTURES AND
STUDENT RESISTANCE

Any programme of vocational education is viewed to some degree as a means to an end. In the case of the LPC, that end is membership of a prestigious and important profession. Central to the interests of the student, therefore, is a programme designed to enable her to attain that end. The importance of this to the student also requires tutors to give it high priority. The extent to which the pragmatic preoccupation of obtaining a qualification is accompanied by an 'educational' objective varies from student to student.

What is certain is that any institution which is able to incorporate a capability approach into a vocational programme is providing a quality outcome. The legal professions are stakeholders in the legal education process and, as I have described above, require an approach which goes beyond summative assessment. Your students are also stakeholders. If you enable your students to develop capability in the vocational part of their programmes, you will be satisfying the real needs of both stakeholders. The public at large are stakeholders, too. And it is they who demand capable and effective professionals. It is this constituency which the Written Standards principally address.

A capability approach will come as just as much of a challenge to many students as it will to teachers. The resistance to it may well be based on the failure to understand the different nature of developmental approaches. Moreover, the need to take greater responsibility for learning could be seen as extremely threatening. The fact that the student has to explain her reasoning processes to the tutor because the latter doesn't already know them may seem to turn the tutor–student relationship on its head.

ROLE CONFUSION FOR TUTORS

The typical role of the teacher in higher education has been that of expert, the discoverer and disseminator of propositional knowledge related to a particular discipline, and the judge of how well that knowledge has been learned. This role inevitably alters when you become a skills teacher: see C Maughan (1996).

The tutor in this situation is no longer the expert. She no longer controls access to the bullion store of knowledge. The power that resource confers is taken away. The power that remains is the power to grant or withhold success through assessment, and I am suggesting that she give some of this power up too!

This calls on the teacher to re-evaluate her own preconceptions about her relationship with the subject matter and the student. Yet in a capability approach we are asking students to learn in ways which may be unfamiliar and threatening to them, and to take responsibility for things which were once the province of the tutor. It doesn't seem to me, at any rate, too much to ask that a tutor should engage in this process, too.

UNFAMILIARITY WITH TECHNIQUES AND PROCESSES

It would be unreasonable to expect a change such as I have described above, without some guidance as to the techniques and processes used in a capability approach. These are concerned with challenging the student to be articulate about her behaviour, its antecedents and consequences, with negotiating agreements about learning, with becoming familiar with novel methods of assessment and evaluation, as well as keeping up with the strict requirements of assessing the DRAIN skills.

This involves a significant developmental process for the teacher. Therefore the second part of this chapter is devoted to a 'toolkit' of approaches the teacher can use, and some suggestions about how to make a gradual transition towards a capability approach.

Conclusion

The starting point for any teacher wishing to adopt a capability approach ought to be from the point of view of what is practicable. An identification of the demands, constraints and choices available may be of some help. By demands, I mean the imperatives of a situation. In the case of the DRAIN programmes, the main demand is that students attain an acceptable level of technical mastery of the skills, as outlined in the Standards. The Standards, however, go well beyond this, and a failure to fulfil their developmental requirements is leaving the job only half done.

The constraints are those factors which put a brake on change, but which are themselves susceptible to change. For our purposes the constraints are teacher and student resistance, lack of confidence, lack of knowledge and resource constraints.

The choices we have in a situation represent those aspects of a situation over which we exercise control. It is likely that the more we reduce the constraints, the greater the area of choice will be.

The second part of the chapter contains a 'toolkit' of techniques and processes that you may wish to introduce step by step, so that you move gradually towards a capability approach. The toolkit is designed to reduce the constraints I mentioned above, and develop the choices available to you. I would emphasise that you are completely free to use my suggestions or not, to modify them and develop them to suit your own style. They are *not* prescriptions of how to do it 'properly'. Your own experience and reflection will inevitably lead you to develop or discard them, and to invent techniques of your own. What I want to do is to give you the basic tools to make a start.

The tool kit

I want to begin by suggesting you construct a matrix. This is designed to set you thinking about how each of the capability elements may be developed and evaluated against the DRAIN skills. Initially, your matrix may look something like this:

	Taking effective and appropriate action	*Saying what you are about*	*Working with others*	*Continuing to learn*
DRAFTING				
RESEARCH				
ADVOCACY				
INTERVIEWING				
NEGOTIATION				

Each of the skills can be subdivided into the activities you use on your programme. Against each of the skills or activities you can then begin to indicate what your students are to do to develop their capability, and how this is to be evaluated. Under 'taking effective action' you will certainly want to include the Law Society performance criteria. The rest is susceptible to whatever degree of negotiation you and your students decide on.

Assessment, however, can only take place if there is some clarity about what it is you are assessing. Within the matrix I would recommend that you write objectives in the way that you would for any other programme. The main difference will be that the objectives will vary somewhat from student to student. Each student will be assessed both on achieving the objective and on *how* they achieved it. It will therefore be a matter of negotiation between student and assessor about the mechanisms to be used to explore and reflect on the individual's learning.

The matrix, if you use one, can be as detailed or general as you want. The one outlined above would only really be appropriate for indicating the methods and techniques for developing, assessing and evaluating each of the capability categories. So the entry for 'Interviewing' might contain something like:

Taking effective and appropriate action

Research, prepare and carry out four interviews, one in each of the following areas: conveyancing, probate, personal injury, criminal litigation.
Assessment: Law Society Standards, tutor observation.

Saying what you are about

Student process report.

Working with others

Feedback from interviewee, student process report, feedback from observers on agreed criteria.

Continuing to learn

Student process report, student action plan.

Some of this will look strange. What is a 'process report', or an 'action plan'?

There are a number of techniques and processes you can make use of, which are explained below. A key issue, though, is who takes responsibility for what in terms of assessment and evaluation. You will see that in the section 'taking effective and appropriate action' the onus is on the tutor to evaluate performance. The reason for this is that you are responsible for maintaining basic technical standards for the Law Society programmes. The Law Society sets the standards and the assessment criteria. It is not a responsibility that can comfortably be delegated to the students. You may naturally wish to feed back to the student your views on the effectiveness and appropriateness of the performance to facilitate further development, but the burden of fair and reliable summative assessment is on you.

The student's share of responsibility for the other capability factors can be much greater, since this evaluation is developmental. It is open ended, as there are no formal descriptions of what the end point of this development will be. Her ability to 'say what she is about' is not assessed by the Law Society, but it is a key factor in self-development. Initially, you will need to give feedback on such reflection, but I show below some processes you can use to transfer such evaluation to the student herself or to her peers.

Under the 'working with others' section, I have involved the interviewee(s) to give some indication of the extent to which expectations were or were not met. Again, students need some initial guidance until they are confident enough to give (and receive) feedback. The process report enables the student to reflect on the feedback and to re-evaluate her action theories about interviewing.

The whole point of capability is to promote autonomous learning. The 'continuing to learn' section is crucial to capability development. To make the most of opportunities, however, most students need an initial methodology to enable them to conceptualise the process. The greater the clarity about what tutors want them to do, the more easily they will accept greater responsibility. The action plan is designed to indicate where improvements to performance should be sought in similar situations. It is not so much an assessment instrument as a means of establishing new working hypotheses to test in action when the opportunity arises.

Techniques and processes

So far I have suggested using a matrix as a starting point. This can be as simple or complex as you wish. Indeed, you may wish to have several: one for each stage of skill development, perhaps, or an integrated one for more 'holistic' development activities. At the least, however, the matrix needs to show the assessment or evaluation process, who is responsible for it and any necessary criteria.

Below I list some typical approaches that are being used in capability development. I try to indicate the values and drawbacks of each and show what they are best used for. Feel free to experiment with them. They are tools to aid learning, they are not dogma! If something doesn't suit you as it is, then try changing it. Above all don't think you need to take them all up. I know that many of you are already using some of these techniques, as well as others. If you have any successes or failures you would like to share with us, both the editors and I would be delighted to hear from you.

THE LEARNING CONTRACT OR LEARNING AGREEMENT

Writing this chapter for lawyers makes me a little reluctant to use a term like learning contract, though this is what most management developers call it. Therefore I have also introduced the term 'learning agreement', which I hope will have fewer strictly legal resonances.

I mentioned in Part 1 that one aspect of capability assessment involved transferring responsibility for evaluation from the tutor to the student. This arises because the path of an individual's development is personal. It is completely unlike anyone else's. Therefore, both the process and the evaluation need to be individualised.

The learning agreement is one way of making learning personal. It is essentially a means of articulating the expectations that tutor and student have of each other, and indicating opportunities which can help fulfil those expectations. It also indicates how assessment and evaluation will take place.

You might consider it advisable to use your matrix as a starting point and as an integral part of the agreement. The matrix has, at least, an indication of activities and assessment and evaluation processes. It shows the break-down in responsibilities between tutor and student as well as the things the student needs to do to produce work that can be evaluated.

Those activities and processes can be negotiated between the tutor and student, to accommodate the student's preferences. Not all, for example, will want to produce a process report. Some may use a learning diary approach, others will produce a portfolio of varied evidence to support their development.

In addition, the learning agreement will deal with timescales for work to be completed.

The tutor (or tutor team collectively) will agree their role as assessor and facilitator, depending on the needs of the student, and will undertake to fulfil these roles. Many learning agreements have within them the means to vary the terms of the agreement, and the conditions in which this might take place. For example, students often underestimate the time taken to achieve their aims, and consequently need to renegotiate times. Occasionally, students will over-commit themselves. This can be a source of stress and defensive behaviour, especially where a written agreement exists, and it is better to soften the terms of the agreement than to set people up to fail.

If you want to follow up the idea of the learning agreement, I would advise you to read George Boak's (1991) *Developing Managerial Competences: The Management Learning Contract Approach.* Although it specifically deals with management development, the principles hold good for almost any capability approach.

ACTION LEARNING SETS

In 1980 Reg Revans published his book *Action Learning.* In it he describes and promotes the notion of 'action learning sets'. For Revans, these are located firmly in the workplace and are intended to act as learning support groups designed to keep managers away from the business schools, which Revans regards with some distaste. While for reasons of ideology and self-interest I do not fully concur with Revans in this, I have found learning sets, adapted for the educational environment, to be valuable, stimulating and supportive of their members. Moreover, an effective group will underwrite the responsibilities of the individuals within it, and will police and monitor those responsibilities. It can also take on some of the assessment burden by helping set objectives, evaluating performance and giving feedback to its members.

Learning sets don't just happen, though. You need to help set them up. They have to have the time and space to develop their own internal relationships and ways of working before they can operate effectively. Occasionally, it becomes plain that a group is not going to work. This happens for a number of reasons. Possibly there are relationship problems within the group that they find difficult to deal with, so that personality clashes overshadow the other activities. Sometimes there are leadership struggles and other power games.

When this happens a skilled facilitator might be able to help the group rescue itself, or it may have to fold.

Usually, however, groups tend to do well when there are clear aims for them to pursue. Where their members have a clear agenda of skills development, I would expect most groups to commit themselves to that agenda.

The initial facilitation may consist in helping groups to clarify their agenda, and to allocate roles and tasks. If you would like to explore the facilitation of learning sets, I would recommend that you look at *Joining Together* by David W Johnson and Frank P Johnson: Chapter 10 will give you some insights into how the tutor can help start and develop the group. You will also find a number of useful activities in the book to help groups deal with conflict and decision-making, to develop creativity and problem-solving skills. An important spin-off from using learning sets is that they develop the capability elements of 'working with other people'. It therefore becomes legitimate to use the group as part of the evaluation process.

One important point to remember is that once a group gets under way, it tends to follow its own aims and objectives. Each group will therefore be different, and the tutor needs to be prepared to let this happen and trust the group. Remember, these groups are going to be playing an important part in the development of their members' capability. They need to be trusted.

A number of points need to be borne in mind when initiating learning sets:

- There is no ideal number of members, though between six and eight seems to work well. There are enough to carry on if one or two individuals leave, but not enough to let the group deteriorate into factions. This is also a reasonable number to make keeping in contact a relatively simple process.

- When sets are first formed make sure they all agree where and when they will next meet, that they all exchange contact information and that one of them will undertake to act as co-ordinator for the next meeting.

- At the first meeting encourage the group members to come up with provisional guidelines for the conduct of the learning set. For example, they should discuss how frequently they will meet. In my experience, it has been helpful to groups to have a policy of allocating tasks at one meeting to be completed or reported on at the next. This gives the meeting a clear focus, and generates commitment from individuals.

• As facilitator, make it clear that the principal responsibility for maintaining and developing the group lies with the members. You might draw attention to the requirements of individual learning agreements, where the learning set can collectively take responsibility for aspects of evaluation.

If you have never been involved with learning sets before, you will need to give the process some thought. For example, the learning set lends itself to a problem-based learning approach: see Cruickshank (1996). It might thus be possible, for instance, to set up a scenario where the notes of an initial interview have been left by an absent solicitor for the student to deal with. The learning set as a whole could assume the role of 'the student'. Through the allocation of tasks and reporting back, they could carry out the necessary research and prepare for the next stage. This would enable much more substantial problems to be dealt with than would be the case with individual student work. It would also have the effect of widening and deepening students' experience of the relevant areas of law and skill.

A learning set can also provide a 'rehearsal studio' for students preparing interviews, negotiations and advocacy. Provided that they are able to give effective and positive feedback, this would be a crucial developmental process.

Many students also use a group as a waystage towards taking individual control of their development. The learning set is obviously designed to take on that role. On the other hand, not all learning sets work according to (the tutor's) plan. Some take on a wider function as a social group, leaving the disciplined learning aspects behind. Others just fold because the dynamic of the membership can't sustain them. Generally, however, they operate well in the short and medium term (by which I mean over a period of an academic year), although I know of one learning set from a Diploma in Management Studies group from four years ago which has gone on to learn to sail sea-going cruisers. The members never refer to themselves or think of themselves as a learning set, but they continue to learn together.

LEARNING DIARIES

Learning diaries come with many names: learning logs, skills diaries, personal development journals, etc. What they have in common is that they all attempt to document learning and development from experience. They range from extremely free form to extremely structured, and from being subject to high levels of tutor control to being completely in the control of the learner.

This is in part a negotiated process, depending on the students' preferences. Those unfamiliar with competence development processes, in my experience, want a great deal of initial support. It is often unclear to students how to structure such a diary or how to decide what should go in it. A useful start is to divide pages into four sections, headed by the stages of the Kolb learning cycle: Experience; Reflection; Conceptualisation and Planning/testing. This provides a practical approach to understanding and articulating the stages of the learning cycle. In particular the processes of reflection and conceptualisation give students problems initially and they need guidance and reassurance.

This is because documenting our learning is an onerous task. We are not used to interrogating ourselves in this way, and some people find it very difficult to do. I have to confess that I am one of them. I have tried keeping a learning journal on several occasions, mainly because I was asking my students to keep one and felt I should do the same. On each occasion it petered out. I didn't so much decisively abandon it as fail to keep it up regularly. Consequently, I am fairly sympathetic to students who suffer the same problems. I usually put some pressure on them to have a go, however. One of the other phenomena I have found with learning diaries is that some students who are initially resistant to them become very enthusiastic, even to the point of continuing to maintain some form of diary after it has become unnecessary for assessment reasons.

The central question is: What is it going to be used for? A diary that follows the learning cycle will, if the student is able to articulate well, identify the three aspects of learning: thinking, feeling, doing. You will, over several entries, begin to get an idea of the student's cognitive processes, values and feelings. You begin to get a sense of her decision-making abilities when faced with ordinary or out of the ordinary situations. It is rare that a single entry can give you great insights into the student's capability, but a number of entries usually can.

Typically, students confine their entries to study-related matters, but this needn't be the case. The ability to spot and document opportunities for learning in other contexts is a valuable ability and should be encouraged.

In the past I have made the keeping of a learning diary a compulsory part of programmes. I no longer do that. If a student is compelled to keep one, then ownership of the process is in dispute. It could

hardly be said to be a true reflection of someone's personal development if the method of that development was prescribed. Making it
compulsory also required that it should be assessed, and that causes
major problems. Was I assessing the ability to keep a diary, or the
student's learning that the diary revealed? If the latter, then would a
capable learner be penalised for not being expert in articulating that
learning through this medium? I regarded these problems as insur-
mountable, both practically and ethically. The only element of
compulsion I operate now is to ask people to keep a diary for a
month. Then they can decide to incorporate it or not into their learning agreement.

PROCESS REPORTS

If students find keeping a learning diary problematic, they might
consider 'process reports'. These are very similar to learning diary
entries, but they are focused on specific activities or events in the
programme. You might agree, for instance, that a student produces a
process report to accompany a piece of drafting, or a series of interviews. The report should begin with a self-evaluation, that is, an
identification of the student's starting point for that particular competence. This could take the form of a reflection of events similar to
the one being dealt with that the student has been involved with in
the past. The remainder of the report could follow the learning cycle
format, with several entries demonstrating how new theories of
action were put into practice. It should ideally end with another self,
peer, or tutor evaluation of performance.

The benefit of a process report is that it is centred around more
formal learning activities and consequently has greater face validity
for students. It also removes the responsibility for students to identify their own learning opportunities. This is of course a loss, but in
my experience it is certainly more comfortable for students. In the
pressured environment of the LPC, pragmatism in this respect may
be the better part of purity.

PORTFOLIO OF LEARNING

Portfolios of 'evidence of development' are the order of the day for
many competence-based programmes like NVQ. Moreover, more
and more professions are asking members to demonstrate continuing professional development through this process.

A portfolio is a combination of process reports and self-evaluation. There is often an element of peer evaluation, too. An NVQ portfolio provides evidence of competent performance against assessment criteria that are the same for all candidates. I am not suggesting that a portfolio for development of capability is the same thing. It is more like a collection of process reports, linked by narrative and containing a variety of evaluation processes.

I admit to having a prejudice against portfolios. I have found them to be cumbersome and disliked by students. I have experience from both sides of the fence, as assessor and as student. However, some students like the process of taking a disparate collection of documents and putting them into an ordered portfolio which tracks their development. A portfolio can contain all the methods of documenting development that I have mentioned. The burden comes in linking them all together into a coherent whole. This is where students need to exercise their creativity and imagination. Unless you are able to set clear criteria in students' learning contracts about what the portfolio is for, how it is to be maintained and what the content is to be, then I would recommend that you do not use the portfolio as a means of evaluating capability.

If you do use it, then it seems to me that its best use is as a means of integrating skills development with other aspects of the LPC programme, promoting the breakdown of the 'knowledge/skills divide'. Since the DRAIN skills are already learned in an integrated way, the portfolio provides a vehicle for integrating the assessment.

It can do this by incorporating material and assessments from other parts of the LPC and identifying the skills outputs required. These can then be assessed and evaluated. As part of a capability approach this has much to recommend it. It encourages a holistic approach to the study and practice of law, and all the aspects of a capability approach can be effectively incorporated into other parts of the programme.

However, I suspect that, unless the skills tutors want a thoroughly unreasonable assessment load, a portfolio approach needs to be integrated across the whole LPC programme, and assessment and evaluation principles and processes agreed and operated.

Thinking differently about assessment

Assessment for capability is developmental assessment, from which the tutor can build up a picture of confidence about future 'real-world' performance. There are no certainties about this kind of assessment. We have no benchmarks for making inferences about the future, beyond our own judgment and experience. I don't, however, make any apology about this. I have not suggested a methodology for saying 'this person will perform effectively, whilst that one will not'. Assessment of development is as personal as the process of development itself.

The skill of the tutor lies therefore in the ability to give challenging feedback to students, which helps them to:

- be articulate about their theories of action;
- see how these develop in the light of experience;
- bring personal value conflicts to the surface and work through them;
- personalise their professional knowledge;
- become confident and autonomous learners.

This, of course, is not assessment in anything like the traditional sense. No one is awarded marks or grades, and there are no internal or external checks to ensure a reasonable level of reliability, while validity is satisfied because you are directly evaluating the abilities you want to develop. The purpose is different. You are not looking for a definitive result which will enable you to predict future performance in a determinist sense. Rather you are using your evaluative skills to give the individual student confidence in their ability to cope effectively, and to continue learning. I maintain that from the point of view of the new practitioner and of the profession at large, such a process is at least as valuable as the summative assessments you carry out on the technical aspects of the DRAIN skills.

References

C Argyris (1989) *Reasoning, Learning and Action*, Jossey Bass, San Francisco.

G Boak (1991) *Developing Managerial Competences: The Management Learning Contract Approach*, Pitman, London.

R Boyatzis (1982) *The Competent Manager: A Model for Effective Performance*, Wiley, New York.

H Brayne (1994) 'LPC Skills Assessments: A Year's Experience', 28 *Law Teacher* 227.

Centre for Legal Education (1994) *The Cost of Legal Education in Australia. The Achievement of Quality Legal Education: A Framework for Analysis*, Centre for Legal Education, Sydney.

D A Cruickshank (1996) 'Problem-based learning in legal education', this collection.

E H Greenebaum (1991) *Coping With a Turbulent Environment: Development of Law Firm Training Programs*, Legal Skills Working Papers, Institute of Advanced Legal Studies, London.

D W Johnson & F P Johnson (1991) *Joining Together: Group Theory and Group Skills*, Prentice-Hall International, Englewood Cliffs, NJ.

P Jones (1996) 'We're all reflective practitioners now: reflections on professional education', this collection.

D Kolb (1984) *Experiential Learning: Experience as the Source of Learning and Development*, Prentice-Hall, Englewood Cliffs, NJ.

E O Laumann & J P Heinz (1977) 'Specialisation and Prestige in the Legal Profession: The Structure of Deference', 155 *American Bar Foundation Research Journal.*

Legal Practice Course Board (1995) Written Standards, version 3, Law Society, London.

C Maughan (1996) 'Learning how to learn: the skills developer's guide to experiential learning', this collection.

C Maughan, M Maughan & J Webb (1995) 'Sharpening the Mind or Narrowing It: The Limitations of Outcome and Performance Measures in Legal Education', 29 *Law Teacher*, forthcoming.

M Pedler, J Burgoyne & T Boydell (1994) *A Manager's Guide to Self-Development*, McGraw Hill, Maidenhead.

R Revans (1980) *Action Learning*, Blond and Briggs, London.

D Schön (1987) *Educating the Reflective Practitioner*, Jossey-Bass, San Francisco.

J Stephenson and S Weil (1992) *Quality in Learning: A Capability Approach in Higher Education*, Kogan Page, London.

Chapter 14

Developing student evaluation of courses
Joanna Shapland

Methods of evaluating courses

In this chapter, I am concentrating on just one means by which courses and coursework can be assessed – student evaluation. It must be emphasised at the outset that student evaluation cannot, by itself, be the sole means by which any course is evaluated. Effective evaluation and assessment require the use of several methods which tap the different perceptions of those involved with the course. The emphasis which those delivering a course will wish to place upon the differing methods for its evaluation should depend upon the purpose of the course itself. It needs careful consideration before the package of different evaluation measures is finalised – which should be well before the course is delivered!

Some of the most tricky moments which I have observed or experienced in post-mortem meetings with staff or students in relation to the delivery of courses and their success (or failure) have stemmed from people holding different perceptions about the weight being placed on the different methods of evaluation of the courses. Essentially, the stress being placed in the overall evaluation on different people's perceptions sends messages about how important those people seem to be to those who control the shape of the course or who are influential in the organisation. So, for example, if all the stress is being put on the results of student evaluations, then staff delivering the course may feel their expertise and contributions being ignored. If, on the other hand, student evaluations are not undertaken, or the results appear to be ignored, then students will start seeing the institution as unresponsive to their needs and may start to take more drastic action.

This is a specific application of the general principle that all evaluation, like all social research, has a political element. Evaluation is a powerful tool for change. If the results are published, then those reading them are empowered to act on the lessons they imply. If the evaluation results show up some difficulties, then it will be expected that those who are in charge of the course or those who are in power in the institution will make changes (or at least explain why such changes will not be made). If the evaluation shows satisfaction with the course, making the results public proclaims the success of the institution. If, however, the results are not published (or not made available to both staff and students), there may be allegations of cover-ups or of ignoring student views. The process of carrying out the evaluation itself will give out powerful messages to those who are affected by the course about the management style of course and institution leaders.

The lesson is that, before the nature and form of evaluation are decided, the following aspects need to be thought through:

- the balance of the kinds of evaluation which will be used;
- those who will be involved in that evaluation and whose views will be tapped;
- those who need to agree to the forms of evaluation to be used;
- how the results will be published and how much detail will be made available to whom;
- the mechanisms through which the results will be considered and action taken to implement changes suggested by the results.

Furthermore, some important practical matters need to be considered:

- the costs of the evaluation methods to be used;
- the staff and student time and resources that will be taken up in administering the evaluation, in analysing the results and in considering the implications;
- the expertise available to undertake the kinds of evaluation proposed.

Striking a balance over methods of evaluation

Student perceptions of a course, although, to my mind, extremely important, cannot be the only way in which the course is judged. Staff perceptions are equally important. So is the judgment of those outside the course who will look either at the course itself (such as quality assessors and the Higher Education Funding Council), or its products – the successful candidates (for example, employers). Which groups need to be concerned and what dominance each of their perceptions should have depends upon the purpose of the course itself.

If one considers a course done entirely for pleasure, then student perceptions might be the most apposite in judging this. If the course is intended to impart intellectual skills or a particular branch of knowledge, then those who are seen as capable of judging whether this has happened (often these are deemed to be staff – at least by staff!) will be important. If it is a course with a vocational element, particularly a vocational training course, then the judgments of those who receive the trained students into their profession or occupation will have relevance, as will the perceptions of the students once they have become members of that profession. Evaluators should think about how to tap into these different groups.

I would argue, however, that student perceptions and staff perceptions still must play a major role in assessing the course – neither learning nor teaching will be most effective if their views are untapped or ignored. Staff perceptions have tended to be tapped in fairly informal ways – staff meetings, course appraisal meetings of course teachers, informal discussions between teachers. For courses involving small numbers of staff, providing any conclusions reached are acted upon (which means they normally need to be formally recorded), such informal discussion group methods of evaluation are the most suitable. If, however, large numbers of staff are involved, it may be necessary to tap their views by more formal questionnaires, sets of discussion groups, or face-to-face interviews, in a similar way to student evaluation.

Student evaluation has tended historically to be neglected in course evaluation in the United Kingdom. Partly this may have been because staff perceptions were far more valued than those of students, whereas the increasing move to student-centred learning, and realisation that it is necessary to attract students to obtain funds, has changed the political balance. I suspect, however, that another reason has been that tapping student perceptions means acquiring the views of large numbers of people, which needs professional social science empirical research skills. There is no doubt that designing and analysing questionnaires is a highly skilled activity and there are many traps: Oppenheim (1992) is an excellent guide to the traps and pitfalls of questionnaires; Gilbert (1993) is a more basic introductory guide to social science research skills and methods. However, in relation to the student evaluation of existing higher education courses or degrees, social scientists with such skills are now far more widespread throughout higher educational establishments. Departments or schools may be able to tap into expertise in other parts of the institution. I feel, however, that entirely new vocational courses or new methods of delivery (such as courses delivered entirely by distance learning) may require independent evaluation, using professional social science expertise, at the start of the course, with the institution then being enabled to take on the ongoing evaluative function after a year or so.

It was this latter role of independent evaluator which we took on in relation to the new vocational course at the Council of Legal Education. The course provides vocational training for those intending to become barristers in private practice in England and Wales. In this chapter, I shall draw upon our experience and results in setting up that evaluation and carrying it out; the results have been published in Shapland et al (1993), (1995); Shapland and Sorsby (1995). I shall also be using the experience we have gained from undertaking full student evaluations of the undergraduate law degrees in the Department of Law at the University of Sheffield from 1991 (there are now over 800 such students in the department).

The first major requirement when designing student evaluation (or any other evaluation, for that matter) is to consider what purpose the course is designed to achieve, so that the methods chosen for the evaluation are able to measure that purpose.

The vocational course at the Council of Legal Education

Students coming to the Council of Legal Education (CLE) in September 1989 were the first to experience the entirely new vocational course for the Bar. The intention of the course is that a student who has successfully completed it should possess a framework of essential skills for competent practice *in the first few years* in private practice at the Bar. In addition, the course aims to equip students with knowledge of legal procedure and practice, and to build on their knowledge of substantive law acquired during the academic stage.

The crucial eventual test for evaluating such a course is obviously whether students have been trained in the relevant areas so that they are able in pupillage and in the first years in practice to build on their training and to perform competently as barristers. For the 1989/90 course, therefore, the major stage of evaluation needed to come when the students from that course went through pupillage in 1990/91 and became barristers thereafter. The evaluation of the

TABLE 1
THE STRUCTURE OF THE EVALUATION OF THE
NEW VOCATIONAL COURSE AT THE CLE

1988/89	Study of the work of the junior Bar to feed into the development of the new course: see Johnston and Shapland (1990).
Sept 1989	The new course starts.
1989/90	Student evaluation of the first year of the course. Questionnaires sent out May 1990, preliminary results fed back Oct 1990, full report Dec 1990: see Shapland et al (1993).
1990/91	Student evaluation of the second year of the course. Questionnaires sent out May 1991, preliminary results fed back Oct 1991, full report Dec 1991: see Shapland et al (1993).
1991	Evaluation of the course by first year students, now pupils (second six months pupils). Questionnaires sent out July 1991, received back over whole period to May 1992. Report by end 1992: see Shapland et al (1995).
1991	Evaluation of the course by pupil masters and mistresses of first year students, now pupils. Questionnaires sent out mid-1991. Report by end 1992: see Shapland et al (1995).
1993	Evaluation of the course by first year students, now two to three years into practice. Questionnaires sent out June 1993, received back by October 1993. Report by end 1993: see Shapland and Sorsby (1995).

course (see Table 1) has hence been designed to follow up the students in 1991 and again in 1993 (pupillage and early years in practice stages), and to compare their views and those of senior members of their chambers with the results of the research on the previous vocational course: see Johnston and Shapland (1990). Student evaluations of the course at the end of that course have, therefore, been compared with the same students' perceptions of the course once they had gone into practice. In this paper, however, I shall restrict myself to the student evaluation done at the end of the course for the 1989/90 and 1990/91 courses.

Deciding on methods of evaluation

Questionnaires, interviews or discussion groups?

If there are large numbers of students taking the course (there were over 800 both at the CLE and at Sheffield) then the only practical method of tapping student views is to use a self-completion questionnaire. If a course has smaller numbers of students, interviews or small discussion groups may be feasible options. However, if evaluation is to be undertaken during a course, or before final assessment results are known, then it is important that students should be able to provide results anonymously. Interviewers or discussion group facilitators will need to be independent and seen to be independent of staff who will be assessing students. Student interviewers is one possibility. Using independent interviewers is normally too expensive an option.

Deciding on sampling

The next choice is on sampling. Should there be a 100% sample (all students have the opportunity to fill in the questionnaire) or is it possible to pick a restricted sample? The answer depends again on the purpose of the evaluation. It is often politically imperative, as with the CLE, that all students' views should be heard. Student evaluation is an opportunity for students to feed back their reactions and suggestions into the development of the course.

If a restricted sample is chosen, it is important to consider whether this should be a random sample (say picking 30% of the student body) or whether it should be a stratified sample (making sure that there are adequate numbers of certain kinds of students in the sample, for example, men and women, or people with different educational qualifications, or people from different ethnic minorities). If responses are likely to vary according to particular background characteristics of students (students living at home, those living in halls of residence, or whatever), then the way in which the sample is chosen should reflect these characteristics, so that there are sufficient numbers responding from each relevant group to be able to look at their particular responses. Obviously, if it is a new course, it may well not be known what are likely to be the significant background characteristics. It is often preferable to take a 100% sample of a completely new course the first time it is evaluated. It may then be possible to decrease the sample size for subsequent evaluations.

For the CLE course, it was possible that different students with different previous experience would evaluate the course entirely differently. We therefore decided to attempt a 100% sample, so that every student had the opportunity to comment. This ruled out interview methods, because of the time and personnel needed, and so pointed to the use of a questionnaire.

Automatic questionnaire coding devices

Given the large numbers of students, we had to think considerably about the time required to analyse the questionnaires and the methods we should use. There are, unfortunately, no short cuts in reducing the time required for undertaking evaluations. It is possible to minimise analysis time by having only very few 'open' questions in the questionnaire (open questions are those which permit a free text response, closed questions being precoded so that students tick boxes). However, closed questions mean that time has to be spent in sorting out the codes to be used for all the questions before printing the questionnaire. Similarly, analysis time can be reduced considerably by adopting automatic coding mechanisms. These involve:

- the students entering their answers directly into a computer, which automatically codes the answers (this requires both access to a large number of computers and considerable computer literacy amongst *all* the students, both of which are not yet very common in law schools);
- or the students entering their answers on cards which are fed into a card reader;
- or the questionnaire being printed and set up so that the questionnaire sheets themselves can be fed through an automatic reading device (this is the method adopted by survey companies).

The last two methods, in our experience, definitely save overall staff time taken up in analysing the questionnaires. Both require the appropriate technology to be available and also expertise to programme the automatic reading device and create the software to analyse the resulting coded data. As multiple choice questions for assessment and the National Lottery become more common, students may have experience with entering answers on cards. At the time at which we were carrying out the CLE evaluation, we judged that the students would find it difficult to use cards (especially since they would be filling in the evaluation forms at home, without readily available help). We hence used an automatic reading device which takes questionnaire pages and programmed a stand-alone PC to display the resulting data, allow the person feeding the pages to correct any misread data, and then store the results in the format suitable for our computer's statistical analysis package. Once all the pages had been fed in (a relatively fast task), the results were then in a form which permitted immediate analysis.

Open questions and closed questions

It is unwise to remove all open questions from a student questionnaire. A complete set of closed questions both implies that the course directors know it all already (so why should students bother to give their views?) and also does not allow for the 'protest' function of student evaluation. Student evaluation questionnaires are often useful as an outlet for grievances and as a channel for communication of difficulties, which otherwise will surface in staff–student meetings, student protests and poor course completion rates.

On the other hand, too many open questions also produce drawbacks. They take a very large amount of time to analyse, since it is necessary to draw out overall themes from students' free text responses and then go through all the questionnaires to count how many students have brought up that item. More seriously, it becomes impossible to work out whether the majority of students take a particular view, or whether certain kinds of students do so, without asking students to give quantitative answers of a Yes/No, ranking or rating type (rating scales, such as 'very satisfied, satisfied, neither satisfied nor dissatisfied, dissatisfied, very dissatisfied', are commonly used in evaluations). Use of solely open questions tends to overweight the responses of the emphatic and those with a good turn of phrase and to lead to ignoring the less concerned majority.

We have, therefore, always adopted the position that we should use closed questions for all issues where we wish to know what all students feel, but we have also always included a general open question at the end where students can bring up any issues we have missed.

When and how should questionnaires be distributed?

The next decision relates to the time at which the questionnaire should be given to students and so the method of distribution and collection that could be used. At the CLE, we needed the evaluation to cover as much of the course as possible – so it would have been best had the questionnaire been sent to the students immediately after the end of the course in July 1990. However, by then many students would not only have left the CLE, but also have left their term-time addresses and gone off home or away for a well-deserved holiday. We would no longer be able to contact them. In fact, once examinations started, students tended to work from home, coming in only for assessments, exams, etc. So distribution at the CLE was impracticable. We also had to make sure that the survey was seen as being independent – and confidential. So it was necessary for the questionnaire to be sent to students' term-time home addresses and for them to send it back directly to Sheffield University.

The compromise was a decision to send the questionnaire and accompanying letter to students' home addresses in late May for the 1989/90 study. We are aware that it arrived in the middle of the revision/examination period – and that this may have adversely affected our response rate. Some questionnaires probably went straight into the bin, as stressed students put all their effort into their assessments.

One of the other problems was that the CLE only had up-to-date addresses for students if students themselves had notified changes of address since the beginning of the year. For students without necessarily much money in London, changes of address are frequent. The advent of the poll tax in 1990 may also not have assisted notification of any changed address (since colleges were required to give the relevant tax authorities students' addresses). We sent a follow-up letter to students who had not returned questionnaires. We also put up posters in the CLE to advertise the evaluation and the opportunity it provided to comment on the course. A supply of questionnaires was provided in the CLE for anyone who had not received one or who had lost it. Our experience both at Sheffield and at the CLE, as well as in other research, is that follow-up letters, posters and an easy supply of questionnaires for those who have lost them are important – they can increase response rates by 10–15%.

Length of questionnaire

The length of the questionnaire is probably the issue about which evaluators worry most. As a general principle, people are more likely to fill in shorter questionnaires. The balance is thus between amount of information that is likely to be able to be obtained and response rates. Students, however, are a committed, interested population. The course they are being asked to evaluate has often been their full-time occupation for many months or years. As long as the questions seem to them to be relevant and as long as they believe that notice will be taken of their views, our experience, both at the CLE and at Sheffield, has been that they are prepared to fill in questionnaires running to over 20 pages and asking about every part of the overall course. Reactions to length and to the kinds of questions asked, however, should be tested – both by undertaking a small pilot exercise in face-to-face interviews or a discussion group to go through the draft questionnaire, and by including a question in the final version which asks the respondents how easy or difficult they found completing the questionnaire.

Response rates

For both the 1989/90 and 1990/91 CLE surveys, the overall response rate is shown in Table 2. For self-completion questionnaires filled in by lawyers away from the institution and needing to be posted back to independent researchers, response rates of 45–55% are commendable, especially since we are not sure whether all our questionnaires reached the students (given the difficulty over addresses).

Where it is not so important that the evaluation be seen to be independent and the results be clearly anonymous, it is possible for students to fill in the questionnaires in class or within the building. Here much higher response rates can be achieved. However, it is important that anonymity be preserved and so it would be better if questionnaires filled in in class be put into a box by the student and be collected by someone other than the lecturer. If questionnaires are given out in class, but are to be returned later, then the response rate does seem to fluctuate considerably according to the apparent enthusiasm of the lecturer for the evaluation. Where lecturers indicate that they don't believe in such evaluation, or that it is just a management exercise, response rates can be as low as 10% (which makes the evaluation results pretty useless).

TABLE 2	
RESPONSE RATES IN THE CLE STUDENT EVALUATIONS	
1989/90	
Number of questionnaires sent out to students' home addresses	822
Number returned by the Post Office as not known	4
Hence number presumed received	818
Completed questionnaires returned	368
Response rate	45%
1990/91	
Number of questionnaires sent out to students' home addresses	887
Number returned by the Post Office as not known	9
Hence number presumed received	878
Completed questionnaires returned	416
Response rate	47%

What can one learn from a student evaluation exercise?

It is important to realise the value and the limitations of any student evaluation exercise. By its very nature, student evaluation, like any other form of evaluation, can only accomplish certain things. The whole of further and higher education is now taking on board the need to find out student views and to design courses in relation to the students who will take them. However, this process is relatively recent and neither the intrinsic constraints of such a process, nor the technical constraints of adopting certain methods, are necessarily yet common knowledge. As such exercises become routine, we shall also acquire a stock of published evaluations of the advantages and disadvantages of different methods. At the moment, the subject is not yet developed within legal education. The disadvantage of being pioneers is that methods have to be developed by reference to other fields and using a general social science methodology of questionnaire design and analysis.

There are, however, a number of points which it is important to bear in mind when considering student evaluations of such a vocational course.

1.   A student evaluation exercise is the only way in which students are able anonymously to express their opinion about the scope of the course, the pressures it puts on them, the ways in which it stretches them or stresses them, the quality of teaching, and the facilities available. With large courses, such as that at the CLE, it is important to gain views across the range of students of different backgrounds. One is forced into a questionnaire method, because any other involves sampling and selectivity, with students likely to feel disenfranchised if they have not been chosen to participate that year. However, a questionnaire method means that it is not possible to enter into a dialogue, or explain verbally the purpose of the questionnaire, or correct any misapprehensions. The results, therefore, are only as good as the questionnaire.

2.   Students can only evaluate what they have experienced. They cannot know of staffing, buildings, timetabling or financial constraints unless they are very obvious, or the students are told about them.

3.   Unlike many other surveys and attempts at feedback, such as standard opinion polls, where people can just make up views if they feel they ought to respond, student evaluations of full-time courses tend to tap strongly held views. Students are being asked to pronounce on the way in which they have spent a considerable amount of their lives to date, and, moreover, on courses which are a necessary part of their progress towards their desired career. In other words, they care. The results of this tend to be:

    (a)   students are quite prepared to be brutally honest in an anonymous, self-completion questionnaire;

    (b)   students expect high standards, particularly if they are paying themselves or feel poor as a result of taking the course.

4.   Students' ratings of courses will be related to their expectations. Where will their expectations come from? Some may relate to the publicity or image of the course. The CLE course, however, was the first vocational legal course to be based strongly on a skills perspective. We suspect CLE students' most likely points of comparison (and this was apparent from their comments) were their previous law courses, the Law Society vocational course, and the previous CLE course. All of these

were different from the new CLE course in that:

- they were largely based on lectures;
- they had relatively little skills input;
- they put most emphasis on substantive law and on legal procedures, as opposed to more practical considerations (dealing with clients, for example);
- they didn't challenge students' opinions of their own abilities.

We suspect that the academic stage still is characterised by these attributes. It would be very interesting to see if students on the new Legal Practice Course show similar expectations – and we would stress that it is vital for teachers of new courses to be aware of those expectations.

On the other hand, some students (a surprising number) had been members of other professions or experienced skills training in other contexts. They were able to compare the CLE course with those courses. This was particularly evident in comments on quality of teaching and assessment methods.

The relation between expectations and the results of student evaluations

In our experience, the results of student evaluations can only be understood by reference to students' prior expectations of the course. Often, any problems of mismatch need to be addressed not by altering the course content itself, but by increasing the flow of information to prospective students about what the course is about, and by addressing those expectations at the start of the course. It is hence very important to ask not only about reactions but about expectations in evaluation questionnaires.

This is clearly illustrated by the experience of the CLE course. We asked the students what they had expected to find on the CLE course and what aspects they themselves felt they would need to learn before starting practice. The results for the 1989/90 evaluation are given in Tables 3 and 4.

The students expected that both legal knowledge and skills training would form a substantial input on the course. Obviously, the prior publicity about the change in the course and the new emphasis on skills training had had an effect. But it did not seem to have displaced expectations about the role of legal knowledge. There was no relation between expectations of legal knowledge and prior legal education: both those who had done law degrees and those who had come to the CLE through other routes were expecting a considerable amount of law teaching.

	Substantial input	Moderate input	Some mention	Would not be in course	Don't know
Legal knowledge	79	20	1	0	0
Academic core subjects	7	49	35	8	1
Skills	78	17	3	1	1
Specialist options	32	39	24	3	2
Office support skills	1	9	35	50	5

TABLE 3

EXPECTATIONS: 'WHEN YOU APPLIED TO COME ON THE CLE COURSE, WHAT ELEMENTS DID YOU EXPECT THE COURSE TO COVER?'

What kind of law teaching were they expecting? A considerable number thought there would be at least a moderate input on the academic core subjects. Rather more emphasis was given to specialist options. Those who had done the CPE foresaw more teaching on specialist options and less on core subjects than those with law degrees, with those who had done joint degrees having greatest expectations of input on the core subjects. The students hence seemed not to make the distinction between academic and vocational phases that both law schools and the CLE have traditionally done. In some senses, this is good: it indicates that students realise the need to build upon their existing knowledge of law, whether in the core subjects or in the specialist options, and take that forward into practice. And of course the CLE course does contain quite a lot on the core subjects – but to be amassed whilst doing the practical exercises, rather than to be taught as straight law in the same way as is common at present in law degrees. But it is an area in which students' expectations might have been unconfirmed.

In contrast, few students expected much on office skills – though around a half thought there would be something on this in the course. It would not surprise us if this expectation grows over the years, in parallel with the use of information technology for processing paper-work and accounts.

Both in 1989/90 and in 1990/91, students' own view of their level of pre-existing skills showed a relatively complacent mindset. Those skills closely linked with the traditional view of practice at the Bar, such as advocacy, drafting and opinion writing, were thought to require a considerable amount of development. Very few thought they already possessed them. Drafting, in particular, sounds technical and everyone clearly felt worried about it.

TABLE 4

EXPECTATIONS: 'DID YOU FEEL PRIOR TO COMING ON THE COURSE THAT YOU MIGHT NEED HELP WHEN YOU STARTED PRACTICE WITH:'

	To a large degree	*Some input*	*Already possessed those skills*	*Don't know*
Communication skills	3	32	63	2
Numeracy skills	8	31	58	3
Advocacy	63	33	4	0
Drafting	91	8	0	1
Fact Management	13	45	34	8
Interviewing/conference skills	14	59	26	1
Legal research	32	44	23	1
Negotiation	23	56	18	3
Opinion writing	74	22	3	1

Students were far less certain they needed help with skills such as interviewing, negotiation, legal research or fact management. Those who had done the CPE were more likely to feel they needed no additional help – with 40% in 1989/90 feeling they needed no help with fact management, and 39% feeling they were already skilled at interviewing. There are several possible reasons why students may not appreciate the need for further acquisition of such skills:

• They may believe that interviewing etc at the Bar is similar to interviewing in other contexts, and that they do all right in those other contexts.

- They may have been trained in these skills in their previous careers or education (remembering that some who did the CPE in particular had come from other professions).
- They may have felt that these skills play only a very small and unimportant part in work at the Bar. This is a common misapprehension, fuelled by TV portrayals of court scenes. Students may be unaware that in civil work, for example, most cases are settled out of court, and that the barrister will be judged on how well that part is done (through interviewing, negotiation, managing the progress of the case, etc). They may not have thought about the difficulties of interaction with clients and solving problems in, for example, family law cases.
- They may have believed that their skills in these areas were already perfect. About 30% of those with law degrees in 1989/90, for example, believed they already possessed all the skills of legal research.

Combating these perceptions is difficult. It is necessary to make students aware of how much all skills can be refined and improved – to make them humble – without destroying their confidence.

What seems essential is to give students early on an accurate picture of work and skills at the Bar. It is probably not sufficient for staff continuously to stress the need to employ negotiation, etc – they could be seen to be biased! Clearly, if the material used in the course is realistic (as it was indeed judged to be), *and* if it shows the place for legal research, fact management, interviewing, and negotiation as a necessary part of coping with the brief, then soon students will realise what place these skills have. It is not possible to rely on practitioners necessarily to give the right impression. As one student said, the practitioners had not been through a skills-based course, and so could not be relied upon as expert skills exponents.

The degree of complacency reached its apogee in relation to the 'basic skills' – communication skills and numeracy. Most students thought they already possessed these to the necessary extent! Though Bar students are already reasonably articulate, it can hardly be said that they – or indeed barristers – are always good at communication, particularly at listening, or at informing clients of what is happening to the case.

Reactions and responding to reactions

Assessing the merits of a course as a whole

The detailed results of our evaluations of the CLE course have been published elsewhere, but it may be helpful, in the context of thinking about how to assess courses as a whole, to provide some results here on the overall verdicts on the new vocational course. We asked questions in detail about each part of the course, about the methods of delivery, about assessment (as far as this was possible, given the time of year the questionnaires had to be given out), and about the practical details of the course (timetabling, facilities etc). We also needed to ask about students' impressions of the overall benefit of the course – as it related to its prime purpose, that of assisting students to practise competently in their first few years. This, however, requires students to put themselves in a context they had only experienced to a limited degree (mini-pupillages etc). Nor can we expect the course to provide *all* the tools, skills and knowledge necessary for practice (otherwise, why have any pupillage/apprenticeship element?). Hence we needed to judge overall reactions at the student evaluation stage from several different questions, which tapped into the extent to which they felt their skills/knowledge had improved, as well as their overall ratings of the basis on which the course had been developed and its success in carrying out its aims.

In 1989/90, the very first year of the course, it was very clear from both ratings and comments in the questionnaire that students felt the new vocational course and its emphasis on skills to be very worthwhile. Everyone also referred to at least some teething troubles – and for some they assumed considerable moment. There were a few very negative reactions, largely ascribed by their authors to the amount of work on the course and the stresses of untried timetabling and assessment methods. The overall reaction to the course, however, was positive; for example:

> As a relatively lazy, non-worker whose boredom with education had reached intolerance level, I have learnt more on this course than I could imagine ever learning on the previous course (or the Law Society finals). I am glad to have done this course, but there have been serious teething difficulties this year.

These verdicts are reflected in the ratings, which also enable us to work out whether any particular groups of students had greater difficulty.

This was corroborated by the answers to the overall success of the course question: 'Do you now feel more confident in your ability to tackle the demands of pupillage?'. In 1989/90, 70% of students said they did. Of course, this question reflects not only their view of the course, but also their own confidence in pursuing a career at the Bar, now they know more about it.

By 1990/91, with most of the administrative teething difficulties regarding the workloads at different points of the course and time-tabling improved, there was no doubt that the overall philosophy and aims of the course were almost universally acclaimed by the students. Its practicality, relevance to work at the Bar, and skills basis were all constantly praised. The old course and its principles had almost been forgotten, so wholeheartedly had students embraced the new. There were almost no comparative comments with the old course this time – and the few that made reference to the equivalent course for solicitors were all disparaging about the latter.

The underlying tone was hence positive in terms of the aims of the course. Its practice, however, came in for a considerable amount of criticism – although the kinds of criticism were substantially different from the previous year. Our general conclusion is that the CLE's response to some of the most vociferous parts of the previous year's criticisms had solved those problems, and rendered the whole course now an attractive package, but that this had allowed a number of other points to emerge.

Responding to the results of the evaluation

This is a general lesson for student evaluation. It is vital to respond to students' criticisms, whether by making changes to the course and its delivery, or by discussing with students why an alternative course must be taken. If the first set of criticisms is thus addressed, the second year's evaluation should show that they are no longer such a problem. But it will also indicate a new set of problems. This may discourage staff, who will be feeling that they have not only under-taken all the work in setting up a new course, but have also opened themselves up to criticism, have taken it on board, and have changed – only for new criticisms to emerge. The point to bear in mind is that *all* student evaluation exercises will come up with some criticisms, however excellent the course. If the most serious prob-lems have been removed, the next lot will show through. What should also be occurring, however, is (even) more positive ratings. This is another reason for including quantitative rating scales in such questionnaires. Obviously, the wording of some of the main evaluative questions needs to remain the same between evaluations in order to be able to make comparisons.

In terms of the CLE course, the first year's criticisms centred on the timetabling of the course, imbalance between the workloads in the three terms, dislike of the then 'basic' modules (now redesigned and integrated with other parts of the course), lack of feedback from practical training exercises, and some problems with the final assessment (particularly perceived lack of consistency in marking, plagiarism, and a view that written examinations should not be used to test skills).

1990/91 saw the disappearance of most of those concerns. There was virtually no criticism of timetabling per se. Most of the difficulties with the first and third term seemed to have lessened, leaving only the second term overloaded. The topics for the 'basic' modules did not come in for special mention in their new guise. Feedback from practical exercises had clearly improved. The measures taken to combat any appearance of plagiarism had resulted in a total lack of mentions of it in the second year (except people wondering why there was such an emphasis against it!), though there were still some concerns about consistency in marking some of the skills courses (something that has affected all skills-based courses, to my knowledge).

The new criticisms were the teaching of some staff (which almost always appears in student evaluation results, because they are by nature comparative between staff in the institution); the perceived defensiveness of staff and the lack of staff–student communication (and adequate mechanisms to promote it); the way in which skills subjects were not assessed in a skills-only way (periodic assessment during the year using practical exercises), but remained assessed to some extent by traditional written examinations; lack of facilities (exacerbated by numbers, and exercises requiring too many students to chase too few books), and general feelings of stress for some students. The CLE then moved to address these concerns – and the subsequent evaluations carried out by them for each year of the course since then have shown that these criticisms have decreased.

It is important to note that none of the above criticisms question in any way the fundamental principles of the course, or the respondents' commitment to the Bar or, indeed, what they were being taught. This is quite different from the reactions of students to the *previous* vocational course: see Johnston and Shapland (1990). The concern is with the quality of delivery of the course, a major step on from the concerns in 1989/90, though a topic which is far more sensitive for those trying to cope with the demands of teaching the course. Interestingly, students' concerns are that the course did not totally match its assessment techniques to its philosophy, showing that they had both understood and welcomed its purpose and aims.

Publishing the results

The real value of student evaluation to those responsible for designing and running a course is to make it an iterative process. The points raised one year can be addressed in the next and then reactions obtained on that – and so forth. Student evaluation which uses core questions on expectations, outcomes and individual teaching ratings can be used to compare changes from one year to the next. Other questions can be added to cope with new demands or changes (library facilities, IT provision, etc). In my opinion, both at the CLE and at Sheffield, the detailed results have been found to be one of the most useful aids to working out the overall design of teaching and the course. Student evaluation doesn't replace other forms of staff–student contact about the course (such as staff–student committees and grievance procedures). But it allows input from *all* students over a wide range of issues.

However, the value of student evaluation can only be realised if people know about the results. Some of the most delicate questions about such evaluations arise in relation to publishing or making known the results. Who should see them and when?

Staff will wish to know the results of any evaluation of their own performance before they are given to students or published outside the institution (or given to senior managers outside the immediate course/cost structure). Allowing this to occur also encourages debate about the results and any factors which may be affecting them – which is itself part of the necessary iterative process. It needs to be recognised that such results, in the academic context, are emotionally still highly charged. The process of evaluation and appraisal/review of performance against set criteria, or in a quantitative way, is not yet as commonplace in academic circles as it is in commercial or public sector ones. Student evaluation can be the principal way in which a teacher receives *any* feedback on their performance. When student evaluation starts in an institution, there can be pressure for results which could be seen to reflect on individual performance to be kept confidential to that teacher. As student evaluation becomes more common and accepted, that pressure seems to ease.

In my opinion, it is essential that all the results should be made available to the teaching team responsible for delivering that particular part of the course. Only then can they assess how that part of the course is developing. Overall results should be made available to all staff teaching that course or related courses and to the whole student body. Ideally, however, providing as many results as possible to as many people as possible is the most helpful. It allows staff to appreciate that no one ever gets perfect ratings (because some people always rate in the middle of scales, some at the ends; and because it is impossible to teach in the ideal way for the whole of a varied student body). It allows freer discussion about different methods of teaching and delivering courses.

Above all, I believe that student evaluation begins to empower students to be more concerned with their course and to improve what they take away from it, *provided* that note is taken of the results (which means of course that the results, and proposed action, need to be fed back to the students). The course is then not just the staff's responsibility. However, perhaps I'm just a hopeless idealist!

References

N Gilbert (1993) *Researching Social Life*, Sage, London.

V Johnston and J Shapland (1990) *Developing Vocational Legal Training for the Bar*, Faculty of Law, Sheffield.

A Oppenheim (1992) *Questionnaire Design and Attitude Measurement*, Pinter Press, London.

J Shapland, V Johnston and R Wild (1993) *Studying for the Bar*, Institute for the Study of the Legal Profession, Faculty of Law, Sheffield.

J Shapland and A Sorsby (1995) *Starting Practice: Work and Training at the Junior Bar*, Institute for the Study of the Legal Profession, Faculty of Law, Sheffield.

J Shapland, R Wild and V Johnston (1995) *Pupillage and the Vocational Course*, Institute for the Study of the Legal Profession, Faculty of Law, Sheffield.

Index

Authors whose work is discussed in the text appear in the index; authors merely quoted do not.